BUILDING GHOSTS

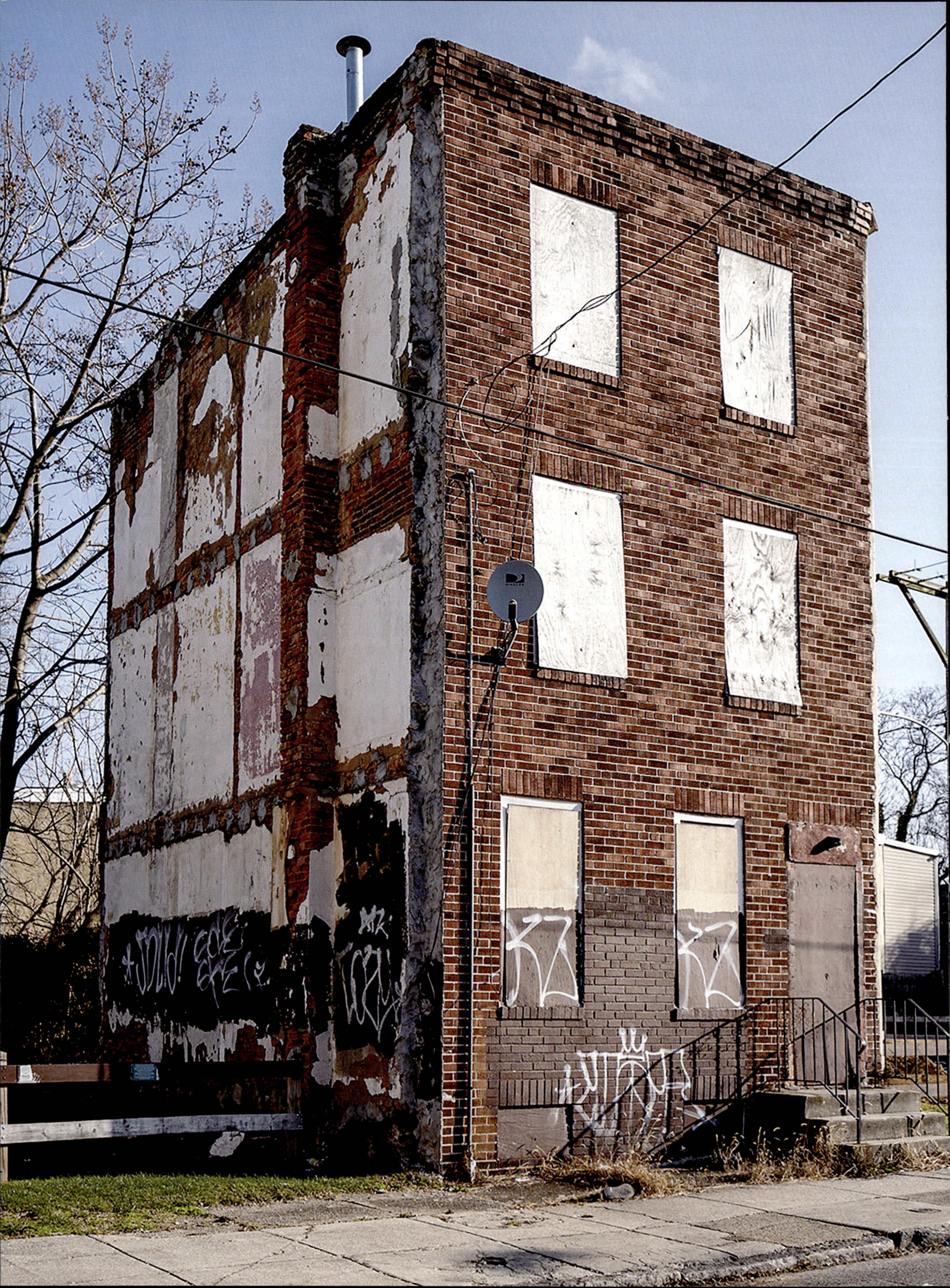

BUILDING GHOSTS

Past Lives and Lost Places in a Changing City

Written by **Molly Lester**

Photographs by **Michael Bixler**

TEMPLE UNIVERSITY PRESS   Philadelphia | Rome | Tokyo

TEMPLE UNIVERSITY PRESS
Philadelphia, Pennsylvania 19122
tupress.temple.edu

Design by Kate Nichols

Published 2024

Library of Congress Cataloging-in-Publication Data

Names: Lester, Molly, 1986– author. | Bixler, Michael, 1977– photographer.
Title: Building ghosts : past lives and lost places in a changing city / written by Molly Lester ; photographs by Michael Bixler.
Description: Philadelphia : Temple University Press, 2024. | Includes bibliographical references and index. | Summary: "Portrays and examines imprints and impressions of demolished buildings found on the walls of neighboring structures. Includes architectural street photography, vignettes of the ghosts' histories, and reflections on their social significance"— Provided by publisher.
Identifiers: LCCN 2024006729 | ISBN 9781439924099 (cloth)
Subjects: LCSH: Lost architecture—Pennsylvania—Philadelphia. | Ruined buildings—Pennsylvania—Philadelphia. | Land use—Pennsylvania—Philadelphia—History. | Philadelphia (Pa.)—Buildings, structures, etc.
Classification: LCC NA735.P5 L47 2024 | DDC 720.9748/11—dc23/eng/20240620
LC record available at https://lccn.loc.gov/2024006729

♾ The paper used in this publication meets the requirements of the American National Standard for Information Sciences—Permanence of Paper for Printed Library Materials, ANSI Z39.48–1992

Printed in the United States of America

9 8 7 6 5 4 3 2 1

To Kate and Elizabeth, who make me whole,
and to my mom and dad, because I remember
whose I am (ML)

To my wife, Kate, who supplies me with endless
encouragement, love, and support (MB)

CONTENTS

Preface

In 2013, I was wandering with a friend through the Northern Liberties neighborhood of Philadelphia. We strolled up North 2nd Street, sidling up alongside the broad Baroque front of St. Michael's Church and the brick buildings that flank it. The parish is an undeniably monumental presence in the neighborhood, and yet it was a different pile of bricks that caught my eye just beyond the church. In a vacant lot at a quiet intersection, an unassuming heap of blocks foregrounded—and were clearly responsible for—a building ghost at the edge of the parcel. I'd lived in Philadelphia for several years at this point, and I'm sure it wasn't the first ghost I'd ever passed, but it was the first one I *saw*: a stair that snaked its way up the wall; the outline of a former foyer; a series of lines in the attic gable, clearly left over from a set of shelves.

The ghost mesmerized me, just as my first college course in architectural history had done several years before, when I first fell in love with the history of old buildings and cultural landscapes. But where my coursework and jobs to this point had mostly focused on grand structures with unquestioned significance, this building ghost of a modest rowhouse claimed a different sort of authority. When you live in an old place like Philadelphia, lavish buildings such as St. Michael's Church may be accents in the streetscape, sparking a thrill when you encounter them, but it's the commonplace buildings such as this erstwhile rowhouse that actually define the everyday. I wanted to know more about this utterly mundane building, to draw on all the same detective skills that I need for my higher-profile research subjects but deploy them for a building with no name or famous residents.

But in the weeks that followed, I somehow lost the ghost. I went back to Northern Liberties alone, wandering in search of the exposed wall I'd stood in front of so recently. I couldn't orient myself, and there were no empty lots to be found as I radiated out from the starting point of the church. Belatedly, I realized that the active construction site at 2nd and Jefferson streets and "my" empty lot were one and the same. The building ghost was no longer visible as a new structure rose to take its place. It was an unfortunate lesson about the nature of building ghosts, which may vanish as quickly as they once materialized.

In the years that followed, I researched the former ghost anyway and wrote a piece about its idiosyncratic history for *Hidden City Philadelphia*. Various work projects took me to every corner of the city, and I documented other building ghosts as I found them (having learned my lesson about trying to return later to a building ghost). I started noticing patterns: what kinds of buildings become ghosts; how long the ghosts last; where ghosts do and do not occur in the broad reaches of the city. I started an Instagram account (@buildingghosts) to chronicle my ghostly wanderings and found that plenty of friends and strangers were enamored by them, too.

Among them was my friend Michael Bixler, photographer and managing editor of *Hidden City Philadelphia*, the publication in which I'd first reflected on this phenomenon. He would send me photos of ghosts from his own travels, hooked with the same curiosity I shared. Eventually, I decided to explore this passion project with more rigor, and I enlisted him and his photographic expertise. I applied for funding from the Sachs Program for Arts Innovation, an interdisciplinary arts initiative at the University of Pennsylvania, and received a seed grant in early 2020.

When the world shut down in the face of the COVID-19 pandemic, I took solace in dreaming about the project that would take shape when we could venture out again. Confined to my house and immediate vicinity, I missed my city. I went months without seeing neighborhoods (and people!) I loved. As many of us hunkered down, building ghosts became emblematic for me of the moment in which we found ourselves: suspended in time, they symbolized some inherent measure of loss and absence.

Finally, in fall 2020 Michael and I launched the project that would become this book. (For more on that process, see the Introduction.) Hungry for exploration, we trekked all over Philadelphia in our spare time, in search of ghosts. For all the pain of that period of 2020, there was something appropriate about embarking on this venture, in that moment. The pandemic reframed so many aspects of our lives, and building ghosts wield a similar power, forcing a reexamination of their context. They have a way of making even familiar places look strange, exposing a rift between what we think we remember of a building and what we see after it's gone. This book exists in that uncertain interlude, dwelling on these lost buildings and found ghosts as an invitation to see the city around us in a new way.

—*Molly Lester*

BUILDING GHOSTS

INTRODUCTION

"Building ghosts" are the imprint and last impressions of a demolished building, left behind on the walls of the neighboring structures. Physically, they are architectural remnants that can be found only in a rowhouse city such as Philadelphia, where the loss of one structure leaves a tangible mark on its neighbors. These ghosts can be ephemeral or enduring, quickly revealed and replaced in a neighborhood seeing rapid change or unveiled and exposed indefinitely in a neighborhood that hasn't seen new construction in a long time.

In the simplest sense, these ghosts are artistic objects: beautiful, sometimes legible, and confounding—all at once. But these vestiges (of structures, stairs, wallpaper, closets) are also legacies, hinting at the lives lived within these walls, the communities shaped around these buildings, and the ways in which we create and erase history in our changing cities. This book investigates, mourns, and celebrates these ghosts in our midst, retracing their structures and selves and dwelling in the moment between a place's loss and its erasure.

Making Sense of Building Ghosts

We should open by defining our terms, beginning with the choice to refer to this type of remnant as a **building ghost** rather than a "ghost building," as it is sometimes known. (We didn't coin either term.) We've opted to use the former, as it places the emphasis on the "ghost"—as in, all the ephemeralities that overlap in these traces—rather than the literalness of just the structure itself.

It is important to note that a building ghost is not simply a building that is in the process of being demolished; if that structure does not abut its neighbor(s), it is not

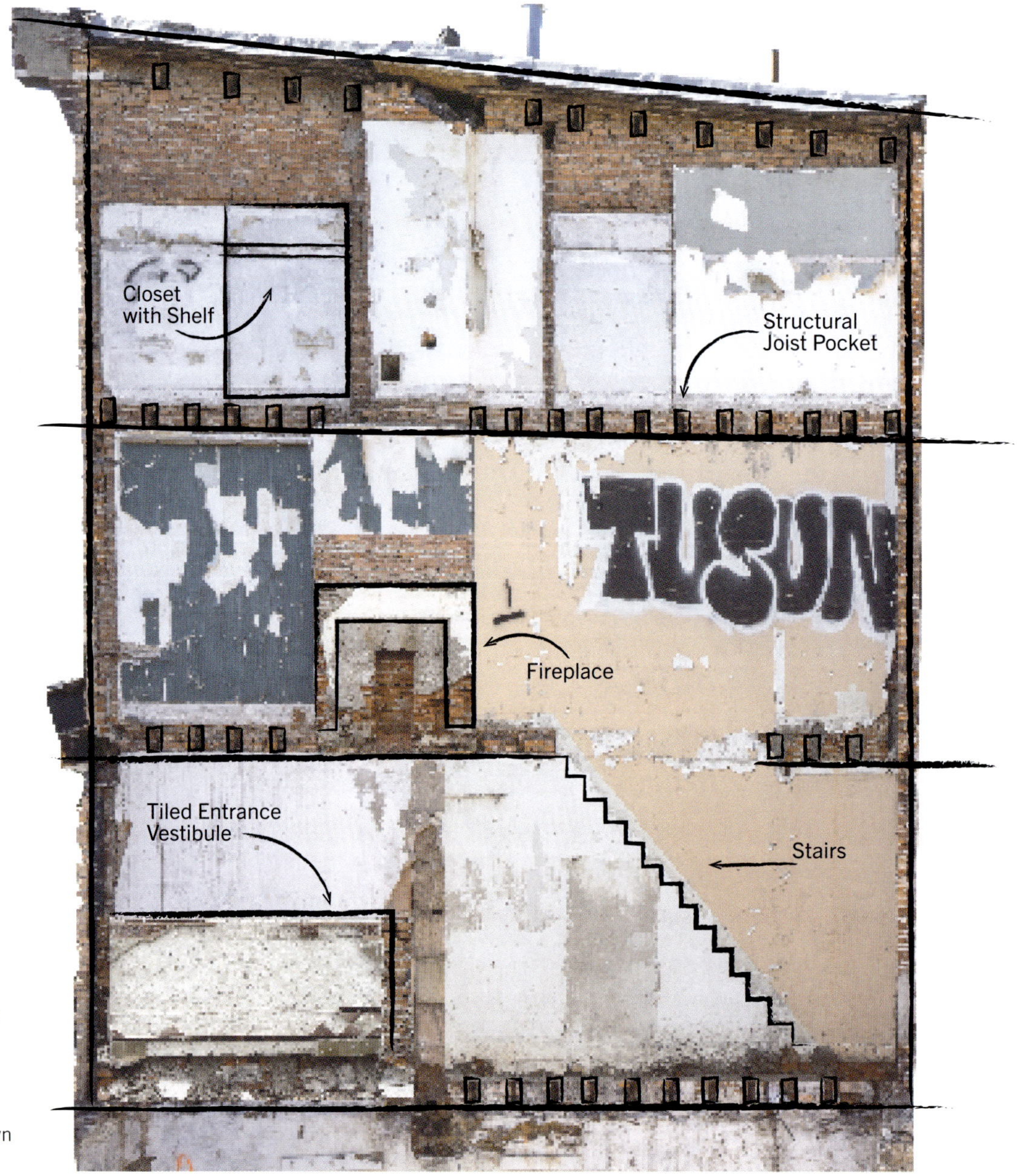

Typical features of a building ghost. (Photomontage designed by Kaitlyn Levesque.)

capable of creating a building ghost. A building ghost (or ghost, for short) is, by definition, the trace of a demolished building *that remains on the shared party wall of its neighbor(s)*, even after it is gone. A building ghost is also distinct from a "ghost sign"—the paint traces of faded advertisements, which are ubiquitous in many cities with older building stock.

The further we got into this project, the more we found that we needed words to define two recurring phenomena related to building ghosts. Thus, we *did* invent two phrases that you'll find in this book. When we say **double ghost**, we are referring to a lot in which there is a ghost on each side. In other words, the demolished building was located in the middle of the block; thus, its empty parcel features two ghosts rather than one. See the ghost of 333 N. 11th Street (page 43), for an example of a double ghost.

Finally, when we allude to a **legacy ghost**, we mean a building ghost whose presence is so long-standing as to suggest permanence. The simplest kind of legacy ghost is one that overlooks an empty lot that remains available for new construction and has been poised that way for some time. The more complex type of legacy ghost survives in spite of new construction that might have supplanted it. In the case of the latter, the ghost of a three-story building might become a legacy ghost if a two-story building is constructed in its place; the legacy ghost (left raw or finished with stucco in a way that still articulates the former building) remains visible above the new structure. This precise scenario played out at 519 South 4th Street (see page 24).

Building ghosts can be hard to interpret, as we're forced to "read" a building based on mere fragments of its former structure. To help make sense of the details that show up on many building ghosts, refer to the photomontage on page 4 and keep an eye out for these same features on the building ghosts throughout the book.

Making Meaning of Building Ghosts

Each building ghost is not merely an artistic object unto itself (although many of them create an odd and beautiful sort of art) but a palimpsest of the artists who created the demolished building over generations of people and time. Building ghosts juxtapose the solidity of the wall and the void of the vacant lot left behind, the tangible and the missing, the past and the present and the pending (or suspended) future. We look to building ghosts, then, to point out the voids of people and place to confront the ghosts we've inherited and the ghosts we've made.

Our intention is to turn urban heritage inside out, making a study of the built environment by looking at what is not built at all. In doing so, the book starts where most interpretations of architecture stop: the moment a structure is demolished. The project has required a blend of archival research and contemporary photography—but first, it required seeing every corner of our beloved city. In late 2020, funded by a seed grant from the Sachs Program for Arts Innovation at the University of Pennsylvania, we scoured the city for building ghosts. (It is worth noting that our survey coincided with the COVID-19 pandemic and all of the socioeconomic turmoil it awakened; some of the photographs and ghosts speak to those overlapping events.) Together and alone, we walked, biked, bussed/trolleyed/trained, and drove all over the city, noting every instance of a building ghost we could find (including several that were crowdsourced by friends and strangers). It would be impossible to count the miles we covered between the two of us, but the surveyed number was clear: 194 building ghosts observed in four months.

Some existed for mere hours, others (according to older photographs) have been around for decades. Such is the nature of building ghosts. But we mapped every single ghost that we found, establishing a timestamp and creating a census—for those four months, at least. If you tried to find all 194 ghosts today, you would not be able to; sometimes we couldn't even revisit a ghost from one day to the next. The timestamp of a city's building ghosts refreshes every moment.

The maps throughout this book reflect the results of that census. You'll see a point for every ghost that we found. We hope that you, too, will notice the patterns that we did—where they show up by the dozens, and where they are not present at all—and start to draw your own conclusions about the intangible themes of community history, demolition, dislocation, and neighborhood change that building ghosts bear out.

Conscious of those implications, we have reconstructed the history of forty of those ghosts (presented throughout the book on white backgrounds). These vignettes, as we refer to them throughout the book, are stories, but they are not fiction. Some recount the full trajectory of the building, from construction to demolition, while others salvage only a fragment of a building's existence. All of them, however, rely on rigorous research in deeds, censuses, city directories, insurance maps, newspapers, genealogical records, aerial photographs, books, magazines, and (in the rarest instances) historical images. Although these archival traces ground our work, we do not include their visual evidence here; instead, this book features only contemporary photographs of the building ghosts as we found them in one particular moment. In this approach, we foreground the fact that the archival record is fractional and often inequitable, shaped by social forces that preserve some narratives while overlooking or destroying others. In other words, the vignettes in this book are inescapably incomplete—as is the encounter with any building ghost.

Forty-one more ghosts from our census are featured throughout the book in photographs only (presented on taupe backgrounds). They are identified on the maps and as "ghost with photograph"—leaving each of us to speculate on the history of those ghosts.

Our census found that ghosts existed in most neighborhoods, but they were not the same in every neighborhood: when it comes to building ghosts, not all communities are created—or destroyed—equally. For this reason, the book is organized geographically (into seven sections), but it is weighted proportionally. For city sections with more surveyed ghosts, we have included more ghosts here; for those with hardly a ghost for miles, our selections reflect that reality.

Building ghosts offer many such realities to reflect on and reckon with. Thus, each section of the book begins with an essay provoked by (but certainly not exclusive to) the ghosts in that section of the city. These reflections—which, we admit, conflate many communities within that broader area of the city—grapple with the present-day resonances of building ghosts and what they might reveal about how cities evolve. Where the vignettes dwell on individual ghosts, the essays examine the connections among many

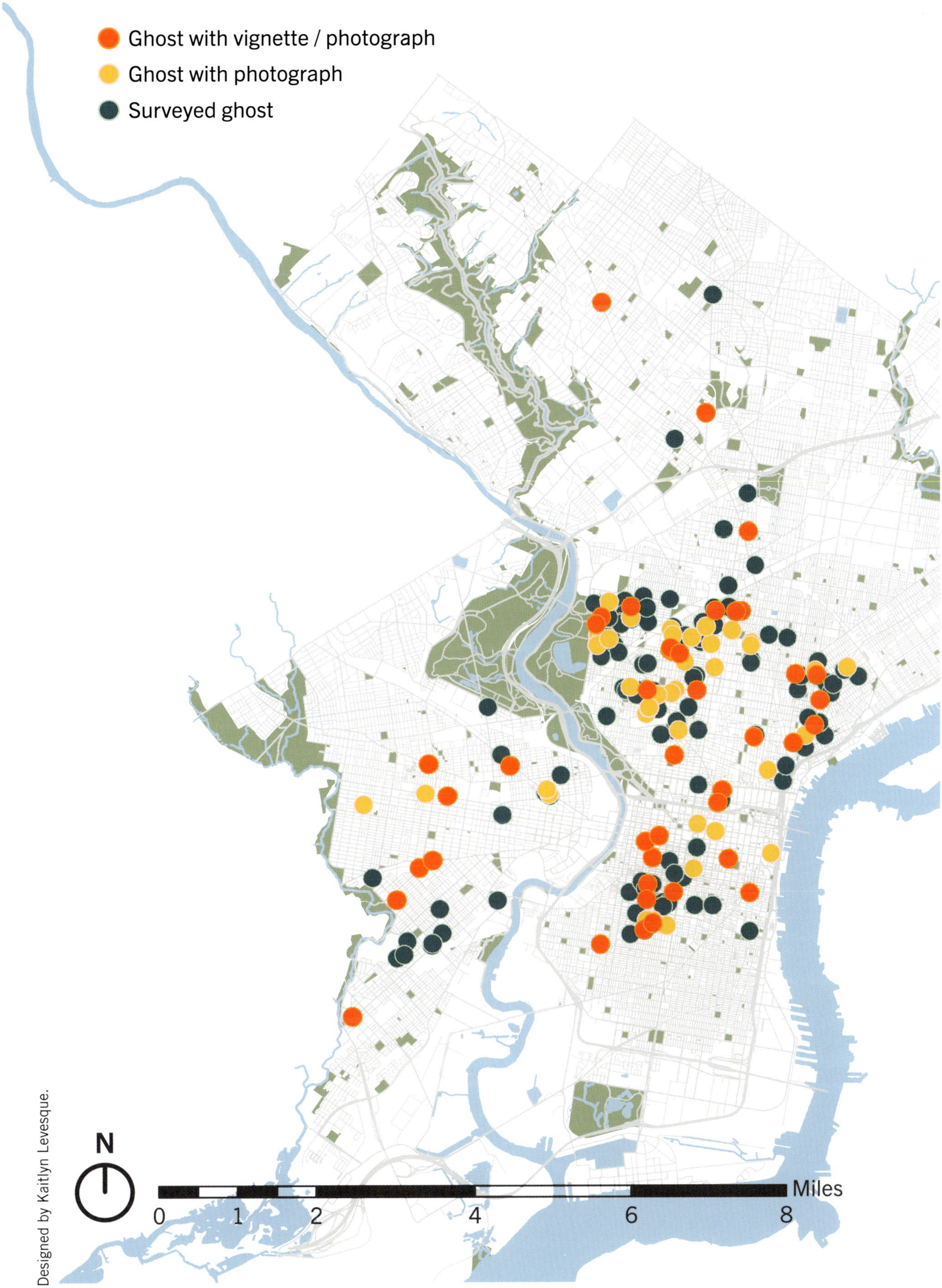

Designed by Kaitlyn Levesque.

ghosts; the vignettes address the more distant past, and the essays consider the present and near-future tense. Building ghosts, and this book about them, are thus stitched together across space and time.

Cities are dynamic places, and demolition within that context is inevitable. (How many preceding structures were torn down to produce these ghosts' buildings?) Amid the disparities of pace and place, building ghosts present an opportunity to pay attention. What can they tell us about our cities—and about *this* city? How is change currently happening? How is it not? And how should we choose to manage those forces going forward? Building ghosts aren't alive on their own (as much as we try to animate them in this book), but they are living pieces of the city.

They are also, paradoxically, a renewable resource: as long as buildings are destroyed, building ghosts may be created. In their ubiquity, then, building ghosts are instructive, sparking a larger conversation about shared experiences and divergent neighborhoods in our cities. We hope that the photographs, vignettes, and community cartographies within this book can ultimately make new art, history, and meaning out of such a tenuous symbol of loss.

CENTER CITY

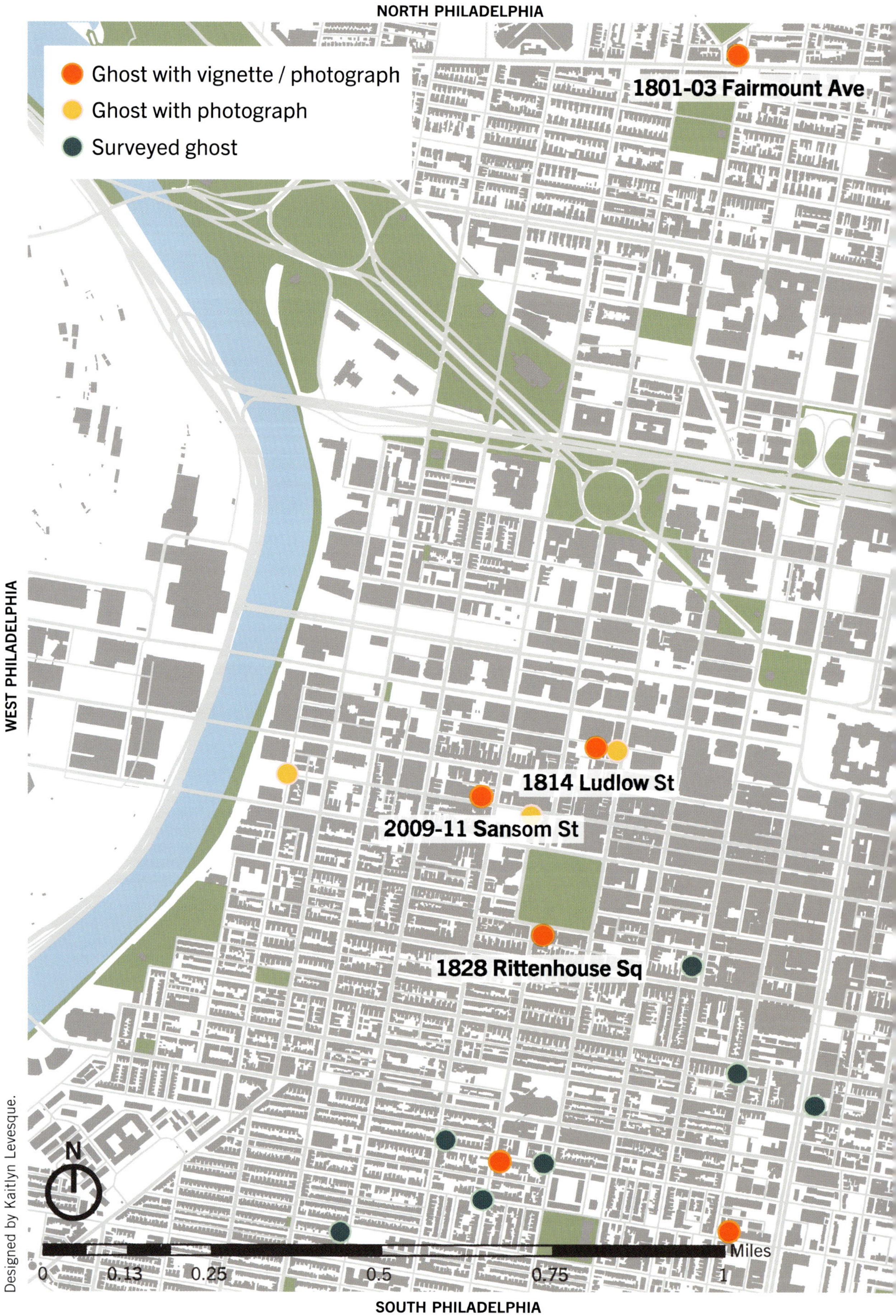

Designed by Kaitlyn Levesque.

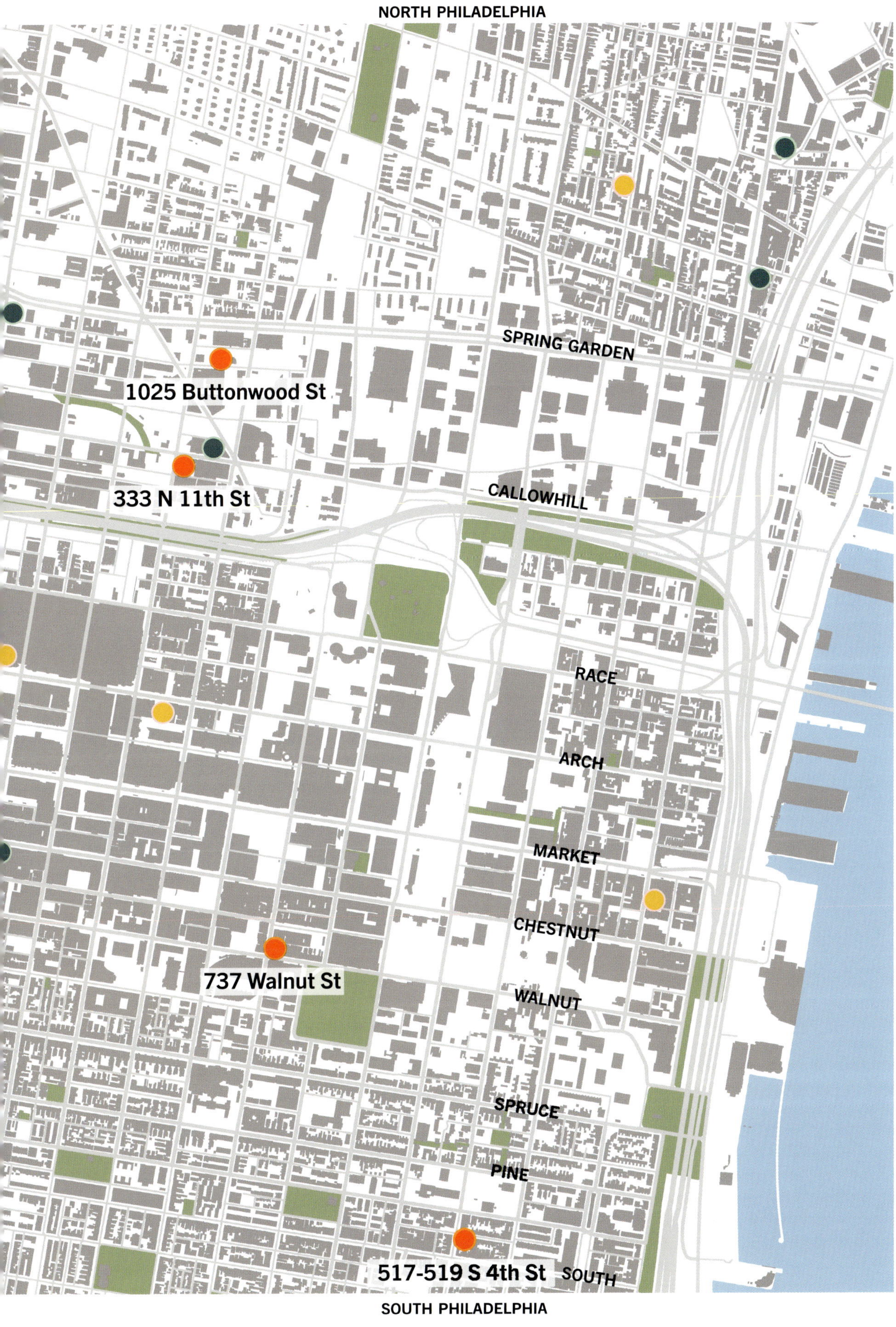
NORTH PHILADELPHIA
SPRING GARDEN
1025 Buttonwood St
333 N 11th St
CALLOWHILL
RACE
ARCH
MARKET
CHESTNUT
737 Walnut St
WALNUT
SPRUCE
PINE
517-519 S 4th St
SOUTH
SOUTH PHILADELPHIA

Center City is a land of fleeting building ghosts. Spot one on a Monday and it might be gone by Wednesday, covered up by scaffolding as a new building races upward. In a city known for its walkable and mixed-use downtown, building ghosts have been the structural fly on the wall to a boom in residents in the past twenty years. Between 2000 and 2020, the population of core Center City surged by 55 percent, compared with 6 percent for the city overall during that same period.[1] All of those incoming residents needed places to live and work and socialize, and new construction has usually been presented as the solution to those pressing needs. Amid such churn, building ghosts are inevitable.

In 2020—the year the photographs for this book were taken—the number of approved demolition permits fell by half in Philadelphia, compared with the previous year.[2] In the face of a pandemic construction shutdown and economic uncertainty, the city's Department of Licenses and Inspections (L&I) fielded just 54 percent of the requests that it had in 2019; one surmises, then, that we would have found twice as many ghosts had we been wandering the streets a year earlier. Yet even at the slower pace of demolition, we found dozens of ghosts in Center City in the span of just a few months and missed many more that proved too ephemeral to track down.

Indeed, in many ways 2020 was just a blip in the overall pace of construction—and demolition—in Center City. By early 2021, the number of new construction permits had

---

1. Center City District and Central Philadelphia Development Corporation, *The Center Holds: Residential Resiliency 2022*, Center City Reports, February 2022, https://centercityphila.org/pressroom/the-center-holds-residential-resiliency-20225.

2. Taylor Allen and Ryan Briggs, "Demolition in Philly Dropped by Half in 2020—Is That a Good Thing?" WHYY, January 2, 2021, https://whyy.org/articles/demolition-in-philly-dropped-by-half-in-2020-is-that-a-good-thing.

not only rebounded but had surged above pre-pandemic levels, factoring in the pent-up demand and a pending change to the long-established ten-year tax abatement in Philadelphia.[3] At the end of 2021, the City Council modified the abatement, a financial carrot created in the 1990s and 2000s to spur investment in a struggling Center City. More than twenty years later, with investment in Center City surging, many Philadelphians believed the abatement had outstayed its welcome, creating an incentive to tear down old buildings and create a tabula rasa for zoning permits and new designs of varying quality.[4]

The abatement does not deserve all the credit or bear all the responsibility for the demolition of many high-profile and substantial sites in the early twenty-first century, but it did help generate the development pressure that disproportionately valued new construction over rehabilitation. The demolition of several buildings on Jewelers' Row, in the heart of Center City, was probably the most painful and galvanizing loss in recent years. But the flurry of abatement-centric projects exacted a more mundane cost, too, in the scores of smaller-scale buildings that were swept up in the financial incentives with little fanfare or outcry. Revealed and re-covered at the midpoint of these rapid transitions, building ghosts have been witnesses to, and markers of, these changes all over Center City.

A preservation task force convened by then-Mayor Jim Kenney released its final report in March 2019. Coupled with the modified five-year tax break that replaced the ten-year abatement two years later, the task force's recommendations were designed to balance the scales between adaptive reuse and new construction. (It would be misguided to think that only new construction qualifies as beneficial "development" for the city.) Even so, at the time of this writing in 2022–2023, the ongoing implementation of the task force's recommendations is up against any number of barriers, including a passive mayor (seemingly waiting out the last years of his administration), a City Council focused on other issues in the midst of significant turnover, existing zoning designations that may not take into account the nuances of older buildings, and more. Some of these conditions can be found in other cities and are responsible for *those* cities' ghosts, too. Others are unique to this place, in this moment. They're a Philly thing.

The now-disbanded task force, and the associated city agencies responsible for implementing the commission's recommendations, did not measure their results in terms of building ghosts—but perhaps they should have. Ghosts are, after all, an indicator of development that favors removal over rehabilitation and replacement over reinven-

---

3. Ryan Briggs and Taylor Allen, "COVID Didn't Stop Philly's Construction Boom, but Signs Point to Slowdown in 2021," WHYY, December 24, 2020, https://whyy.org/articles/covid-didnt-stop-phillys-construction-boom-but-signs-point-to-slowdown-in-2021.

4. Inga Saffron, "As 10-Year Tax Abatement Nears Its End, Philadelphia's Architectural Treasures Are Left Vulnerable," *Philadelphia Inquirer*, August 5, 2021, https://www.inquirer.com/columnists/historic-preservation-demolition-philadelphia-churches-tax-abatement-renovation-st-laurentius-lancaster-avenue-20210805.html.

tion. They rarely exist in cases of infill, where an empty lot is put back into use without extracting an equivalent building cost. Meanwhile, *double* ghosts—where a building is demolished mid-block, leaving ghosts on both sides—are a demonstration of all the conditions that aligned to rationalize the demolition of what was likely an otherwise intact, companionate structure.

But a funny thing happens, despite all this turnover: some building ghosts are too persistent to be erased. They refuse to conform to the expectations of temporality in a changing city and are instead folded into the "permanent" streetscape as legacy ghosts. They insist on remaining on the sides of their neighboring buildings even after the risks of new construction and erasure have passed (at least for now). For just one example, see 519 South 4th Street (page 24). Building ghosts, then, reflect the same elasticity as the changing city around them. Some have a life span of just days; others, we will be living alongside for years.

A few millennia ago, in ancient Greece, the philosopher Heraclitus mused, "No man ever steps in the same river twice, for it's not the same river and he's not the same man." The same can be said for our cities—nowhere more so than the heart of Philadelphia, which metamorphoses every day, for every person in it. In the context of such change, then, are Center City's building ghosts a symbol of the last city or the next one?

1025 Buttonwood Street

Constructed pre-1860
Demolished in 2020

By the time she took lodgings at 1025 Buttonwood Street, twenty-three-year-old Edith Fantini had already called Germany, France, Russia, and Venezuela home. If modern passports had existed then, hers would have had more stamps than the rowhouse had rooms. Born in the town of Breslau (part of Prussia at the time, now known as Wrocław and part of Poland), she studied in Leipzig and Paris, developing a love of languages. When an opportunity to work as a governess arose, she ventured to the city of Odessa, situated on the Black Sea and within Russian borders. At some point, with at least three languages on her tongue, she set out to learn a fourth; this one required a transoceanic crossing, as she set sail for Puerto Cabello, Venezuela. She taught there until 1885, when she continued on to North America. Soon after, she landed in Philadelphia.

During the many years Fantini was traveling the globe, a modest two-and-a-half-story brick rowhouse stood at 1025 Buttonwood Street. Located a block south of the grand Spring Garden Street, the block was lively in its own right, with an uninterrupted line of rowhouses on the north side and a school and police station on the south side, closer to 11th Street. It was also a convenient distance from the office at 10th and Market streets, where Fantini found a job around the same time she began renting at number 1025 in 1888. She had journeyed more than ten thousand miles to earn a commute of just seven blocks.

A fluent multilinguist, Fantini secured a post as a stenographer for French, Richards, and Company, with responsibility for interpreting the company's foreign mail. Although French, Richards was primarily a wholesale drug company (selling legitimate pharmaceuticals alongside whiskey and bottled water to cure various ailments), it also advertised its robust trade in imported wares. The job kept Fantini busy, and she liked it, all the more so when she met Benjamin Franklin Hunter working there, too.

It was a shock, then, when the company suddenly announced in 1890 that it would shut down by the end of the year, after forty-six years in business. Its founder had died suddenly, and the company had stumbled in his absence. Fantini lamented the announcement and helped draft a brief resolution in which the staff thanked the company and parted on good terms. A newspaper remarked, "The relations between the employees and members of the firm (had) always been of the most pleasant character."

Her years at French, Richards were not an entire loss, however. In 1892, Fantini married Benjamin Hunter; a year later, she gave birth to a daughter, Helen. By 1896 (if not earlier), she was once again making use of her language skills, offering private instruction in French and German at a rate of fifty cents per lesson.

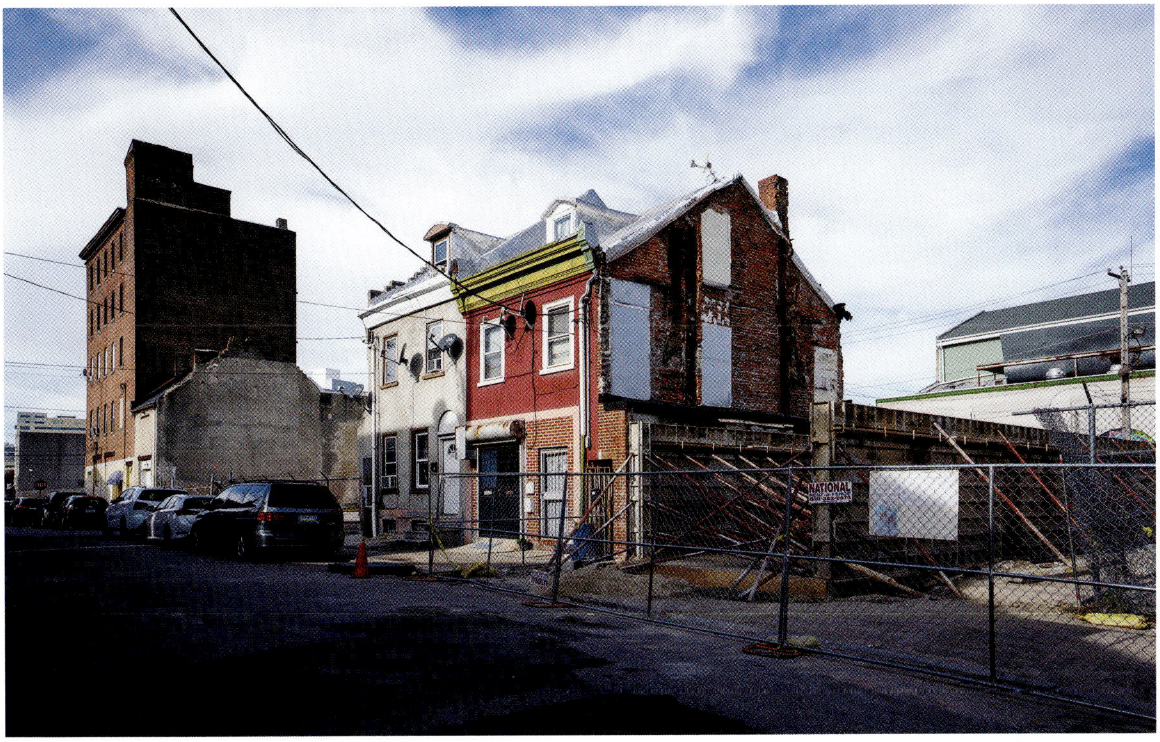

1025 Buttonwood Street. (Photographed December 3, 2020.)

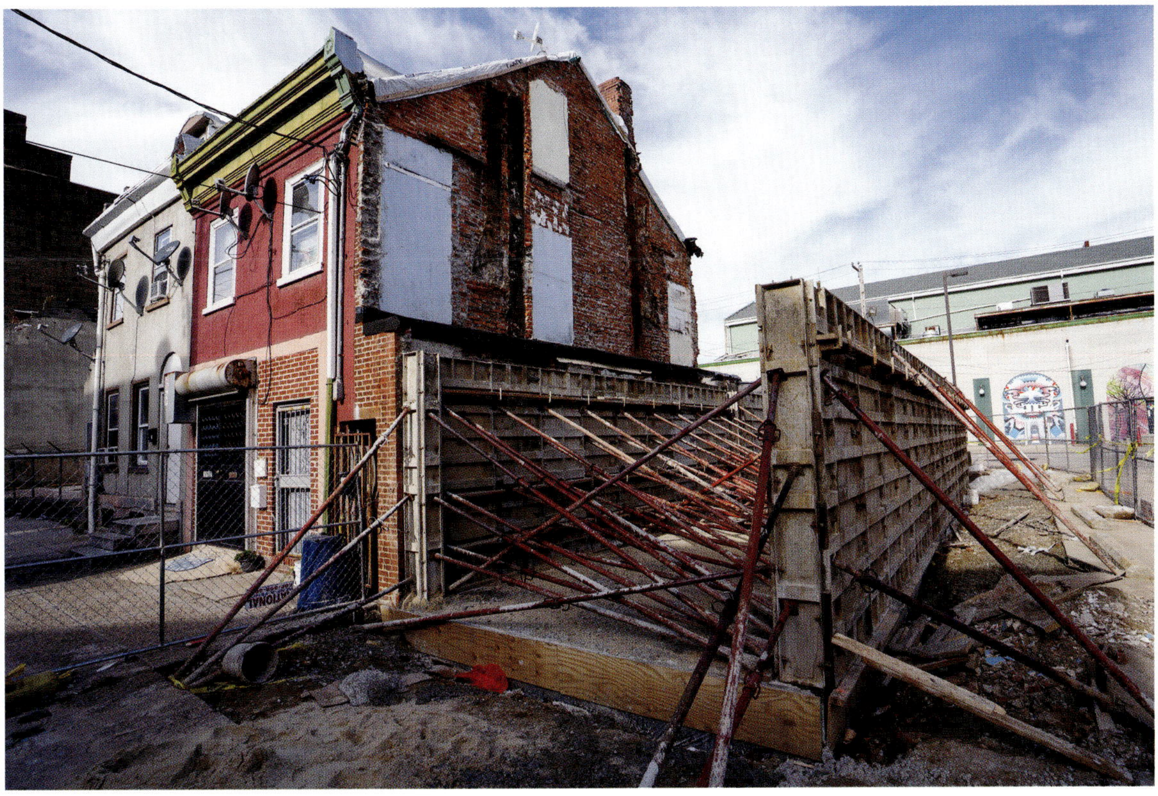

Detail of 1025 Buttonwood Street. (Photographed December 3, 2020.)

It is unclear when Fantini moved out of 1025 Buttonwood Street. (White women were only ever intermittently included in city directories, even when they had professions outside the home to list. Black women and men, meanwhile, were almost always relegated to separate directories altogether.) She definitely lived there in 1888 and 1889, but her name does not appear at all in the city directories that follow. Nevertheless, she may have lived there until her marriage to Hunter in 1892, or perhaps she moved elsewhere in the city in 1890–1891, around the time French, Richards was heading toward insolvency. By 1896 (if not earlier), she lived in West Philadelphia.

French, Richards did not entirely fold in 1890. In the course of its liquidation, a segment of the company was sold off, merging with another outfit to become Smith, Kline, and Company. Eventually, Fantini's company became part of what is now GlaxoSmithKline.

Edith Fantini Hunter, meanwhile, left Philadelphia in the 1890s. Perhaps the wanderlust of her younger years returned, because after about fifteen years in one place, she pulled up roots. Together with her husband and daughter, she once again called Paris home—this time, though, it was Paris, Tennessee. She died there in 1935.

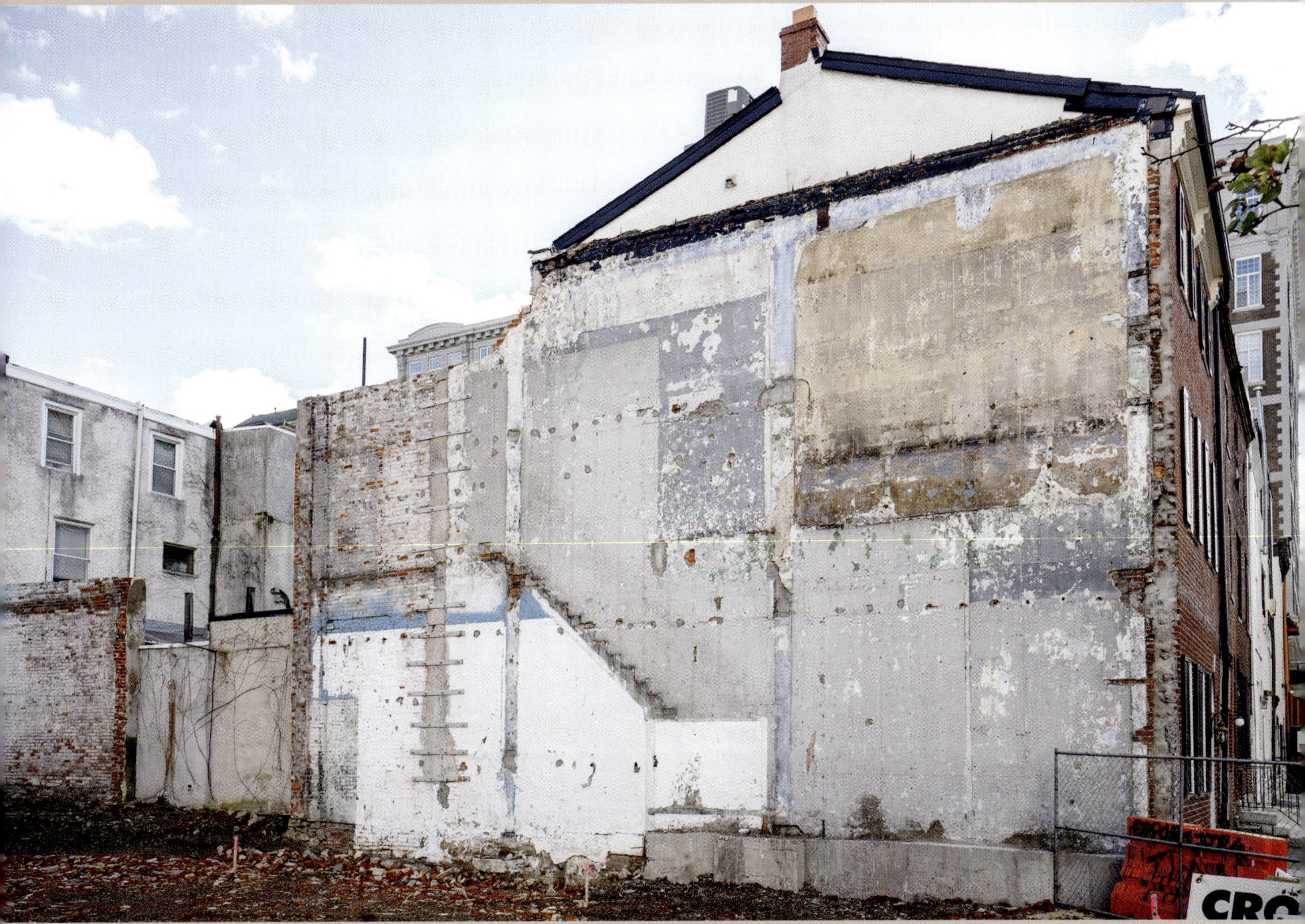

133 South 24th Street. (Photographed September 22, 2020.)

737 Walnut Street

Constructed ca. 1941
Demolished in 2020

From the moment it was erected around 1941, the one-story building at 737 Walnut Street was physically out of sync with its neighbors. Dwarfed by three- and four-story buildings, the structure could claim to be a member of the surrounding jewelers' district (it was a jewelry store of sorts from its birth until its death in 2020), but it otherwise clashed with the older, taller structures that flanked Walnut Street. In style and scale, number 737 was outmatched.

The previous structure on the site had been four stories, each story perfectly aligned with the equivalent floors at 735 and 739 Walnut Street. But during a period of vacancy in May 1939, a fire broke out at number 737 and damaged the building. It was demolished in July.

Within two years, a new owner, Jacob Simon, had purchased the lot and submitted an application to erect a one-story brick store in its place. The application was approved, and by 1942 the jeweler Louis Perloff was operating out of the space, advertising his stock of wholesale wristwatches on a near-monthly basis in *Billboard Magazine* and other outlets. When Perloff moved a few storefronts away in the early 1950s, a stream of other jewelry outlets took his place, one after another: Rieff and Serota, Ben Mazer Diamonds, Brett Jason Jewelry Company, Wolf Jewelry (which would remain associated with the building until its demolition).

Each successive business was part of the larger ecosystem of the Jewelers' Row district, sometimes moving down the street (as Louis Perloff did) or around the corner (like Ben Mazer Diamonds), but almost always staying close to the heart of the district on Sansom Street. The businesses competed with and complemented one another, altering their buildings to show off their products and burnish their sales pitch—a marketing arms race, played out in their architecture. For 737 Walnut Street, this meant a project in 1972 to remove the marble veneer (perhaps it seemed outdated?) and replace it with a brick veneer. (In 1983, the owners added a one-story bump-out at the rear of the building, presumably for additional storage space; unfortunately for that extra storage, three years later robbers escaped with $100,000 worth of the store's cache.)

By the 1990s (and perhaps long before), the building was subdivided into two storefronts: Wolf Jewelry Store, at number 737 proper (the western half), and a few different tenant businesses at what was by this point known as 737A Walnut Street (the eastern half). For a brief period, 737A Walnut Street's occupants bucked the typical patterns of Jewelers' Row, boasting a salon at one point and the textile company Amazulu at another. But by 2006, Marchi Jewelers had moved in, restoring both sides of the storefront to the use befitting the district. It was Marchi that would paint the walls the

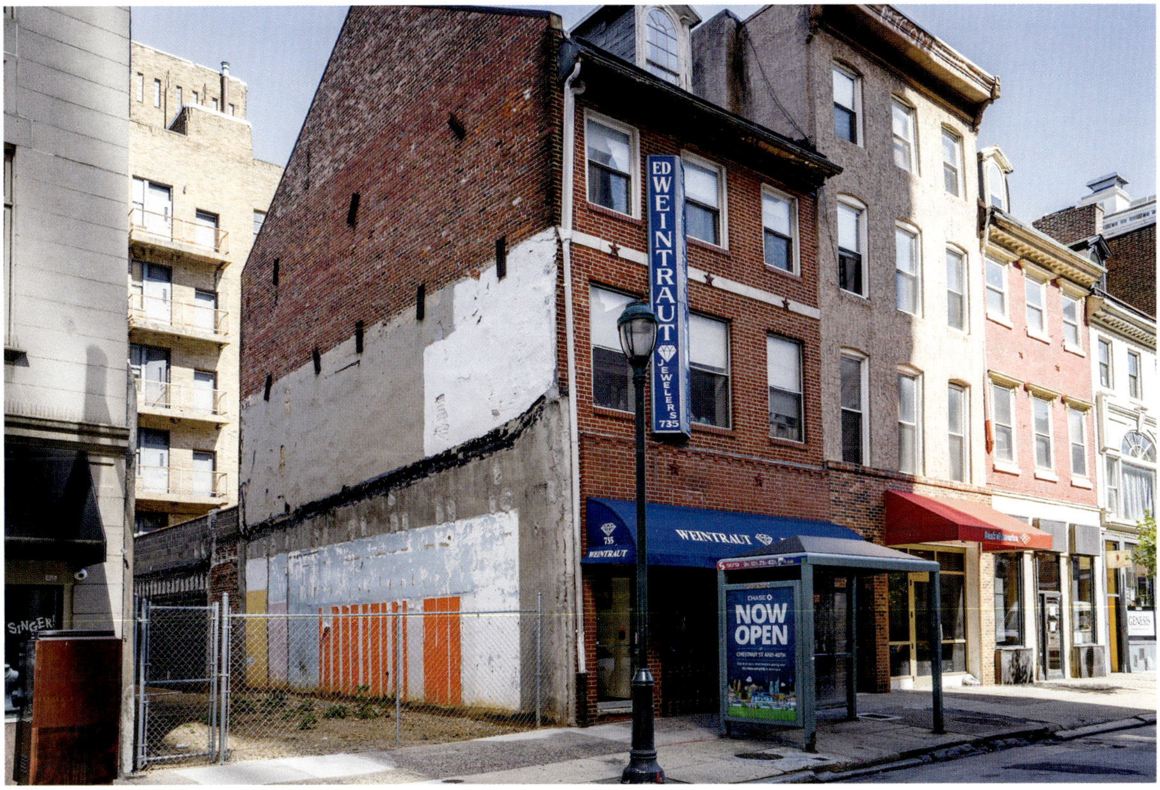

737 Walnut Street. (Photographed September 22, 2020.)

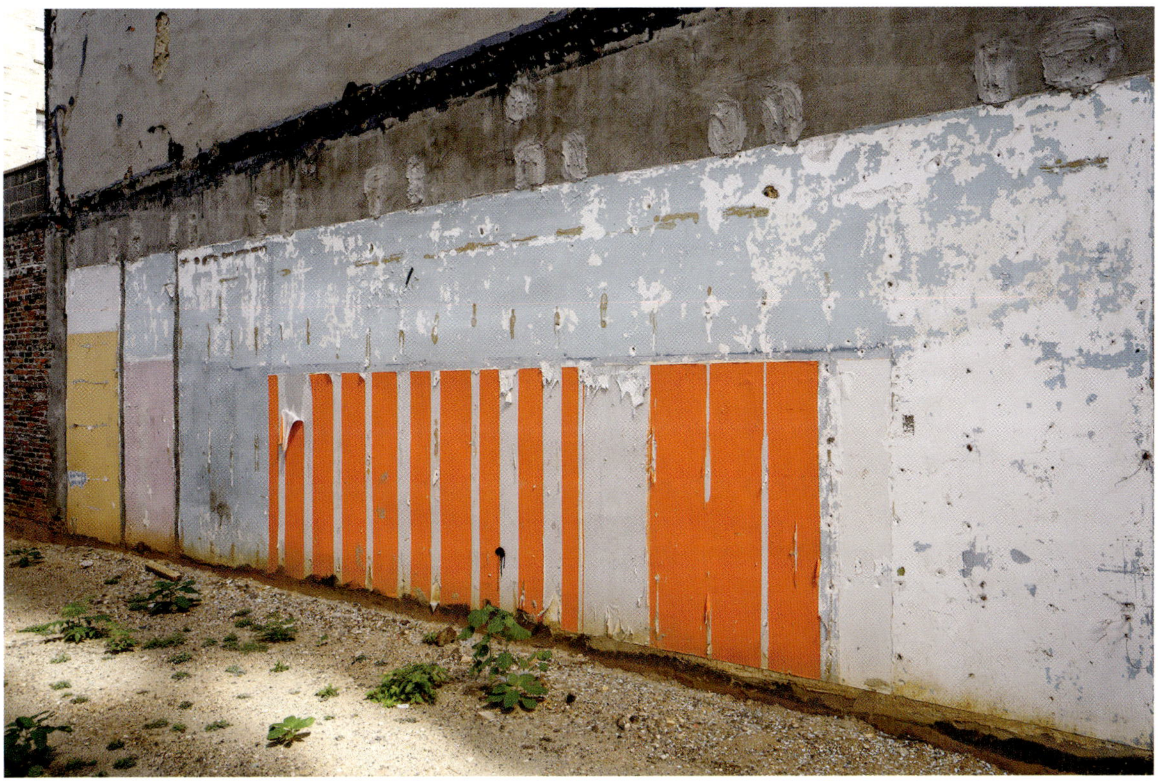

Detail of 737 Walnut Street. (Photographed September 22, 2020.)

vivid shades of orange, blue, pink, and yellow that eventually characterized the site's building ghost.

In 2019, the property changed hands, and a year later, the one-story building at 737/737A Walnut Street was demolished, just as its four-story predecessor had been. Eclipsed as it had always been by its denser neighbors, the building was a prime candidate for redevelopment as a multifamily residence. It would have been easy prey even if the Jewelers' Row area *wasn't* being squeezed by development pressures—which it increasingly was, and still is.

By this time, Robert Wolf of Wolf Jewelry had died, and Marchi had moved a block north, to Sansom Street, relocating within the neighborhood as jewelers had been doing for generations. The stores' inventories were packed away and the site was cleared, leaving only a distinctive paint palette (and a lot of curiosity about it) on the walls of 735 and 739 Walnut Street, both of which remain standing. From construction permit to demolition permit, the building was standing for all of eighty-one years; it was a relatively unremarkable, unprecious building that traded in precious stones. Some of the stores' own wares may last longer than their building ever did.

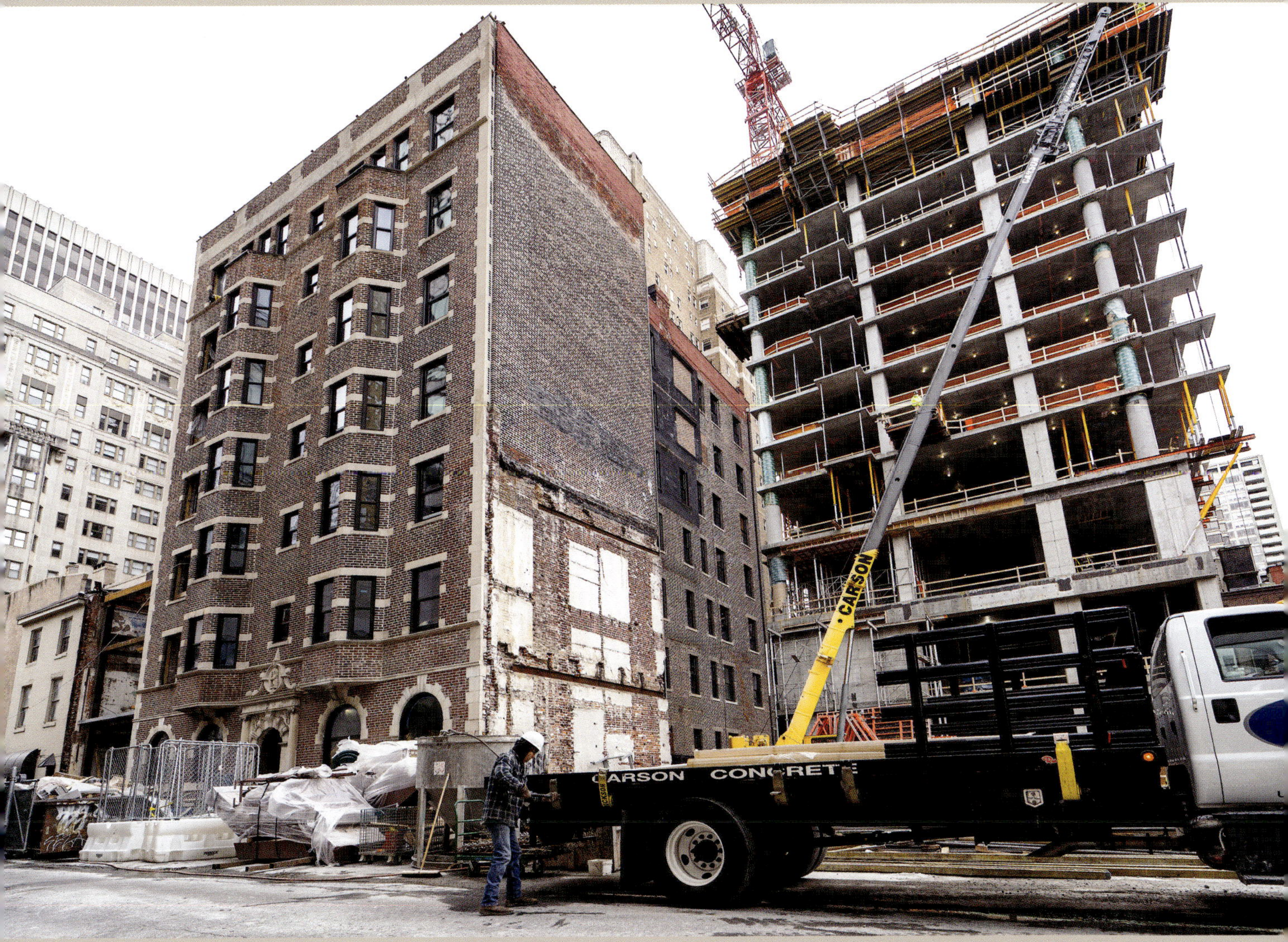

1918–1920 Sansom Street. (Photographed December 2, 2020.)

519 South 4th Street

Constructed before 1858 (likely eighteenth century)
Demolished ca. 1945

The extant two-story building at 517–519 South 4th Street—the structure that continues to occupy the southeast corner of 4th and Gaskill streets today—was constructed in the 1940s, when Israel Forman hired the architect Herman H. Kline to design a building for his meat production facility, the Formost Kosher Sausage Company. Once completed, the manufactory's two-story building sidled up alongside, without ever obscuring, the remnants of the three-and-a-half-story structure that preceded it on the site. A full story taller than its successor, that legacy ghost of 519 South 4th Street was etched in stucco on the neighboring building to the south and is still visible today. It's fitting that both eras would coexist in this way, in this part of Philadelphia, since the building ghost and its descendant structure epitomize the maturation of the Jewish quarter in Philadelphia over the past few centuries.

The older building at 519 South 4th Street was constructed more than a century earlier, possibly in the eighteenth century. In use by the mid-nineteenth century as a dwelling-over-store, the building was a mere "fourth-class" structure, lowlier than the grander houses along Spruce Street and in other, wealthier enclaves. Still, 519 South 4th Street was made of brick, so it (and the surrounding brick buildings) was at least a step up in quality and durability from the frame buildings that remained scattered around Society Hill at the time.

By the second half of the nineteenth century, William Shuman was running his jewelry business out of 519 South 4th Street. Born in Pennsylvania, Shuman predated the waves of immigration that would follow and reshape the neighborhood. After his wife's death in 1868, Shuman leaned especially on his oldest daughter, Emma; in turn, he sold number 519 to her in 1878. Emma apparently became her father's (and family's) landlord, as he maintained his jewelry and watchmaking business at the address for fifteen more years, while many members of the Shuman family lived in the upper stories. In 1903, Emma sold the property again. It was but one of many land exchanges that she made over the course of her lifetime (particularly after her father's death in 1892 left her with a series of generous bequests), giving her enough financial stability to remain unmarried to her death.

Harry Broslavsky (or Baraslavsky, depending on the record) purchased 519 South 4th Street from Emma Shuman in 1903; the house was conveniently located just a block away from his bakery at 605 South 4th Street. Born in Poland during a period of Russian occupation, the Yiddish-speaking Broslavsky lived at number 519 with his wife, Rebecca; three children; and several boarders and servants. With such a full house,

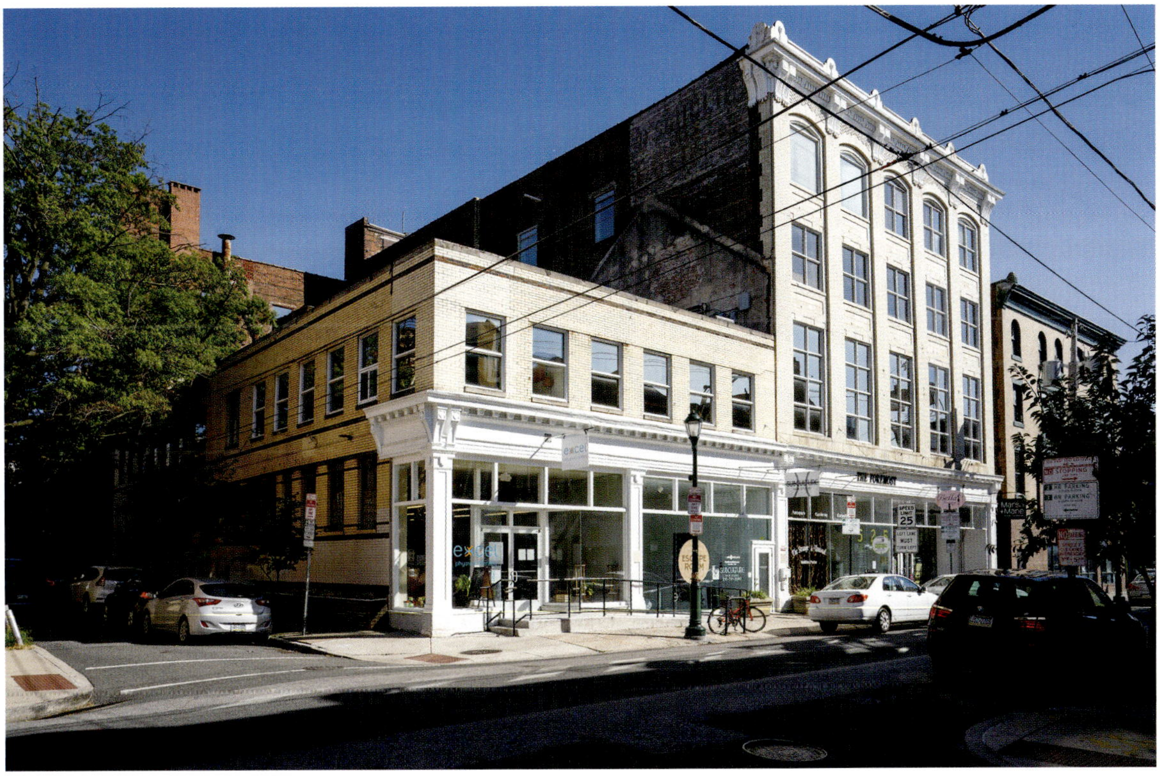

519 South 4th Street. (Photographed September 22, 2020.)

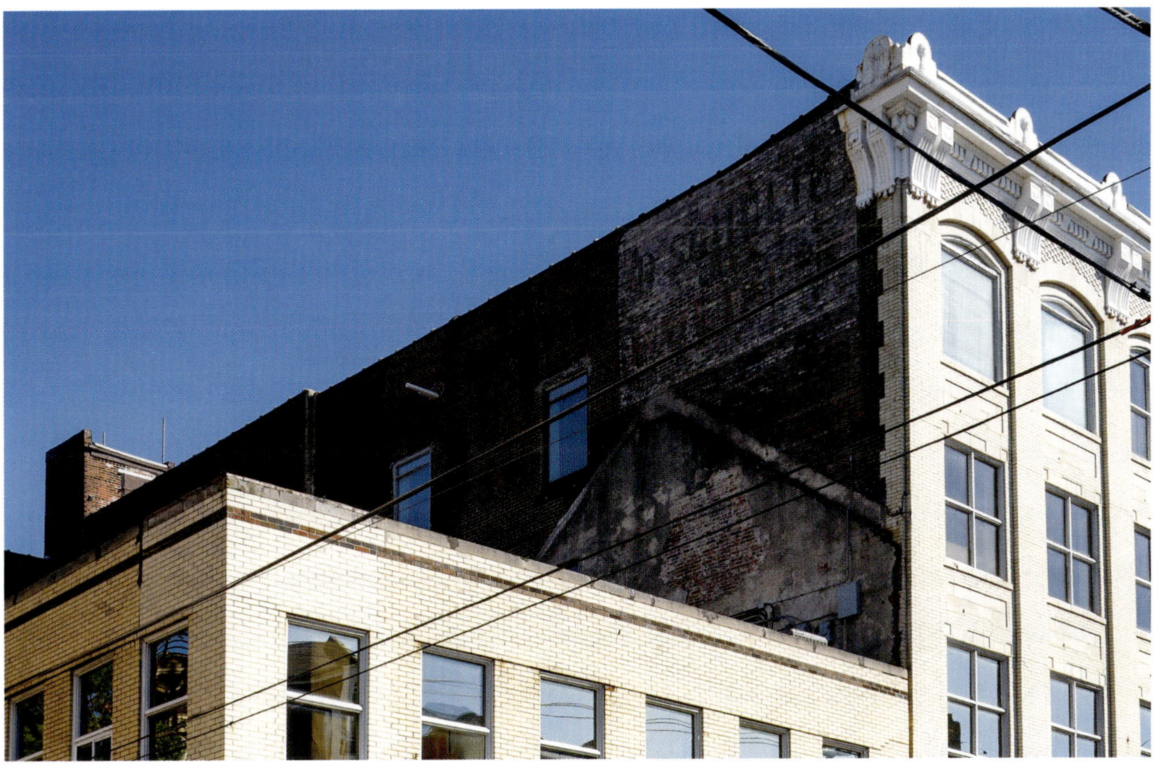

Detail of 519 South 4th Street. (Photographed September 22, 2020.)

Broslavsky, soon after he purchased the building from Emma Shuman, unsurprisingly applied for a permit to construct a two-story brick addition at the rear.

The Broslavskys lived at 519 South 4th Street for sixteen years, selling it in 1919 to Jacob B. Rosenblum, Selig Jaffe, and Louis Jaffe, who operated under the business name Rosenblum and Jaffe Brothers. All three men had immigrated from Russia (it's unclear whether they were from the country itself or an occupied territory, as Broslavsky was). They presumably negotiated the details of the sale with Broslavsky in Yiddish, their shared native tongue.

Rosenblum and the Jaffe brothers held on to number 519 until the 1930s. It changed hands several times within just a few years (including by sheriff's sale, in the midst of the Great Depression) before Israel Forman secured the title in 1937. It was not until the early 1940s, however, that Forman began to make major moves to replace and reshape numbers 517 and 519, engaging in a flurry of land purchases, zoning adjustments, and permit applications to assemble the current parcel. In February 1942, Israel Forman filed paperwork to register the Formost Provisions Company. (Whether the misspelling of "foremost" was intentional or accidental, it did mimic his own surname.) While he worked to get that company off the ground, he began operating Monarch Wine Company out of the address ("all the best quality" Manischewitz wines), and Herman H. Kline began design work for the parcel.

The eighteenth-century iteration of 519 South 4th Street was still standing as of 1944. Over the course of that year, though, Israel Forman purchased and consolidated several parcels along 4th and Gaskill streets, assembling enough land to construct his sausage factory. The proposed use was not without controversy; a wallpaper company at 521 South 4th Street objected to the scheme, concerned (among other issues) that the factory's smells might seep into its products. But Israel Forman would ultimately prevail. He ran the Formost Provisions [aka Kosher] Company until 1970, when he sold it to Riviana Foods.

Today, the accumulated layers of 519 South 4th Street remain in lingering conversation with one another, the older building hovering over its younger, shorter replacement. A trace of the many people, and their shared structure, that came before, the former 519 South 4th Street is more permanent than most building ghosts have the chance to be.

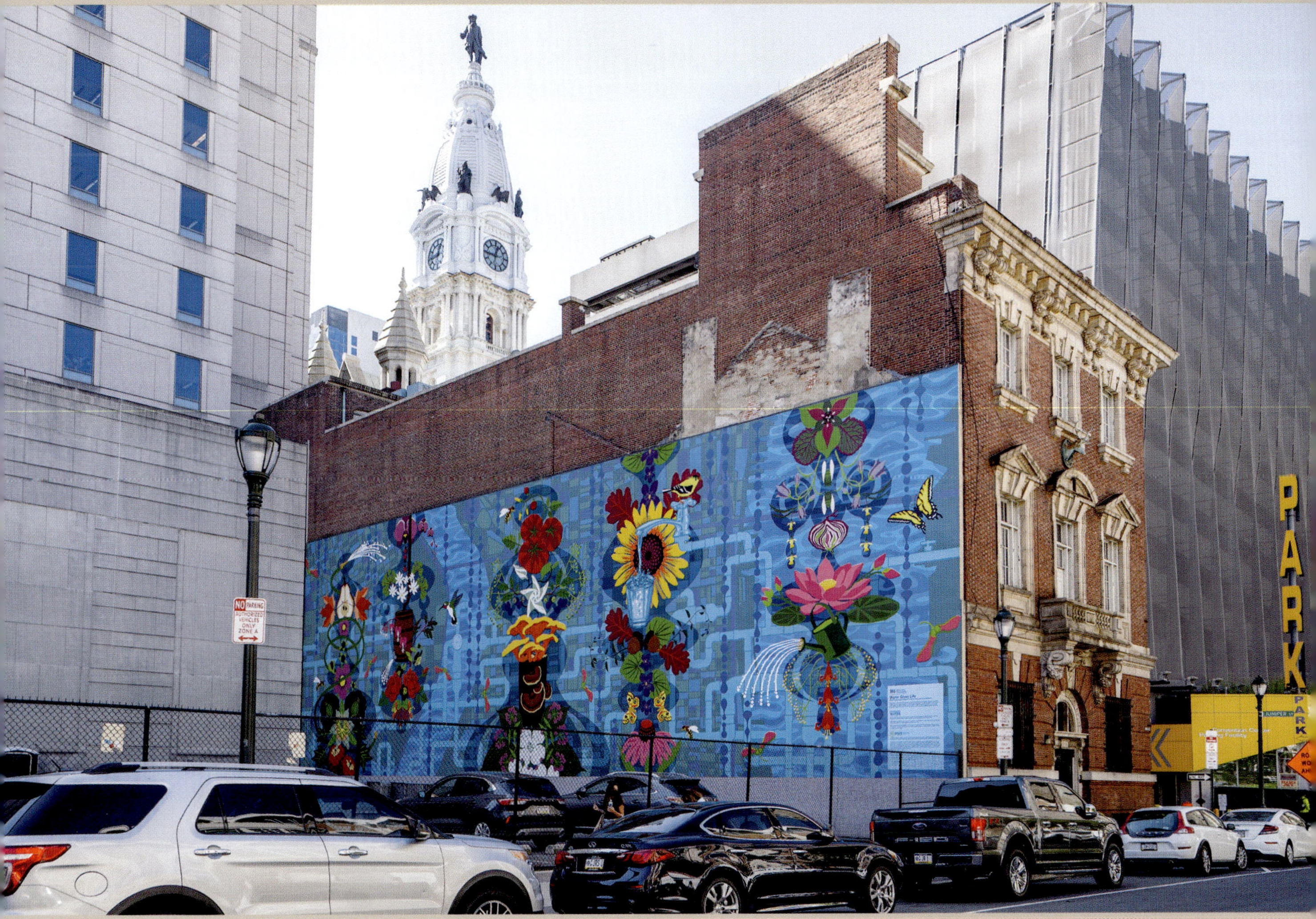

1309 Arch Street. (Photographed September 22, 2020.)

1814 Ludlow Street

Constructed before 1860
Demolished in 2020

For the century and a half that it stood, 1814 Ludlow Street was a relatively nondescript member of the Center City rowhouse class. Its brick façade was anonymous in its ubiquity: the familiar three-story, two-bay arrangement, with a touch of dentil detailing at the cornice to help it blend in with the other houses in the row. It was so modest compared with its robust counterparts on the tree-named streets that both this building and its neighbor at 1812 Ludlow Street were eventually torn down in quick succession with hardly an objection, let alone an outcry. Even the building ghost of 1814 Ludlow Street is unremarkable.

Yet there it stood, for more than 150 years, home to an untold number of people and, increasingly in the twentieth century, a pastiche of businesses. By 1925, Newmark and Brother had moved into the building. (It was a curious moniker for the electrician company, referring to Morris Newmark by name but alluding to his younger sibling Manuel, who shared his surname, simply as "Brother.") When they were just fourteen and twelve, respectively, Morris and Manuel Newmark had emigrated from Russia (or a Russian-occupied territory), arriving in the United States in 1910. By 1920, Morris had set up his own company, and five years later, he and his brother had established offices at 1814 Ludlow Street.

Morris and Manuel Newmark's business was not typically associated with new buildings. Instead, throughout the 1920s and '30s, they were "maintainers," responsible for altering and improving the electrical systems of existing buildings such as Eastern State Penitentiary, the Stephen Girard School, Northeast High School, and the elegant commercial buildings at 1410 Chestnut Street and 1617 Walnut Street. Their reparative work—so essential to ensuring that a city's most prominent buildings remain functional, extant, and even beautiful—originated in the rowhouse on Ludlow Street, part of the much larger universe of utterly mundane buildings.

The brothers rented space on Ludlow Street until 1940, by which time Morris had amassed enough funds to purchase a building several blocks north, at 1924 Arch Street. Unquestionably grander than the brick building at 1814 Ludlow Street, the late nineteenth-century brownstone on Arch Street presented a more distinguished face to the brothers' clients. Their fifteen years on Ludlow Street would be an insignificant chapter of their career in comparison, then, if 1814 Ludlow Street's very mediocrity didn't point to a bigger, utterly vital dimension of the urban fabric: the city's most monumental buildings on its most dignified thoroughfares could not exist without the

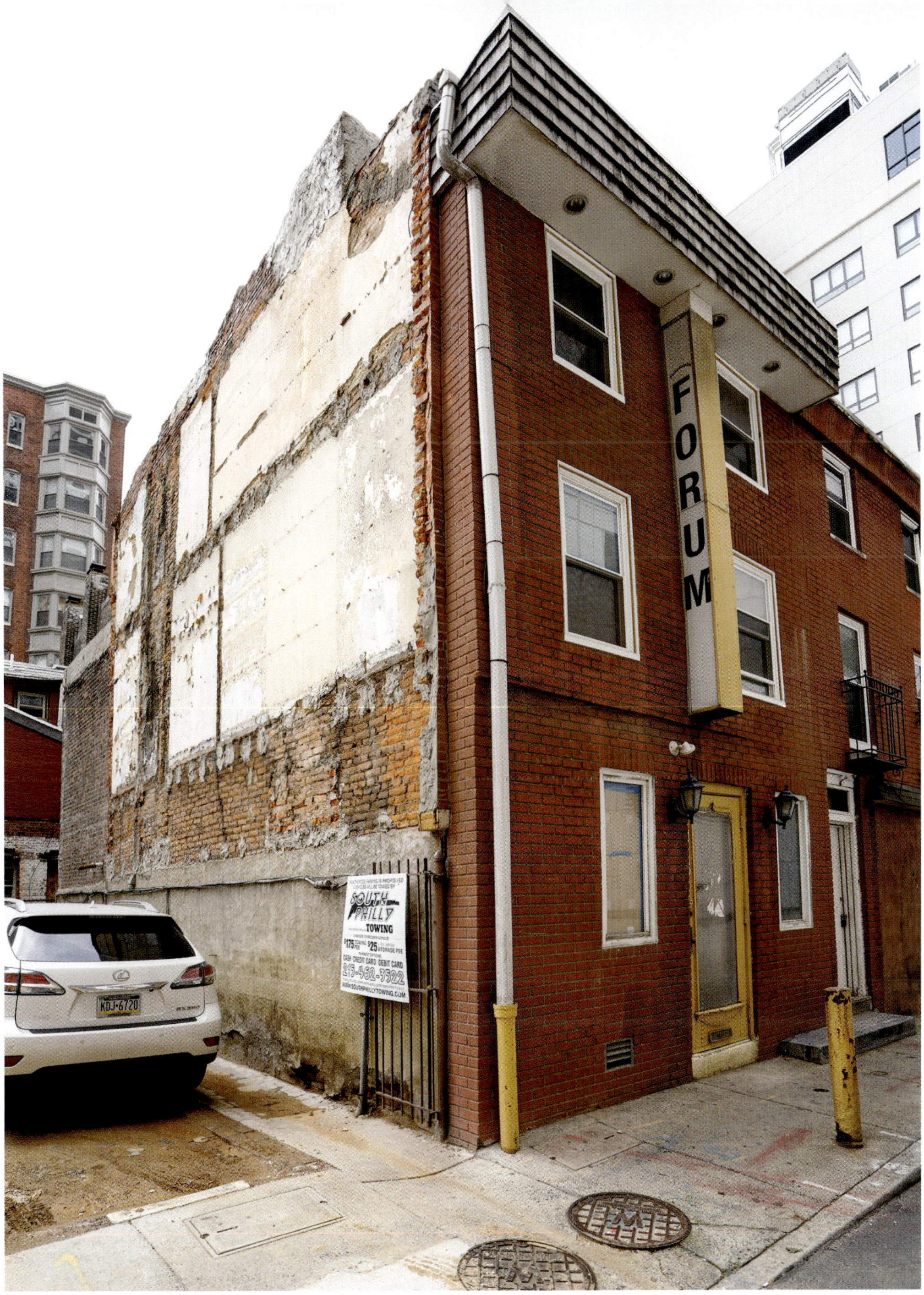

1814 Ludlow Street. (Photographed December 2, 2020.)

infrastructure of its smallest rowhouses on its tiniest side streets—and the people who live and work there.

Even buildings such as 1924 Arch Street are not immune to the wrecking ball that would claim 1814 Ludlow Street. In fact, the Arch Street structure fell first, seven years before its humbler counterpart.

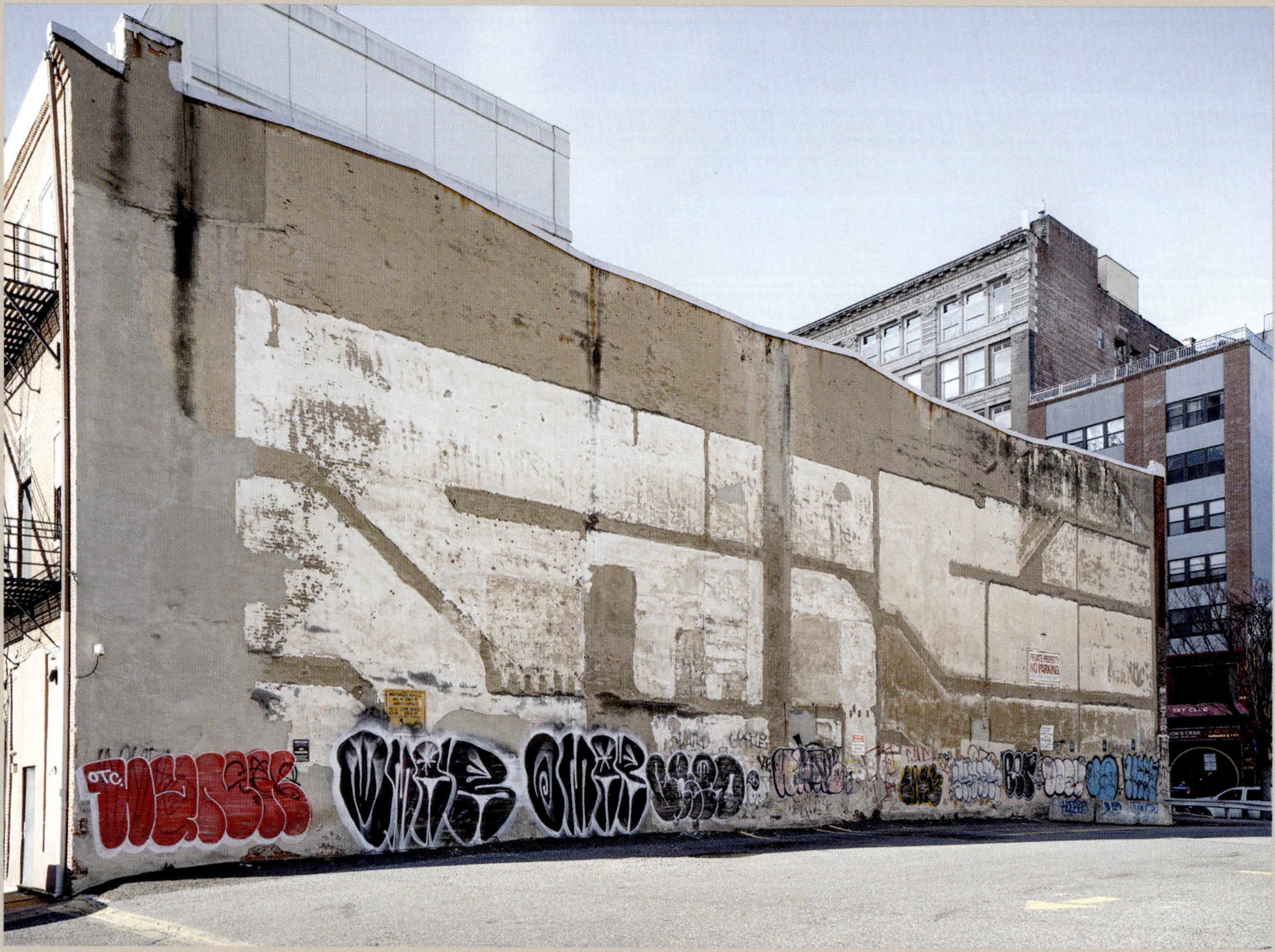

1010–1018 Arch Street. (Photographed December 3, 2020.)

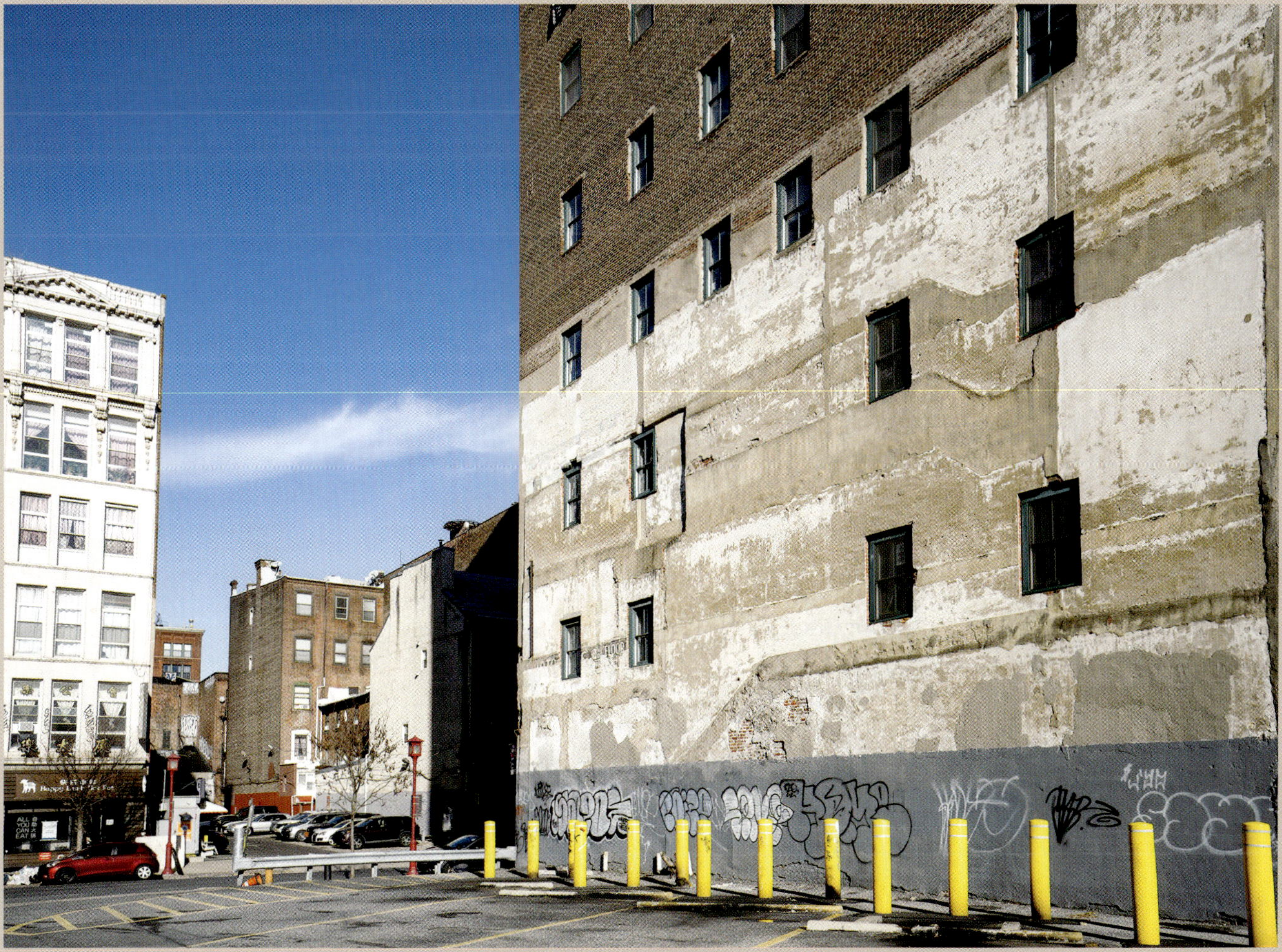

1010–1018 Arch Street. (Photographed December 3, 2020.)

1801–1803 Fairmount Avenue

Earliest section (number 1801) constructed by 1858
Demolished in 2020

The building at 1801–1803 Fairmount Avenue ended in recent years as a hollowed-out crater, but it started in the nineteenth century as solid blocks of brick and marble. As of 1860, number 1801 was, in fact, the only solid presence on the block (along what was then known as Coates Street, until it became Fairmount Avenue in 1873). Its neighbors to the west, including number 1803, did not materialize until later.

The structure at 1801 Coates Street was an oddly shaped building from the start (the street didn't conform to the same grid as most of the city's east-west thoroughfares, resulting in an irregular parcel). It was initially three stories tall and built of brick, despite the fact that for several decades at least, brick was not the specialty at 1801 Coates Street; marble was. From about 1860 (if not earlier) until about 1880, John Preston Kochersperger—the "marble mantle man"—lived there, working out of the marble yard at the rear of the building.

While Kochersperger carved and dressed his marble mantels, residents moved in and out of number 1801; once number 1803 was built, they did the same there. (The two buildings would not share an owner or a floor plan until the mid-twentieth century.) With each wave of tenants, the buildings no doubt saw new coats of plaster and paint; one renter, Charles White, might even have done some of the work himself, as he was a house painter.

Beginning around 1889, the Jefferson Democratic Club held its political meetings in number 1801 for nearly two decades. When the local carpenters' union went on strike in 1890, and eventually won a new contract, it celebrated the victory with its first post-contract job at the club. There the carpenters constructed wood-frame alterations and additions of some kind—perhaps number 1801 needed sprucing up to fit in with its fresher neighbors along what was now Fairmount Avenue.

When the first floor at 1801 Fairmount became a grocery store in the 1890s, the retail counters were, fittingly, topped with a solid slab of marble. In 1902, though, the grocery store operator sold off the marble-top counter; it was no doubt the most expensive item the store ever traded.

In the 1920s and 1930s, the materials at 1801 Fairmount Avenue got greasier and grittier, as an auto parts store took over and a sheet metal business agent moved in. By 1938, the brick wall required repairs, and by 1945 it was beginning to fail on the upper floors. In April 1946, Richard E. Newman purchased 1801 Fairmount; he bought number 1803 in July. The two buildings were both three stories tall at the time.

In 1947, Newman placed ads in the *Inquirer*, seeking union bricklayers for a long-

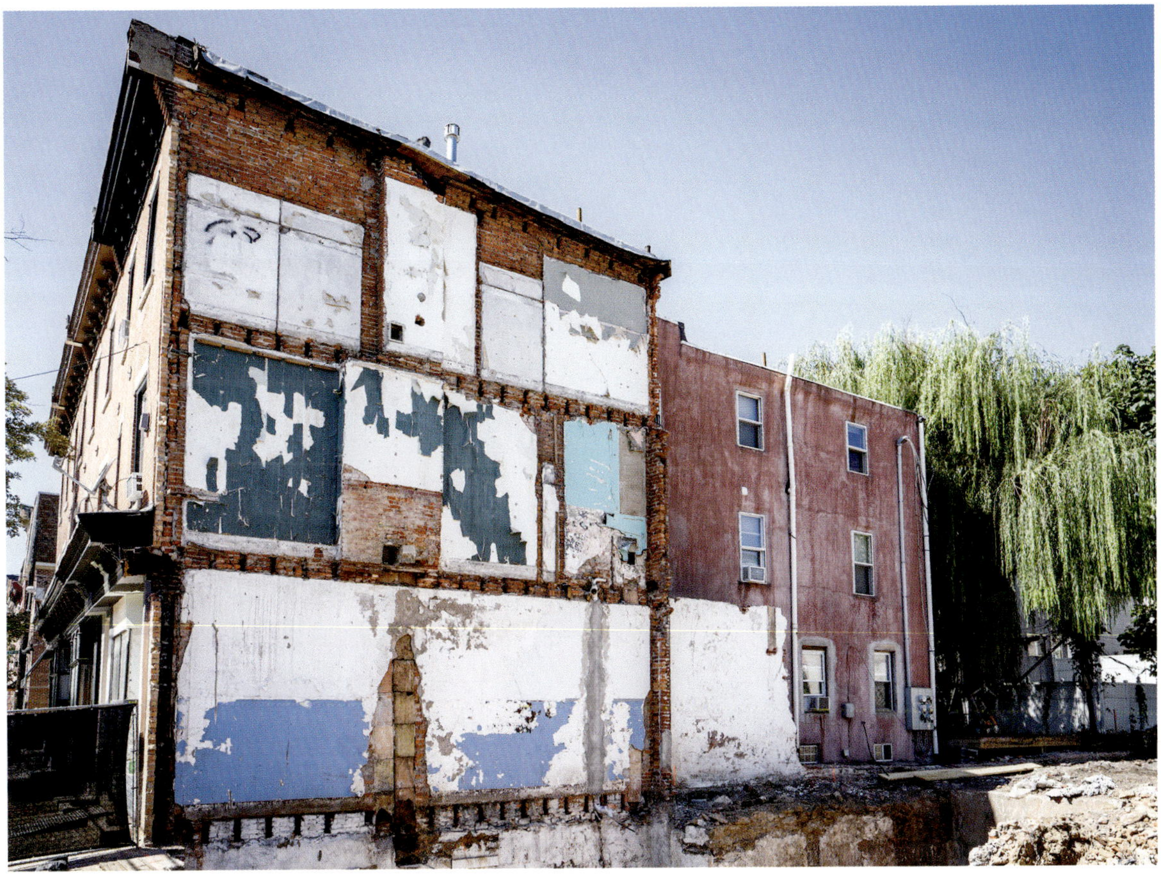

1801–1803 Fairmount Avenue. (Photographed September 22, 2020.)

term job. Soon after, 1801 Fairmount Avenue was whittled down to a third of its original height, as laborers removed the second and third stories and repaired bulges in the remaining walls. In exchange for the loss, the surviving one-story section received an elegantly turned corner at the intersection of 18th and Fairmount streets. Metal trim curved around both sides of the building above the new modern entrance and windows, definitively linking 1801–1803 as one parcel.

In 1952, Newman attempted to recapture some of the demolished square footage, as he applied for a permit to add a second story above the one-story section at number 1801. He won approval but apparently never acted on it. The 1947 job marked the last major alteration to the structure.

For seventy more years, the building's residents and retail operations continued to make their presence felt in material ways. New paint was applied to the walls. (By the time the building was demolished, the interior was finished in deep teals and sky blues.) Grease from the motor rebuilding shop dripped onto the floors, which were no doubt refinished at some point, or perhaps carpets were stapled in for a time.

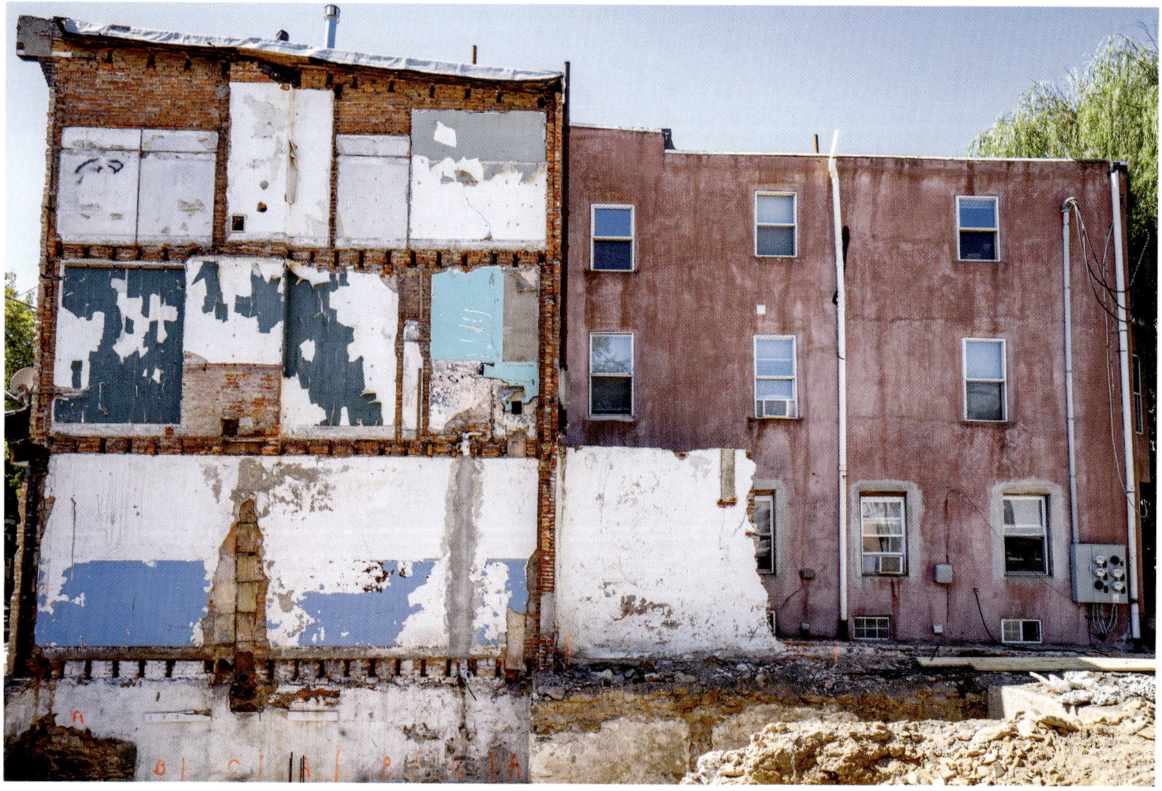

Detail of 1801–1803 Fairmount Avenue. (Photographed September 22, 2020.)

In 2000, the artist Robert Woodward—known as "Peanutbutter"—moved his studio into the building. His palette called on many of the same materials that had accrued on the site for more than a century—ceramic, wood, stone, and metal—and he introduced others, including resin. His large collages made their way from his "Peanut Gallery" at number 1801–1803 to the Girard Avenue subway station, among other places.

In 2020, the site was cleared, and all of its solid scraps were carted away, leaving behind a void of dirt. In the brief interlude before its successor was built, however, the building ghost of 1801–1803 Fairmount Avenue remained visible, insisting that something palpable had been there once and hinting that something new would materialize there again.

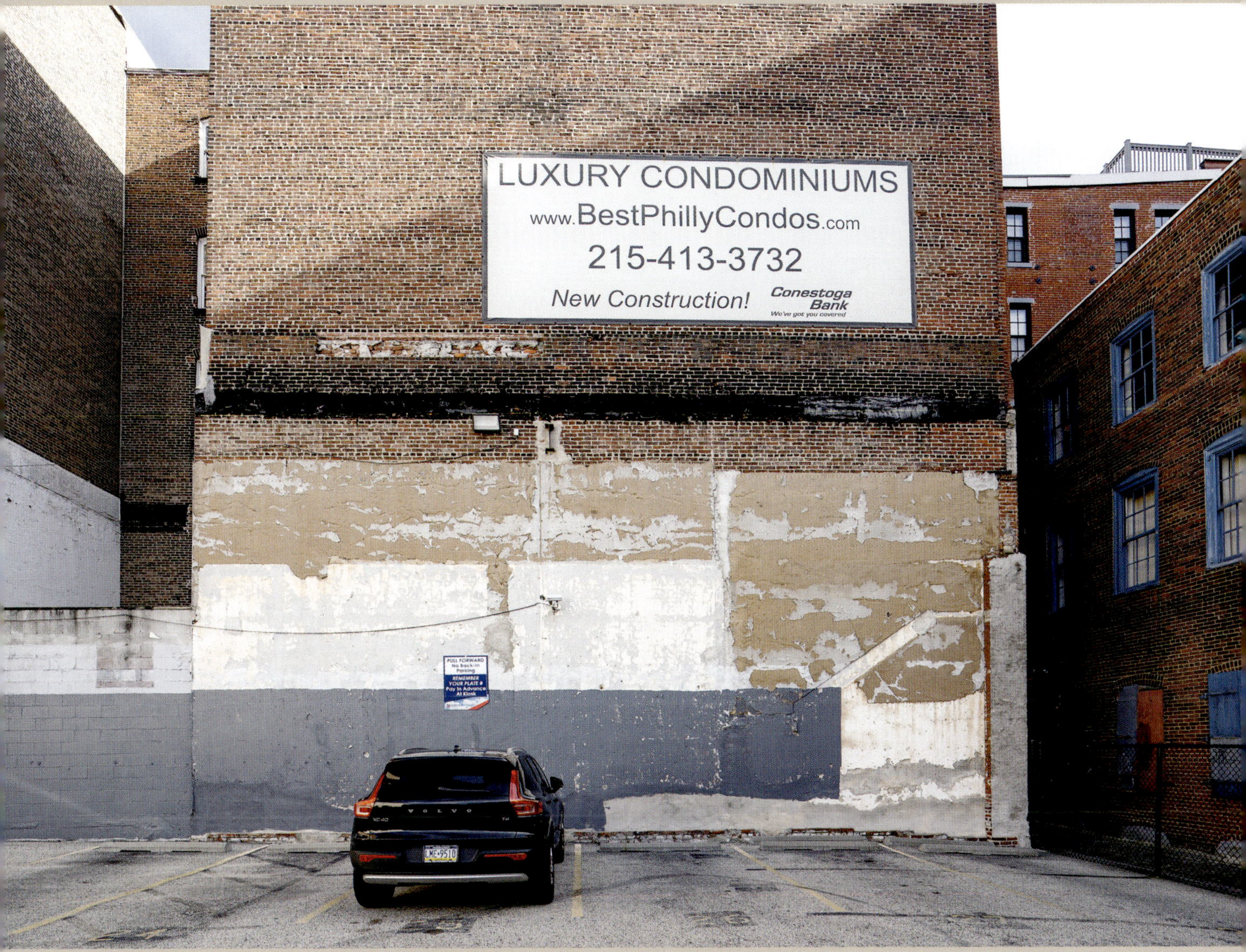

19 South 2nd Street. (Photographed December 3, 2020.)

1828 Rittenhouse Square

Constructed ca. 1856
Demolished ca. 1958

The ghost of 1828 Rittenhouse Square offers fewer traces than most, lingering only as an outline on the east elevation of 1830 Rittenhouse Square. A smooth stretch of stucco over the neighbor's otherwise brick wall, the ghost of number 1828 is accented only by its former chimneys. It reads rather like a blank canvas or, perhaps, an empty drafting board—if one were to read into it the lives of two of its most famous residents, the sculptor Katherine Cohen and the architect Edgar V. Seeler.

Cohen lived there just before venturing to Paris for several years of study; Seeler lived there just after returning home from the City of Light. The rowhouse at 1828 Rittenhouse Square (or 1828 Locust Street, as it was alternately known when Cohen and Seeler each lived there) was the first of many creative homes for both the artist and the architect. Separated in their tenancies by only a decade, they each lived at number 1828 while attempting to launch their creative careers in the United States.

Katherine Cohen's family moved into the four-story brick building around 1866, about a decade after it was constructed overlooking Rittenhouse Square. Like so many of its rowhouse cousins, the building had ample windows—each trimmed with stone lintels and sills—on its north and south elevations. Its east and west elevations, meanwhile, bumped up against number 1826 and number 1830, the latter of which was the fifty-two-room mansion designed by Frank Furness and owned by Colonel Thomas A. Scott, vice president of the Pennsylvania Railroad.

Born in 1859, Katherine Cohen was still young when the family moved in; she grew up there with her two older sisters and two younger brothers. In her teenage years, she became interested in art and eventually enrolled in the School of Design for Women (now Moore College of Art and Design) and, later, the Pennsylvania Academy of Fine Arts. She studied under some of the finest artists of the day, including Thomas Eakins, Augustus Saint-Gaudens, and John J. Boyle. It was Boyle's specialization in sculpture that eventually became Cohen's, as well.

Cohen's family was deeply involved in the congregation of Mikveh Israel, and her Jewish faith found its way into her art career as she created busts of prominent Jewish Philadelphians and incorporated Jewish themes into her work. Her career was relatively unusual among her Jewish counterparts, since traditional interpretations of Jewish texts held that such portraits and figural sculptures were forbidden as "graven images."

Katherine M. Cohen was first listed in Philadelphia city directories in 1884, the year she launched her own artistic studio. As capacious as the house at 1828 Rittenhouse Square was, it could not accommodate both her family and her studio, so she (together with a few artist friends) secured a large workroom on the fourth floor at 1334

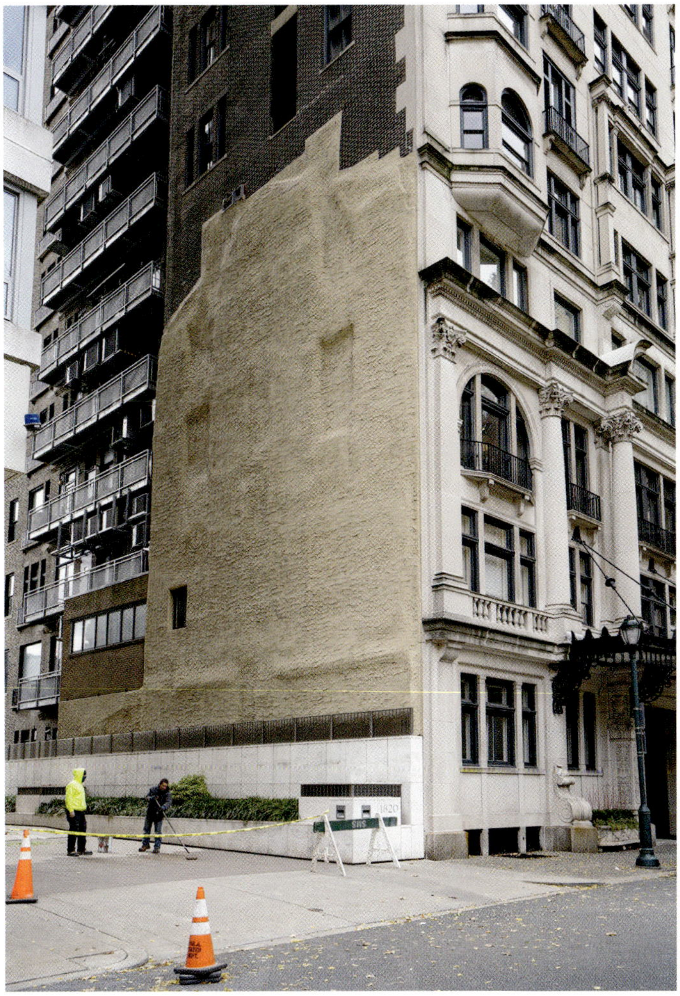

1828 Rittenhouse Square. (Photographed December 2, 2020.)

Chestnut Street, situated above a publishing house on the lower floors. There she could spread out her materials and studies, with no siblings underfoot.

Yet she chafed at the distance between her home on Rittenhouse Square and her studio on Chestnut Street. She maintained the arrangement for four years, until she left around 1888 for further study in Paris. There she got a taste of the possibilities that Paris's built environment offered, which Philadelphia (and so many other American cities) did not: affordable artists' studios with living rooms attached. The proximity was a boon to her artistic life, and the experience lingered even after she left Paris. In 1893, she gave a high-profile speech about the issue in the Woman's Building at the World's Columbian Exposition in Chicago:

> An artist's chief grief is that life is too short for him to accomplish what he wants to do even in his own special line of work, and this is equally true of woman, for talent knows no sex. There is another important consideration, and that is the lack here of studios with living rooms attached, at moderate rents. An artist comes back here from Paris with very little ready money, for

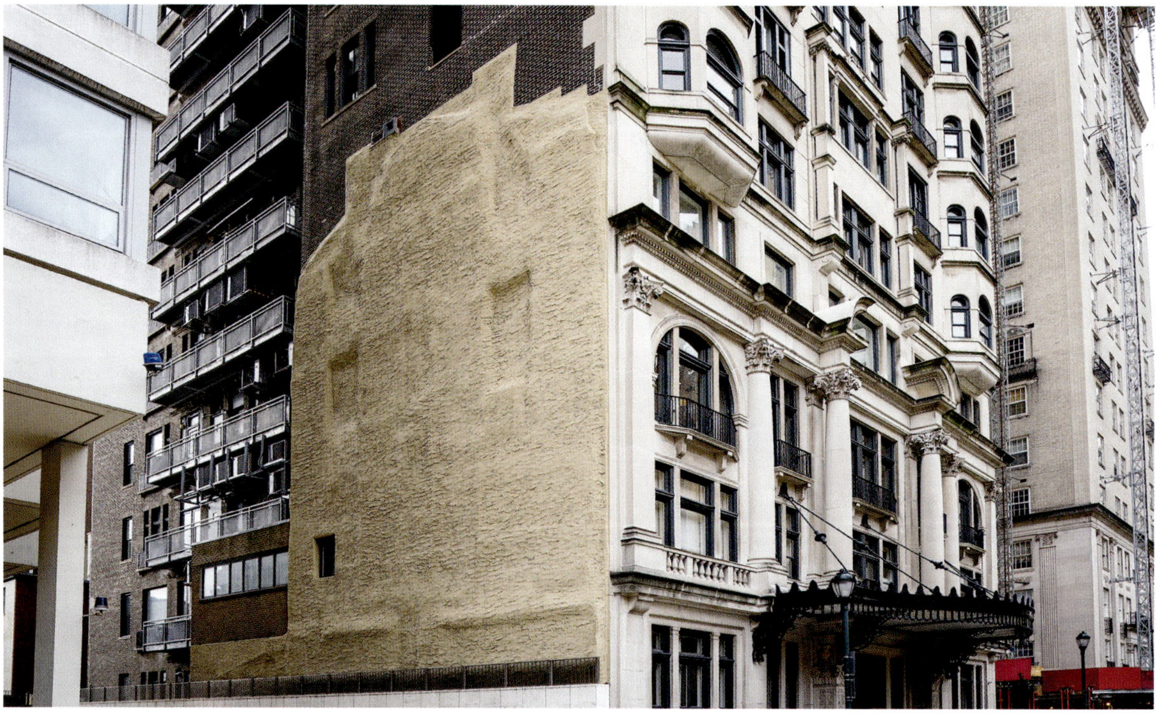

Detail of 1828 Rittenhouse Square. (Photographed December 2, 2020.)

> he has his way still to make. He has had there a studio with a fine light and all necessary fittings, . . . at a very moderate rent. . . . What does he find when he comes here, say in New York or Boston, or Philadelphia or San Francisco, or Chicago? He must take his studio by the year, and it costs a small fortune at that, and there are scarcely any living rooms, except in a very few instances. We hope that some one will recognize this need of the coming artists, and put up studio buildings with small apartments or living rooms attached, and let them at a moderate rent.

Cohen lived a privileged life on Rittenhouse Square, brushing shoulders with high-powered neighbors and overlooking one of the city's toniest public spaces. Yet for all its significance in the years that launched her artistic career, 1828 Rittenhouse Square ultimately laid bare the contrasts between her current creative setup and the artistic life she desired to lead. Upon her return from Paris, she left 1828 Rittenhouse Square to find lodging elsewhere in the neighborhood (her family had left the house by this time, too). In the ensuing years, her home and studio addresses inched progressively closer—and yet, in Philadelphia at least, she apparently never managed to make them one and the same.

The same year Cohen opened her studio, Edgar Viguers Seeler graduated from Central High School. By the time she gave her speech at the 1893 exposition, he had graduated from both the Pennsylvania Museum and School of Industrial Art and the Massachusetts Institute of Technology and had studied for four years in the atelier of Victor Laloux at the École des Beaux-Arts in Paris. He returned to his hometown of Philadelphia in 1894, and he and his brother George (a bookkeeper) rented rooms (or perhaps the entire house) at 1828 Rittenhouse Square. That same year, Edgar Seeler launched his own practice, taking an office at 328 Chestnut Street in Old City, even as he also commuted in the other direction to a new post as an assistant professor of architectural design at the University of Pennsylvania. His were longer commutes than Cohen's, but 1828 Rittenhouse Square was a relatively convenient midpoint between the geographic extremes of Seeler's working life.

In his two years of living on Rittenhouse Square, Seeler secured the first commissions of what would be a productive and illustrious career. Among the earliest of his works was a building for Penn's Dental School (now known as Hayden Hall), the construction of which overlapped perfectly with his time living at number 1828. Fittingly enough, the building that Seeler designed at Penn would house the university's architecture program in the mid-twentieth century.

Edgar (and George) Seeler moved out of 1828 Rittenhouse Square around 1896, and two years later Edgar ended his teaching position at Penn. He would go on to design prominent commercial commissions for the Curtis Publishing Company, Penn Mutual Life Insurance, and the *Philadelphia Bulletin*, as well as several residential and institutional projects. In some ways, then, 1828 Rittenhouse Square was for him the building that launched scores of buildings.

In the decades after the Seelers moved out, development leapfrogged back and forth on both sides of 1828 Rittenhouse Square. As many of its neighbors were replaced by modernist newcomers, number 1828 increasingly looked like a remnant from another century—and it was. In 1913, a seventeen-story tower with forty luxury apartments replaced the Scott family mansion to the west and loomed over the four-story rowhouse at 1828 Rittenhouse Square. Meanwhile, other new apartment buildings went up at the east end of the block at the mid-century mark, creeping closer to number 1828.

Finally, around 1958, development pressures grew too strong, and 1828 Rittenhouse Square was torn down to make way for an apartment building (1820 Rittenhouse Square) that took another decade to materialize. The demolished building did not disappear without a trace, however: it left behind a building ghost on the tower at 1830 Rittenhouse Square, as if the older structure at number 1828 insisted on pulling rank on its more fashionable new neighbor. The building ghost's presence is subtly felt, receding into the cityscape as a stucco imprint that frames a nondescript driveway where the house used to be. Yet in the years that it was present, 1828 Rittenhouse Square cultivated two of Philadelphia's most renowned artisans, lending itself to the accumulated creativity of the city.

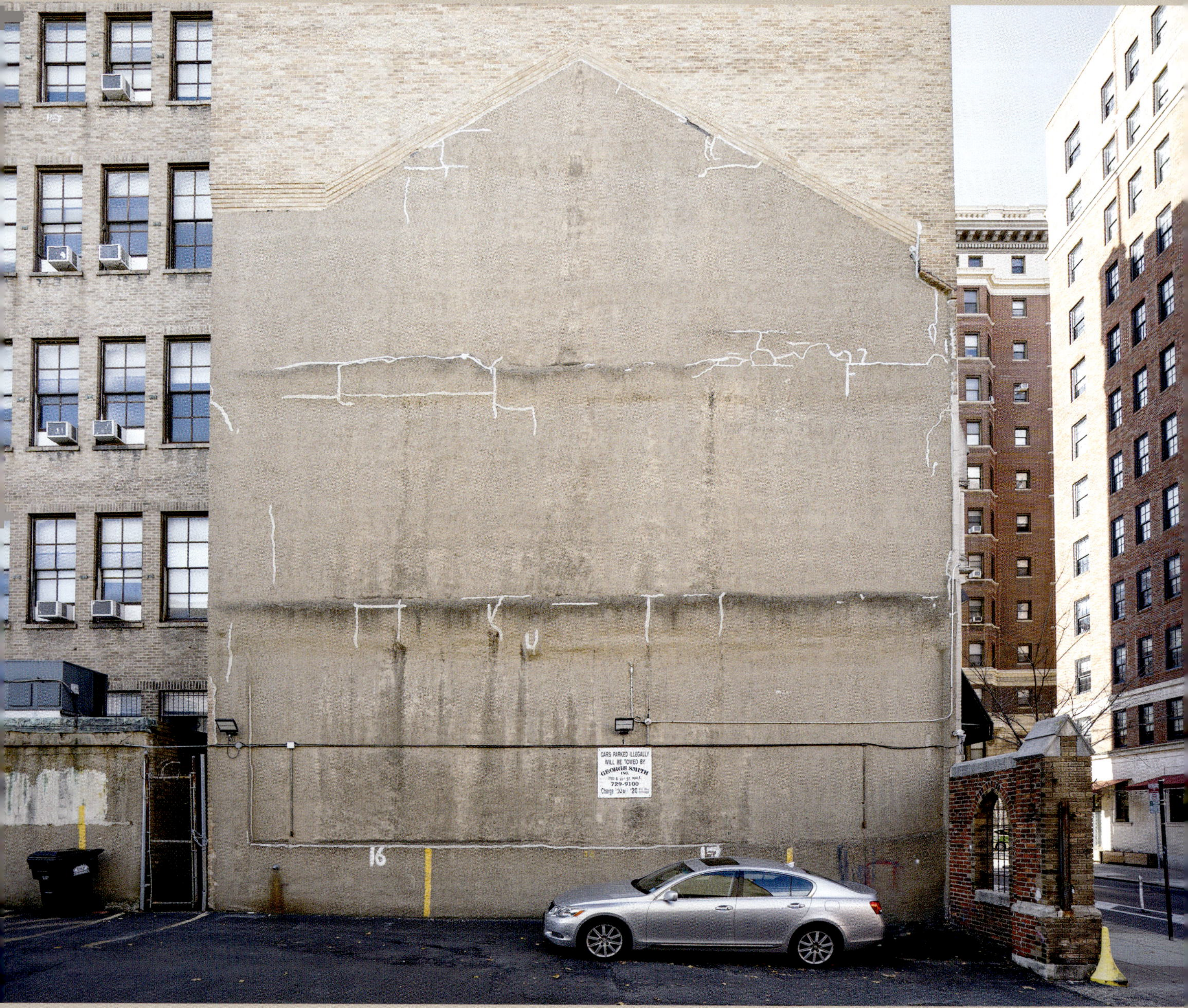

1228 Spruce Street. (Photographed December 3, 2020.)

2009–2011 Sansom Street

2009 Sansom Street constructed as one-story building ca. 1870

2011 Sansom Street constructed before 1860

2009–2011 Sansom Street demolished in 2020; the façade of number 2009 was retained

Originally erected as two separate buildings (one industrial, one residential), 2009 and 2011 Sansom Street were associated for several decades with Thomas E. Cahill, the wealthy businessman who would donate much of his estate to establish the Roman Catholic High School for Boys. By comparison, the women of these buildings led a much less visible existence than their male counterparts. They lived—and in several cases, died—within numbers 2009 and 2011, yet they were rarely acknowledged in official records that tracked Sansom Street's occupants and occupations.

It was not uncommon for women to go unlisted in the city's annual directories—particularly married women, who were considered sufficiently represented by their husbands and sons. When they *were* mentioned in official records, it was typically at the touchpoints of birth, marriage, or death; the years in-between were more often than not left unaddressed. The throughlines of their lives within these buildings are thus more difficult to trace.

It is unsurprising, then, that 2011 Sansom Street could have stood for nearly twenty years before any female names were inscribed in association with it. Even then, we learn only about Margaret Hassett when her parents, John and Bridget Hassett, had to bury her in 1872 at three months old. A few years later, the first mention of Annie Stark emerges shortly before her death. Born in Ireland around 1843, she immigrated to the United States at an unknown date, settled in Philadelphia at some unknown point, married an unknown man, and lived at 2011 Sansom Street for an unspecified amount of time. All that can be proved, definitively, is that she was living at 2011 Sansom Street when she died of cholera in 1879. The rest of her life inside the three-story brick store/residence left no documented trace.

Fifteen years later, Rose Slavin, too, died while living at number 2011. When the *Philadelphia Times* published mention of her death, it noted that her funeral would be held on the morning of February 12 "from her husband's residence." Like Annie Stark, Rose Slavin was born in Ireland (although Slavin was a decade older than Stark). She had married Edward Slavin and settled in Philadelphia by 1860; they may have immigrated to the United States that very year. If she is, indeed, the same "Rose Slavin" who arrived in 1860 (without further documentation, it is impossible to prove), then she made the transatlantic voyage on the *Emerald Isle*—a ship named for the very place she was leaving. Once settled at 2011 Sansom Street, she (and Edward, and their family, and all of the other boarders who overlapped with them) lived on a jumbled block of

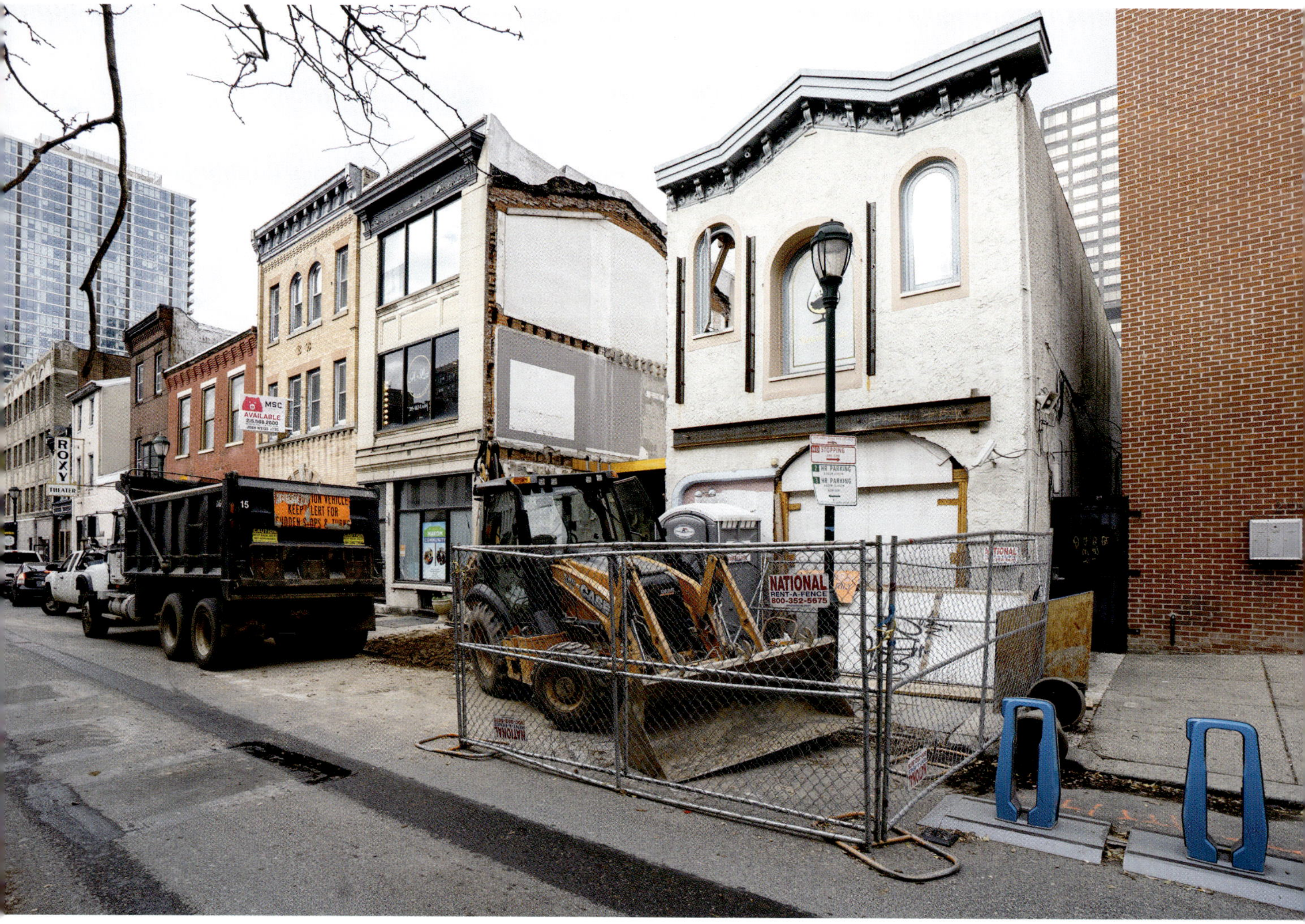

2009–2011 Sansom Street. (Photographed December 2, 2020.)

central Philadelphia, next door to what was for many decades a carpentry shop at 2009 Sansom Street.

Other women came and went from the two buildings as the twentieth century progressed; some, such as Annie Warshavsky and Matilda Roseman, were even included on the deeds. But any progress, however small, that these sales might have signaled with respect to women's financial status and autonomy was somewhat undermined by the sort of advertisement that ran a few times in the *Philadelphia Inquirer* in 1958, on behalf of the Town and Country Cocktail Lounge, which had taken over 2009 Sansom: "Female Help Wanted: Checkroom girl. Attractive." There is no way to know, of course, which woman made the cut. As with so many aspects of the women associated with 2009–2011 Sansom Street, the details remain elusive.

333 North 11th Street

Constructed ca. 1858
Demolished ca. 2008

When it was torn down around 2008 to make way for . . . nothing, 333 North 11th Street left behind an unexpected mid-block breach near Callowhill Street and not one, but two, building ghosts. Sandwiched between intact rowhouses at 331 and 335 North 11th Street, the ghosts are practically a musical score of plaster notes, smoother at the first floor and ascending into increasingly staccato beats of alcoves, bookcases, and closet shelves on the second and third floors. When the ghosts were photographed in September 2020, the party walls loomed over a gaping chasm where the basement had been, leaving little doubt as to the exact footprint this building once occupied. And yet for all that empty space, 333 North 11th Street actually spent much of its existence quite full: for most of the twentieth century, the building was a rooming house with as many as sixteen units. Suddenly, the musical score on the party walls looks even more cacophonous.

The building was constructed in the late 1850s by Samuel Jacobs, a carriage manufacturer who purchased the property in 1856. Once the three-story building was constructed (by 1860 at the latest), Jacobs's family lived there, including his wife, Rebecca, and his children, Catherine, Henry (or Harry), and William. They were joined by Caroline Dorsey and her daughter Mary, who worked as servants for the household. Teenage Henry was a clerk, apparently at the same carriage manufactory where Samuel was employed, as father and son both worked at 617 Arch Street as of the late 1860s.

When Samuel Jacobs sold the building in 1871, the single-family dwelling again became a family seat of sorts, this time for the Riehle family. Catherine Riehle, widow of the physician Henry J. Riehle, was living around the corner at 1020 Callowhill Street when she purchased the building from her neighbor Samuel Jacobs. Her sons moved in first: Frederick and Henry B. Riehle, partners in a business that traded in some sort of scales, lived there by 1872. Within a couple years, their mother joined them; she remained there until her death in 1894. The house would remain in the Riehle family's hands until 1939, when Catherine's daughter-in-law Emma Riehle eventually sold it.

In the wake of Catherine's death, however, the Riehle family's relationship with the property was more distant, as it became a robust rooming house for working-class residents. Ironworkers, cooks, printers, cabinetmakers, teamsters, and other laborers climbed the stoop and passed through the brief foyer in the first decades of the twentieth century. They used the address to look for work, to license their marriages, and to register for the World War I draft (even when they were long past the age of serviceable deployment).

In the 1940s, the building itself was probably on the decline, as it drew tenants with more checkered backgrounds. Among them was Christopher Schiek. Born in Jeru-

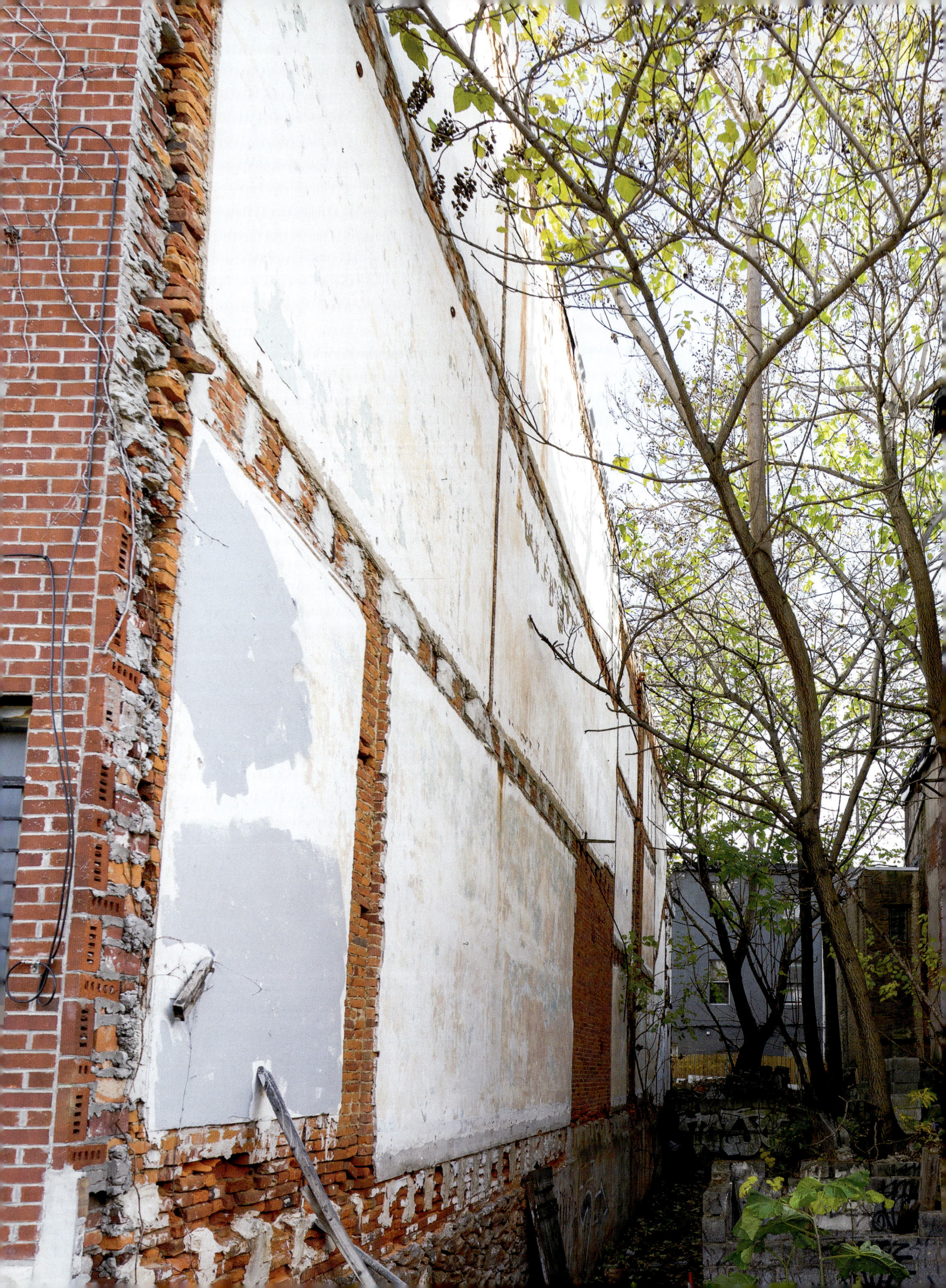

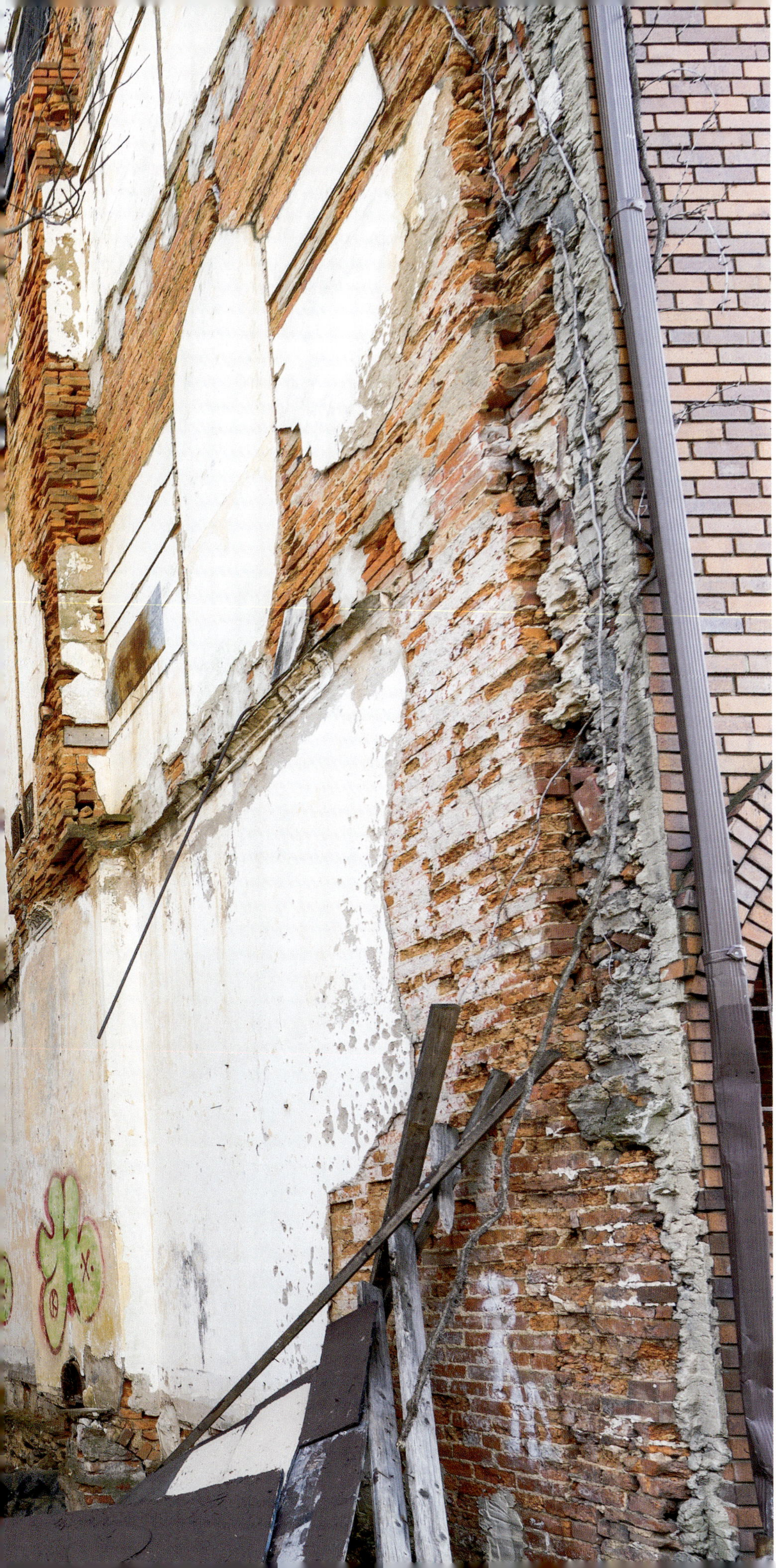

333 North 11th Street.
(Photographed September 22, 2020.)

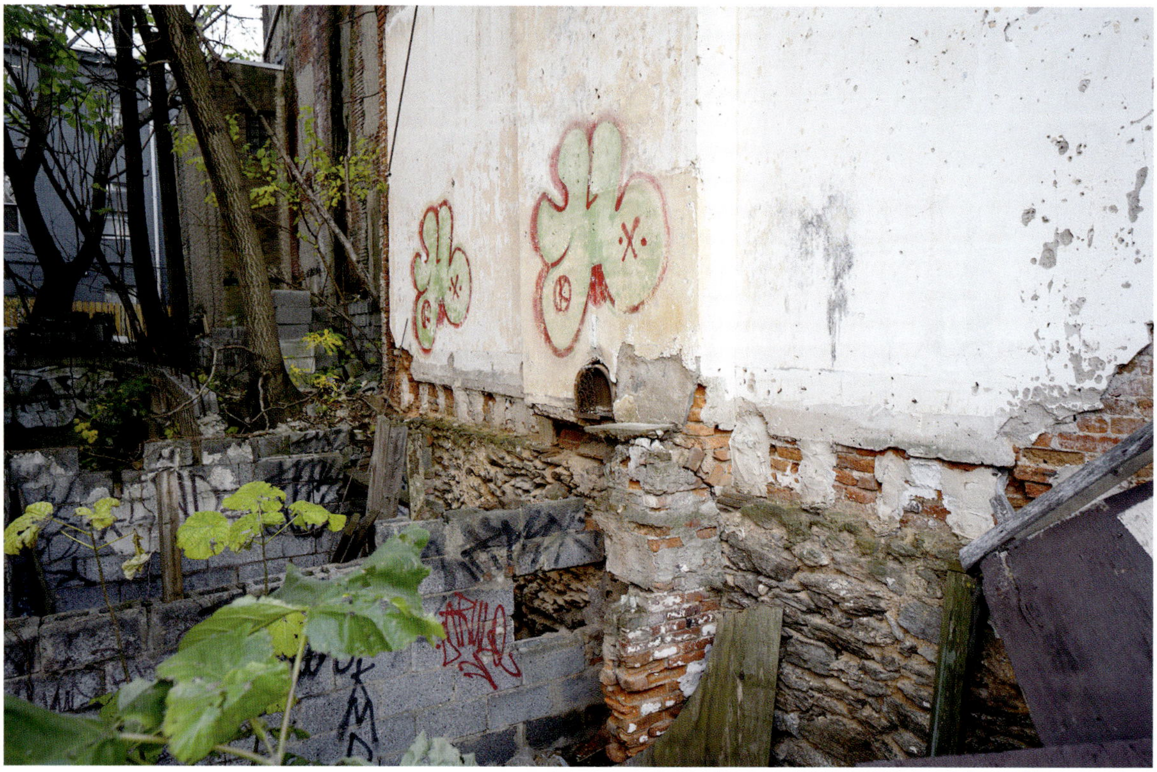

Detail of 333 North 11th Street. (Photographed September 22, 2020.)

salem around 1879, he immigrated to New York in 1889. He lived at various addresses in Pennsylvania's Montgomery County and in Philadelphia, including at 1020 Callowhill Street (the same house around the corner where Catherine Riehle had once lived—that property shared a curiously recurring link with its neighbor at 333 North 11th Street). In 1937, Schiek was living in a rooming house at 728–730 Race Street when a fire broke out, apparently ignited by a candle in Schiek's room. The blaze killed two of his fellow tenants, and Schiek was held criminally responsible. It is unclear what became of those charges, however; he does not appear to have spent time in prison. In the wake of the fatal incident, though, he moved around several times. As of 1940, he lived just a few doors down from number 333, at 329 North 11th Street. By 1944, he had relocated to number 333; he was living there when a coal truck sideswiped him on Ridge Avenue nearby. At first doctors amputated his foot, hoping to save his life, but Schiek eventually died from his injuries.

Two years later, another resident of 333 North 11th Street was killed suddenly—this time in a work accident at a tool factory on Vine Street. Like Schiek, Hovannes Maksoodian was an immigrant, born in Turkey in 1886. Armenian by birth, he arrived in the United States in 1912, escaping the deteriorating conditions in his country as the Ottoman Empire was losing ground in the Balkan Wars and Armenians were increasingly under threat. (After years of persecution, the Armenian genocide began just three years after Maksoodian left; his departure actually may have been a deportation.) Upon arrival, he changed his first name to Henry.

In the three decades that he lived in the United States before his untimely death, Henry Maksoodian had several run-ins with federal authorities. He joined the U.S. Army almost immediately after immigrating but butted heads with an officer who said that Maksoodian had called him a liar. In the early 1930s, he was under surveillance by the Immigration and Naturalization Service for potential (or actual) ties to the Communist Party. In 1935, police in Baton Rouge, Louisiana, arrested him as a suspect in a kidnapping case; his immigration file was updated to include information not just about the arrest, but also about the aliases he was purportedly using. Throughout these incidents, Maksoodian maintained his innocence. "The only trouble I've ever been in was when I was in the Army," he insisted to a reporter in 1937. "I'm no kidnapper." Indeed, he was eventually released without charge and made his way from Louisiana to Philadelphia, where he found work in the tool factory where he would die a few years later.

The boardinghouse at 333 North 11th Street continued to squeeze in new residents in the years after Schiek's and Maksoodian's deaths. In 1955, the building had fifteen units; five years later, it had yet another. Around the same time, the owners applied formstone to the front of the building, obscuring the brick that Samuel Jacobs had used.

In 2004, the building was vacant and needed structural work, including a reconstructed exterior wall and additional supports for the floors and roof; the scoped work would cost more than four times what the contemporary owners had paid for the property. It is unclear whether that work was ever carried out. In any case, the building was demolished about four years later. A property that could count scores of owners and tenants among its residents was now marked only by vacancy.

Center City References

General Resources

Bromley, George. *Atlas of the City of Philadelphia*. Philadelphia: G. W. Bromley, 1895. Athenaeum of Philadelphia, *Greater Philadelphia GeoHistory Network*. http://www.philageohistory.org/tiles/viewer.

Bromley, George W., and Walter S. Bromley. *Atlas of the City of Philadelphia, Central Business Property, 5th, 6th, 7th, 8th, 9th, 10th, & 15th Wards, from Actual Surveys and Official Plans*. Philadelphia: G. W. Bromley, 1908. Zebooker Collection, Athenaeum of Philadelphia, *Greater Philadelphia GeoHistory Network*. https://www.philageohistory.org/rdic-images/view-image.cfm/237%2DMP%2D022.

———. *Atlas of the City of Philadelphia (Central): South Street to Lehigh Ave., Wards 5 to 20, 28, 29, 31, 32, 37 and 47*. Philadelphia: G. W. Bromley, 1922. Athenaeum of Philadelphia, *Greater Philadelphia GeoHistory Network*. https://www.philageohistory.org/rdic-images/view-image.cfm/BRM1922.CentralPhila.005.Plate01.

———. *Atlas of the City of Philadelphia, Complete in One Volume, from Actual Surveys and Official Plans*. Philadelphia: G. W. Bromley, 1910. Athenaeum of Philadelphia, *Greater Philadelphia GeoHistory Network*. https://www.philageohistory.org/rdic-images/view-image.cfm/237%2DMP%2D022.

City Plans Division, Bureau of Surveys and Design, Department of Streets. *Philadelphia Land Use Map, 1962*. Philadelphia: Federal Works Progress Administration for Pennsylvania, 1962. Map Collection, Free Library of Philadelphia, *Greater Philadelphia GeoHistory Network*. http://www.philageohistory.org/rdic-images/view-image.cfm/LUM1962.Title.

Hexamer and Locher. *Maps of the City of Philadelphia, 1858–1860*. Map Collection, Free Library of Philadelphia, *Greater Philadelphia GeoHistory Network*. http://www.philageohistory.org/tiles/viewer.

Hopkins, G. M. *City Atlas of Philadelphia by Wards, Complete in 7 Volumes*. 1875. Private collection of Matt Ainslie, *Greater Philadelphia GeoHistory Network*. http://www.philageohistory.org/tiles/viewer.

"Insurance Maps of Philadelphia, Pennsylvania, Volume 1" (online database). Sanborn Map Company, New York, 1916. *ProQuest Digital Sanborn Maps, 1867–1970*. https://digitalsanbornmaps.proquest.com/browse_maps/39/7881/38451/40224/536312?accountid=10977.

———. Sanborn Map Company, New York, 1951. *ProQuest Digital Sanborn Maps, 1867–1970*. https://digitalsanbornmaps.proquest.com/browse_maps/39/7881/38452/40255/539438?accountid=10977.

Nationwide Environmental Title Research (NETR) Online. *HistoricAerials.com* (online database). Various dates. https://www.historicaerials.com.

Philadelphia Department of Records. *PhillyHistory.org* (online database). Various dates.

Plans and Registry Division, Bureau of Engineering Surveys and Zoning, Department of Public Works. *Philadelphia Land Use Map*. Philadelphia: Federal Works Progress Administration for Pennsylvania, 1942. Map Collection, Free Library of Philadelphia, *Greater Philadelphia GeoHistory Network*. http://www.philageohistory.org/rdic-images/view-image.cfm/LUM1942.Title.

"Sanborn Fire Insurance Map from Philadelphia, Philadelphia County, Pennsylvania, Volume 1" (online database). Sanborn Map Company, New York, 1916–1950. *Library of Congress*. http://hdl.loc.gov/loc.gmd/g3824pm.g3824pm_g07905195001.

Smedley, Samuel. *Atlas of the City of Philadelphia*. Philadelphia: J. B. Lippincott, 1862. Map Collection, Free Library of Philadelphia, *Greater Philadelphia GeoHistory Network*. http://www.philageohistory.org/tiles/viewer.

1025 Buttonwood Street

"Boom in Big Buildings: Notable Increase in the Number of Large Structures." *Philadelphia Times*, July 15, 1893. https://www.newspapers.com/image/53338402.

"Buffalo Lithia Water: Nature's Great Specific." *Philadelphia Times*, April 22, 1888. https://www.newspapers.com/image/52218863.

C. E. Howe Company. *Boyd's Co-partnership and Residence Business Directory of Philadelphia City*. Philadelphia: Boyd's Directory Office, 1900. *Google Books*. https://www.google.com/books/edition/Boyd_s_Co_partnership_and_Residence_Busi/TNIwAQAAMAAJ?hl=en&gbpv=1&dq=%221025+buttonwood%22+philadelphia&pg=PA501&printsec=frontcover.

Department of Records, Philadelphia City Archives. 1025 Buttonwood Street deeds (map registry no. 4N120156). Various dates.

"Dyspepsia, Indigestion and All Wasting Diseases Can Be Cured!" *Philadelphia Times*, March 14, 1865. https://www.newspapers.com/image/53055052.

"Educational." *Philadelphia Inquirer*, December 1, 1896. https://www.newspapers.com/image/168387736.

"French, Richards & Co." *Philadelphia Times*, December 4, 1888. https://www.newspapers.com/image/52213578.

"French, Richards & Co. No More." *Philadelphia Times*, December 17, 1890. https://www.newspapers.com/image/168341090.

GlaxoSmithKline (GSK). "History and Heritage." Accessed May 21, 2023. https://www.gsk.com/en-gb/company/history-and-heritage.

Gopsill's Philadelphia City Directory for 1895. Philadelphia: James Gopsill's Sons, 1895. *Google Books*. https://www.google.com/books/edition/Boyd_s_Philadelphia_Combined_City_and_Bu/YTqVUuo1hMkC?hl=en&gbpv=1.

Gopsill's Philadelphia City Directory for 1901. Philadelphia: James Gopsill's Sons, 1901. *Google Books*. https://www.google.com/books/edition/Gopsill_s_Philadelphia_Business_Director/kexGJtxupMMC?hl=en&gbpv=1&bsq=%221025%20buttonwood%22.

Martindale, J. B. *Martindale's American Law Directory, 1885–6: A Complete Directory of the Practicing Lawyers of the United States and Canada; with an Appendix Containing Brief Synopsis of the Collection Laws of Each State, Territory and Province*. Chicago: J. B. Martindale, 1885. *Google Books*. https://www.google.com/books/edition/Martindale_s_American_Law_Directory/mytOAAAAYAAJ?hl=en&gbpv=1.

McElroy's Philadelphia City Directory. Philadelphia: A. McElroy, 1865. *Google Books*. https://www.google.com/books/edition/_/gKGJ_bh_OZQC?hl=en&sa=X&ved=2ahUKEwj2lO_g14f_AhWPD1kFHbqpBbwQ7_IDegQIEBAD.

"Mrs. B. F. Hunter." *Nashville Tennessean*, September 20, 1935. https://www.newspapers.com/image/168059680.

"1025 Buttonwood Street: Zoning Permit Documents." *City of Philadelphia Atlas*. Accessed October 13, 2022. http://s3.amazonaws.com/eclipse-docs-pdfs/zoning/ZP-2020-003391.pdf.

"Philadelphia, Pennsylvania, U.S., Marriage Index, 1885–1951" (online database). Digital image s.v. "Fantini, Edith Beate Augusta." *Ancestry.com*. https://www.ancestrylibrary.com/discoveryui-content/view/1041293:2536?tid=&pid=&queryId=043774e376d1aeb88041769a7ce00856&_phsrc=VNq225&_phstart=successSource.

Thirty-Seventh Annual Report of the Fire Insurance Patrol of the City of Philadelphia. Philadelphia: Review Publishing and Printing, 1907. *Google Books*. https://www.google.com/books/edition/Annual_Report_of_the_Fire_Insurance_Patr/_CxEAQAAMAAJ?hl=en&gbpv=1.

"U.S., City Directories, 1822–1995" (online database). Digital image s.v. "Fantini, Edith," 1888. *Ancestry.com*. https://www.ancestrylibrary.com/discoveryui-content/view/178031933:2469?tid=&pid=&queryId=10de3e1095fa557b0446f5a8634e0e19&_phsrc=VNq222&_phstart=successSource.

———. Digital image s.v. "Fantini, Edith," 1889. *Ancestry.com*. https://www.ancestrylibrary.com/discoveryui-content/view/146213379:2469?tid=&pid=&queryId=10de3e1095fa557b0446f5a8634e0e19&_phsrc=VNq221&_phstart=successSource.

———. Digital image s.v. "Fantini, Edward," 1889. *Ancestry.com*. https://www.ancestrylibrary.com/discoveryui-content/view/146213379:2469?tid=&pid=&queryId=10de3e1095fa557b0446f5a8634e0e19&_phsrc=VNq221&_phstart=successSource.

"U.S. Federal Census" (online database). Digital image s.v. "Hunter, Edith," 1900. *Ancestry.com*. https://www.ancestrylibrary.com/discoveryui-content/view/60586357:7602?ssrc=pt&tid=78081989&pid=48377441295.

———. Digital image s.v. "Hunter, Edith," 1910. *Ancestry.com* (online database). https://www.ancestrylibrary.com/discoveryui-content/view/136311861:7884.

737 Walnut Street

"Ben Mazer Diamonds." *Philadelphia Inquirer*, November 23, 1973. https://www.newspapers.com/image/185139678.

"Building Permits Granted." *Philadelphia Inquirer*, July 23, 1939. https://www.newspapers.com/image/171090457.

———. *Philadelphia Inquirer*, October 9, 1941. https://www.newspapers.com/image/171552753.

"Bullet Halts Jewel Burglar in Midcity Shop." *Philadelphia Inquirer*, February 11, 1952. https://www.newspapers.com/image/178098903.

"Business Properties Sale." *Philadelphia Inquirer*, July 31, 1974. https://www.newspapers.com/image/173569939.

"Business Prop—Rent." *Philadelphia Inquirer*, December 11, 1994. https://www.newspapers.com/image/177966069.

Department of Records, Philadelphia City Archives. 737 Walnut Street deeds (map registry no. 1S170142). Various dates.

"Fire Delays Traffic at 8th and Walnut." *Philadelphia Inquirer*, May 6, 1939. https://www.newspapers.com/image/171083035.

"For Sale—Misc." *Philadelphia Inquirer*, November 7, 1976. https://www.newspapers.com/image/172509424.

"Grand Opening." *Philadelphia Daily News*, November 2, 1978. https://www.newspapers.com/image/185682880.

"Help Wanted." *Philadelphia Inquirer*, January 5, 1979. https://www.newspapers.com/image/174510392.

Hurdle, Jon. "In Jewelers Row in Philadelphia, Condo Plan Worries Preservationists." *New York Times*, October 12, 2016. https://www.nytimes.com/2016/10/12/realestate/in-jewelers-row-in-philadelphia-condo-plan-worries-preservationists.html.

Leech, Benjamin. *Jewelers' Row Historic District*. Nomination of Historic District, Philadelphia Register of Historic Places. March 10, 2017.

"Male Help Wanted." *Philadelphia Inquirer*, April 9, 1942. https://www.newspapers.com/image/172132072.

———. *Philadelphia Inquirer*, June 27, 1942. https://www.newspapers.com/image/171462962.

Miles, Gary. "Robert Wolf, Philadelphia Jeweler and Family Man, Dies at 91." *Philadelphia Inquirer*, March 29, 2021. https://www.inquirer.com/obituaries/robert-wolf-philadelphia-jewelry-obituary-20210329.html.

"On Jewelers Row, Oral History Project Goes beyond the Bench Work." *Hidden City Philadelphia*, October 12, 2016. https://hiddencityphila.org/2016/10/on-jewelers-row-oral-history-project-goes-beyond-the-bench-work.

Philadelphia Department of Records. *PhillyHistory.org* (online database). Various dates.

Saffron, Inga. "As Toll Brothers Starts Work on Jewelers Row Tower, Merchants Wonder What's Next." *Philadelphia Inquirer*, October 17, 2019. https://www.inquirer.com/real-estate/inga-saffron/jewelers-row-historic-preservation-diamond-district-architecture-toll-brothers-20191017.html.

"737 Walnut Street: Zoning Permit Documents." *City of Philadelphia Atlas*. Accessed January 10, 2023. http://s3.amazonaws.com/eclipse-docs-pdfs/zoning/ZP-2021-009158.pdf.

"Shop on the Row." *Philadelphia Daily News*, September 10, 1987. https://www.newspapers.com/image/186249927.

"Shopping on the Continent." *Philadelphia Daily News*, June 9, 2000. https://www.newspapers.com/image/331533104.

"Skin Care, Nails, Body Man and Women Beaute Salon." *Philadelphia Daily News*, April 9, 1997. https://www.newspapers.com/image/186225657.

"10,000 Government Surplus Bulova-Waltham-Elgin Gents' Wrist Watches." *The Billboard*, June 7, 1947, 95. https://books.google.com/books?id=WkUEAAAAMBAJ&pg=PA95&lpg=PA95&dq=%22louis+perloff%22+%2B%22737+walnut%22+philadelphia&source=bl&ots=YcCtZrFkev&sig=ACfU3U20QyxiT6SmNUqwxsV6bndZY7jKdg&hl=en&sa=X&ved=2ahUKEwiavtqW68z8AhXvLFkFHdzeDUoQ6AF6BAgIEAM#v=onepage&q=%22louis%20perloff%22%20%2B%22737%20walnut%22%20philadelphia&f=false.

"U.S., City Directories, 1822–1995" (online database). Digital image s.v. "Perloff, Louis," 1950. *Ancestry.com*. https://www.ancestrylibrary.com/discoveryui-content/view/1197846891:2469?tid=&pid=&queryId=5f84d06543f8073ead4f1ebfc617a8f6&_phsrc=VNq134&_phstart=successSource.

White, Meghan. "Diamonds Are Forever, but Jewelers Row Might Not Be." *National Trust for Historic Preservation*, June 2, 2017. https://savingplaces.org/stories/the-history-of-philadelphia-jewelers-row.

519 South 4th Street

"Activities of the Day in Real Estate." *Philadelphia Inquirer*, December 7, 1931. https://www.newspapers.com/image/176083414.

"Advance Construction News." *Philadelphia Real Estate Record and Builders' Guide*, June 8, 1921. *Greater Philadelphia GeoHistory Network*. http://www.philageohistory.org/rdic-images/view-book-uv.cfm/PhilaBuildersGuide_v36_1921#?ft=&q=%22519%20s%20fourth%22&c=&m=&s=&cv=451&xywh=1950%2C3358%2C2566%2C869.

"Alterations and Additions." *Philadelphia Real Estate Record and Builders' Guide*, May 10, 1911. *Greater Philadelphia GeoHistory Network*. http://www.philageohistory.org/rdic-images/view-book-uv.cfm/PhilaBuildersGuide_v26_1911#?ft=&q=%22519%20s%20fourth%22&c=&m=&s=&cv=371&xywh=-3495%2C0%2C14545%2C4927.

Atkinson, William B., ed. *Philadelphia Medical Register and Directory*. Philadelphia: Collins, 1875. *Google Books*. https://books.google.com/books?id=mk22oTvu_F4C&newbks=1&newbks_redir=0&dq=%22521%20s%204th%22%20st%20philadelphia&pg=PP5#v=onepage&q&f=false.

Board of Fire Commissioners. "Report." In *Eighth Annual Message of William S. Stokley, Mayor of the City of Philadelphia, with the Accompanying Documents*, 254. Philadelphia: E. C. Markley and Son, 1880. *Google Books*. https://books.google.com/books?id=GDEtAQAAMAAJ&pg=PA254&dq=%22517+south+fourth%22+philadelphia&hl=en&newbks=1&newbks_redir=0&sa=X-&ved=2ahUKEwiCyrPBloX_AhXGElkFHaCHDs4Q6AF6BAgIEAI#v=onepage&q=%22517%20south%20fourth%22%20philadelphia&f=false.

Boonin, Harry. *Jewish Quarter of Philadelphia: A History and Guide, 1881–1930*. Philadelphia: Jewish Walking Tours, 1999.

"Building Permits." *Philadelphia Real Estate Record and Builders' Guide*, December 2, 1903. *Greater Philadelphia GeoHistory Network*. http://www.philageohistory.org/rdic-images/view-book-uv.cfm/PhilaBuildersGuide_v18_1903#?ft=&q=%22519%20s%204th%22&c=&m=&s=&cv=791&xywh=19%2C245%2C2839%2C1571.

Dallin Aerial Survey. *Aerial Survey of Philadelphia, PA*, ca. 1930. Map Collection, Free Library of Philadelphia, *Greater Philadelphia GeoHistory Network*. https://www.philageohistory.org/rdic-images/view-image.cfm/DAL1930.PhilaMetroAerials.009.

Davis, Allen Freeman. *The Peoples of Philadelphia: A History of Ethnic Groups and Lower-Class Life, 1790–1940*. Philadelphia: University of Pennsylvania Press, 1998.

Department of Records, Philadelphia City Archives. 519 South 4th Street deeds (map registry no. 4S070255). Various dates.

"Died." *Philadelphia Inquirer*, October 23, 1909. https://www.newspapers.com/image/169056005.

"519 S. 4th Street: Zoning Permit Documents." *City of Philadelphia Atlas*. Accessed January 10, 2023. https://s3.amazonaws.com/lni-zoning-pdfs/27-164167.pdf.

"For Sale." *Philadelphia Inquirer*, December 30, 1936. https://www.newspapers.com/image/176073125.

Friedman, Murray. *Philadelphia Jewish Life, 1940–2000*. Philadelphia: Temple University Press, 2003.

"General Manufacturing: Middle Atlantic." *American Machinist*, March 14, 1912. *Google Books*. https://www.google.com/books/edition/American_Machinist/mLBLAQAAIAAJ?hl=en&gbpv=1&bsq=d.%20shultz.

Hills, John. *Plan of the City of Philadelphia and Its Environs Shewing* (sic) *the Improved Parts . . . 1796*. Zebooker Collection, Athenaeum of Philadelphia, *Greater Philadelphia GeoHistory Network*. http://www.philageohistory.org/tiles/viewer.

"Israel Forman, Sausage Executive." *Jewish Exponent*, April 30, 1976. https://www.proquest.com/docview/901442959/BA391545D893454EPQ/1?accountid=14707&parentSessionId=u0jigottH4GlfiN9yyghoHBmV5S3gh0nMjQfmPaYqf0%3D.

McElroy's Philadelphia City Directory for 1863, Containing the Names of the Inhabitants of the Consolidated City, Their Occupations, Places of Business, and Dwelling Houses; A Business Directory; A List of the Streets, Lanes, Alleys, City Offices, Public Institutions, Banks, Etc., Twenty-Sixth Edition. Philadelphia: E. C. and J. Biddle, A. McElroy, and C. Sherman and Son, 1863. *Google Books*. https://books.google.com/books?id=_J46AAAAcAAJ&newbks=1&newbks_redir=0&printsec=frontcover&source=gbs_ge_summary_r&cad=0#v=onepage&q&f=false.

["Monarch Wine Co."] *Jewish Exponent*, March 20, 1942. https://www.proquest.com/docview/900054658/AEBED0317CD4C59PQ/6?accountid=14707&parentSessionId=AN2xXzAfzzhrJtmi1spLu%2FuhXf6w9CJbU6p7mekv7Xs%3D.

Nelson, Raymond. "Residential Deals Dominate Activity of Local Market." *Philadelphia Inquirer*, July 26, 1936. https://www.newspapers.com/image/176114322.

"Pennsylvania and New Jersey, U.S., Church and Town Records, 1669–2013" (online database). Digital image s.v. "Burial Register: New Cathedral Cemetery." *Ancestry.com*. https://www.ancestrylibrary.com/imageviewer/collections/2451/images/42154_331369-00609?treeid=&persoid=&hintid=&queryId=deea91a19a590df8cd149e4592c7911f&usePUB=true&_phsrc=NyU49&_phstart=successSource&usePUBJs=true&pId=2021337113.

Pennsylvania Department of Factory Inspections. *Seventh Annual Report of the Factory Inspector of the Commonwealth of Pennsylvania for the Year 1896*. Harrisburg[?]: Clarence M. Busch, 1897. *Google Books*. https://books.google.com/books?id=bsVNAAAAMAAJ&newbks=1&newbks_redir=0&dq=%22517%20s%204th%22%20philadelphia&pg=PP8#v=onepage&q=%22517%20s%204th%22%20philadelphia&f=false.

"Pennsylvania, U.S., Death Certificates, 1906–1969" (online database). Digital image s.v. "Baby boy Forman." *Ancestry.com*. https://www.ancestrylibrary.com/discoveryui-content/view/25233161:6482?tid=&pid=&queryId=b32fb4530e16298239f7734134638014&_phsrc=VNq813&_phstart=successSource.

"Pennsylvania, U.S., Wills and Probate Records, 1683–1993" (online database). Digital image s.v. "Schuman, William." *Ancestry.com*. https://www.ancestrylibrary.com/discoveryui-content/view/2493520:8802.

"Philadelphia, Pennsylvania, U.S., Death Certificates Index 1803–1915" (database online). Digital image s.v. "Sarah Hartman." *Ancestry.com*. https://www.ancestrylibrary.com/discoveryui-con

tent/view/1035831:2535?indiv=1&tid=&pid=&queryId=deea91a19a590df8cd149e4592c7911f&usePUB=true&_phsrc=NyU49&_phstart=successSource.
"Plan for Meat Plant Attacked in Court." *Philadelphia Inquirer*, October 26, 1944. https://www.newspapers.com/image/172137720.
"The Runaway Scrivener." *Philadelphia Times*, April 24, 1878. https://www.newspapers.com/image/52211764.
Stewart, Caroline. "Buzz." *Philadelphia Daily News*, July 12, 1985. https://www.newspapers.com/image/185897049.
Tatman, Sandra L. "Kline, Herman H. (fl. 1915–1956)." *Philadelphia Architects and Buildings*. Accessed May 20, 2023. https://www.philadelphiabuildings.org/pab/app/ar_display.cfm?ArchitectId=A0777.
"U.S. Federal Census" (online database). Digital image s.v. "Braslavsky, Hyman," 1920. *Ancestry.com*. https://www.ancestrylibrary.com/discoveryui-content/view/51805735:6061?tid=&pid=&queryId=e612580c949db7ee1365030e9a245ddf&_phsrc=VNq817&_phstart=successSource.
———. Digital image s.v. "Broslovsky, Harry," 1910. *Ancestry.com*. https://www.ancestrylibrary.com/discoveryui-content/view/25269810:7884.
———. Digital image s.v. "Forman, Israel," 1950. *Ancestry.com*. https://www.ancestrylibrary.com/discoveryui-content/view/237001067:62308?tid=&pid=&queryId=bc6f6e34cd6b668ff988502b6239b33a&_phsrc=VNq823&_phstart=successSource.
———. Digital image s.v. "Rosenblum, Jacob," 1910. *Ancestry.com*. https://www.ancestrylibrary.com/discoveryui-content/view/25250537:7884?tid=&pid=&queryId=738a6c3504e1cc62de449a1deba81080&_phsrc=VNq263&_phstart=successSource.
———. Digital image s.v. "Shuman, Emma," 1900. *Ancestry.com*. https://www.ancestrylibrary.com/discoveryui-content/view/37437443:7602?tid=&pid=&queryId=c0704089825daee7bd2bba584c0fb8d8&_phsrc=VNq811&_phstart=successSource.
———. Digital image s.v. "Shuman, Emma," 1910. *Ancestry.com*. https://www.ancestrylibrary.com/discoveryui-content/view/25243710:7884?tid=&pid=&queryId=f07418396d69910f8637555c2d91cab0&_phsrc=VNq339&_phstart=successSource.
———. Digital image s.v. "Shuman, William," 1850. *Ancestry.com*. https://www.ancestrylibrary.com/discoveryui-content/view/5178461:8054?tid=&pid=&queryId=44f1d521899a71088f15501ce346b3ab&_phsrc=VNq801&_phstart=successSource.
———. Digital image s.v. "Shuman, William," 1880. *Ancestry.com*. https://www.ancestrylibrary.com/discoveryui-content/view/339521:6742?tid=&pid=&queryId=c1599f38221328ab03a16dff3c75cf8d&_phsrc=VNq807&_phstart=successSource.
"U.S., World War I Draft Registration Cards, 1917–1918" (online database). Digital image s.v. "Braslavsky, Harry." *Ancestry.com*. https://www.ancestrylibrary.com/discoveryui-content/view/25233161:6482?tid=&pid=&queryId=b32fb4530e16298239f7734134638014&_phsrc=VNq813&_phstart=successSource.
———. Digital image s.v. "Braslavsky, Hyman." *Ancestry.com*. https://www.ancestrylibrary.com/discoveryui-content/view/25233162:6482?tid=&pid=&queryId=e612580c949db7ee1365030e9a245ddf&_phsrc=VNq816&_phstart=successSource.
"U.S., World War II Draft Cards Young Men, 1940–1947" (online database). Digital image s.v. "Forman, Israel." *Ancestry.com*. https://www.ancestrylibrary.com/discoveryui-content/view/5375941:2238?tid=&pid=&queryId=c05cf8ef14c4ad356c4453c554f85f16&_phsrc=VNq819&_phstart=successSource.

1814 Ludlow Street

"Advance Construction News." *Philadelphia Real Estate Record and Builders' Guide*, March 13, 1935. *Greater Philadelphia GeoHistory Network*. http://www.philageohistory.org/rdic-images/view-book-uv.cfm/PhilaBuildersGuide_v50_1935#?ft=&q=%221814%20ludlow%22&c=&m=&s=&cv=56&xywh=-187%2C559%2C12398%2C2677.

——. *Philadelphia Real Estate Record and Builders' Guide*, July 17, 1935. *Greater Philadelphia GeoHistory Network*. http://www.philageohistory.org/rdic-images/view-book-uv.cfm/PhilaBuildersGuide_v50_1935#?ft=&q=%221814%20ludlow%22&c=&m=&s=&cv=120&xywh=-2355%2C0%2C12218%2C4889.

"A. H. Geuting Company Store." *Philadelphia Architects and Buildings*. Accessed May 20, 2023. https://www.philadelphiabuildings.org/pab/app/pj_display.cfm/43234.

American Institute of Architects, Philadelphia Chapter. *Yearbook of the Twenty-Sixth Annual Architectural Exhibition: Philadelphia*. Philadelphia: Joint Exhibition Board of the Philadelphia Chapter A.I.A. and the T Square Club, 1923. *Google Books*. https://www.google.com/books/edition/Yearbook/00YMAQAAMAAJ?hl=en&gbpv=1&dq=%22the+arvon+company%22+philadelphia&pg=PA214&printsec=frontcover.

"Arvon for Waterproofing." *Philadelphia Real Estate Record and Builders' Guide*, July 12, 1922. *Greater Philadelphia GeoHistory Network*. http://www.philageohistory.org/rdic-images/view-book-uv.cfm/PhilaBuildersGuide_v37_1922#?ft=&q=%221814%20ludlow%22&c=&m=&s=&cv=545&xywh=-129%2C2013%2C3330%2C1128.

"Business Properties Sale." *Philadelphia Inquirer*, April 13, 1975. https://www.newspapers.com/image/173359409.

"Contracts Awarded." *Philadelphia Real Estate Record and Builders' Guide*, July 14, 1926. *Greater Philadelphia GeoHistory Network*. http://www.philageohistory.org/rdic-images/view-book-uv.cfm/PhilaBuildersGuide_v41_1926#?ft=&q=%22newmark%20%26%20brother%22&c=&m=&s=&cv=552&xywh=4154%2C457%2C2997%2C1802.

——. *Philadelphia Real Estate Record and Builders' Guide*, April 13, 1927. *Greater Philadelphia GeoHistory Network*. http://www.philageohistory.org/rdic-images/view-book-uv.cfm/PhilaBuildersGuide_v42_1927#?ft=&q=%221814%20ludlow%22&c=&m=&s=&cv=288&xywh=-2638%2C-1%2C12929%2C4886.

Department of Records, Philadelphia City Archives. 1814 Ludlow Street deeds (map registry no. 1S110011). Various dates.

"Died." *Philadelphia Inquirer*, October 2, 1903. https://www.newspapers.com/image/168998338.

——. *Philadelphia Inquirer*, October 7, 1904. https://www.newspapers.com/image/169009001.

"Eating." *Philadelphia Inquirer*, December 12, 1976. https://www.newspapers.com/image/171485654.

"1814 Ludlow Street: Zoning Permit Documents." *City of Philadelphia Atlas*. Accessed January 10, 2023. http://s3.amazonaws.com/eclipse-docs-pdfs/zoning/ZP-2020-002441.pdf.

"Help Wanted." *Philadelphia Inquirer*, November 20, 1988. https://www.newspapers.com/image/169295298.

"Hide Tough as Rhino's, Mayor Tells Bridge Session." *Philadelphia Inquirer*, October 23, 1937. https://www.newspapers.com/image/171100510.

"Male Help Wanted." *Philadelphia Inquirer*, May 17, 1922. https://www.newspapers.com/image/170694805.

——. *Philadelphia Inquirer*, March 16, 1924. https://www.newspapers.com/image/171041150.

Mattern, Shannon. "Maintenance and Care." *Places*, November 2018. https://placesjournal.org/article/maintenance-and-care/?cn-reloaded=1.

"Morene Art Cement." *Philadelphia Real Estate Record and Builders' Guide*, November 11, 1922. *Greater Philadelphia GeoHistory Network*. http://www.philageohistory.org/rdic-images/view-book-uv.cfm/PhilaBuildersGuide_v37_1922#?ft=&q=%221814%20ludlow%22&c=&m=&s=&cv=925&xywh=-457%2C1890%2C4575%2C1550.

"Morris Newmark and Brother." *Philadelphia Inquirer*, May 17, 1929. https://www.newspapers.com/image/172732739.

"Office and Desk Space." *Philadelphia Inquirer*, January 6, 1955. https://www.newspapers.com/image/176209895.

"Opening of Victor's New Store at 1617 Walnut St." *Philadelphia Inquirer*, March 3, 1940. https://www.newspapers.com/image/167456168.

"Pennsylvania, U.S., Death Certificates, 1906–1969" (online database). Digital image s.v. "Newmark, Morris." *Ancestry.com*. https://www.ancestrylibrary.com/imageviewer/collections/5164/images/42410_2421406272_0908-00499?treeid=&personid=&hintid=&queryId=f802d61ac1c4112c44f3b3d1c41e579a&usePUB=true&_phsrc=VNq311&_phstart=successSource&usePUBJs=true&pId=7133528.

"Philadelphia Contracts Awarded." *Philadelphia Real Estate Record and Builders' Guide*, February 3, 1932. *Greater Philadelphia GeoHistory Network*. http://www.philageohistory.org/rdic-images/view-book-uv.cfm/PhilaBuildersGuide_v47_1932#?ft=&q=%221814%20ludlow%22&c=&m=&s=&cv=40&xywh=3293%2C1392%2C8152%2C1760.

"Real Estate for Rent: City." *Philadelphia Evening Public Ledger*, December 16, 1921. https://www.newspapers.com/image/150214303.

"These Dealers Sell American Blower Comfort Cooling." *Philadelphia Inquirer*, May 23, 1939. https://www.newspapers.com/image/171070799.

"U.S. Federal Census" (online database). Digital image s.v. "Newmark, Morris," 1920. *Ancestry.com*. https://www.ancestrylibrary.com/discoveryui-content/view/70654923:6061?tid=&pid=&queryId=f802d61ac1c4112c44f3b3d1c41e579a&_phsrc=VNq311&_phstart=successSource.

"U.S., World War I Draft Registration Cards, 1917–1918" (online database). Digital image s.v. "Newmark, Morris." *Ancestry.com*. https://www.ancestrylibrary.com/discoveryui-content/view/25387826:6482?tid=&pid=&queryId=ca067c2b77d4413e8ec5ee42de709783&_phsrc=VNq310&_phstart=successSource.

"U.S., World War II Draft Registration Cards, 1942" (online database). Digital image s.v. "Newmark, Morris." *Ancestry.com*. https://www.ancestrylibrary.com/discoveryui-content/view/1654413:1002?tid=&pid=&queryId=ca067c2b77d4413e8ec5ee42de709783&_phsrc=VNq310&_phstart=successSource.

1801–1803 Fairmount Avenue

"Accessories, Parts, Repairs." *Philadelphia Inquirer*, January 6, 1946. https://www.newspapers.com/image/171453714.

"Application for Liquor Licenses." *Philadelphia Inquirer*, February 17, 1892. https://www.newspapers.com/image/168311799.

"Auction Sales." *Philadelphia Inquirer*, June 11, 1881. https://www.newspapers.com/image/247889220.

"Birthday of Jefferson." *Philadelphia Times*, April 3, 1889. https://www.newspapers.com/image/52215500.

Boyd's Philadelphia City Business Directory. Philadelphia: Central News Company, 1860. *Google Books*. https://www.google.com/books/edition/Boyd_s_Philadelphia_City_Business_Direct/-4QSAAAAYAAJ?hl=en&gbpv=0&bsq=kochersperger%20marble%20philadelphia.

"Business Opportunities." *Philadelphia Inquirer*, September 30, 1900. https://www.newspapers.com/image/167229656.

——. *Philadelphia Inquirer*, October 7, 1923. https://www.newspapers.com/image/170624278.

C. E. Howe Company. *Boyd's Co-partnership and Residence Business Directory of Philadelphia City*. Philadelphia: Boyd's Directory Office, 1900. *Google Books*. https://www.google.com/books/edition/Boyd_s_Co_partnership_and_Residence_Busi/TNIwAQAAMAAJ?hl=en&gbpv=1&dq=%221025+buttonwood%22+philadelphia&pg=PA501&printsec=frontcover.

Dairy and Food Bureau. "Oleomargarine Licenses." *Monthly Bulletin of the Pennsylvania Department of Agriculture*, vol. 17, nos. 1–2, 1919, 83.

"Democrats Who March." *Philadelphia Times*, August 20, 1888. https://www.newspapers.com/image/52219715.

Department of Records, Philadelphia City Archives. 1801–1803 Fairmount Avenue deeds (map registry nos. 7N080150, 7N080239). Various dates.

"Don Cameron's Call." *Philadelphia Inquirer*, July 11, 1890. https://www.newspapers.com/image/168029906.

Dribben, Melissa. "The Artist behind SEPTA Station's Makeover." *Philadelphia Inquirer*, March 19,

2012. https://www.inquirer.com/philly/living/20120319_The_artist_behind_SEPTA_station_s_makeover.html.
"1801–1803 Fairmount Avenue: Zoning Permit Documents." *City of Philadelphia Atlas*. Accessed January 10, 2023. https://s3.amazonaws.com/lni-zoning-pdfs/219-150648.pdf.
"Fictitious Name Notices." *Philadelphia Inquirer*, June 4, 1997. https://www.newspapers.com/image/187293504.
"Fifteenth Ward Democrats." *Philadelphia Times*, September 2, 1876. https://www.newspapers.com/image/54231192.
"The First Contract." *Philadelphia Inquirer*, May 15, 1890. https://www.newspapers.com/image/168142377.
"For Sale." *Philadelphia Inquirer*, April 20, 1902. https://www.newspapers.com/image/168398479.
———. *Philadelphia Inquirer*, April 14, 1912. https://www.newspapers.com/image/168290453.
Gopsill's Philadelphia City Directory for 1887. Philadelphia: James Gopsill's Sons, 1887. *Google Books*. https://www.google.com/books/edition/Gopsill_s_Philadelphia_City_Directory/46JIAQAAMAAJ?hl=en&gbpv=0&bsq=%221801%20fairmount%22%20philadelphia.
Gopsill's Philadelphia City Directory for 1895. Philadelphia: James Gopsill's Sons, 1895. *Google Books*. https://www.google.com/books/edition/Boyd_s_Philadelphia_Combined_City_and_Bu/YTqVUuo1hMkC?hl=en&gbpv=1.
Kelly, Autumn N. "New Art Gallery on Fairmount Ave.—'They Know Me as "Peanut Butter."'" *Philadelphia Inquirer*, January 1, 2013. https://autumnnoelkelly.wordpress.com/2013/01/01/they-know-me-as-peanut-butter.
"Machinery and Tools." *Philadelphia Inquirer*, November 2, 1945. https://www.newspapers.com/image/171455566.
"Male Help Wanted." *Philadelphia Inquirer*, September 6, 1898. https://www.newspapers.com/image/167919159.
———. *Philadelphia Inquirer*, March 14, 1900. https://www.newspapers.com/image/167487717.
———. *Philadelphia Inquirer*, October 29, 1900. https://www.newspapers.com/image/168153491.
———. *Philadelphia Inquirer*, September 11, 1902. https://www.newspapers.com/image/169005190.
———. *Philadelphia Inquirer*, October 14, 1913. https://www.newspapers.com/image/168761374.
———. *Philadelphia Inquirer*, November 3, 1947. https://www.newspapers.com/image/174120401.
———. *Philadelphia Inquirer*, February 24, 1951. https://www.newspapers.com/image/177952414.
———. *Philadelphia Inquirer*, November 23, 1952. https://www.newspapers.com/image/177934308.
McElroy's Philadelphia City Directory. Philadelphia: A. McElroy, 1863. *Google Books*. https://www.google.com/books/edition/Philadelphia_Directory_for_containing_th/_J46AAAAcAAJ?hl=en&gbpv=0.
"Philadelphia, Pennsylvania, U.S., Death Certificates Index, 1803–1915" (online database). Digital image s.v. "Breen, George J.," 1895. *Ancestry.com*. https://www.ancestrylibrary.com/discoveryui-content/view/1473811:2535?indiv=1&tid=&pid=&queryId=0c67fcd89596d0d4b6c61348e6172ddb&usePUB=true&_phsrc=NyU57&_phstart=successSource.
———. Digital image s.v. "Campbell, James," 1902. *Ancestry.com*. https://www.ancestrylibrary.com/discoveryui-content/view/903618:2535?tid=&pid=&queryId=548fbbc059d69ec0f7a5169e44e56ac9&_phsrc=VNq129&_phstart=successSource.
"Portrait of Jefferson." *Philadelphia Times*, March 27, 1890. https://www.newspapers.com/image/52216847.
"U.S., City Directories, 1822–1995" (online database). Digital image s.v. "Breen, George J.," 1881. *Ancestry.com*. https://www.ancestrylibrary.com/discoveryui-content/view/178031933:2469?tid=&pid=&queryId=10de3e1095fa557b0446f5a8634e0e19&_phsrc=VNq222&_phstart=successSource.
———. Digital image s.v. "Breen, George J.," 1888. *Ancestry.com*. https://www.ancestrylibrary.com/imageviewer/collections/2469/images/2872421?usePUB=true&_phsrc=NyU58&_phstart=successSource&usePUBJs=true&pId=177992472.
———. Digital image s.v. "Kochersperger, John P.," 1888. *Ancestry.com*. https://www.ancestrylibrary

.com/discoveryui-content/view/178031933:2469?tid=&pid=&queryId=10de3e1095fa557b0446f5a8634e0e19&_phsrc=VNq222&_phstart=successSource.
———. Digital image s.v. "Oilman, William," 1905. *Ancestry.com*. https://www.ancestrylibrary.com/discoveryui-content/view/173767070:2469?tid=&pid=&queryId=f6fffcfe496ca87537cc4431e138ff13&_phsrc=VNq124&_phstart=successSource.
———. Digital image s.v. "Weyl, Hamilton D.," 1904. *Ancestry.com*, https://www.ancestrylibrary.com/discoveryui-content/view/160017141:2469?tid=&pid=&queryId=f6fffcfe496ca87537cc4431e138ff13&_phsrc=VNq124&_phstart=successSource.
———. Digital image s.v. "Weyl, Hamilton D.," 1909. *Ancestry.com*. https://www.ancestrylibrary.com/discoveryui-content/view/166694354:2469?tid=&pid=&queryId=f6fffcfe496ca87537cc4431e138ff13&_phsrc=VNq124&_phstart=successSource.
"U.S. Federal Census" (online database). Digital image s.v. "Kochersperger, John P.," 1870. *Ancestry.com*. https://www.ancestrylibrary.com/discoveryui-content/view/8916925:7163?tid=&pid=&queryId=48ecdd218b81e592b95f8784e31ec954&_phsrc=VNq239&_phstart=successSource.
"U.S., World War I Draft Registration Cards, 1917–1918" (online database). Digital image s.v. "Breen, George Warren J.," *Ancestry.com*. https://www.ancestrylibrary.com/imageviewer/collections/6482/images/005270407_05272?treeid=&personid=&hintid=&queryId=0c67fcd8996d0d4b6c61348e6172ddb&usePUB=true&_phsrc=NyU57&_phstart=successSource&usePUBJs=true&pId=26753465.

1828 Rittenhouse Square

Ashton, Dianne. "Crossing Boundaries: The Career of Mary M. Cohen." *American Jewish History* 83, no. 2 (June 1995): 153–176.
Cohen, Katherine M. "The Israelite." *Monumental News* 11, no. 4 (April 1899): 224. *Google Books*. https://www.google.com/books/edition/The_Monumental_News/Xcg7AQAAMAAJ?hl=en&gbpv=1&dq=katherine+m.+cohen&pg=PA224&printsec=frontcover.
———. "Life of Artists." In *The Congress of Women, Held in the Woman's Building, World's Columbian Exposition, Chicago, U.S.A., 1893*. Edited by Mary Kavanaugh Oldham Eagle. Kansas City, MO: Thompson and Hood, 1894. *Google Books*. https://www.google.com/books/edition/The_Congress_of_Women_Held_in_the_Woman/qT8SAQAAMAAJ?hl=en&gbpv=1&dq=katherine+m.+cohen&pg=PA428&printsec=frontcover.
Department of Records, Philadelphia City Archives. 1828 Rittenhouse Square deeds (map registry nos. 2S210003, 2S210058). Various dates.
Eagle, Mary Kavanaugh Oldham, ed. *The Congress of Women, Held in the Woman's Building, World's Columbian Exposition, Chicago, U.S.A., 1893*. Kansas City, MO: Thompson and Hood, 1894. *Google Books*. https://www.google.com/books/edition/The_Congress_of_Women_Held_in_the_Woman/qT8SAQAAMAAJ?hl=en&gbpv=1&dq=katherine+m.+cohen&pg=PA428&printsec=frontcover.
Fairmount Park Art Association. *Fairmount Park Art Association: An Account of Its Origin and Activities from Its Foundation in 1871, Issued on the Occasion of Its Fiftieth Anniversary, 1921*. Philadelphia: Fairmount Park Art Association, 1922. *Google Books*. https://www.google.com/books/edition/Fairmount_Park_Art_Association/nmUAAAAAYAAJ?hl=en&gbpv=1&dq=katherine+m.+cohen&pg=PA201&printsec=frontcover.
Gopsill's Philadelphia City Directory for 1895. Philadelphia: James Gopsill's Sons, 1895. *Google Books*. https://www.google.com/books/edition/Boyd_s_Philadelphia_Combined_City_and_Bu/YTqVUuo1hMkC?hl=en&gbpv=1.
Heinzen, Nancy M. *The Perfect Square: A History of Rittenhouse Square*. Philadelphia: Temple University Press, 2009.
Higgins, Charles T. "Aerial View, Rittenhouse Savoy Apartments," December 1953. Print and Picture Collection, Free Library of Philadelphia. https://libwww.freelibrary.org/digital/item/18612.

Koehler, S. R. *The United States Art Directory and Year Book (Second Year)*. New York: Cassell, 1884. *Google Books*. https://www.google.com/books/edition/The_United_States_Art_Directory_and_Year/o9lLAQAAMAAJ?hl=en&gbpv=1&dq=%221828+rittenhouse+sq%22&pg=PA173-IA2&printsec=frontcover.
McElroy's Philadelphia City Directory for 1863, Containing the Names of the Inhabitants of the Consolidated City, Their Occupations, Places of Business, and Dwelling Houses; A Business Directory; A List of the Streets, Lanes, Alleys, City Offices, Public Institutions, Banks, Etc., Twenty-sixth Edition. Philadelphia: E. C. and J. Biddle, A. McElroy, and C. Sherman and Son, 1863. *Google Books*. https://books.google.com/books?id=_J46AAAAcAAJ&newbks=1&newbks_redir=0&printsec=frontcover&source=gbs_ge_summary_r&cad=0#v=onepage&q&f=false.
Seeler, Edgar V. "The Relations of Specialists to Architects." *American Architect and Building News*, February 11, 1905, 87, 1520.
Siegel, Michele. "Katherine M. Cohen: March 18, 1859–December 18, 1914." *Shalvi/Hyman Encyclopedia of Jewish Women*. Accessed March 22, 2023. https://jwa.org/encyclopedia/article/cohen-katherine-m.
University of Pennsylvania. *Catalogue of the University of Pennsylvania, 1894–95. Google Books*. https://www.google.com/books/edition/Undergraduate_Courses_of_Study/ODxHAQAAMAAJ?hl=en&gbpv=1&dq=%221828+rittenhouse+sq%22&pg=PA376&printsec=frontcover.
"U.S., City Directories, 1822–1995" (online database). Digital image s.v. "Cohen, Henry," 1875. *Ancestry.com*. https://www.ancestrylibrary.com/discoveryui-content/view/176538492:2469?tid=&pid=&queryId=90e5a6b43520eb78d880ed0c6eb57627&_phsrc=VNq103&_phstart=successSource.
———. Digital image s.v. "Cohen, Katherine M.," 1886. *Ancestry.com*. https://www.ancestrylibrary.com/discoveryui-content/view/172796429:2469?tid=&pid=&queryId=7412e341435466bb55f57d9c864dd40a&_phsrc=VNq98&_phstart=successSource.
———. Digital image s.v. "Cohen, Katherine M.," 1888. *Ancestry.com*. https://www.ancestrylibrary.com/discoveryui-content/view/178007597:2469?tid=&pid=&queryId=7412e341435466bb55f57d9c864dd40a&_phsrc=VNq101&_phstart=successSource.
———. Digital image s.v. "Cohen, Katherine M.," 1891. *Ancestry.com*. https://www.ancestrylibrary.com/discoveryui-content/view/145569544:2469?tid=&pid=&queryId=7412e341435466bb55f57d9c864dd40a&_phsrc=VNq98&_phstart=successSource.
"U.S. Federal Census" (online database). Digital image s.v. "Cohen, Kate M.," 1870. *Ancestry.com*. https://www.ancestrylibrary.com/discoveryui-content/view/10504274:7163?tid=&pid=&queryId=7412e341435466bb55f57d9c864dd40a&_phsrc=VNq98&_phstart=successSource.
Wharton, Anne H. "Some Philadelphia Studios." *Decorator and Furnisher*, vol. 7, no. 6, March 1886, 178.

2009–2011 Sansom Street

Department of Records, Philadelphia City Archives. 2009–2011 Sansom Street deeds (map registry no. 1S240030). Various dates.
"Died." *Philadelphia Times*, July 29, 1879. https://www.newspapers.com/image/52220700.
———. *Philadelphia Times*, February 12, 1894. https://www.newspapers.com/image/52375740.
"Female Help Wanted." *Philadelphia Inquirer*, October 4, 1958. https://www.newspapers.com/image/177662097.
"Pennsylvania and New Jersey, U.S. Church and Town Records, 1669–2013" (online database). Digital image s.v. "Slavin, Rose." *Ancestry.com*. https://www.ancestrylibrary.com/discoveryui-content/view/2023123882:2451?tid=&pid=&queryId=56117b90b20239c50689d9be5c26479f&_phsrc=VNq352&_phstart=successSource.
"Philadelphia, Pennsylvania, U.S., Death Certificates Index, 1803–1915" (online database). Digital image s.v. "Hassett, Margaret," 1872. *Ancestry.com*. https://www.ancestrylibrary.com/discoveryui-content/view/1951180:2535?tid=&pid=&queryId=173f022ebbf91864d1646841b35d9b11&_phsrc=VNq348&_phstart=successSource.

———. Digital image s.v. "Slevin, Rosie," 1894. *Ancestry.com*. https://www.ancestrylibrary.com/discoveryui-content/view/1344690:2535?tid=&pid=&queryId=0ee25fa61e75f8a793cfe2b168550a06&_phsrc=VNq268&_phstart=successSource.
———. Digital image s.v. "Stark, Annie," 1879. *Ancestry.com*. https://www.ancestrylibrary.com/discoveryui-content/view/2119281:2535?tid=&pid=&queryId=5710ae9a1d13a6b28cc5ef67e7c871d7&_phsrc=VNq249&_phstart=successSource.
———. Digital image s.v. "White, Annie," 1885. *Ancestry.com*. https://www.ancestrylibrary.com/discoveryui-content/view/2245209:2535?tid=&pid=&queryId=173f022ebbf91864d1646841b35d9b11&_phsrc=VNq348&_phstart=successSource.
"2009 Sansom Street: Zoning Permit Documents." *City of Philadelphia Atlas*. Accessed January 10, 2023. https://s3.amazonaws.com/lni-zoning-pdfs/219-323406.pdf.
"U.S., City Directories, 1822–1995" (online database). Digital image s.v. "Brogan, Isabella," 1887. *Ancestry.com*. https://www.ancestrylibrary.com/discoveryui-content/view/145264476:2469?tid=&pid=&queryId=97bd12ff59352dd7344c93b19e826484&_phsrc=VNq344&_phstart=successSource.
———. Digital image s.v. "Brogan, Isabella," 1888. *Ancestry.com*. https://www.ancestrylibrary.com/discoveryui-content/view/177993871:2469?tid=&pid=&queryId=173f022ebbf91864d1646841b35d9b11&_phsrc=VNq346&_phstart=successSource.
———. Digital image s.v. "Clark, Mary," 1892. *Ancestry.com*. https://www.ancestrylibrary.com/discoveryui-content/view/1195348857:2469?tid=&pid=&queryId=97bd12ff59352dd7344c93b19e826484&_phsrc=VNq344&_phstart=successSource.
———. Digital image s.v. "Shirley, Annie J.," 1890. *Ancestry.com*. https://www.ancestrylibrary.com/discoveryui-content/view/174689299:2469?tid=&pid=&queryId=173f022ebbf91864d1646841b35d9b11&_phsrc=VNq345&_phstart=successSource.
———. Digital image s.v. "Shirley, Annie J.," 1892. *Ancestry.com*. https://www.ancestrylibrary.com/discoveryui-content/view/174418894:2469?tid=&pid=&queryId=173f022ebbf91864d1646841b35d9b11&_phsrc=VNq345&_phstart=successSource.
———. Digital image s.v. "Slavin, Rose," 1867. *Ancestry.com*. https://www.ancestrylibrary.com/discoveryui-content/view/173514013:2469?tid=&pid=&queryId=0fb18b4f3cdd5e7e1d8ed6953fa7dcbc&_phsrc=VNq270&_phstart=successSource.
"U.S. Federal Census" (online database). Digital image s.v. "Slavin, Rose," 1860. *Ancestry.com*. https://www.ancestrylibrary.com/discoveryui-content/view/23044968:7667?tid=&pid=&queryId=6919d8119de6c90f3ead81d2efc85fa8&_phsrc=VNq342&_phstart=successSource.
———. Digital image s.v. "Slavin, Rose." 1880. *Ancestry.com*. https://www.ancestrylibrary.com/discoveryui-content/view/277422:6742.
"U.S. Federal Census Mortality Schedules, 1850–1885" (online database). Digital image s.v. "Stark, Annie," 1880. *Ancestry.com*. https://www.ancestrylibrary.com/discoveryui-content/view/2275422:8756?tid=&pid=&queryId=5710ae9a1d13a6b28cc5ef67e7c871d7&_phsrc=VNq249&_phstart=successSource.

333 North 11th Street

"Connecticut, U.S., Federal Naturalization Records, 1790–1996" (online database). Digital image s.v. "Maksoodian, Hovannes Bagdasar." *Ancestry.com*. https://www.ancestrylibrary.com/discoveryui-content/view/135860:61195?tid=&pid=&queryId=32bbf5d33b819f668969072567ea3db7&_phsrc=VNq157&_phstart=successSource.
Department of Records, Philadelphia City Archives. 333 North 11th Street deeds (map registry no. 2N230071). Various dates.
"Farmer Held for Fire That Took Lives of Two Roomers." *Plain Speaker* (Hazleton, PA), December 13, 1907. https://www.newspapers.com/image/104789788.
"Philadelphia Rooming House Fire Fatal to Two." *Evening News* (Wilkes-Barre, PA), December 13, 1937. https://www.newspapers.com/image/396217034.

"333 N. 11th Street: Zoning Permit Documents." *City of Philadelphia Atlas*. Accessed January 10, 2023. https://s3.amazonaws.com/lni-zoning-pdfs/219-23776.pdf.

"Two Burn to Death in Fire at Phila. Rooming House." *News Journal* (Wilmington, DE), December 13, 1937. https://www.newspapers.com/image/161729551.

"U.S., City Directories, 1822–1995" (online database). Digital image s.v. "Jacobs, Henry L.," 1870. *Ancestry.com*. https://www.ancestrylibrary.com/discoveryui-content/view/197439259:2469?tid=&pid=&queryId=4e71b946f9397551c983d58a988024db&_phsrc=VNq143&_phstart=successSource.

———. Digital image s.v. "Jacobs, Samuel W.," 1862. *Ancestry.com*. https://www.ancestrylibrary.com/discoveryui-content/view/177058283:2469?tid=&pid=&queryId=4e71b946f9397551c983d58a988024db&_phsrc=VNq142&_phstart=successSource.

———. Digital image s.v. "Jacobs, S. W.," 1866. *Ancestry.com*. https://www.ancestrylibrary.com/discoveryui-content/view/1189754861:2469?tid=&pid=&queryId=c26dafe53ce4f9b8946fd06b9c3ab3f5&_phsrc=VNq141&_phstart=successSource.

———. Digital image s.v. "Riehl, Caroline A.," 1900. *Ancestry.com*. https://www.ancestrylibrary.com/discoveryui-content/view/177632099:2469?tid=&pid=&queryId=4e71b946f9397551c983d58a988024db&_phsrc=VNq142&_phstart=successSource.

———. Digital image s.v. "Riehl, Catharine," 1873. *Ancestry.com*. httpshttps://www.ancestrylibrary.com/discoveryui-content/view/177274106:2469?tid=&pid=&queryId=4e71b946f9397551c983d58a988024db&_phsrc=VNq142&_phstart=successSource.

———. Digital image s.v. "Riehl, Catharine," 1881. *Ancestry.com*. https://www.ancestrylibrary.com/discoveryui-content/view/145175893:2469?tid=&pid=&queryId=c26dafe53ce4f9b8946fd06b9c3ab3f5&_phsrc=VNq141&_phstart=successSource.

———. Digital image s.v. "Riehl, Ellen," 1895. *Ancestry.com*. https://www.ancestrylibrary.com/discoveryui-content/view/146064585:2469?tid=&pid=&queryId=c26dafe53ce4f9b8946fd06b9c3ab3f5&_phsrc=VNq141&_phstart=successSource.

———. Digital image s.v. "Riehl, Frederick A.," 1876. *Ancestry.com*. https://www.ancestrylibrary.com/discoveryui-content/view/176773496:2469?tid=&pid=&queryId=4e71b946f9397551c983d58a988024db&_phsrc=VNq142&_phstart=successSource.

"U.S. Federal Census" (online database). Digital image s.v. "Schiek, Christopher," 1910. *Ancestry.com*. https://www.ancestrylibrary.com/discoveryui-content/view/186483338:7884?tid=&pid=&queryId=f9d4535b9fa0fee1c542cbb18acee8f1&_phsrc=VNq825&_phstart=successSource.

"U.S., Subject Index to Correspondence and Case Files of the Immigration and Naturalization Service, 1903–1959" (online database). Digital image s.v. "Maksoodian, Hovannes B." *Ancestry.com*. https://www.ancestrylibrary.com/discoveryui-content/view/300325:1946?tid=&pid=&queryId=58edb32b014c844069ec94912f5b8437&_phsrc=VNq156&_phstart=successSource.

"U.S., World War I Draft Registration Cards, 1917–1918" (online database). Digital image s.v. "Schiek, Christopher Frederick." *Ancestry.com*. https://www.ancestrylibrary.com/discoveryui-content/view/9884280:6482?tid=&pid=&queryId=044690c17a6150663e48cdbedc69892c&_phsrc=VNq828&_phstart=successSource.

NORTH PHILADELPHIA

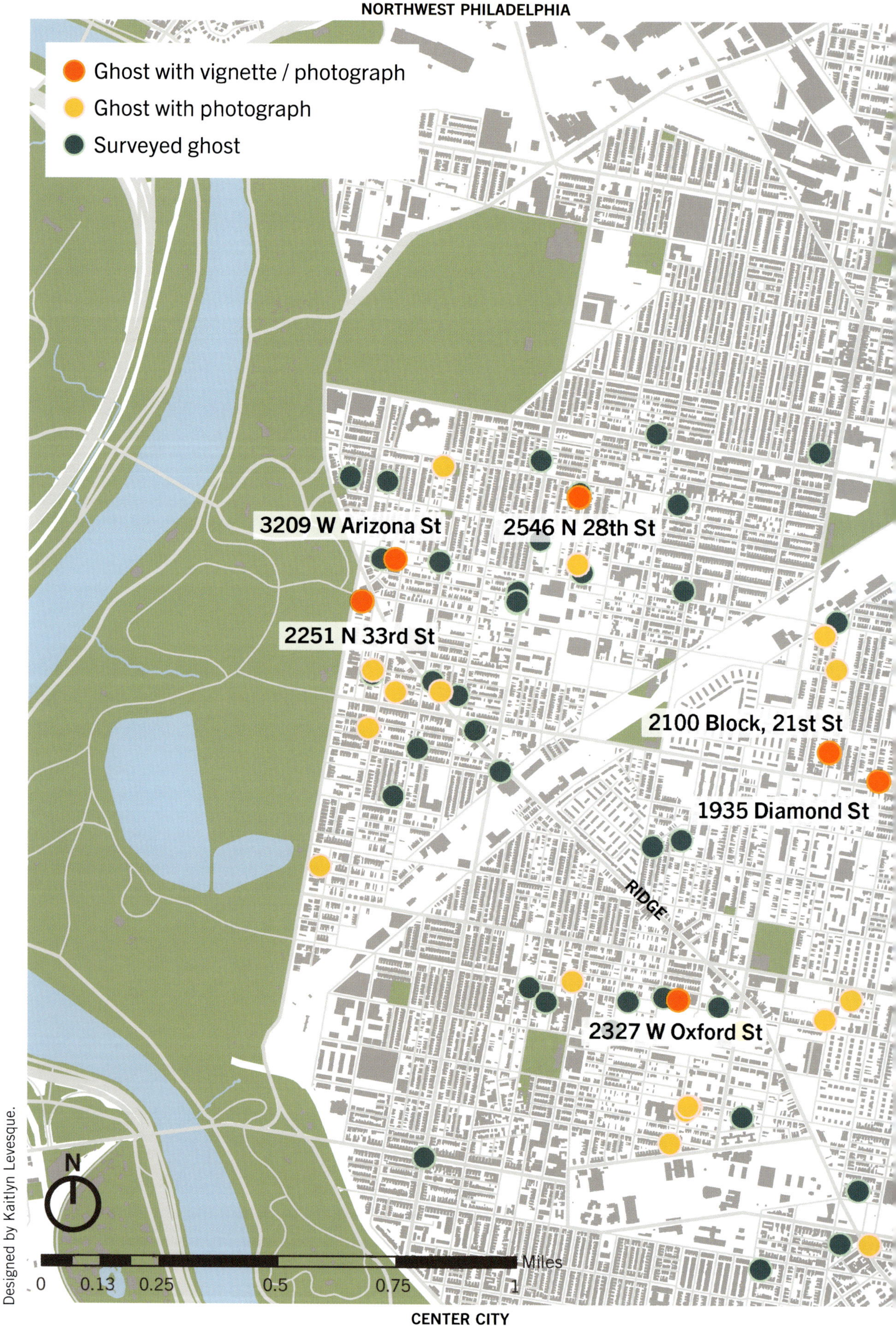
NORTHWEST PHILADELPHIA
Ghost with vignette / photograph
Ghost with photograph
Surveyed ghost
3209 W Arizona St
2546 N 28th St
2251 N 33rd St
2100 Block, 21st St
1935 Diamond St
RIDGE
2327 W Oxford St
N
0
0.13
0.25
0.5
0.75
1
Miles
CENTER CITY
Designed by Kaitlyn Levesque.

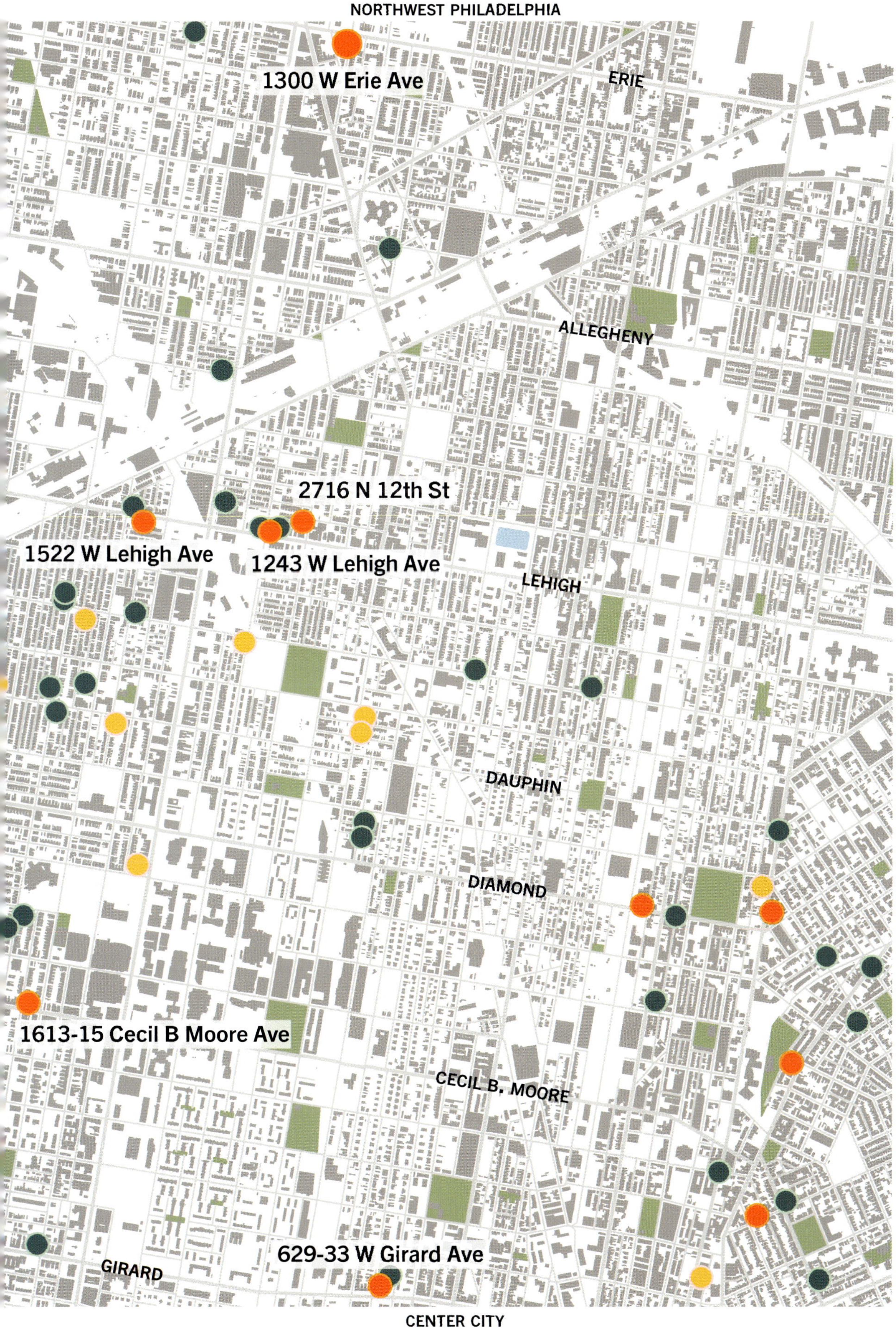
NORTHWEST PHILADELPHIA
1300 W Erie Ave
ERIE
ALLEGHENY
2716 N 12th St
1522 W Lehigh Ave
1243 W Lehigh Ave
LEHIGH
DAUPHIN
DIAMOND
1613-15 Cecil B Moore Ave
CECIL B. MOORE
629-33 W Girard Ave
GIRARD
CENTER CITY

North Philadelphia is rife with building ghosts, some of which have lingered for so many decades that they have become longtime neighbors in their own right. In four months of meticulous ghost hunting throughout Philadelphia for this project—and a preceding decade's worth of casual observations—the area between Girard and Lehigh avenues, and between Front and 33rd streets, was home to more ghosts than any other part of the city. Nowhere was this more evident than on the 2100 block of North 21st Street: in one single block between Diamond Street and Susquehanna Avenue, five ghosts lined both sides of the street at the same time. These lost buildings and their razed interior lives would be enough to mourn on their own, but in researching the circumstances of their demolition, it became clear that there is more to condemn in North Philadelphia than merely the structures. We did this.

That is, the City of Philadelphia's Department of Licenses and Inspections (L&I) did, razing some or all of eleven different houses on a single block as the agency carried out its taxpayer-funded mandate to "conduct [a] demolition program for imminently dangerous buildings."[1] And it's not just the buildings on North 21st Street. Between 2010 and 2020, L&I demolished some or all of 5,458 buildings throughout Philadelphia, a whopping 56 percent of which were in North Philadelphia alone—this despite the fact that North Philadelphia hosts only 13.8 percent of the city's population and only 14 percent of its buildings.[2] This may mean that North Philadelphia is home to more im-

1. "L&I Demolitions," City of Philadelphia, accessed September 22, 2021, https://data.phila.gov/visualizations/li-demolitions; Licenses and Inspections, City of Philadelphia, *Start Right: A Guide to L&I Services*, March 1, 2019, https://www.phila.gov/media/20220616124113/StartRight-FINAL-6.16.2022.pdf, 2.

2. These statistics are calculated based on L&I's demolitions data, at https://data.phila.gov, and from the American Community Survey's data from 2019, at www.censusreporter.org. Both datasets were culled for North Philadelphia using the following census tracts (which overlap with the city's

minently dangerous buildings than any other part of the city, but if that's true, then how did we get here? And with an honest look at the history of this predominantly Black neighborhood, what responsibility do we have to seek different outcomes in the present? When they are the work of the city—with nothing constructive introduced in their place—building ghosts are evidence of collective failure, not success, in a neighborhood. By that measure, we have failed North Philadelphia most of all.

L&I's demolition program exists to raze buildings that are a risk to public safety. The very same characteristic that makes building ghosts possible—the cheek-by-jowl construction of attached rowhouses—can also become a threat. If one building is on the verge of collapse, it can affect an entire block of buildings that share party walls; the 2100 block of North 21st Street bears this out. This is the precipitating reason that 94 percent of the 5,458 buildings that L&I demolished between 2010 and 2020 were the result of a violation case for an "imminently dangerous," structurally hazardous building. In demolishing them, L&I was simply carrying out its responsibility, with few alternatives available to the agency.[3] The thorny issue of tangled titles can mire the situation further, confusing the matter of a building's ownership (and responsibility for its maintenance) even as the structure continues to deteriorate. As of August 2021, the Pew Charitable Trusts estimated that Philadelphia had 10,407 tangled titles, of which 1,716 (or 17 percent) were in North Philadelphia.[4]

Lower North and North planning districts): 137–141, 144–149, 151.01–151.02, 152–153, 156–157, 162–166, 167.01–167.02, 168, 169.01–169.02, 170–171, 172.01–172.02, 173–175, 176.01–176.02, 177.01–177.02, 190–192, 195.01–195.02, 197–200, 201.01–201.02, 202–205, 287–288, 289.01–289.02, 377, 383, 9805.

"L&I Demolitions," U.S. Census Bureau (2015–2019), "Units in Structure [Table B25024, by Census Tracts]," *American Community Survey Five-Year Estimates*, CensusReporter.org, accessed September 27, 2021, https://censusreporter.org/data/table/?table=B25024&geo_ids=16000US4260000,05000US42101,140|16000US4260000&primary_geo_id=16000US4260000#valueType|estimate; U.S. Census Bureau (2015–2019), "Total Population [Table B01003, by Census Tracts]," *American Community Survey Five-Year Estimates*, CensusReporter.org, accessed September 27, 2021, https://censusreporter.org/data/table/?table=B01003&geo_ids=16000US4260000,140|16000US4260000&primary_geo_id=16000US4260000.

3. "L&I Demolitions."

4. Even this high number is undoubtedly an undercount, according to Pew, based on data and methodology limitations. See also Garrett Hincken, *How "Tangled Titles" Affect Philadelphia* (Philadelphia: Pew Charitable Trusts, August 2021), 3. Pew's boundaries for North Philadelphia differ slightly from the boundaries we used for our building ghosts census/analysis, which rely on the city's Planning Commission's district boundaries and census tracts. The Pew report's definition of "North" is bounded by Germantown Avenue to the east, Route 1 and Roberts Avenue to the north and northwest, Ridge Avenue and 33rd Street to the west, and Poplar Street to the south. For a visualization of these boundaries, see Hincken, *How "Tangled Titles" Affect Philadelphia*, 1, 4, 6 (map). According to the Philadelphia City Planning Commission's planning district boundaries, the Lower North planning district is bounded by Poplar Street to the south; 6th Street/Front Street and Frankford Avenue/Kensington Avenue to the east; Lehigh Avenue to the north; and 33rd Street to the west. The North planning district is bounded by Lehigh Avenue to the south, Kensington Avenue to the east, Frankford Creek/Roosevelt Boulevard/Wingohocking Street/Route 1 to the north, and the Schuylkill River to the west.

But how did North Philadelphia come to have so many teetering, imminently dangerous buildings in the first place? And with a longer view, and a broader lens, what does it really mean to be a risk to public safety? The United States has a long history of analogizing Black neighborhoods and risk—most notoriously, in the form of the Federal Housing Administration's influential *Underwriting Manual* and discriminatory lending practices that made their way into the "redlined" maps created by the Home Owners' Loan Corporation (HOLC).[5] But states and cities also participated in segregationist practices based on the perceived risk of Black neighborhoods, as they enabled racial covenants that restricted the sale of property to Black (and Jewish) residents and passed local zoning codes that diverted the placement of industrial facilities and other environmental hazards toward Black neighborhoods.[6] The current condition of North Philadelphia's buildings—and the preponderance of its building ghosts—cannot be isolated from the insidious specters of Philadelphia's, and America's, segregationist policies that historically constrained Black Philadelphians to certain sections of the city and then punished them for living there.

In Philadelphia specifically, these policies confined Black residents primarily to sections of West, South, and North Philadelphia. Those constrained geographies resulted in many close-knit enclaves with deep cultural, religious, and entrepreneurial communal ties, but it also left their residents vulnerable to predatory property owners. Landlords and lenders capitalized on the limited housing options available to Black Philadelphians, charging them higher rents and mortgage rates (a widespread practice that drew little objection from any branch of government for decades).[7] It follows, then, that as predatory lenders siphoned off their disposable income, Black residents had less money available to make repairs to their homes. Over decades and generations of these patterns (compounded by all of the other facets of structural racism), the result is a disproportionate share of the city's "imminently dangerous" buildings in North Philadelphia in particular.

---

5. "Redlining" refers to the act of mapping segregationist restrictions by neighborhood and demographics. The maps produced by the HOLC and others used the color red to refer to neighborhoods that were predominantly Black (in contrast with green and blue neighborhoods, which were predominantly white). This practice, and the maps it produced, coined the term *redlining* to describe the breadth of segregationist policies and the systematic denial of services to residents in these neighborhoods.

6. In *The Color of Law,* Richard Rothstein documents these actions and the many other ways in which the United States—at all levels of government—actively pursued segregation for much of the twentieth century. However, Rothstein and others have pointed to the HOLC redlining maps as the root cause (or one of the root causes) of discriminatory lending practices. Upon further analysis, several scholars have argued instead that the FHA bears more direct responsibility for those practices, while the HOLC simply represented existing conditions. See also: Amy Hillier, "Redlining in Philadelphia," in *Past Time, Past Place*, edited by Anne K. Knowles (Redlands, CA: ESRI, 2002); Jake Blumgart, "Redlining Didn't Happen Quite the Way We Thought It Did," *Governing*, September 21, 2021, accessed September 21, 2021, https://www.governing.com/context/redlining-didnt-happen-quite-the-way-we-thought-it-did.

7. Amy Hillier, "Searching for Red Lines: Spatial Analysis of Lending Patterns in Philadelphia, 1940–1960," *Pennsylvania History* 72, no. 1 (Winter 2005): 42–43.

This is not to argue that deteriorating buildings do not present a problem. The condition of one building can indeed harm many more. But we *would* like to ask why we so often seem to veer consistently toward the most destructive solution—demolition—rather than finding ways to intervene earlier and fund rehabilitation. As the cultural historian Francesca Ammon asks in *Bulldozer: Demolition and Clearance in the Postwar Landscape*: How did we come to associate widespread destruction with the achievement of progress?[8] And, we would add, why does that approach persist today?

The social rupture of large-scale demolition and wholesale clearance cannot be dismissed as a past event. Even now, we treat it as a good solution (and, too often, the only solution) to decades of structural problems in predominantly Black neighborhoods. As recently as 2015, Philadelphia was wrapping up the final phase of the Neighborhood Transformation Initiative (NTI), former Mayor John Street's solution to the issue of vacant buildings and blighted neighborhoods. The controversial program spent $300 million and demolished around seven thousand buildings, with the goal of clearing the path (and the lots) for redevelopment.[9] Even today, the modern urban renewal project of the Philadelphia Housing Authority (PHA) continues in the Sharswood neighborhood of North Philadelphia.[10] There, in the name of public safety, the PHA demolished not only two towers of deeply disinvested public housing, but also hundreds of privately owned buildings that it commandeered through eminent domain, including seventy-three rowhomes that were occupied at the time they were claimed for demolition.[11] The PHA is quick to say that it has replaced these demolished properties with hundreds of new housing units to date (the project was in its final stages in 2023).[12] But those new units come at the cost of $675 million, scores of displaced residents (some of whom have returned years later, but others who have not), a mountain of landfilled debris in an era of climate crisis, and a community's social fabric. It's urban renewal by a different name: "There goes the neighborhood," but in the most literal, bulldozed sense.

While the NTI and the Sharswood project represent the gouging use of public funds for demolition, L&I's ongoing demolition program is death by a thousand cuts. What L&I shares with the NTI and Sharswood, however, is that it, too, is disproportion-

8. Francesca Ammon, *Bulldozer: Demolition and Clearance in the Postwar Landscape* (New Haven, CT: Yale University Press, 2016), 3.

9. Aaron Moselle, "Fifteen Years Later, Appraising $300 Million Effort to Transform Philly Neighborhoods," WHYY, July 20, 2015, https://whyy.org/articles/15-years-later-appraising-300-million-effort-to-transform-philly-neighborhoods.

10. Claudia Vargas, "Philly Housing Authority Adding New Streets in Sharswood Redevelopment," *Philadelphia Inquirer*, December 20, 2017, https://www.inquirer.com/philly/news/pennsylvania/philadelphia/philly-housing-authority-sharswood-redevelopment-20171220.html.

11. Ryan Briggs, "Remaking Sharswood: Taking a Neighborhood through Eminent Domain in the Name of 'Transformation,'" *PlanPhilly*, March 7, 2016, https://whyy.org/articles/remaking-sharswood-taking-a-neighborhood-through-eminent-domain-in-the-name-of-transformation.

12. "PHA Joins with Mosaic Development and SHIFT Capital to Break Ground on Sharswood Ridge," press release, Philadelphia Housing Authority, October 14, 2020, http://www.pha.phila.gov/pha-news/pha-news/2020/sharswood-ridge-groundbreaking.aspx.

ately active in Philadelphia's Black neighborhoods. If a building receives a violation notice and poses a risk of collapse, city officials have the power to intervene and demolish the property but very little analogous opportunity to repair it. The agency is carrying out its directive, with few alternatives to alter the outcome from demolition—and not because cost is a limiting factor or the department needs a clear chain of title to act. As of 2021, L&I's demolition program operated with a $10 million budget (excluding inspectors' salaries and other personnel costs); it recouped costs where possible but demolished the imminently dangerous building regardless of the owner's ability to pay.[13] Even in cases with a tangled title and an unconfirmed or absent owner, then, the city is empowered to move forward with demolition to protect public safety. Why can it not take similar steps to repair the building rather than demolish it? When Mayor Jim Kenney's Historic Preservation Task Force published its recommendations in 2019 about the barriers to preservation in Philadelphia, it noted that "current City policy provides no incentives targeted at historic properties."[14] If only rehabilitation contractors could benefit from the same city funding scenarios as demolition contractors.

When all you've got is a hammer, everything looks like a nail—or, in this case, when all L&I has to work with is a bulldozer, everything looks like a demolition notice. In some cases, neighbors undoubtedly prefer the empty lot (and its building ghost) to the former deteriorated building. But if that is so, what a sad commentary it is on the limited tools in our toolbox. In the end, in the absence of anything productive to replace them, or any stucco to erase them, these building ghosts remain the only signature of the city's work.

The balance is finally starting to shift in favor of several programs that allocate money for rehabilitation and repair, and more than one has had demonstrably positive results. The Basic Systems Repair Program (BSRP), which has been operational since 1995, provides free services (up to $20,000 worth) to address electrical, plumbing, heating, structural, and roofing emergencies.[15] In 2021, researchers at the University of Pennsylvania found that a single home repaired under the BSRP was associated with a 21.9 percent drop in crime for the entire block.[16] Meanwhile, the city's Restore, Repair, Renew initiative, launched in 2019, provides direct low-interest loans to help homeowners improve their properties. In 2022, the City Council doubled the loan limit, to $50,000.[17] The newest city

13. Karen Guss, e-mail communications to the author, September 20, 2021, September 22, 2021.

14. Philadelphia Historic Preservation Task Force, *Final Report: Key Recommendations of the Philadelphia Historic Preservation Task Force,* April 2019, https://www.phlpreservation.org/reports.

15. The operational date and maximum value of services are cited in Eugenia C. South, John MacDonald, and Vincent Reina, "Association between Structural Housing Repairs for Low-Income Homeowners and Neighborhood Crime," *JAMA Network Open*, July 21, 2021, https://doi.org/10.1001/jamanetworkopen.2021.17067.

16. Ibid.

17. Between 2019 and 2020, the Restore, Repair, Renew program originated 109 loans totaling $1,991,849: Philadelphia Housing Development Corporation, *PHDC Report, 2018–2020,* revised April 2021, https://phdcphila.org/who-we-are/publications/phdc-report-2018-2020; Aaron Moselle, "Philly Refreshes Home Repair Program with Hopes of Preserving More Properties," *PlanPhilly,* July 13, 2022, https://whyy.org/articles/philly-refreshes-home-repair-program-with-hopes-of-preserving-more-properties.

program, the Philadelphia Housing Development Corporation's Rental Improvement Fund, launched in 2023; it offers loans of up to $50,000 per unit to small landlords in exchange for certain restrictions on rent increases.[18] At the state level, the Whole Home Repair Program passed in 2022, spearheaded by State Senator Nikil Saval, of Philadelphia.[19]

In the program most relevant for building ghosts (and the quest to preempt them), Philadelphia's City Council passed a bill in October 2021 that would create a citywide emergency repairs program to resolve outstanding code violations. The bill would require property owners with violations to make repairs in thirty days. If they failed to do so, L&I would step in to resolve the issue. Like the demolition program, L&I would bill the property owner or place a lien on the property to recoup the money. In terms of mitigating the costs of demolition—financial, social, structural, environmental, and otherwise—this approach is very promising, and it was encouraging that the City Council passed it unanimously. However, L&I has raised concerns about its implementation, as the agency (like many others in the city) faces staffing shortages and other hurdles.[20] As a result, Mayor Kenney opted to take no action on the bill, and there have been no public signs of movement since the bill's initial passage.

These programs—and others for more targeted audiences—are much more fruitful alternatives to demolition, intervening earlier and prioritizing incremental repair over wholesale, late-stage removal.[21] Yet all of these programs are at a disadvantage in the race to forestall demolition, with funding constraints and specific eligibility requirements.[22] Meanwhile, as long as the city's demolition program is funded at current levels, in the millions of dollars, we must continue to work toward more constructive, equitable solutions for the city's deteriorating buildings. After centuries of disinvestment and structural racism that have treated neighborhoods such as North Philadelphia as more dangerous, more destructible, and more disposable, we must invest our public wealth and willpower in better outcomes than the creation of building ghosts. If we fail to do so, what else is to be concluded than that we are more willing to pay to raze a place than to repair and restore it?

---

18. Michaelle Bond, "Philly Is Offering Loans for Landlords to Repair Properties and Maintain the City's Affordable Housing," *Philadelphia Inquirer,* August 23, 2023, https://www.inquirer.com/real-estate/housing/home-repair-landlord-loan-philadelphia-rental-improvement-fund-phdc-20230823.html.

19. Katie Meyer, "In a Rare Bipartisan Move, the P[ennsylvani]a Legislature Approves a New Home Repair Assistance Program," WHYY, July 8, 2022, https://whyy.org/articles/pennsylvania-legislature-home-repair-assistance-program-bipartisan.

20. Aaron Moselle, "Philly Council Passes Bill to Create New Emergency Repair Program for Neglected Buildings," *PlanPhilly,* October 28, 2821, https://whyy.org/articles/philly-council-passes-bill-to-create-new-emergency-repair-program-for-neglected-buildings.

21. These city programs are complemented by nonprofit programs such as Rebuilding Together Philadelphia, Habitat for Humanity, LISC Philadelphia, among others. Some of these nonprofit programs receive limited city funding to support their work.

22. Meir Rinde, "Making a 'Hard Situation Even Worse,'" *PlanPhilly,* June 9, 2020, https://whyy.org/articles/making-a-hard-situation-even-worse-philadelphians-ask-mayor-to-rethink-housing-cuts.

2327 West Oxford Street

Constructed ca. 1876
Demolished ca. 2000

There is a strange disruption in the history of 2327 West Oxford Street—a silence that sets in, in certain records, as of the early 1920s. Up to that point, the research and retracing is relatively unremarkable: the three-story building was erected around 1876, part of a development on the former estate of Amos Ellis, with J. Clifford Schoch likely responsible for its construction. "With the house thereon erected," as the deeds read, it changed hands a few times in the late 1870s. An elderly woman (Rachel Garrigues) died at the address in 1890; a younger couple (J. Clarence Smyth and Esther H. Walliser) got married there the following year. These life events would repeat in the early twentieth century, with another death (Mary Kelly Barnes) and another young couple (Rose Montgomery and Thomas Harris Jr.). Each of these traces of life at 2327 West Oxford Street had a public presence, morsels of acknowledgment and communal witness that were featured in the *Philadelphia Inquirer.*

After a certain point, however, there are no such traces of life at number 2327 in the *Inquirer*: practically none of the familiar funeral announcements or notices of marriage licenses or classified ads that are routine clues for this kind of vernacular research. The drop-off occurs in the first half of the 1920s, circa 1922–1923. Why the cliff in coverage—in this newspaper, at least? What happened in the life of this building to explain such a clear before and after?

As it turns out, in April 1923 Samuel and Sylvia Gourley sold 2327 West Oxford Street to William and Sarah Montgomery. The Gourleys were white; the Montgomerys were Black.

From this point on, 2327 West Oxford Street is primarily addressed in the *Philadelphia Tribune* (the primary newspaper for Black Philadelphia), not the *Philadelphia Inquirer* (which, according to its own recent contrition, had a history of privileging white Philadelphians and ignoring the news of Black Philadelphians). With respect to 2327 West Oxford Street, the *Tribune* compensated for the silence of the *Inquirer*: the Rodriques-Hill wedding took place at number 2327 in 1934. Charles L. Hill Jr. held a surprise birthday party at the house in 1936 for his wife. In 1944, Mrs. Margaret I. Willis sang several hymns at the Piedmont Club while staying with her friend on Oxford Street.

This pattern emerged across many of the building ghosts researched for this book, a testament to the ways in which the archival record is an inequitable actor in the research process. White owners and tenants—for this building ghost and so many others—are more readily found in the records, their lives deemed that much more worthy of chronicling. (For deeds in particular, the recorded owners obviously were much more

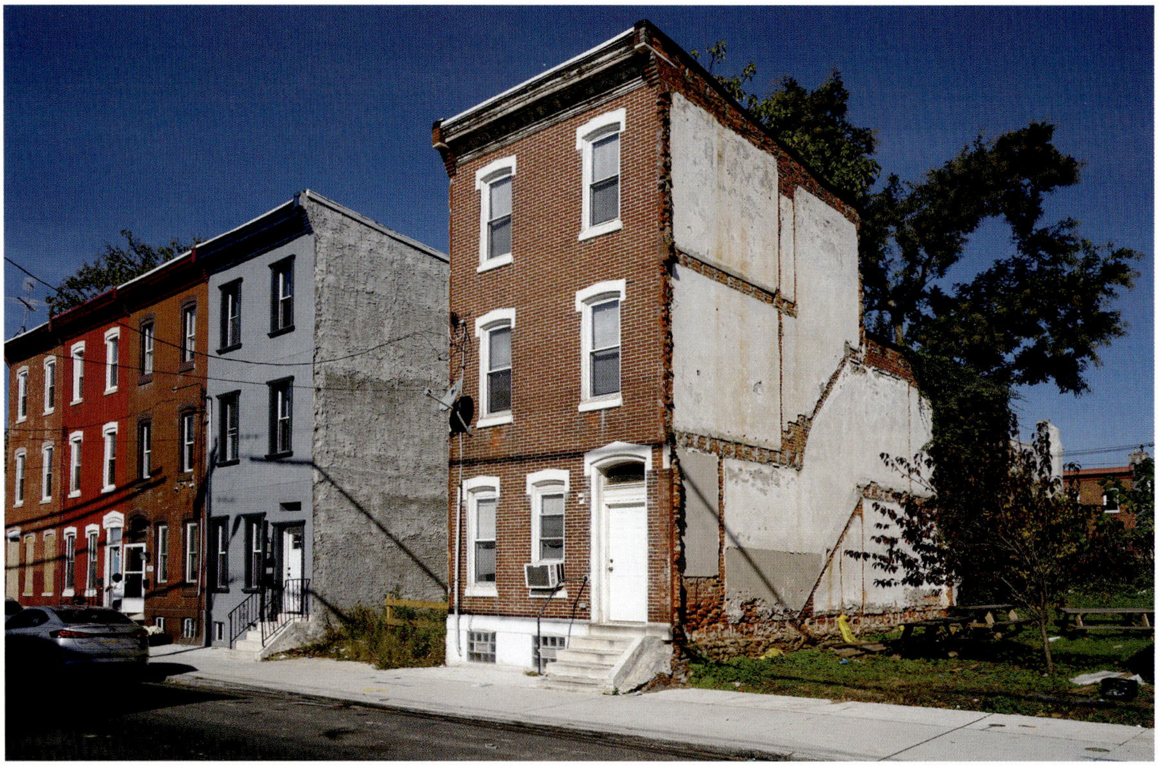

2327 West Oxford Street. (Photographed November 7, 2020.)

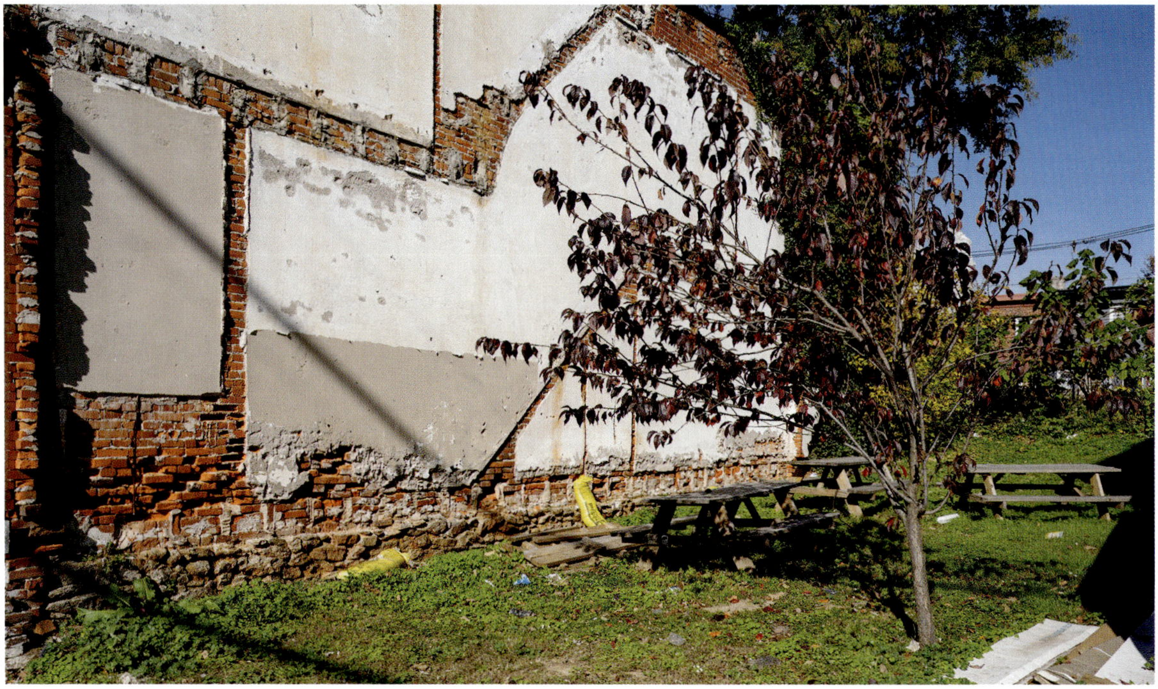

Detail of 2327 West Oxford Street. (Photographed November 7, 2020.)

likely to be white, given the history of property ownership in the United States.) In contrast, Black property owners and residents, on Oxford Street and elsewhere, were all too often minimized in, or omitted from, the archives, as they lived comparatively unacknowledged lives.

The Oxford Street house and its owners are also emblematic of the demographic changes in North Philadelphia in the twentieth century. The Montgomerys were both born in South Carolina before moving to Pennsylvania; in that small fact, this one house's particular history exemplifies the broad sweep of the century's Great Migration, which ushered an estimated 1.6 million Black Americans from the South to the North in the early twentieth century. Between 1910 and 1920, the Black population in Philadelphia climbed from 84,000 to 134,000; the Montgomerys may have been among them that decade. By 1930, when the Montgomerys lived at number 2327, the Black population had swelled to 219,000. More than half of those residents had moved to Philadelphia from just four states, all located south of the Mason-Dixon Line: Virginia, Georgia, Maryland, and the Montgomerys' own South Carolina. Settled in their house on Oxford Street, the Montgomerys were in good company in Philadelphia.

In this light, the seeming disruption in the building's informal archive is actually not strange at all (it's utterly predictable); nor was it ever a disruption. Instead, one small rowhouse played its part in the sweep of social history, whether or not all of the records of that history acknowledged it.

1522 West Lehigh Avenue

Constructed in 1895
Demolished in 2016 under the auspices of the L&I Demolition Program

The house at 1522 West Lehigh Avenue looked down on its northern neighbors with a yawn. It was but one in a long row of statuesque yellow-brick houses with decorative stone lintels over the windows and an arrhythmic staccato of pointed pediments—1522 West Lehigh Avenue being one of the accented notes. The three-story house overlooked its diminutive counterparts across the street with a broad arch that spanned the full width of the house and cloaked a deep front porch. It was the work of John Serrill and his much younger brother, William—or, more accurately, their laborers, because the Serrill brothers were far too busy in the 1890s to build every house themselves. In their hands, entire blocks of houses sprang to life like the awakened pages of a pop-up book, and so it was that in 1895, 1522 West Lehigh Avenue took shape.

In April 1895 alone, John and William Serrill needed someone to build staircases in 184 different houses. The house at 1522 West Lehigh Avenue was one of them, and it needed two. This pace was both relentless and unremarkable for the brothers, who were separated by twenty years in age (and their membership in different Quaker meeting houses) but, in most other ways, were inextricably linked in their mission to transform North Philadelphia west of Broad Street. As their developments accelerated in the 1880s and 1890s, their mailing addresses hopscotched around the neighborhood and between projects. They deployed a handful of different designs for their developments; 1522 West Lehigh Avenue and its neighbors on the south side of the block were at the higher end of their work, with "ornate fronts of various material" and "best interior work and accommodations." The house was complete and ready for sale within a year, and in early 1896, John Serrill sold the building to Augustus Pfaff, a retired machinist born to German immigrants, and his wife, Anna.

Augustus and Anna's time in the house together was short-lived, though. Augustus set foot in the vestibule of his new home in April 1896; by August, he was dead. It was several more years before Anna settled into the house without her husband. Once she did in 1899, it was with her adult son Charles. At seventy, Anna Pfaff had lived an exhausting life by the time she moved into number 1522. She had given birth to seven children—the youngest, Augustus Jr., when she was forty-five—but buried five of them. Only Charles and Augustus Jr. outlived their parents. Anna lived in the house for ten years, with Charles at her side the entire time. He never married.

By 1902, the house had been subdivided into apartments. That may have been true from the start, but more likely Anna and Charles partitioned the building because they could not care for all three stories and five bedrooms on their own. Dr. Frank Na-

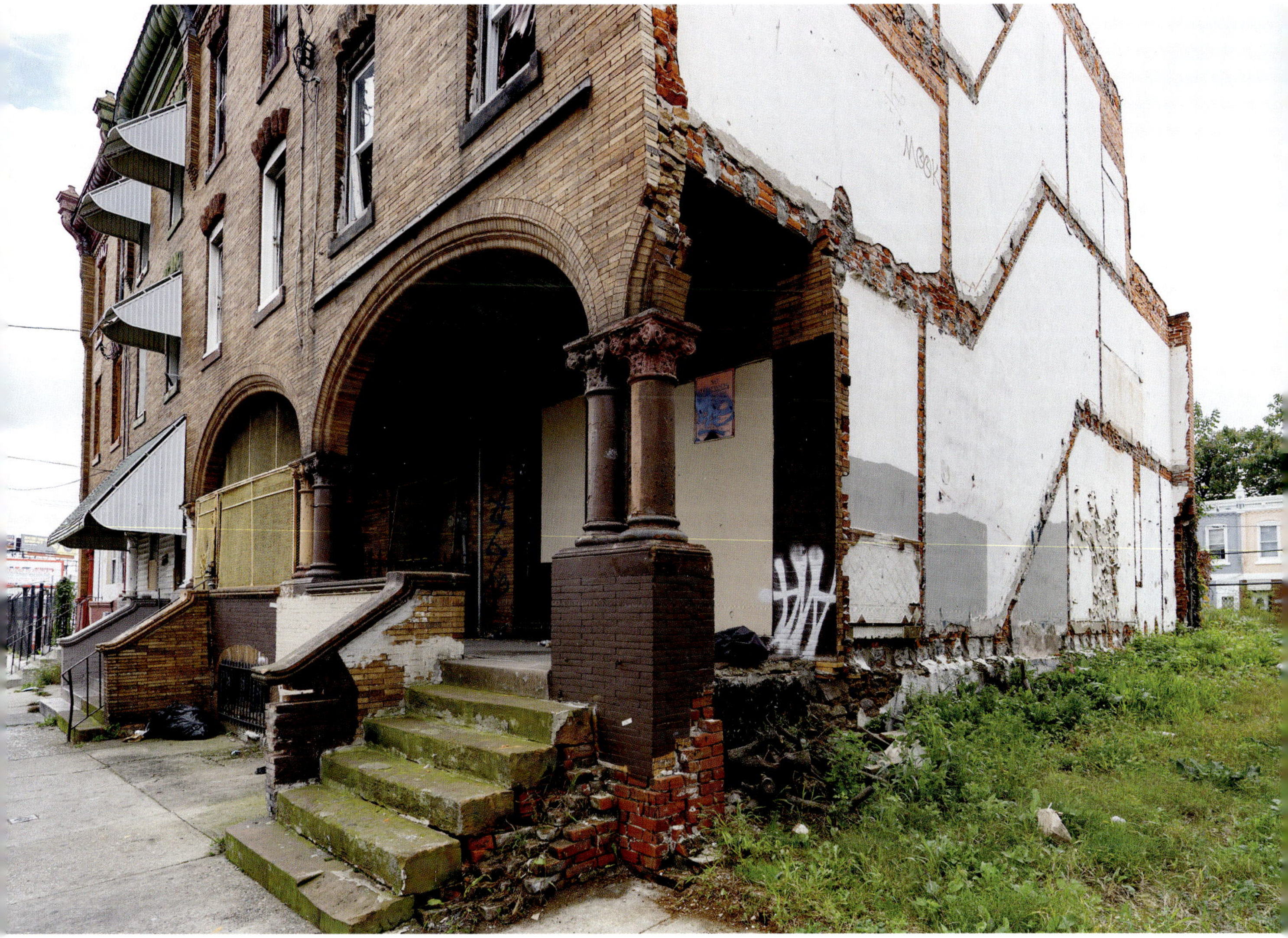

1522 West Lehigh Avenue. (Photographed January 13, 2021.)

than Pampinella joined them in 1902. (It was an easy move for Dr. Pampinella, who came from next door, at 1524 Lehigh Avenue.) The son of Spanish immigrants, he had graduated from New York Homeopathic College in 1883 and had married Lizzie Winpenny in 1886. By 1898, though, he was a thirty-six-year-old widower living with his in-laws before relocating to Lehigh Avenue a few years later. Once he moved in with the Pfaffs, he advertised his practice at this address; presumably, Anna and Charles retreated from the living room, ceding the space next to the vestibule and overlooking the porch to Dr. Pampinella and his patients.

Within a few years, Ernst Kohl and his son Ernst Jr. lived with the Pfaffs at 1522 West Lehigh Avenue. (Whether they overlapped with Dr. Pampinella or replaced him as

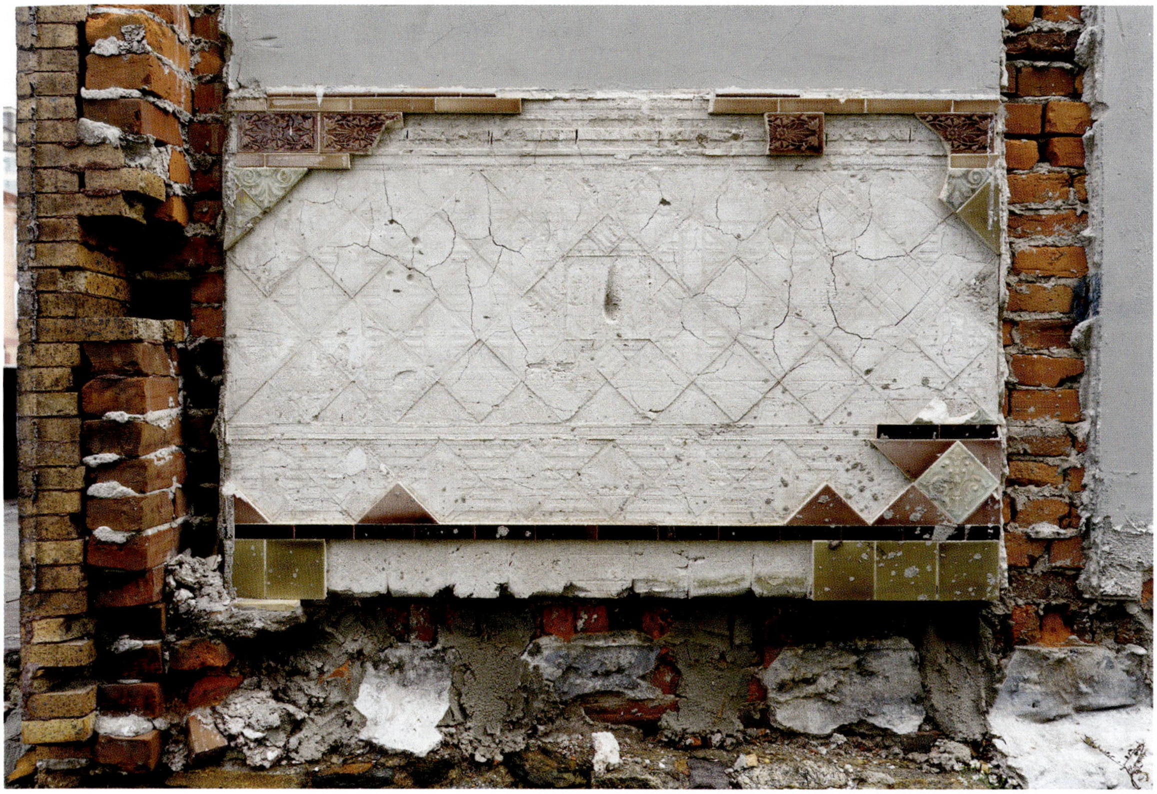

Detail of 1522 West Lehigh Avenue. (Photographed January 13, 2021.)

tenants is unclear.) Ernst Sr., a German immigrant as Augustus's parents had been, was one of the premier wholesale dry goods merchants in the city, while his son graduated with a degree in engineering and held several skilled positions with the Philadelphia and Reading Railroad.

The Kohl father and son lived on the upper floors of the house—most likely using the two bedrooms on the second floor—and shared the first floor's common spaces with the Pfaffs. The arrangement made the two generations and the two families close. It was the Kohls who appraised the contents of the house when Anna died in 1909 and bequeathed the property to Charles, and when Charles died, in turn, the house passed to Ernst Jr.'s older sister, Emma. (It is unclear whether Emma herself ever lived in the house, as the record is—once again—incomplete.) Ernst Sr. died in 1916 at seventy-two, and his memorial service was held at the house. When Ernst Jr. took a job in Cuba in 1909 and subsequently opened his own company there, he clung to 1522 West Lehigh Avenue as a permanent address back home.

Emma Kohl held on to the house for thirty years. She never married, and the building's rental income was probably useful to her for those three decades. In 1948, a man named Jesús William Haughey bought the building. He was born in Cuba in 1911, and his purchase of the house at 1522 West Lehigh Avenue hints at the changing demographics of North Philadelphia in the mid-twentieth century, as white residents fled for the exclusive suburbs and immigrants and Black Philadelphians took their place in the city's increasingly segregated neighborhoods. Haughey tried to convert the building from three apartments to four so his mother could live comfortably and independently on the top floor. But his permit application was denied, and he settled for just modernizing the first-floor bathroom instead.

In the last few decades of 1522 West Lehigh Avenue's life, a rotating roster of tenants crossed the front porch: Harry, Inez and Ida, Garcia, James, Elaine, Shirley. . . . They took turns moving in and out of the three apartments; such subdivision was typical as buildings got older, servants grew scarcer, and neighborhoods got poorer. By 1994, all of the building's tenants had moved on. The triplex was empty and for sale.

In June 2015, L&I noticed a bulging wall on the building and declared it imminently dangerous. By September 2016, the building was gone—a yawning gap in the block of the Serrill brothers' homes. Perhaps the ghost's tile traces in the entryway were part of the "best interior work" promised by John and William Serrill; several years later, in the room with the plastered wall at the back of the first floor, Anna and Charles shared a kitchen with Ernst Sr. and Jr. and became friends in the process. Up the stairs, Dr. Pampinella retreated from his patients to his private room, and up another flight of stairs, J. William Haughey worried about how his mother would age in place in this home. The ghosts of all of them linger in the simple, crisply plastered wall at 1522 West Lehigh Avenue, 120 years' worth of living that defies the empty expanse of a grassy lot.

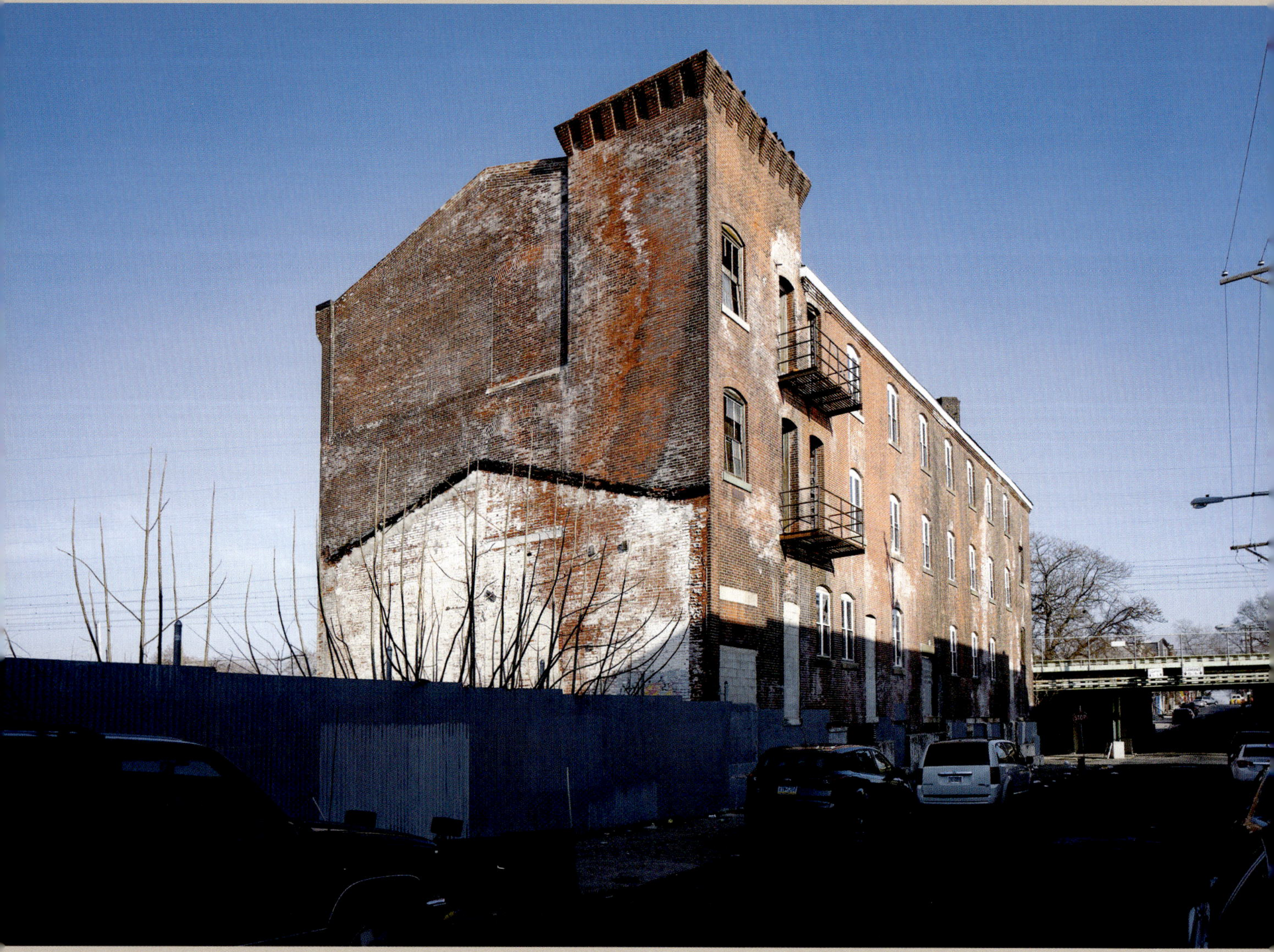

1315–1325 West Cumberland Street. (Photographed January 13, 2021.)

2546 North 28th Street

Constructed ca. 1906
Demolished in 2020 under the auspices of the L&I Demolition Program

At the turn of the twentieth century, William Gegenheimer was both a butcher and a real estate agent in the Strawberry Mansion neighborhood of North Philadelphia. When he wasn't running a shop on Ridge Avenue, he spent his time buying and selling properties, appealing to the potential customers that came with them. Gegenheimer and his family lived nearby at 3005 Susquehanna Avenue, which meant that, with each real estate transaction, he was handpicking his neighbors as well.

Gegenheimer was relatively new to the neighborhood himself, and not just because Strawberry Mansion was urbanizing around this time. A German immigrant, he had arrived in the United States in 1892 and filed his naturalization petition in Manhattan in 1899. He must have settled in Philadelphia in the first few years of the twentieth century, around the same time that Malcolm Briggs Jr. purchased (and built on?) several lots on 28th Street. Gegenheimer bought thirteen lots in total from Briggs, including number 2546. It is unclear which of the two men was responsible for the block of rowhouses—they were already individually addressed when Gegenheimer purchased them in January 1906—but it is certain that by June of that year, 2546 North 28th Street featured a two-story brick building. Gegenheimer sold the house that month to Charles Roedmann and his wife, Minnie May, who quickly resold it to Henry and Rhoda Kalbach in October 1907.

Gegenheimer's transactions as a real estate agent were not the last—or the most egregious—instance of someone trying to prescribe who would live at 2546 North 28th Street. On January 17, 1923, Rhoda Kalbach (now widowed) and at least fifty-four of her neighbors up and down the block banded together to file a petition covenant with the City of Philadelphia. The agreement was entirely voluntary, initiated by the property owners themselves, and stipulated:

> We the Undersigned for ourselves . . . and for our several and respective heirs, Executors and Administrators . . . do covenant each for himself and his Heirs . . . THAT in those lots or pieces of ground with the buildings and improvements thereon situate [*sic*] upon the East and West side of Twenty-eighth Street and included between Huntingdon Street and Cumberland Street . . . *we hereby bind ourselves as above severally and jointly not to grant sell or convey lease or sublet our respective premises of which we are the owners in fee or any portion thereon* . . . for a slaughter house bone boiling establishment blacksmiths shops *or to any member of the negro race*. [Emphasis added]

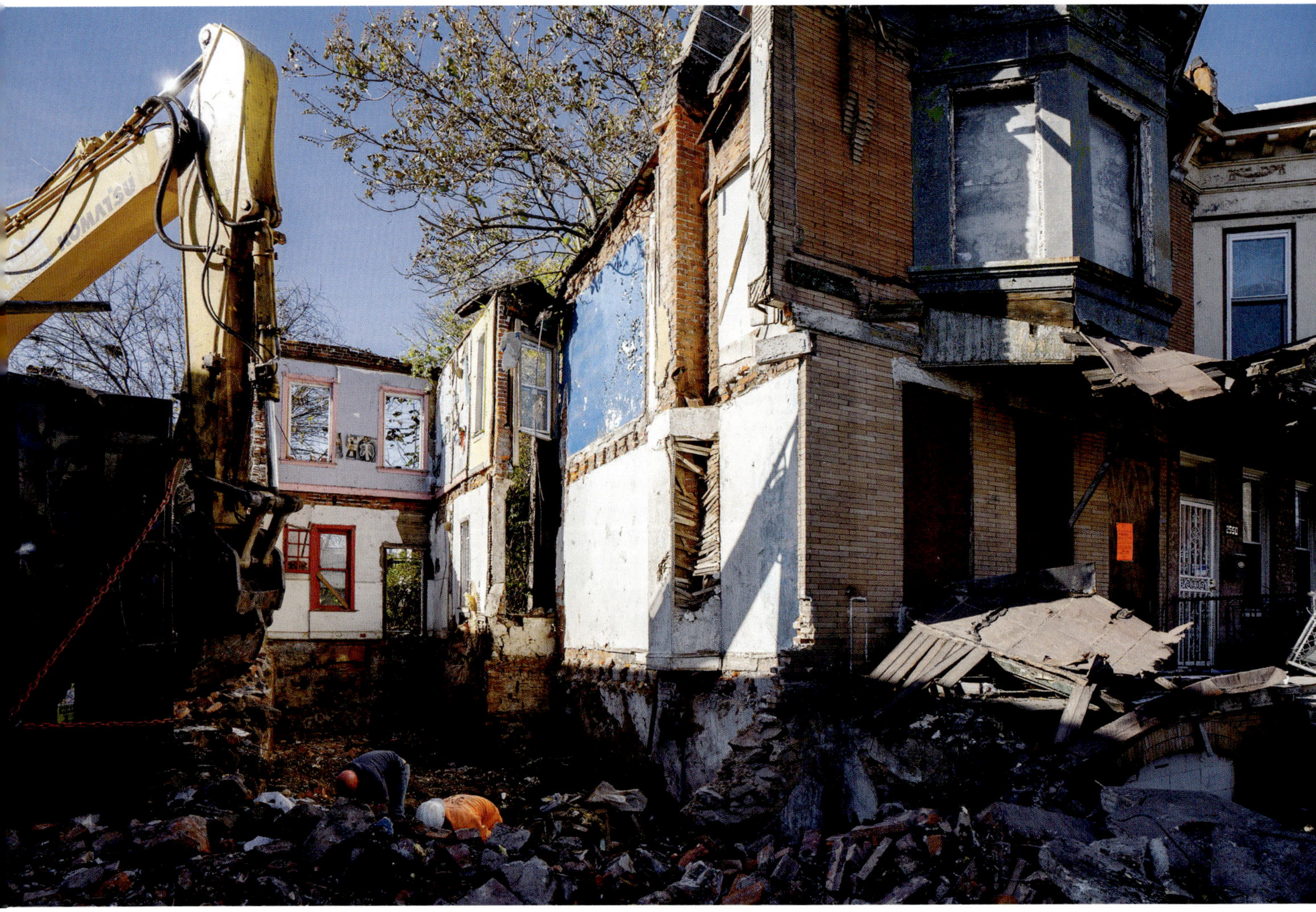

2546 North 28th Street. (Photographed November 20, 2020.)

To bind themselves to their segregationist pact, the 28th Street property owners self-imposed a fine: $1,000 for each instance of violating the agreement (the equivalent of $18,160 today).[23]

There is some irony that Rhoda Kalbach cosigned a covenant barring any slaughterhouse activity at number 2546, given what had been Gegenheimer's job (well, one of them) and his role in the early sales of the building. But the covenant was more odious than just trivial irony. It was Jim Crow in its most flagrant form, and it was legally sanctioned in Philadelphia and elsewhere.

Three years after the 28th Street households signed their restrictive covenant, the U.S. Supreme Court affirmed their right to do so. In its 1926 decision in *Corrigan v.*

23. Federal Reserve Bank of Minneapolis, "Inflation Calculator," accessed May 8, 2023, https://www.minneapolisfed.org/about-us/monetary-policy/inflation-calculator.

Buckley, the court held that this kind of agreement was legal and constitutional, since it was privately enacted. It was not until 1948, in the *Shelley v. Kraemer* decision, that the Supreme Court overturned the 1926 precedent, acknowledging that the enforcement of such covenants—which relied on state and police power—was not private at all and, in fact, violated the 14th Amendment. In other words, people like Rhoda Kalbach and her neighbors could still create private agreements for places like 2546 North 28th Street, but they could not turn to any arm of government—including the courts or law enforcement—to implement them. Without those powers, the covenants were unenforceable.

Kalbach held on to 2546 North 28th Street until 1940, when she sold it to Anne M. Cohen. It is unclear whether the covenant remained in place when she sold the house. At the time of the sale, *Corrigan v. Buckley* continued to bless its existence—for eight more years, at least. The house sold twice more before *Shelley v. Kraemer* rendered moot any lingering 28th Street contract.

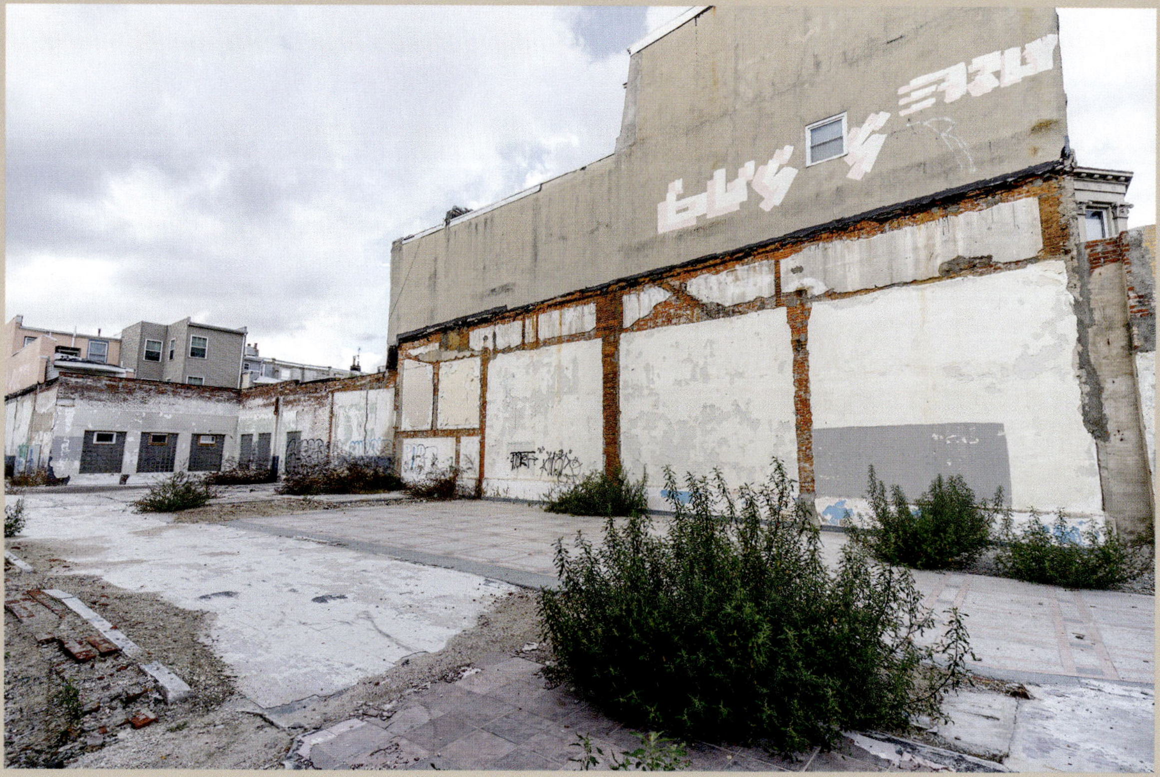

2008 North Broad Street. (Photographed October 23, 2020.)

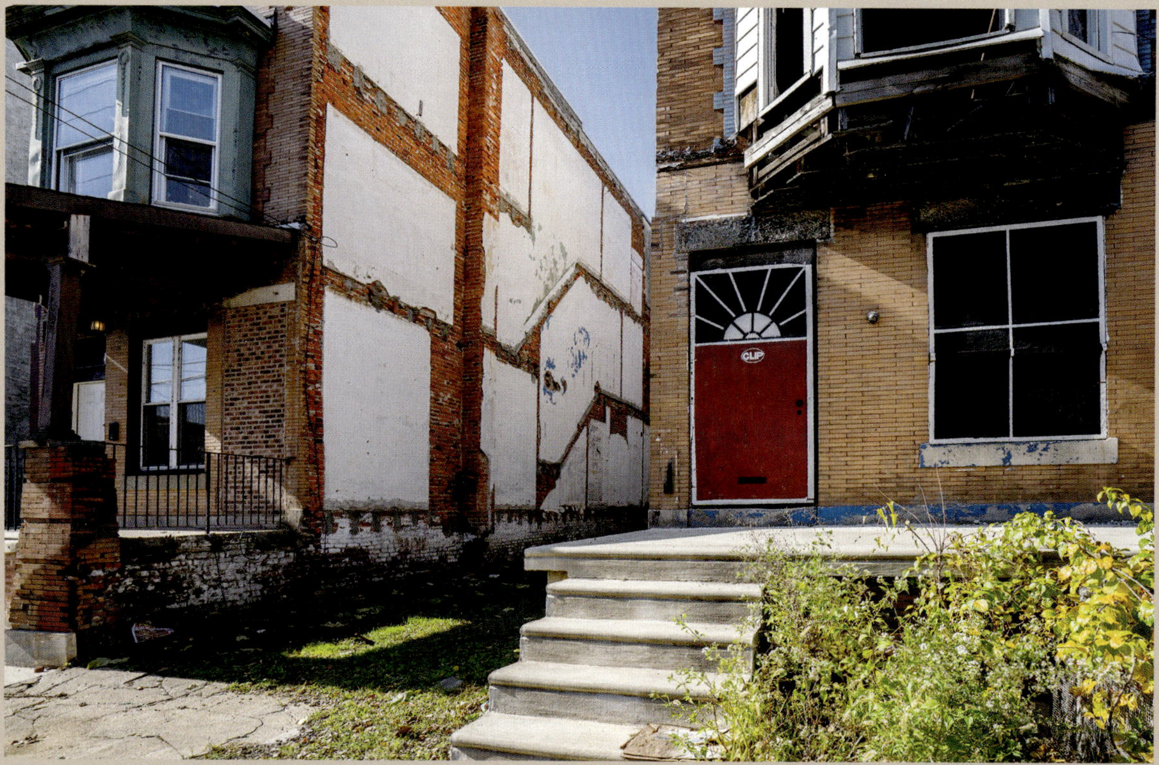

2026 North 32nd Street. (Photographed November 16, 2020.)

2716 North 12th Street

Constructed in 1901
Demolished ca. 2002

In 1926, Miss Elizabeth Cornog rented a room at 2716 North 12th Street, just two doors away from her secretarial job at Cookman United Methodist Church—and on the night of August 7, it was very lucky that she did. That evening, a policeman on patrol noticed flames shooting out of the steeple of the two-story stone church. He sounded the alarm, but by the time the firefighters arrived, the blaze had escalated to a two-alarm, and then a three-alarm, fire. Four firemen were injured, caught on a collapsing stair and buried under the subsequent debris. Even the battalion chief, Joseph Hughes, suffered severe cuts to the face when a mass of window glass shattered on him as he stood on the sidewalk outside, directing his men.

But none of these circumstances could apparently stop Elizabeth Cornog from rushing into the church in the midst of the fire. The minister, Reverend Ernest Bawden, was away on vacation in Maine with his family. In his absence, Cornog was likely the most knowledgeable about the layout of the church and the location of the most critical congregational records. She was almost certainly the closest, rushing down the block that night in who knows what clothes. While the building was still burning, she ran inside to salvage as many records as possible—a feat that became all the more impressive in the light of day the next morning, as firefighters, neighbors, and newspaper photographers surveyed the tremendous damage to the wrecked interior.

Firefighters ultimately determined that the fire had been caused by electrical wires in the organ room. The church's wood paneling and draperies didn't help matters. Within two days of the blaze, Cookman's board of trustees committed to rebuilding, and in October 1926 (just two months after the fire), the congregation hired the architect George E. Savage to oversee the reconstruction.

Elizabeth Cornog could not be there for the rebuilding process, though. On April 1, 1927, she resigned her position as church secretary due to poor health. Whether her medical issues were related to her heroic efforts during the fire is unclear. As she surrendered her position, she likely also vacated her room at 2716 North 12th Street, as by 1930 she was no longer living there.

Even after her tenure at Cookman, though, Cornog remained a Methodist through and through. She eventually recuperated enough to take a job as a host at Methodist Episcopal Hospital (at Broad and Ritner streets), and she occasionally sang for services at various Methodist churches in Philadelphia. In 1939, she married for the first time, at fifty-five, to a widower in Burkeville, Virginia. The minister conducting the ceremony was Reverend Warren A. Smith, her sister's husband and a former minister of Cookman United Methodist Church.

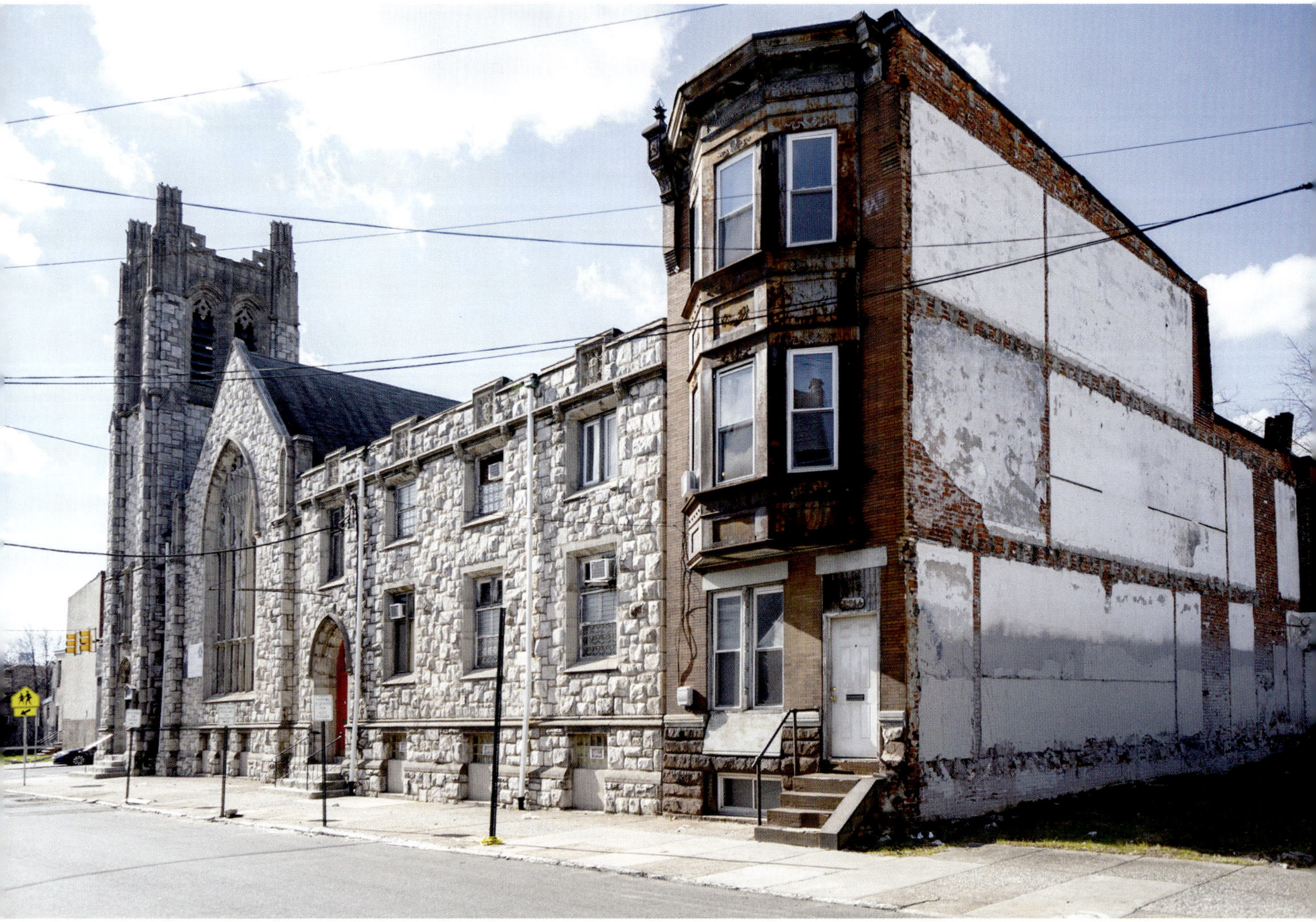

2716 North 12th Street. (Photographed January 13, 2021.)

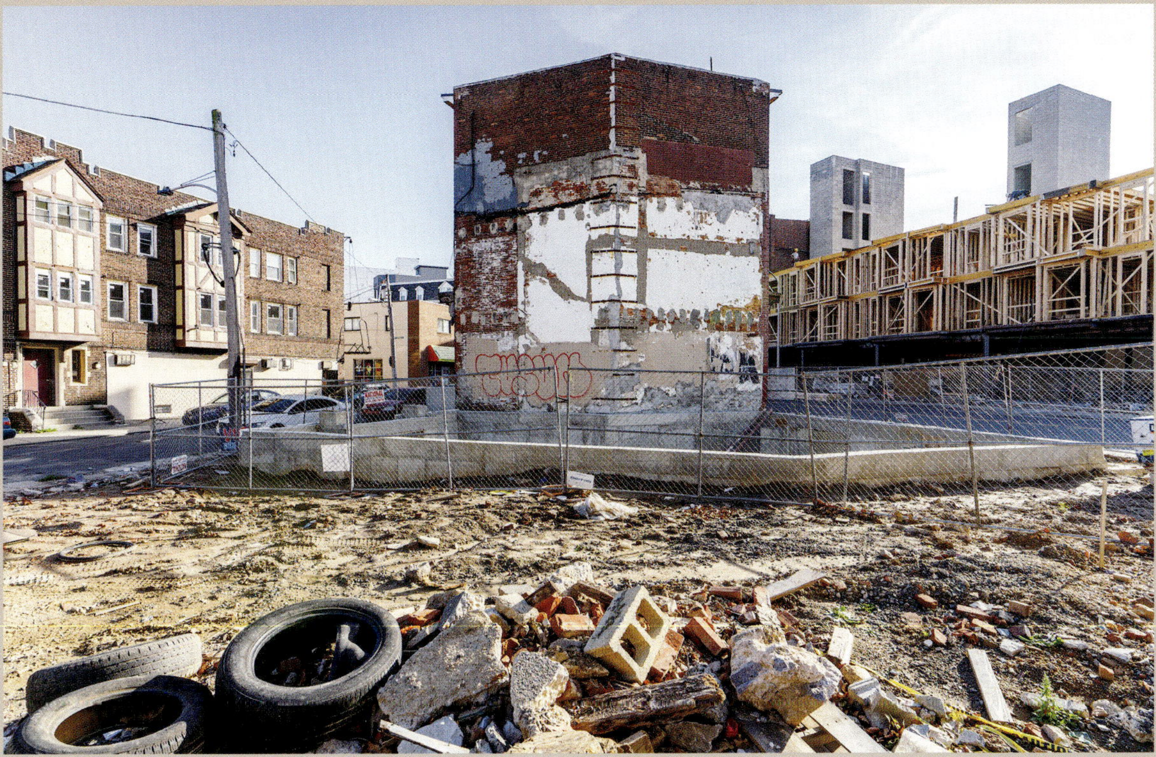

1803 Ridge Avenue. (Photographed November 5, 2020.)

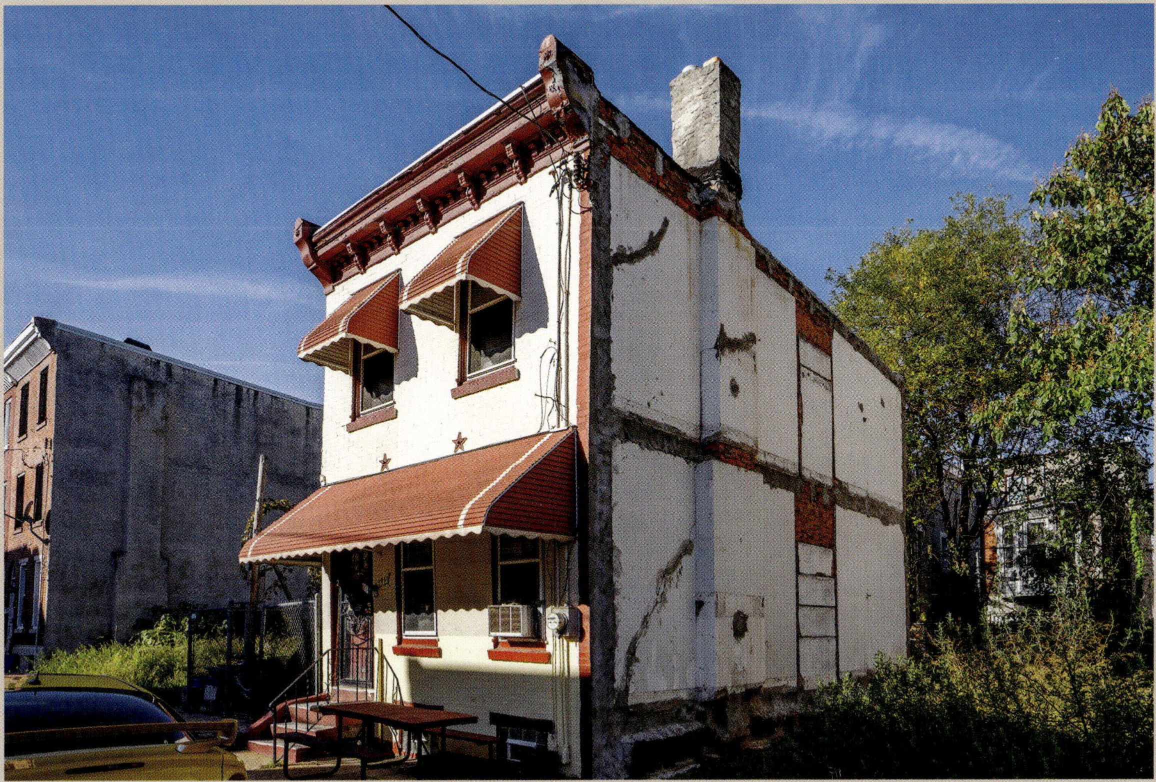

1931 Nicholas Street. (Photographed November 5, 2020.)

2100 Block, North 21st Street

2115 North 21st Street: Constructed ca. 1887; Demolished ca. 2017
2121 North 21st Street: Constructed ca. 1887; Demolished in 2017
2124 North 21st Street: Constructed ca. 1887; Demolished ca. 2017
2127 North 21st Street: Constructed ca. 1887; Demolished in 2017
2140 North 21st Street: Constructed ca. 1887; Demolished in 2017
All five buildings were demolished under the auspices of the L&I Demolition Program

The five houses on the 2100 block of North 21st Street—numbers 2115, 2121, 2124, 2127, and 2140—began together. The builder John Sharp constructed them all around 1887, as he developed this and many other blocks in North Philadelphia.

They ended together, too, when L&I's Demolition Program swept up their structural deficiencies and conditions issues in or around 2017. (Four of the five buildings were privately owned at the time of their demolition, but number 2124 was owned by the Philadelphia Housing Authority [PHA], and had been since 1968.)

But in the decades between the buildings going up and coming down, the neighbors on this block shared—or, at least, witnessed—all of the milestones and mundanity of life in close quarters.

The block's first generation of owners and residents consisted primarily of laborers: machinists in numbers 2115 and 2124 (Charles Lavis Sr. and Jacob Hoff, respectively); a foreman named William Myers in number 2121; patternmaker and foreman Edward W. Barton in number 2140; and more. They left for their mill jobs in the morning and returned in the evening to life with their tenants, housemates, and families. But not all could grow their households as they hoped. Edward Barton and his wife, Thomson, gave birth to a son, Arthur, in 1889, only to lose him at fourteen months old. He was buried on New Year's Eve in 1890.

Sarah Reid, in number 2127, was also working class. Already widowed by the time she moved to 21st Street, she purchased the house in 1888 from two sisters: Katharine Russell Pettingill and Louise Russell. Sarah Reid lived in the three-story, mid-block brick house with Ida Reid, who was almost certainly a relation, but it is unclear of what sort. Sarah owned the house for six years, eventually selling it to a lawyer (George Milgus) in 1895. In a fascinating bit of building ghost coincidence, she subsequently lodged with the Pfaffs at 1522 West Lehigh Avenue (see that house's story on page 74).

George Milgus was one in a wave of white-collar workers who began moving to the block in the 1890s. He was joined by an architect, a draughtsman, and a printer—Byron C. Dickson, Richard L. Vansant, and Joshua J. Daugherty—all of whom lived at number 2124. They did not entirely supplant the working-class residents of the street, though, as masons and machinists continued to live in numbers 2127 and 2140, for instance. At

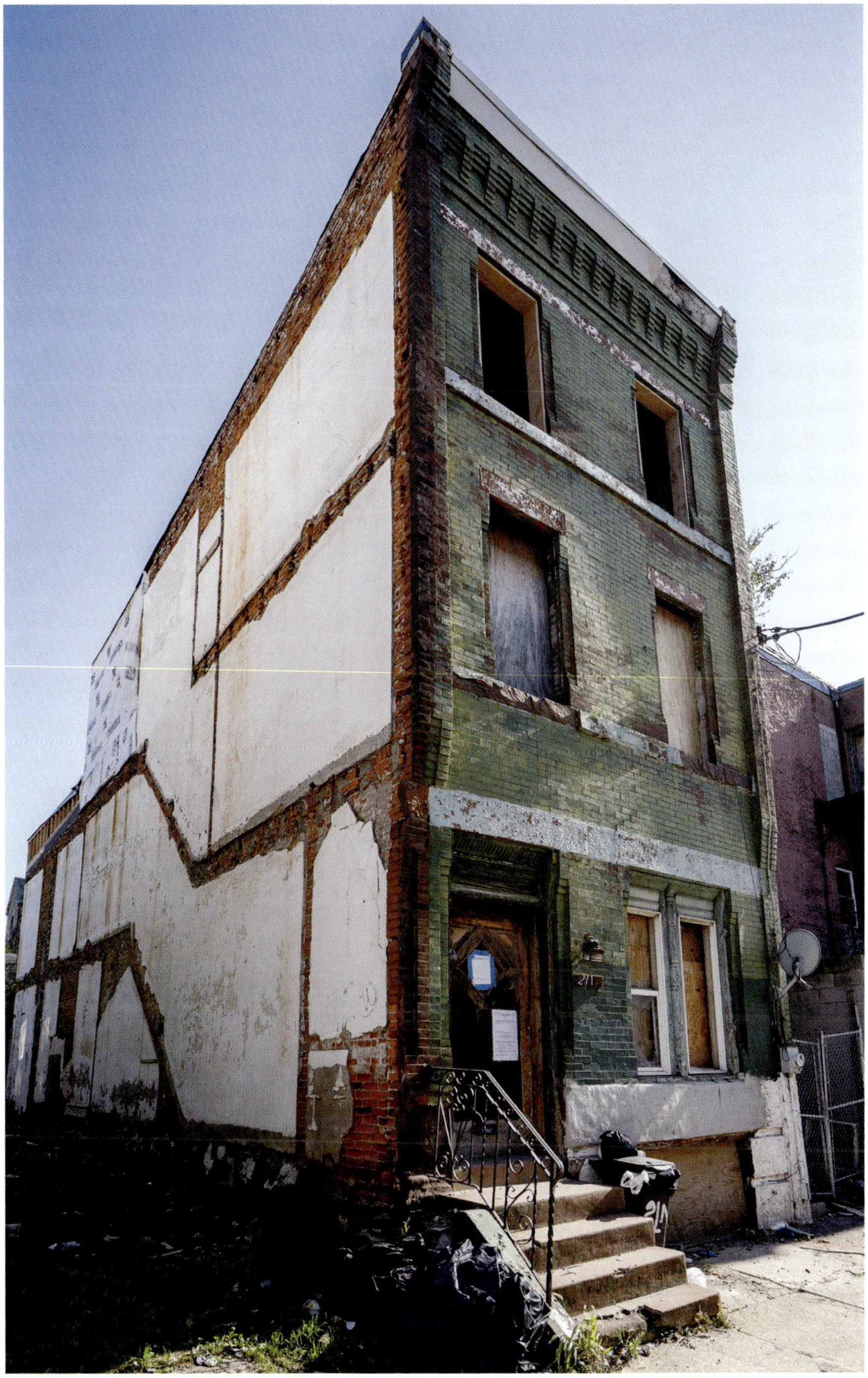

2115 North 21st Street. (Photographed November 6, 2020.)

number 2115, Charles Lavis Sr. was by this point the master mechanic of the Philadelphia Mint; he lived on 21st Street along with his wife, Anna; three sons (and possibly some of his three daughters, although at least two of them were married); and his sons' business partner, Robert Dahlgren. (The firm of Lavis, Dahlgren, and Lavis sold bedding nearby, on West Columbia—now Cecil B. Moore—Avenue.) Even after Charles Lavis Sr. died in 1899, his widow remained in the house. His sons held on to number 2115 until 1914.

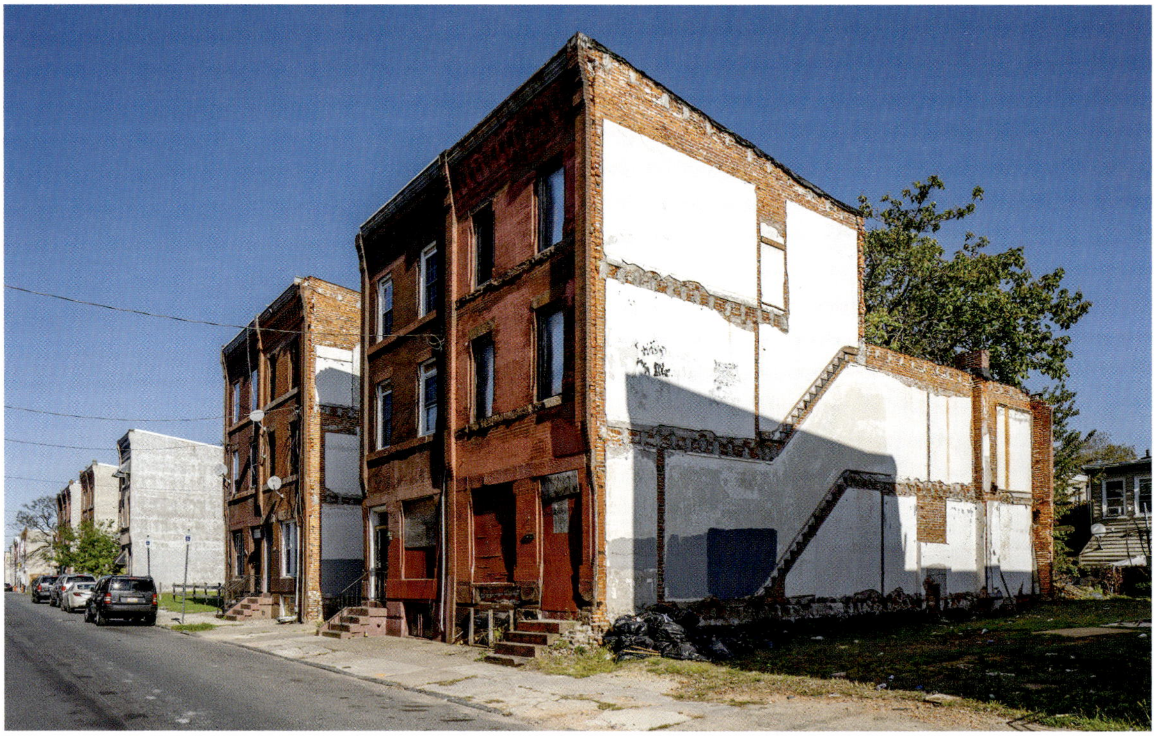

2121 North 21st Street. (Photographed November 6, 2020.)

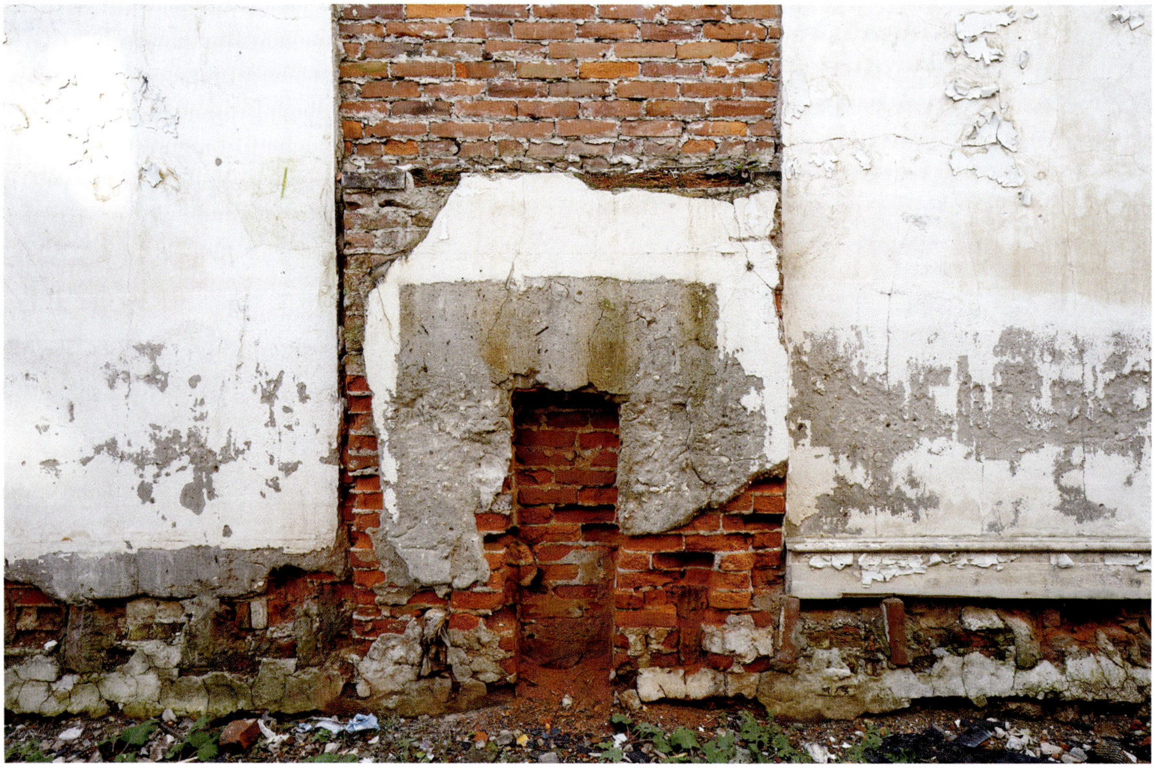

Detail of 2121 North 21st Street. (Photographed November 6, 2020.)

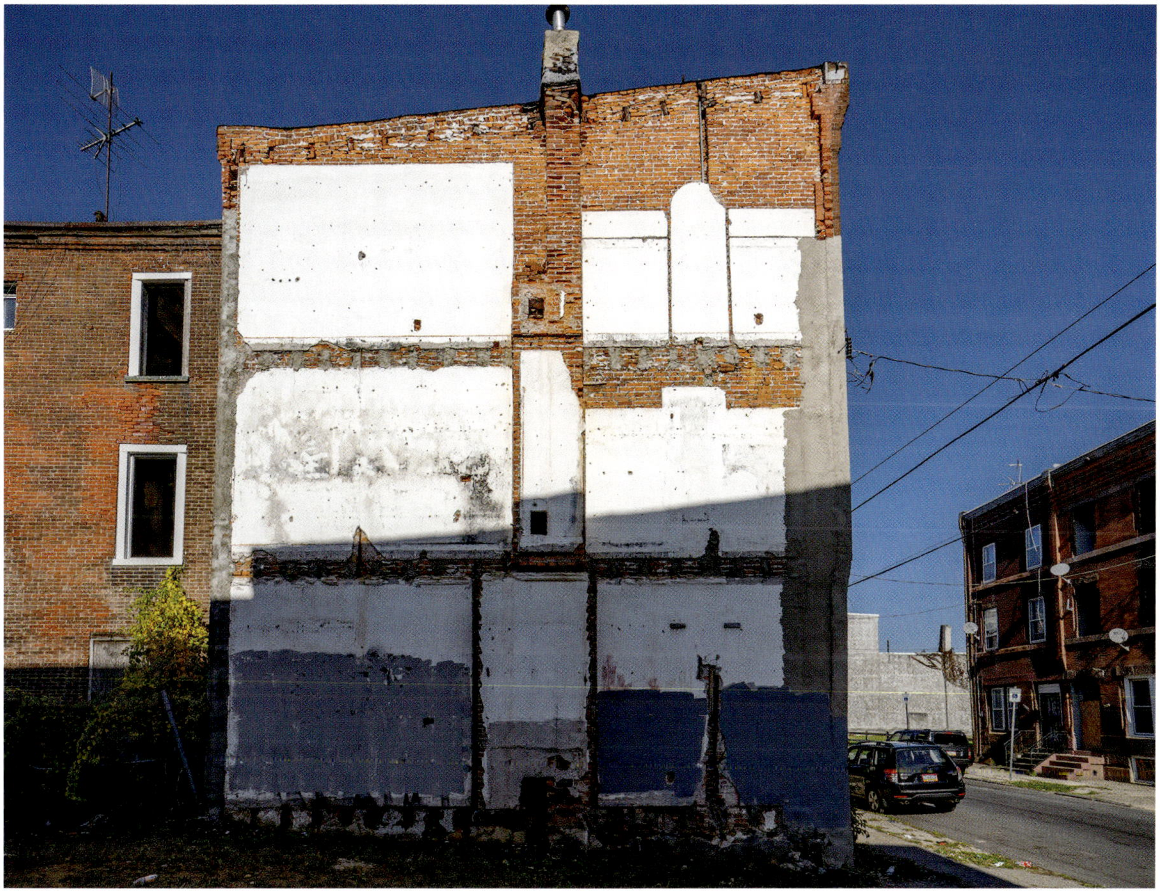

2124 North 21st Street. (Photographed November 6, 2020.)

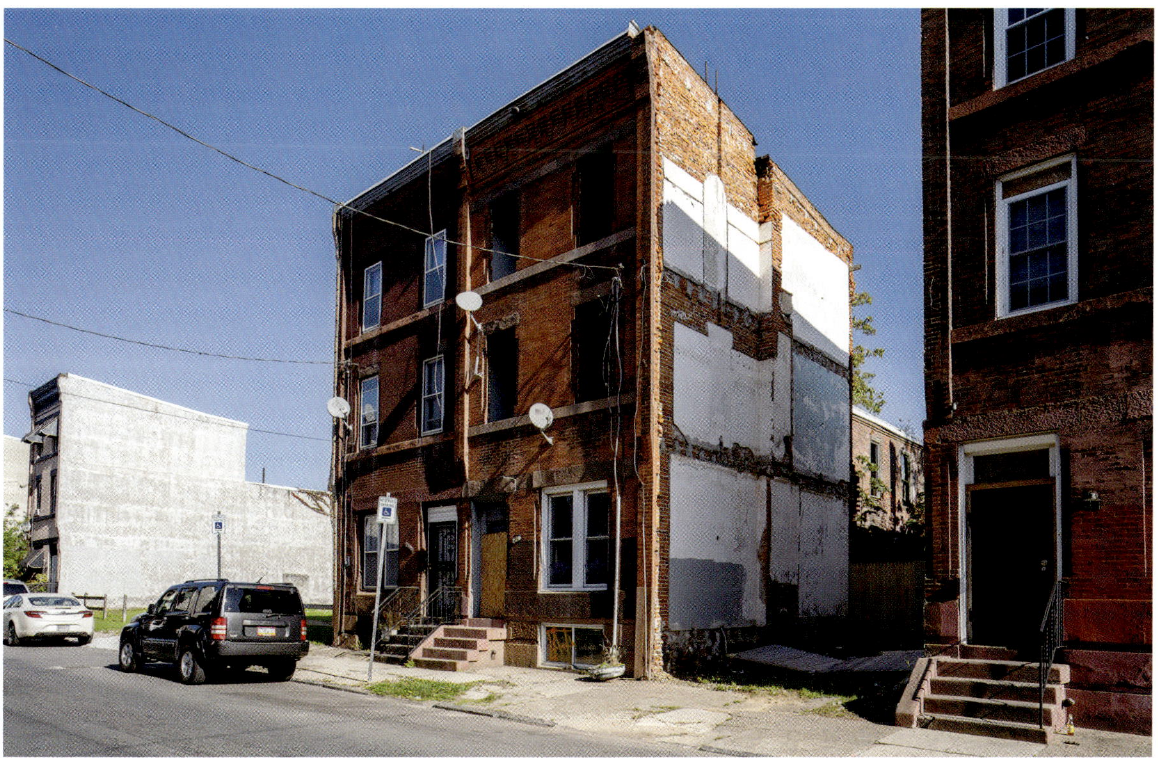

2127 North 21st Street. (Photographed November 6, 2020.)

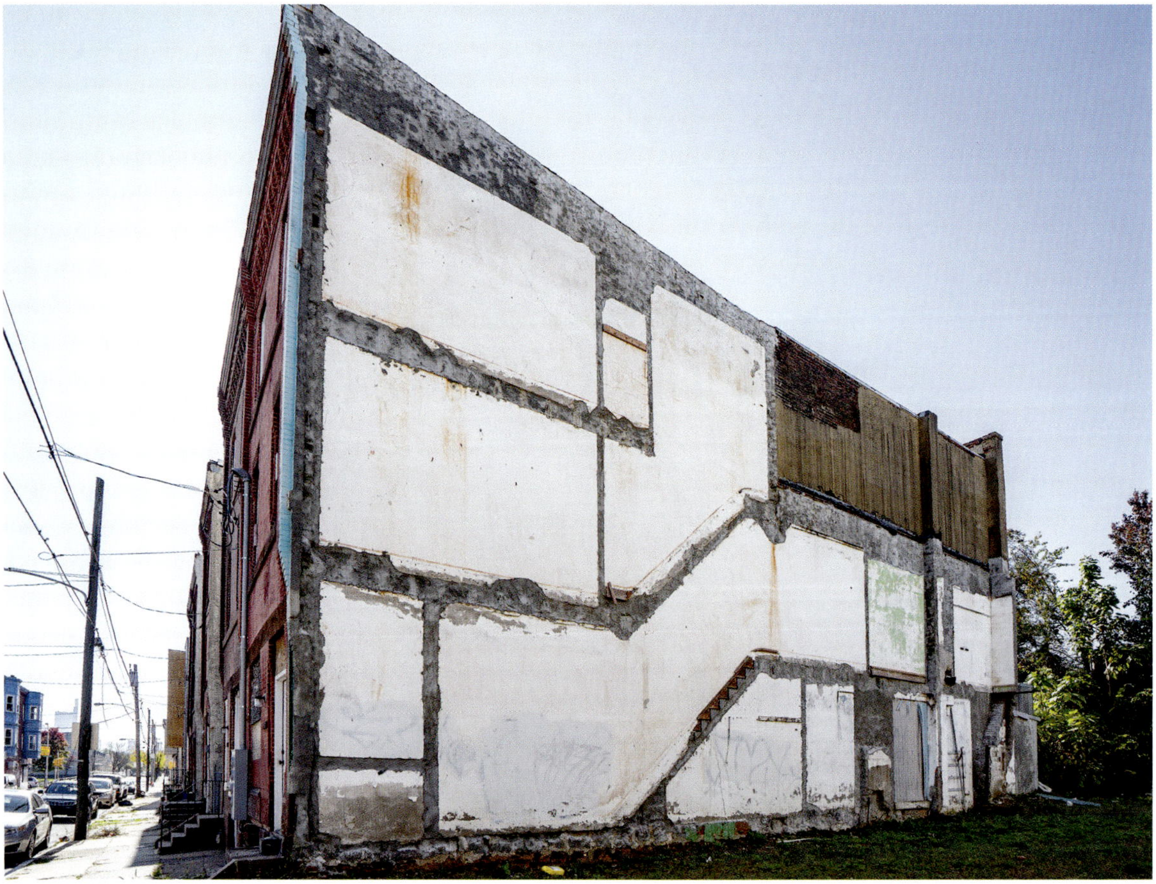

2140 North 21st Street. (Photographed November 6, 2020.)

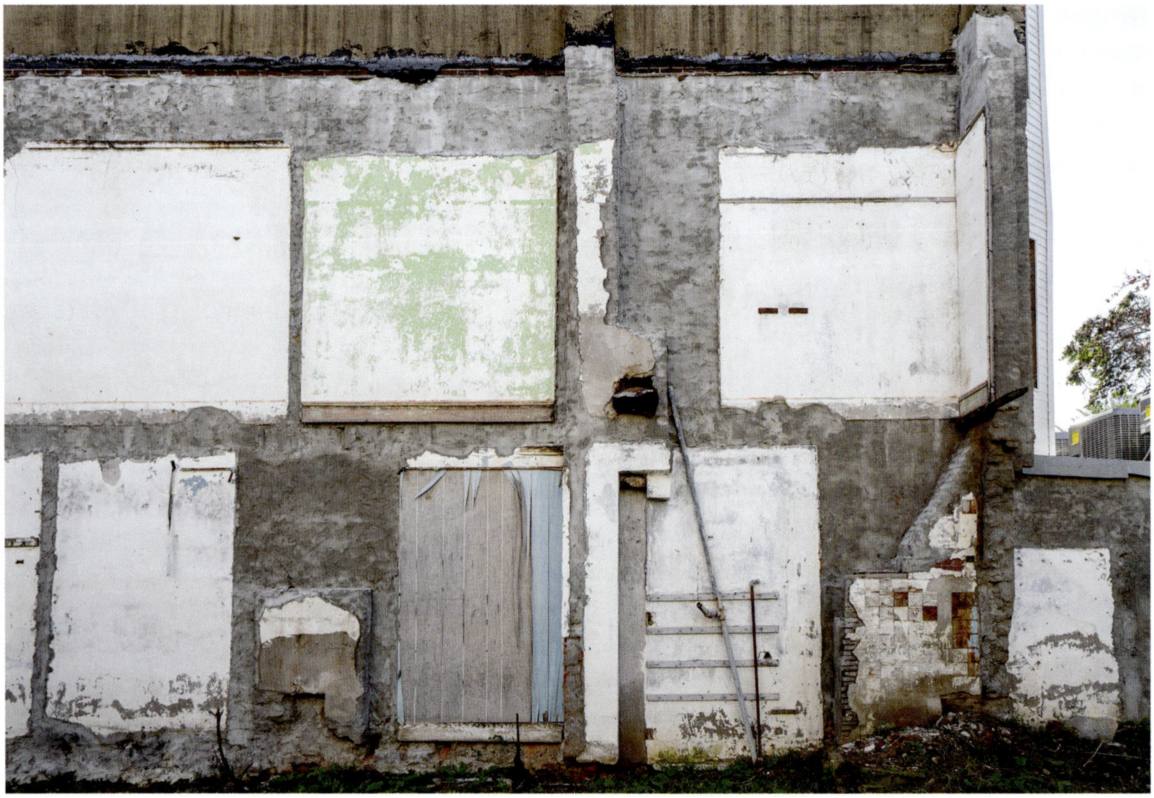

Detail of 2140 North 21st Street. (Photographed November 6, 2020.)

The block's residents were predominantly white through the early twentieth century. Based on a 1903 ad seeking a white woman for housework at number 2127, that pattern wasn't at all accidental. It was not until the 1930s that the demographics of the block began to shift, as new residents in numbers 2121, 2124, and 2127 (and perhaps other homes) were Black. In the broader context of Jim Crow and its impacts on homeownership in America, it is worth noting that the Black residents of 21st Street were most often tenants rather than owners. (In earlier decades, the homes were generally owner-occupied.)

There were grim moments in the life of the block. In 1932, while Grace Moore was living at 2127 North 21st Street, her ex-boyfriend stalked and eventually murdered her. He received a life sentence for the crime. In 1945, three residents of the block were involved in two different trolley crashes: Etta Johnson and Susie Holman, who both lived at number 2121, would survive their injuries, but two-year-old Matthew Watson, of number 2124, would not.

Still, the neighbors enjoyed parallel celebrations, too. Thomas Murray (number 2115) and Robert Watson (number 2124) both got married in 1945. Pearl and Eugene Williams (presumably siblings; they lived at 2127 North 21st Street) each marked the same occasion in 1959 and 1960, respectively.

All five houses were slow to change hands in the first few decades of the century—then all of them began turning over relatively frequently starting in the 1930s, as they were bequeathed in wills or transferred in sheriff's sales during the Great Depression. The house at 2124 North 21st Street was even owned by a bunch of Presbyterians (first by an individual congregation, and then by the broader Presbytery of Philadelphia) for several decades; it may have served as a manse. Some buildings saw additions or alterations, including repairs made to number 2124 in the 1950s, after the Presbytery sold the building. For the most part, though, these five houses appear to have maintained a relatively consistent existence from the time John Sharp first developed them.

By the first decades of the twenty-first century, though, these houses on the 2100 block of North 21st Street had begun to deteriorate. In the 2000s and 2010s, the buildings started to accumulate code violations and face the prospect of sheriff's sales. The PHA was cited in 2008 for unlicensed vacancy at number 2124 and again in 2017 for failing to secure the still-vacant structure. In 2016, classified ads threatened sheriff's sales for numbers 2127 and 2140. Both would indeed meet that fate soon after.

All five houses were demolished in or around 2017; 2127 North 21st Street was the last to fall. In their absence, what had been a dense urban block became accidentally suburban in feel, as piecemeal demolition created detached houses with inadvertent "side yards." Now the density of the 2100 block of North 21st Street can be measured in building ghosts as much as buildings.

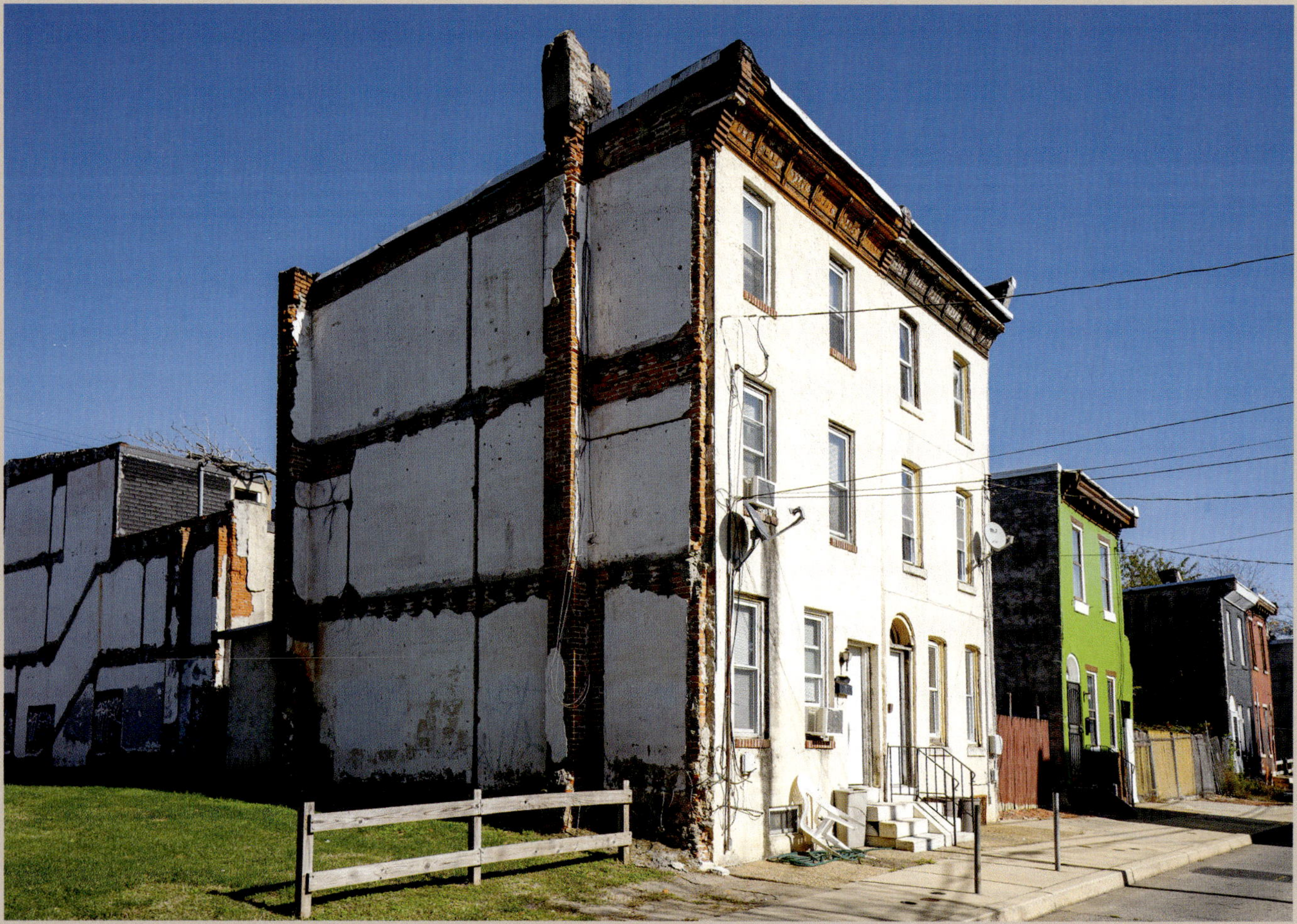

2251 Ingersoll Street. (Photographed November 7, 2020.)

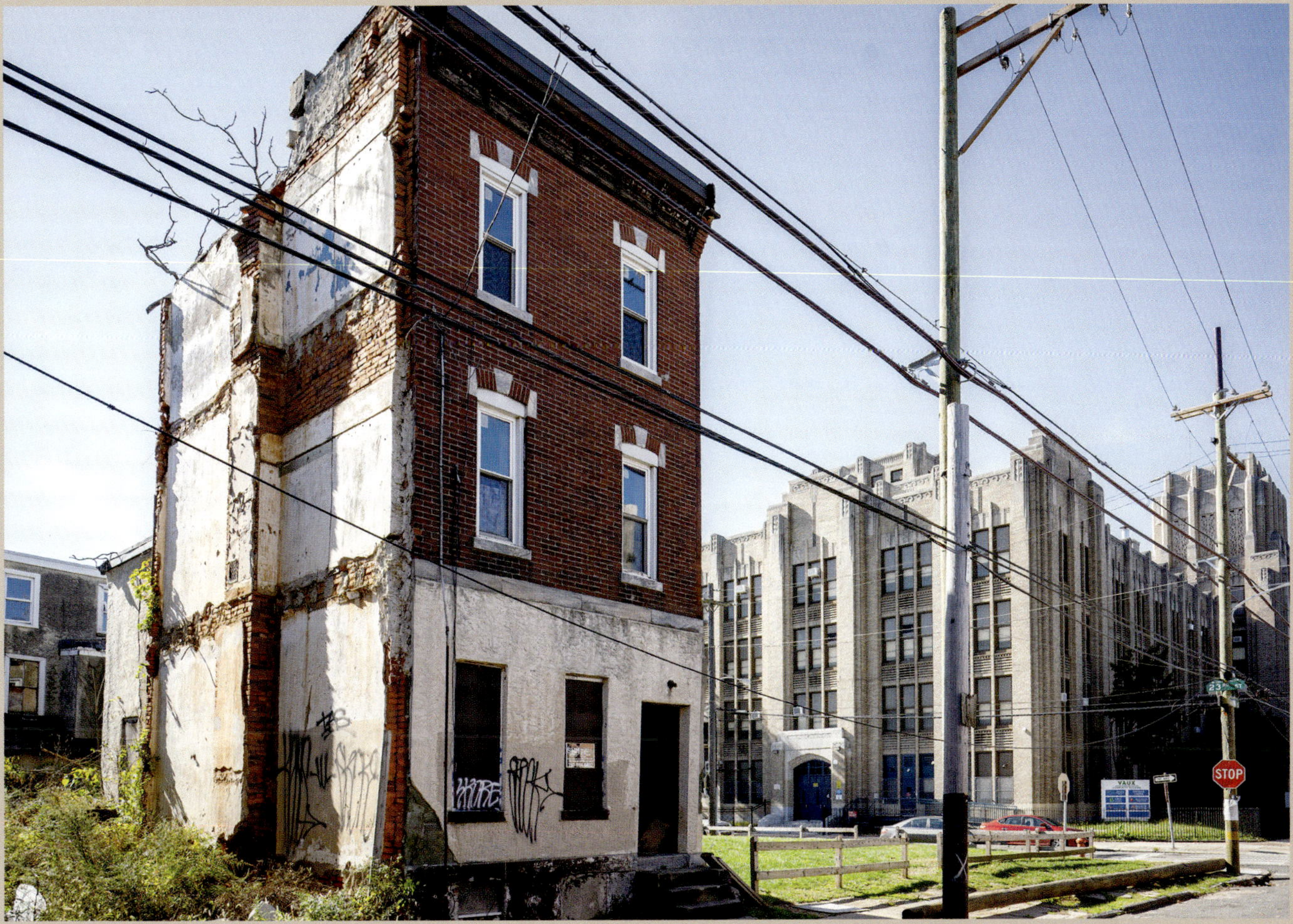

2240 Master Street. (Photographed November 7, 2020.)

1935 Diamond Street

Constructed ca. 1886
Demolished in 2018 under the auspices of the L&I Demolition Program

Number 1935 Diamond Street was not the highest-profile commission in Willis G. Hale's career. (How could it be when compared with the gargantuan, extravagant North Broad Street mansion he designed around the same time for Peter A. B. Widener?) It barely even registered when it was announced in the *Philadelphia Real Estate Record and Builders' Guide*, arriving last in a litany of projects he was working on contemporaneously for the builder Colonel E. H. Flood: twenty-two houses at Fountain and Diamond street; thirty-five others on Van Pelt, north of Diamond; thirty-two more residences on Uber Street; twenty-two on Page Street; and eleven on Norris Street. Oh, and a block of ten houses on Diamond Street—"also ten rooms." Even among those ten, number 1935 was a recessive design. The third-westernmost house on the street, it was decidedly shorter than the block's most muscular members. Still, those more assertive designs could not be understood without their deferential counterparts, such as number 1935.

Trained under the famous local architects Samuel Sloan and John McArthur Jr., Willis G. Hale embraced the popular eclecticism of his day as he amassed commissions for the city's wealthiest speculators and tycoons. Philadelphia was an adopted hometown for the Seneca Falls, New York-born designer, who had apprenticed in Buffalo and Rochester before landing in Philadelphia in the 1860s. After a brief stint practicing in northeastern Pennsylvania, he returned to the city for good in 1876. (Perhaps he, like many, could not resist the Centennial Exhibition that Philadelphia hosted that year.)

In addition to his livelihood as an architect, Hale was an amateur musician, which may explain why so many of his ensembles—including the one in the 1900 block of Diamond Street—read like a staff of music, in terms of both rhythm and stylistic flourishes. (The word *flourish* is inevitable when discussing Hale's designs.) Certain buildings served as accents in the row—1939 Diamond Street, for instance, continues to anchor the northeastern corner of 20th and Diamond streets—while other, quieter beats repeated. The house at number 1935 fell into the latter class, deferring to its weightier neighbors and echoing the configuration of number 1925. Taken all together, the ensemble had an A-B-B-B-A-A-B-B-B-A pattern, in which the four-story buildings ("A") and their three-story complements ("B") were mirrored across a central axis.

But what may have seemed, at first glance, like a measure with just two notes actually incorporated much more nuance. Hale made a habit of foreshortening individual features within his designs, which is to say that he exaggerated some elements closer to the ground while scaling down some details at the upper floors, with the designed effect of making a building seem taller. Two of his more famous surviving buildings—the Divine Lorraine Hotel and what is now known as the Hale Building, at Juniper

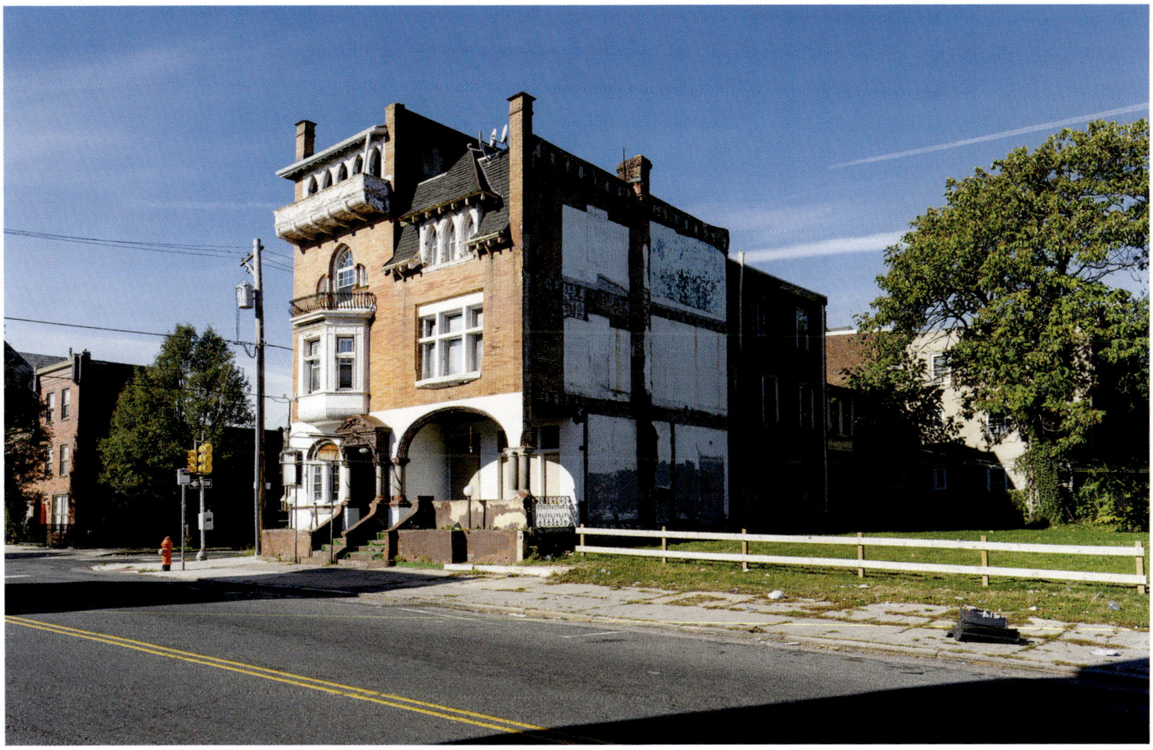

1935 Diamond Street. (Photographed November 5, 2020.)

and Chestnut streets—demonstrate this foreshortening prowess on a much larger scale. But 1935 Diamond Street once did, too: the archway of the porch was as broad as the building, wryly exaggerating the opening at the ground floor, while the second- and third-story windows winked to passersby at a much smaller scale. (The surviving residence at number 1937 employs similar windows at the third story, so in that floor, at least, the building ghost's neighbor offers some echoes of its missing counterpart.) The total effect was one of quirky complexity, and the Diamond Street block took a self-assured place amid the asymmetry and eccentricity that characterized much architectural work of the day, particularly in Philadelphia, where Frank Furness could be said to set the tone.

The Diamond Street houses were constructed with bricks produced by the Eastern Hydraulic Press Brick Company. The manufacturers were so eager to show off their product and associate themselves with Hale and his Diamond Street houses that they featured photographs of the residences in their advertisements for several years.

Number 1935 Diamond Street began as one in a block of ten houses. By the time it was demolished in 2018, just four of the houses—the bookends of the block—remained. None of the surviving buildings deploys the same design that number 1935 once did. Its loss, then, not only chipped away yet another house in the original block (another beat in the rhythm); it stamped out any possibility of understanding Hale's full composition.

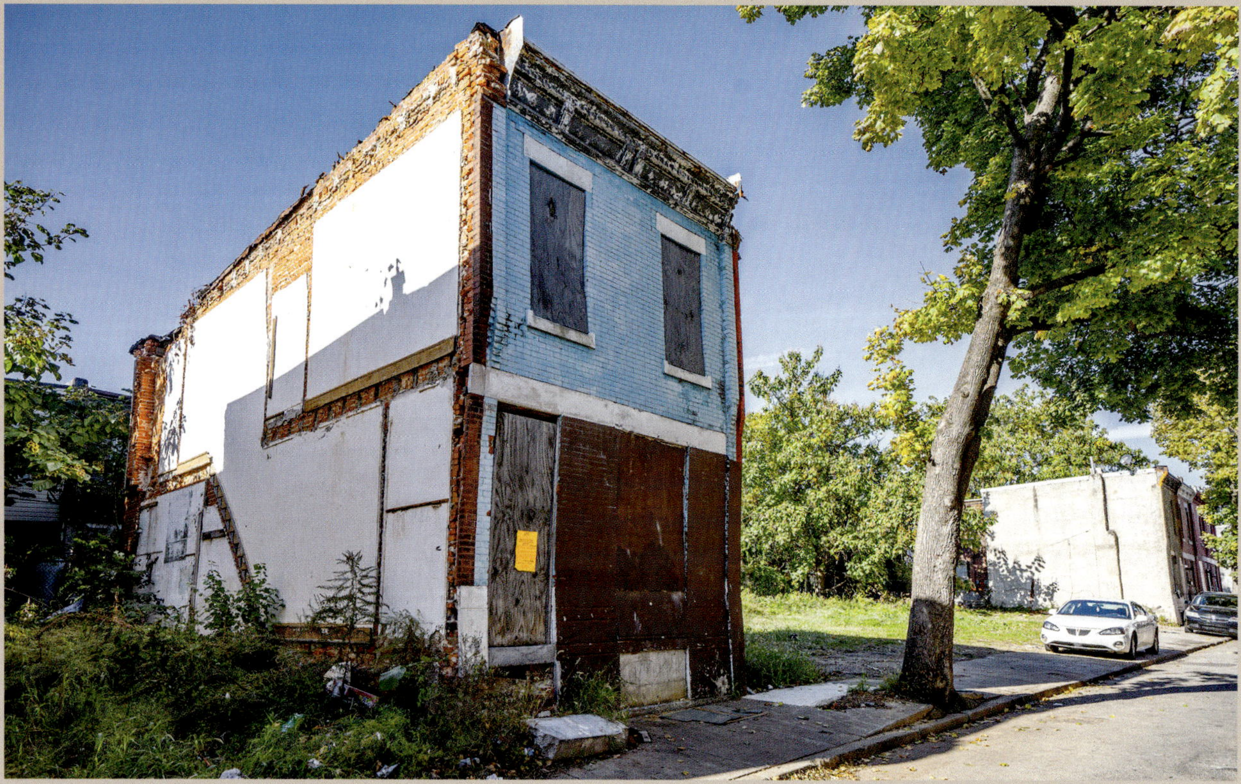

2312 Cleveland Street. (Photographed November 5, 2020.)

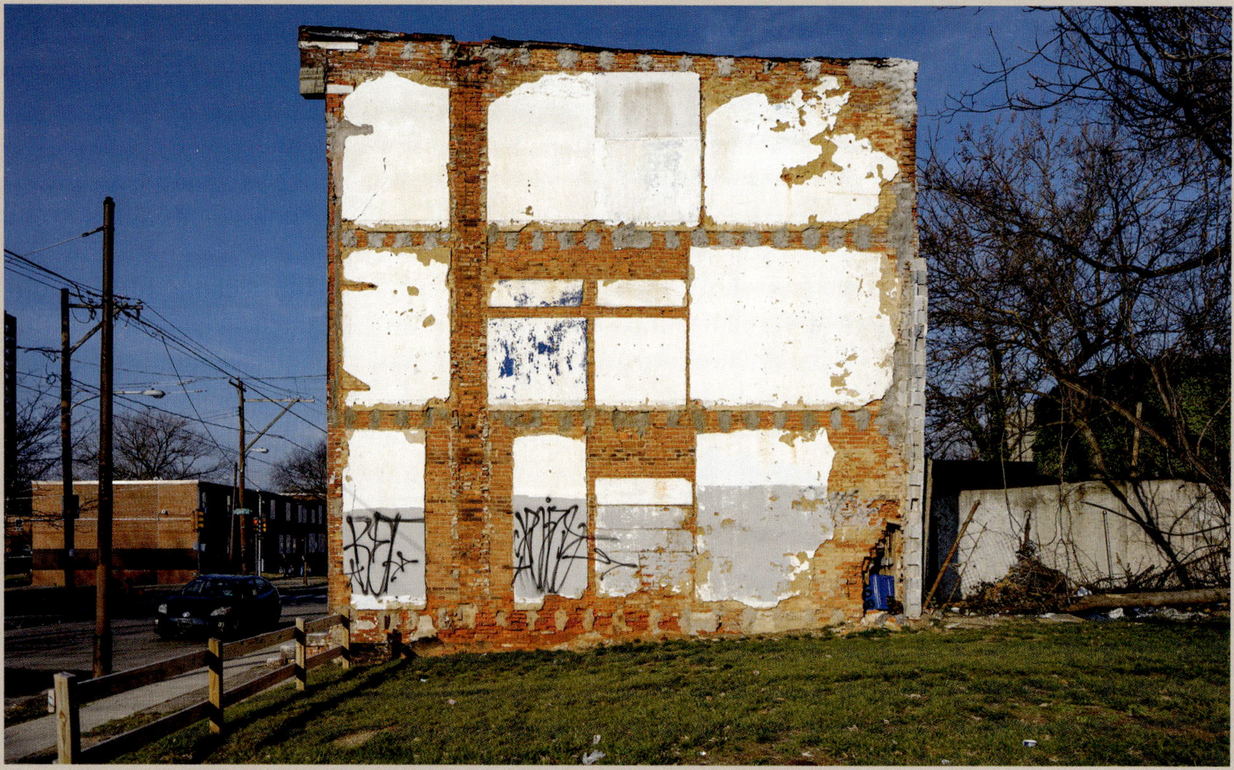

2341 North 10th Street. (Photographed January 13, 2021.)

1613–1615 Cecil B. Moore Avenue

Both sections (1613 and 1615) constructed ca. 1871
Both sections demolished ca. 2017

The buildings at 1613 and 1615 Cecil B. Moore Avenue (known as West Columbia Avenue until 1986) came down together around 2017, and they went up the same way around 1870. In the nearly 150 years that they were standing, their fates and functions proceeded in parallel. Sometimes they shared an owner (with a party wall that was apparently porous), while at other times, they simply coexisted. William Guier was the likely developer for both buildings, as he sold each of them in separate sales in the same month—December 1871. *Guier sold number 1613 to Catherine D. Lukens* and number 1615 to Watson Malone.

Number 1613 West Columbia Avenue traded hands a few more times before the end of the century. In 1901, it became the site of many more property transactions, as C. Harry Showaker moved his real estate business into the building. He would maintain an office there until 1909, sharing space at times with a dressmaker.

Meanwhile, Laura V. Carpenter purchased number 1615 from Watson Malone in 1884 and lived there for a time with her husband, William, and her widowed mother, Zipporah Hooper. Laura Carpenter's name was the only one on the deed of purchase, yet of the three adults it is Laura who weaves in and out of contemporary city directory listings for the household. William Carpenter (who was white and male) and Zipporah Hooper (white and widowed) are much more consistently named. By the time number 1615 sold again in 1894, William had joined Laura on the paperwork. Still, this was clearly not the only property in her possession, with or without William's involvement. When she died three years later, Laura left behind an estate valued at a sizeable $18,200 (an estimated $667,000 in today's dollars), which she bequeathed to William (he would live eighteen more years).

In 1895, Miss Annie Freeman opened a hair salon at 1615 West Columbia Avenue. She promised that she could restore gray and bleached hair to its natural color, assisted by a "full line of up-to-date hair goods." The shop proved so successful that by 1901 she had launched a second location in Atlantic City, opening a hairdressing and manicure parlor right off the beach, at the intersection of New York Avenue and the boardwalk. With a grand opening in June of that year, Miss Annie Freeman's shop springboarded from Columbia Avenue to the Jersey Shore just in time for the summer crowds. By 1903, she had shut down her first location, and her former space at number 1615 became a dress shop.

In the years after C. Harry Showaker sold number 1613, it resold practically every other year, if not more often: to Mary C. Noell (1909); to Catharine M. Diehl (1912); to Frank J. Eustace, then John F. Donnelly, then Harry C. King, then Frank J. Eustace again

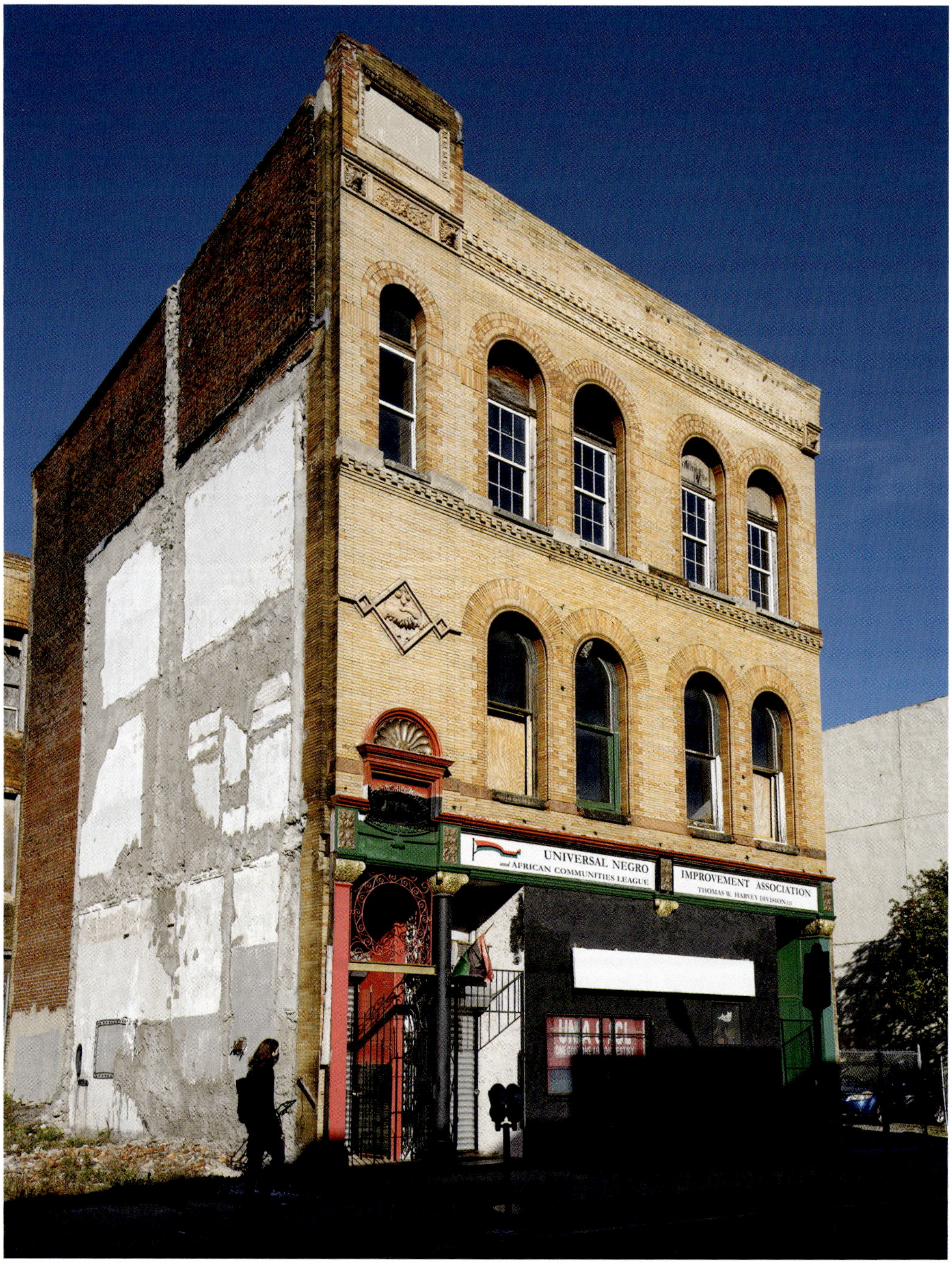

1613–1615 Cecil B. Moore Avenue. (Photographed November 5, 2020.)

(1917); to Rose Kleiman (1919); to Samuel Rosner (1920); etc. As of 1923, the building hosted a barbershop, although the only evidence of that business is a notice of sale, so there is no indication how long before or after that year number 1613 served that purpose.

The 1930s were tough for the owners of both buildings, as was true for so many other places during that decade: *in July 1933, 1613 West Columbia Avenue was offloaded in a sheriff's sale*, and in August 1936, the same was true for number 1615.

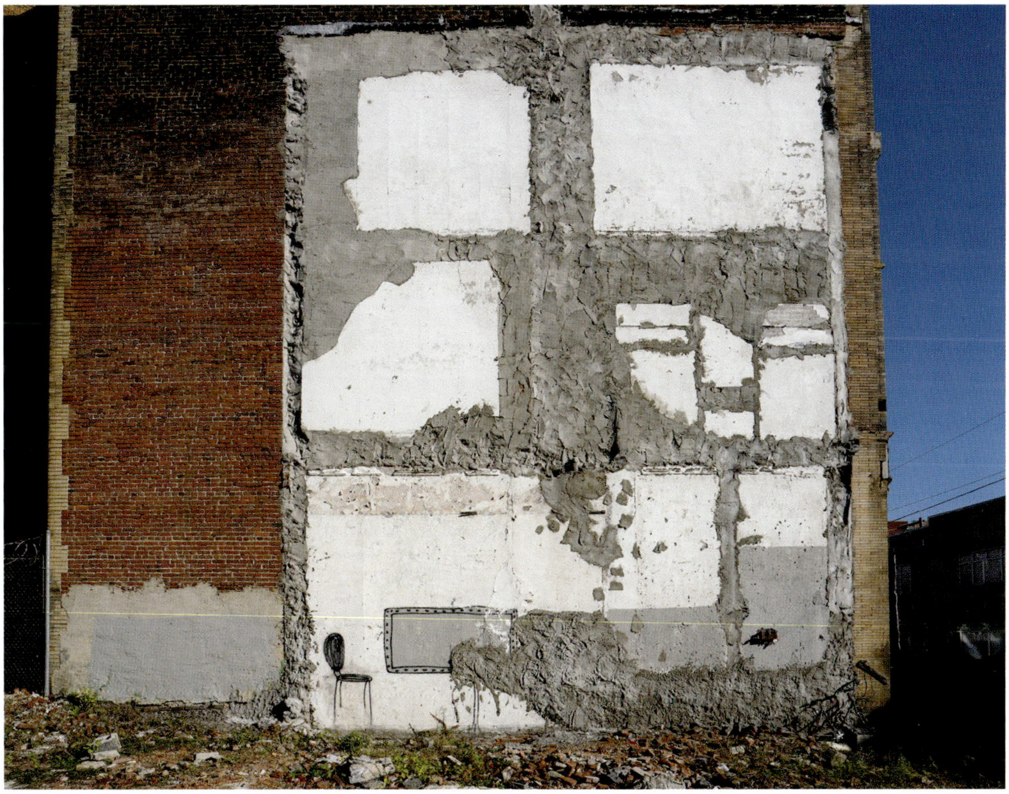

1613–1615 Cecil B. Moore Avenue. (Photographed November 5, 2020.)

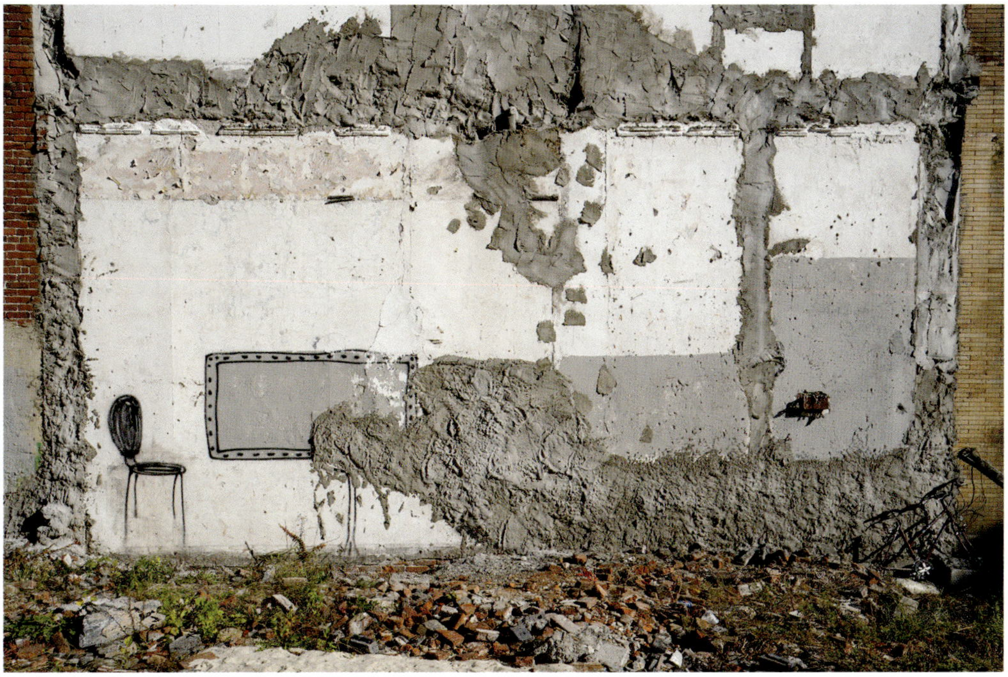

1613–1615 Cecil B. Moore Avenue. (Photographed November 5, 2020.)

By this time, number 1613 was a three-family residence. There was no business in place around the time of the sheriff's sale—perhaps a further effect of the Great Depression. In September 1937, though, Adolph Bock and his wife, Marion, purchased the building. They would run Bock's Dress Shop at 1613 West Columbia Avenue for nearly two decades, until 1954 or so.

Next door, Jacob and Frieda Lipschutz purchased number 1615 in 1944 and opened the "Hollywood Shop," selling shoes. *(Frieda lived at 1613 West Columbia Avenue as of 1943, so it is unclear how intertwined the buildings' ownership and uses were from this point forward.)* There were four apartments above the Hollywood Shop by the late 1950s, *which was also true of number 1613 by this time (marking an increase from three apartments as of 1933).*

In 1964, both buildings had a front-row seat to the heated events of late summer. On August 28, a domestic dispute blocking the intersection of 22nd Street and Columbia Avenue initially drew a police response, and then a crowd. As the police handcuffed the woman involved in the dispute, the crowd grew angry and agitated, questioning the mistreatment of her. The unrest escalated, fueled by police radio calls that claimed their lives were being threatened, as well as rumors that spread within the disquieted crowds, saying that it was the police who were threatening lives. The city eventually deployed 1,800 officers to disperse the protesters and punish looters. In the context of a suppressed, segregated neighborhood marked by high unemployment and systemic poverty, the presence of so many police officers ignited existing tension and anger. Within three days, one person was killed (twenty-one-year-old Robert Green) and an estimated 340 people were injured, including about 240 civilians and 100 police officers. In terms of property damage, more than six hundred businesses were damaged up and down the avenue (it is unclear whether Hollywood Shoes was among them), fracturing the community and devastating its commercial corridors.

In the aftermath of the August 1964 clashes, 1613 West Columbia Avenue had relatively brief bouts of retail. As of 1967, Joe Davis Records was based there, but by 1969 the storefront was vacant, and a used furniture business was trying to make a go of it.

Hollywood Shoes, however, remained a stalwart. Based at number 1615 since the early 1940s, *it apparently expanded into number 1613 around 1971.* The combined buildings remained standing for another half-century, segueing from a presence as 1613–1615 West Columbia Avenue, to 1613–1615 Cecil B. Moore Avenue, to no presence at all.

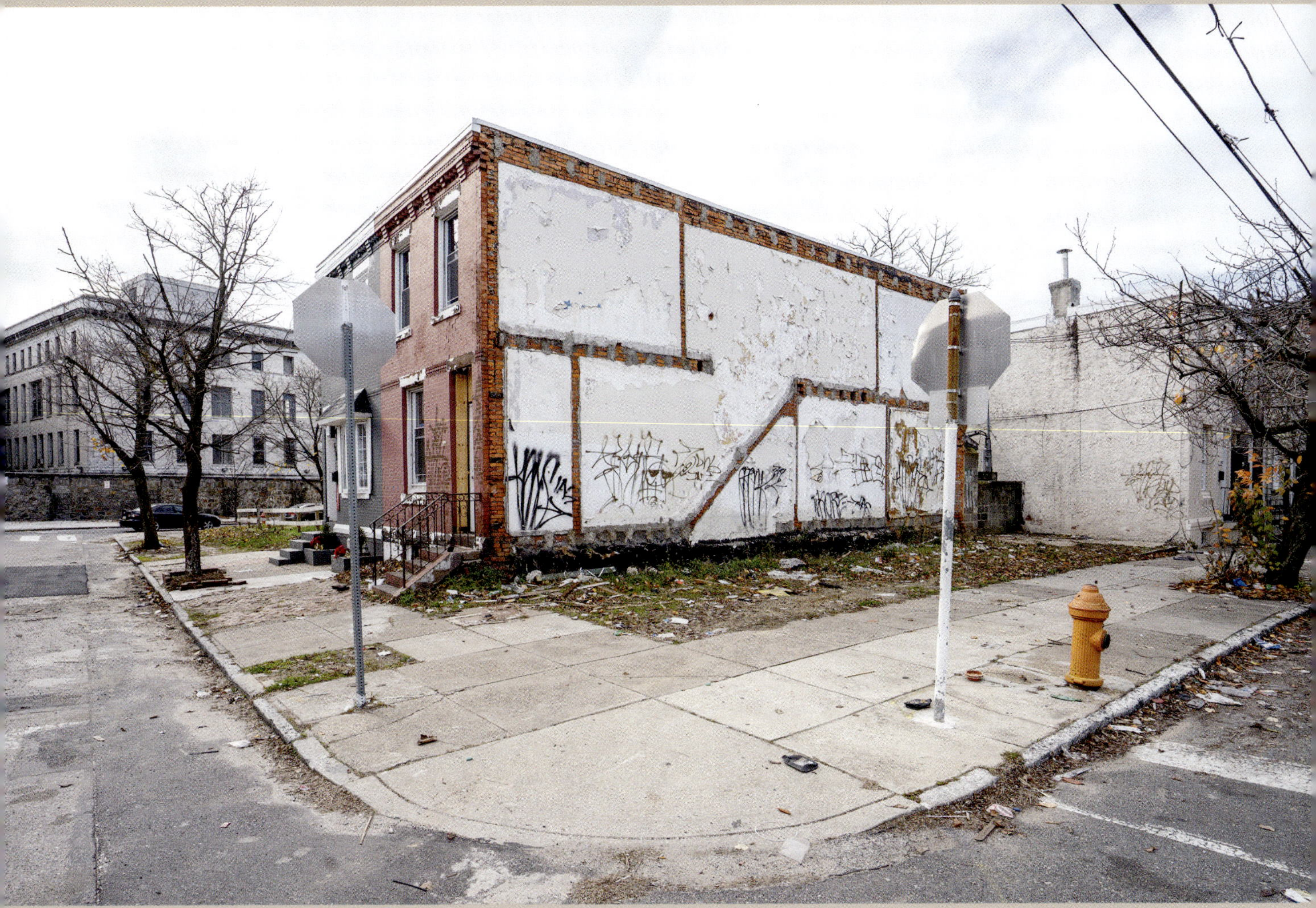

1264 North 23rd Street. (Photographed December 3, 2020.)

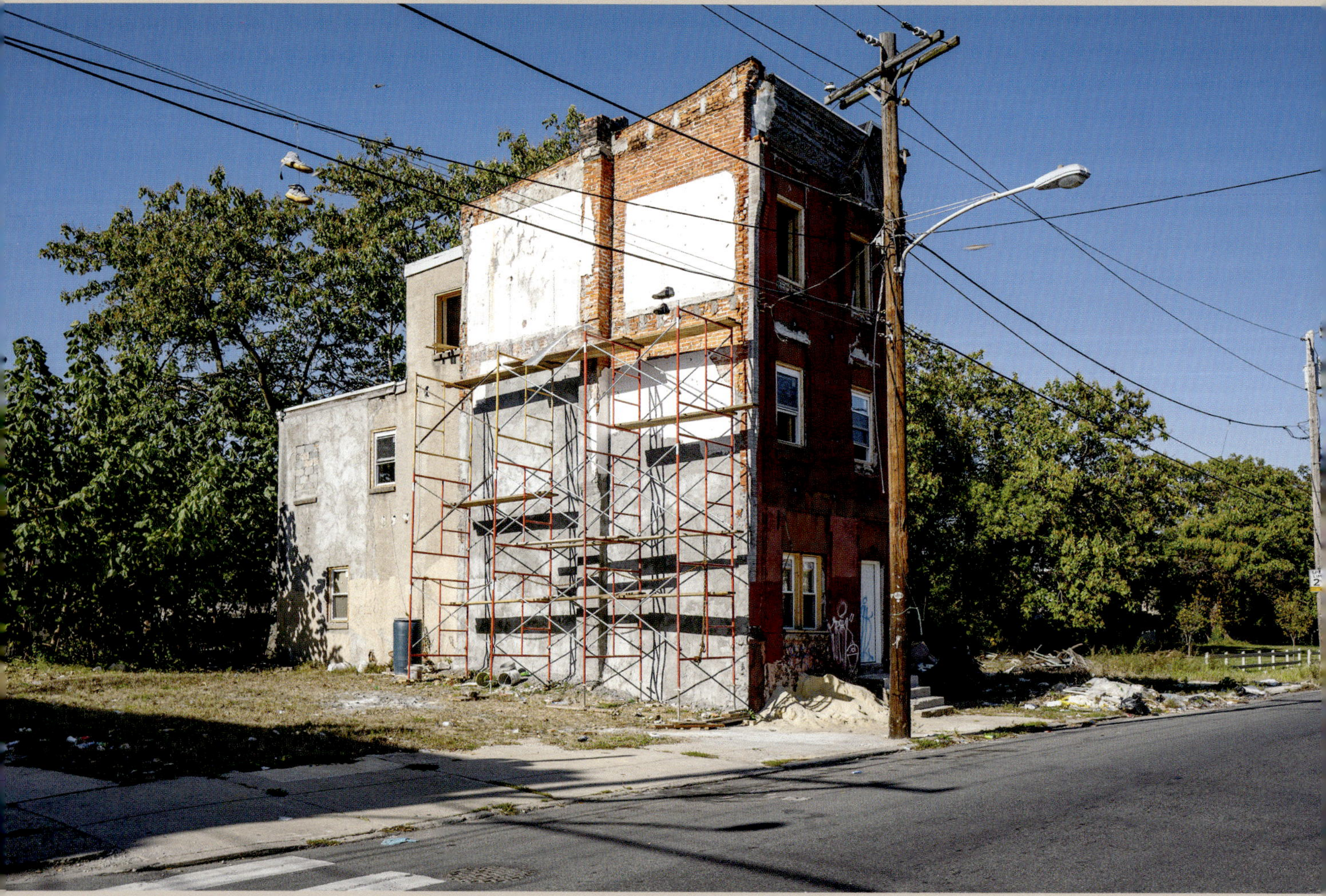

2304 North 21st Street. (Photographed November 6, 2020.)

3209 West Arizona Street

Constructed in 1894
Demolished ca. 2020 under the auspices of the L&I Demolition Program

The house at 3209 West Arizona Street was just one of the four thousand homes that the builder J. Franklin Moss constructed in his lifetime. Tucked away on a small street in North Philadelphia, the modest two-story house may not have stood out even among the twenty-four houses Moss constructed in this particular development project. But it was an early test of his business acumen, taking shape within the first five years of operations for J. Franklin Moss and Company. It also set the stage for the developer's later large-scale operations, such as when he participated in a government program to construct more than 560 houses in the Elmwood section of Southwest Philadelphia during World War I.

The Arizona Street houses were complete in 1894, and Moss sold number 3209 to Benjamin and Agnes Forrest in April of the following year. (With the Arizona Street houses complete, he worked his way northward to vacant lots around the intersection of 33rd and Cumberland streets.) A carpenter rented the brick rowhouse in 1897, before the Forrests sold the house in 1898, and the Johnsons moved in.

Born in Sweden in 1873, Axel Johnson arrived in the United States at twenty-three. In 1897—shortly before moving into number 3209—he met and married Cecilia (her maiden name is unknown), a natural-born citizen born to Swedish-born parents. Axel worked as a machinist, and Cecilia was soon pregnant with their first child, a son named Carl who was born around September 1898. He lived just ten months.

The Johnsons shared number 3209 for a time with a man named Gustave Vidlund. His biography overlapped in many significant ways with Axel Johnson's: both were born in Sweden and immigrated in 1896; both were machinists; and they were close in age. This suggests they knew each other in their home country or met on the transatlantic journey. By the time he boarded alongside the Johnsons around 1900, Vidlund was a recent widower. Between his wife's death and the loss of baby Carl Johnson, 3209 West Arizona Street must have been suffused with grief.

It would only become more so. Gustave Vidlund died in December 1900, on the day after Christmas. Within a matter of weeks, Cecilia learned she was pregnant once again and gave birth a second time in mid-August 1901. But William Johnson died even younger than Carl: on January 1, 1902, the Johnsons' second child—but their "only son," as the newspaper obituary poignantly noted—died, "aged 4 months and 17 days." For some unknowable reason, the infant brothers were buried in separate cemeteries: Carl at Greenwood, in Delaware County, and William in Mount Peace, at 33rd Street and Lehigh Avenue.

Having lived through the death of their two children and their friend while at 3209 West Arizona Street, Axel and Cecilia Johnson remained at the house for just one more year. After 1902, there are no traces of them in association with the address. In their

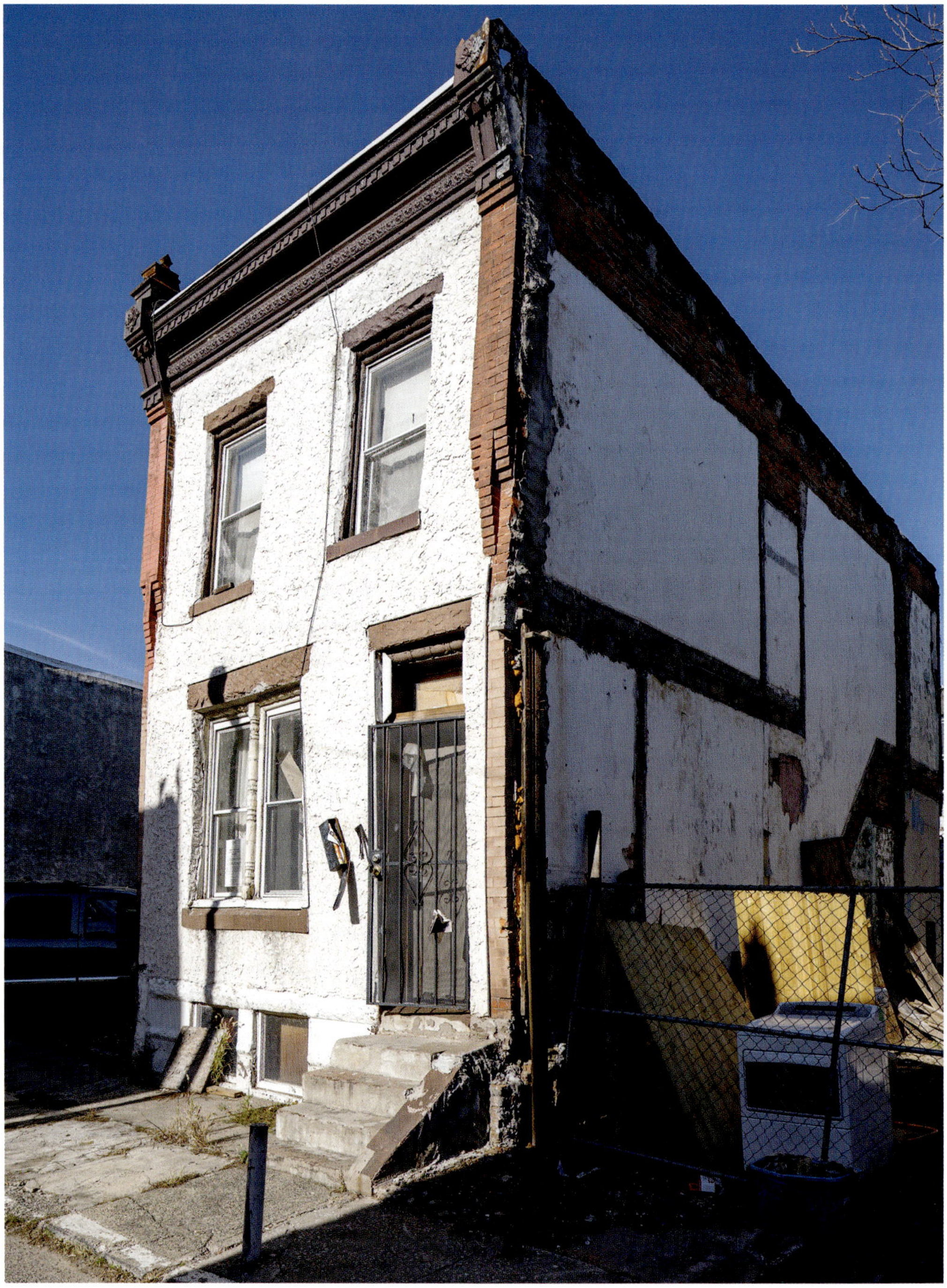

3209 West Arizona Street. (Photographed November 20, 2020.)

place, other working-class tenants rented the house from middle-class property owners in the first few decades of the twentieth century.

In September 1936, Nathan and Miriam Schockert purchased the house and quickly resold it to Nathan's mother, Ida. The Yiddish-speaking Ida Schockert had been born in 1885 in Russia (or, perhaps, one of the countries invaded by Russia in the nineteenth century, since the U.S. Federal Census did not always note the difference). She had mar-

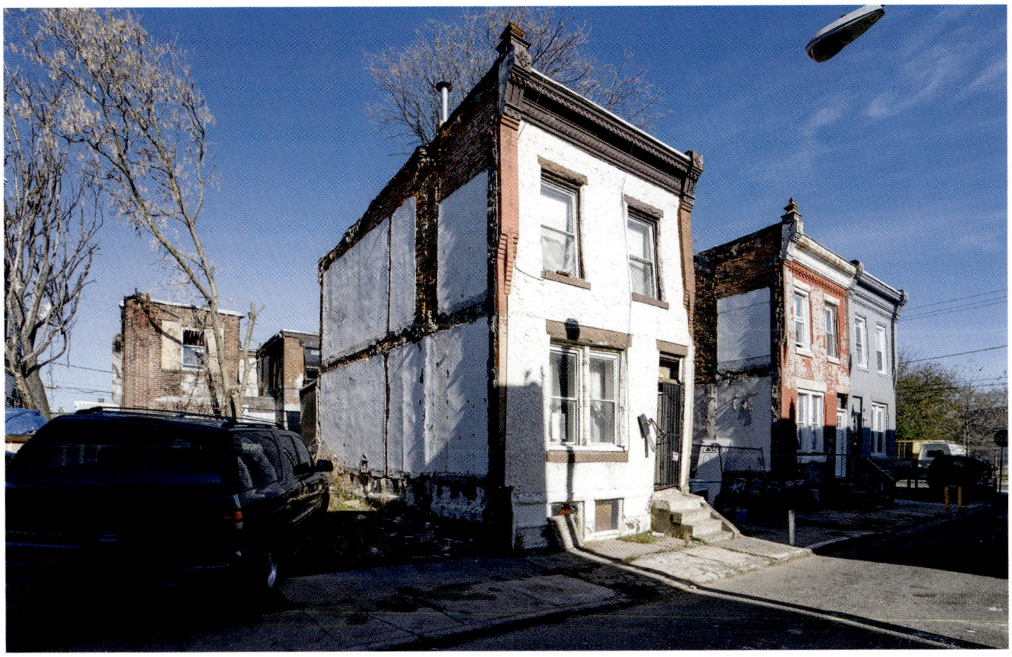

3209 West Arizona Street. (Photographed November 20, 2020.)

ried David Schockert, a brush maker, and given birth to three children, of whom Nathan was the middle child and the only son. At some point in the 1920s, Ida and David's marriage appears to have splintered; in 1920, the whole family was living at 3108 West York Street, but by 1930, Ida had moved with Nathan and her younger daughter, Frances (known as Fay), to 3206 West Arizona Street, down the block from number 3209.

Ida rented the house at number 3206 while she worked as an operator at a dress shop and Nathan worked odd jobs, saving enough money between the two of them to buy and swap the house down the street in September 1936. The family would hold on to the house for the next two decades, trading it among the generations in a manner that allowed Ida to remain in place in the home, joined at various points by two of her three grown children. The rowhouse saw everything from marriage to divorce in that time, as Fay got married at the house in 1940, Nathan got divorced (and subsequently remarried), and Ida herself was officially separated from David as of 1950. On March 10, 1958, Ida Schockert died at the house, and her children subsequently put the vacant house up for sale.

Once it left the Schockerts' hands, the more recent history of the house is spotty. In 2014, it started earning violations as a vacant property, and by 2016 it was subject to a sheriff's sale. The inspections escalated to a determination of "Unsafe" conditions in 2018. The following year, the structure had deteriorated to the point of being "Imminently Dangerous" (an official classification). By March 2020, the matter was "Resolved"—torn down at the site, and tidied up in the paperwork.

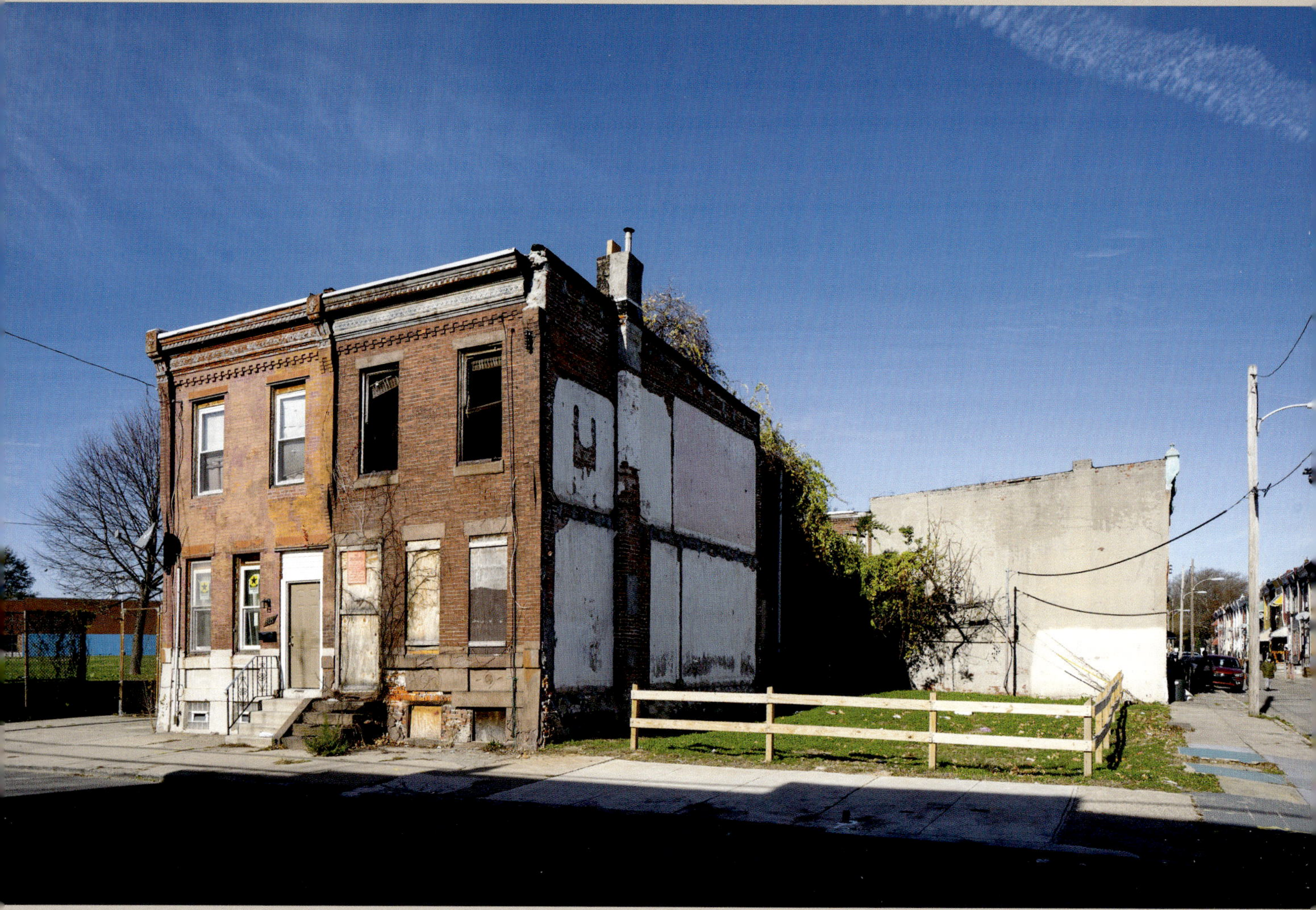

2562 Napa Street. (Photographed November 20, 2020.)

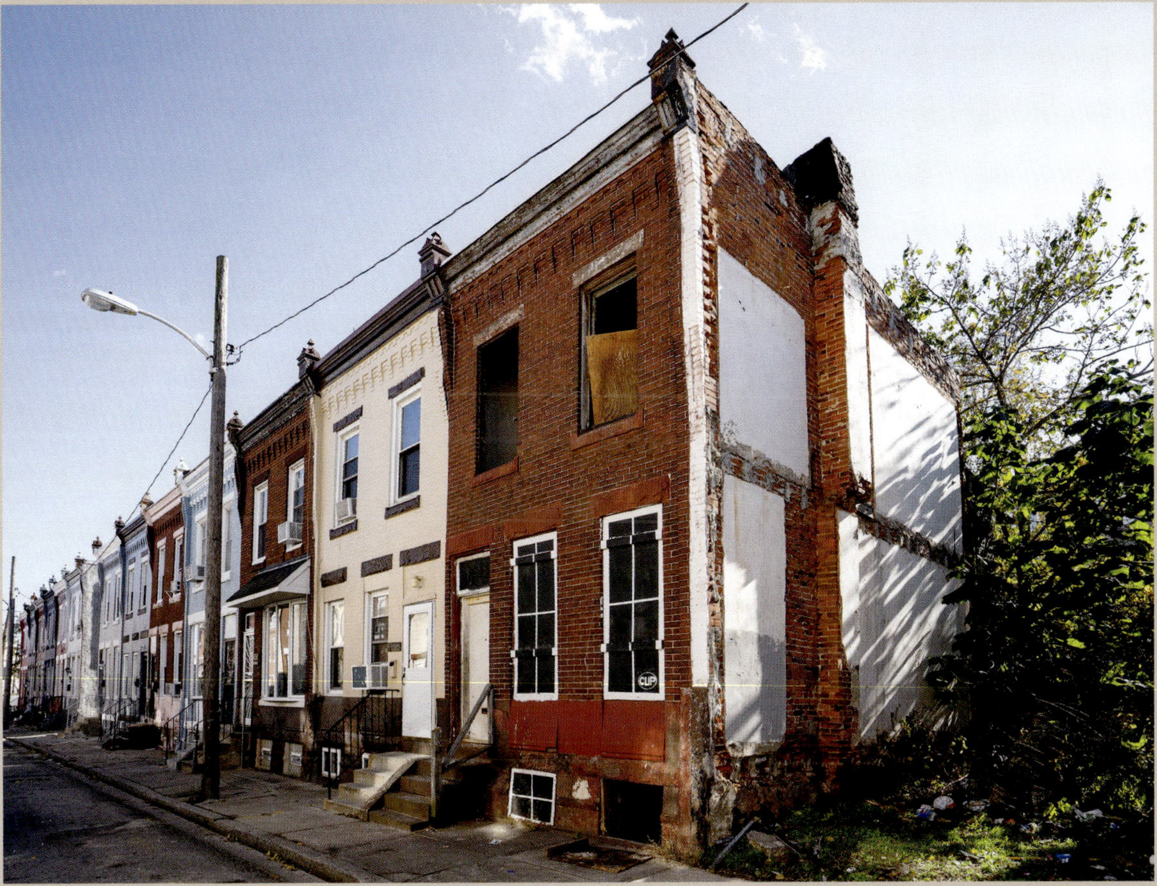

3136 Westmont Street. (Photographed November 16, 2020.)

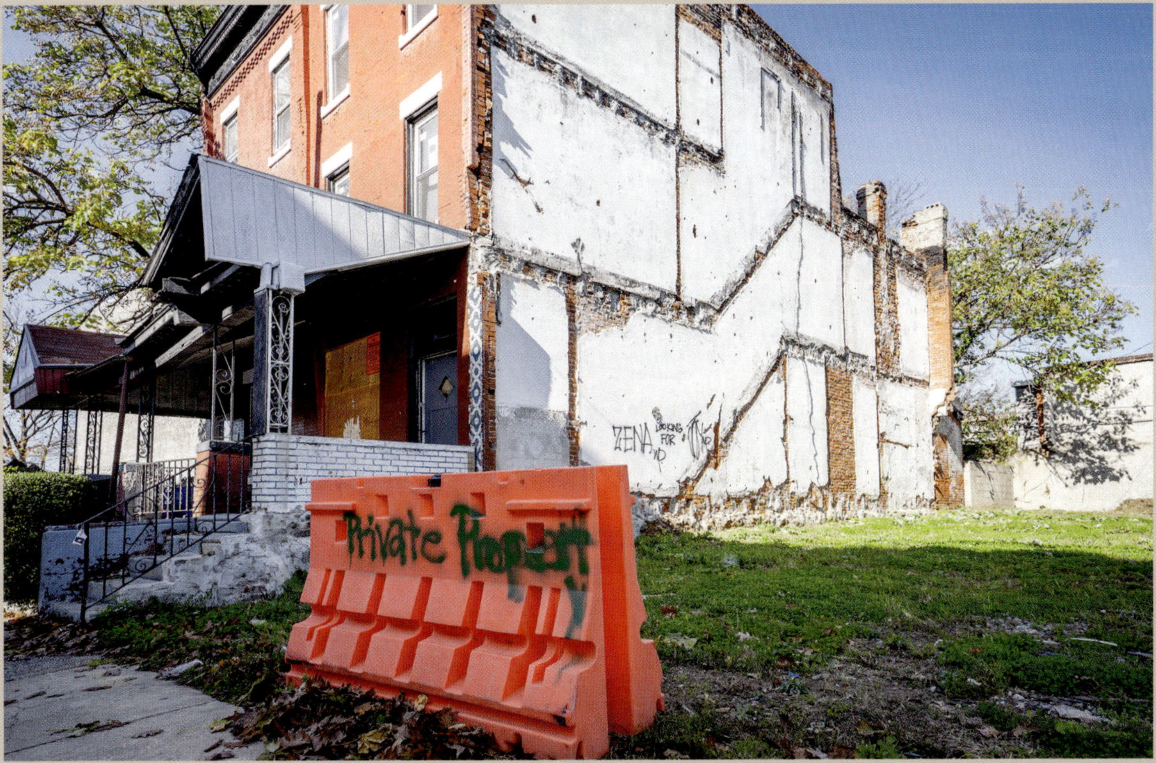

3229 Clifford Street. (Photographed November 16, 2020.)

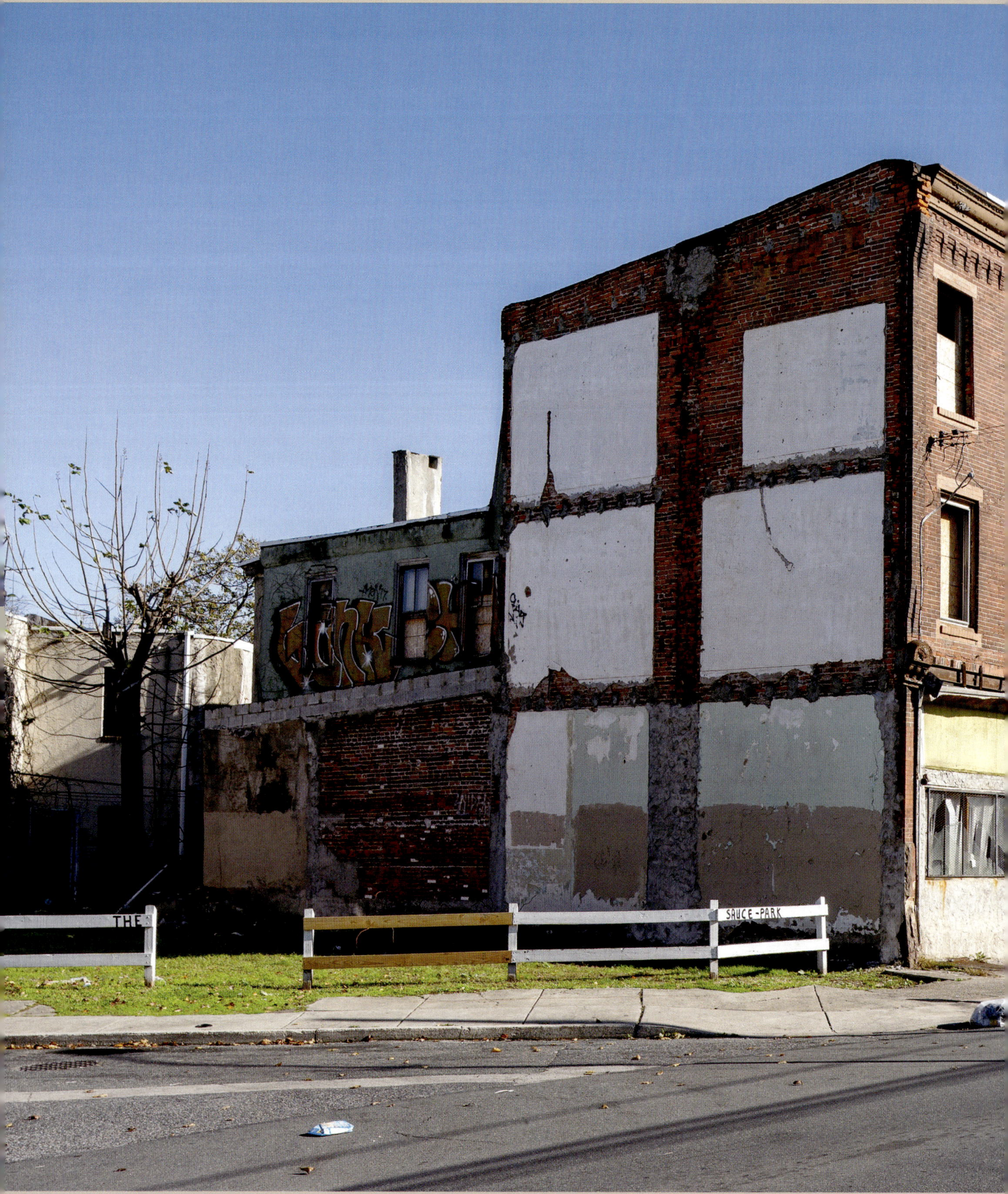
THE
SAUCE-PARK

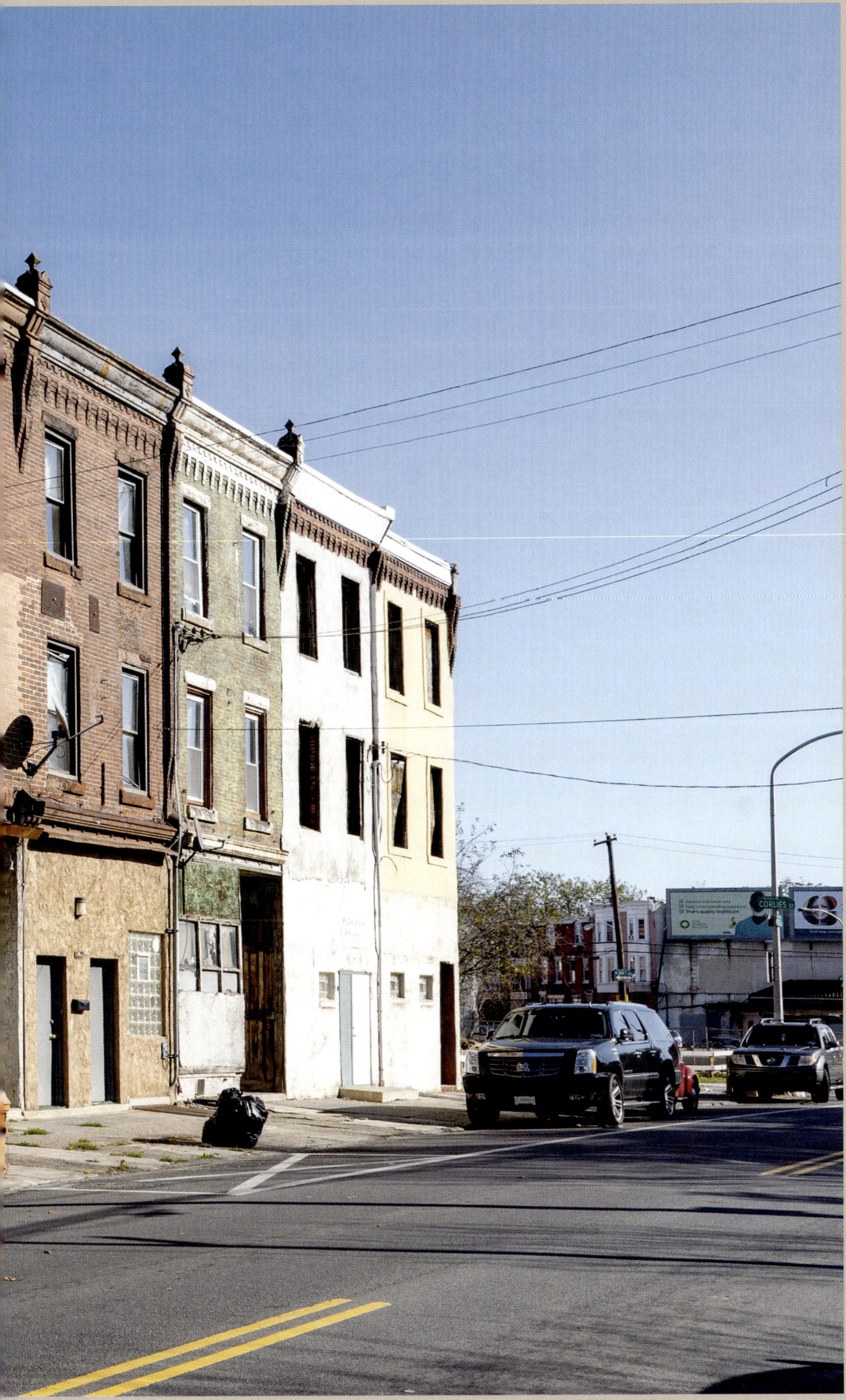

3029 Ridge Avenue.
(Photographed November 16, 2020.)

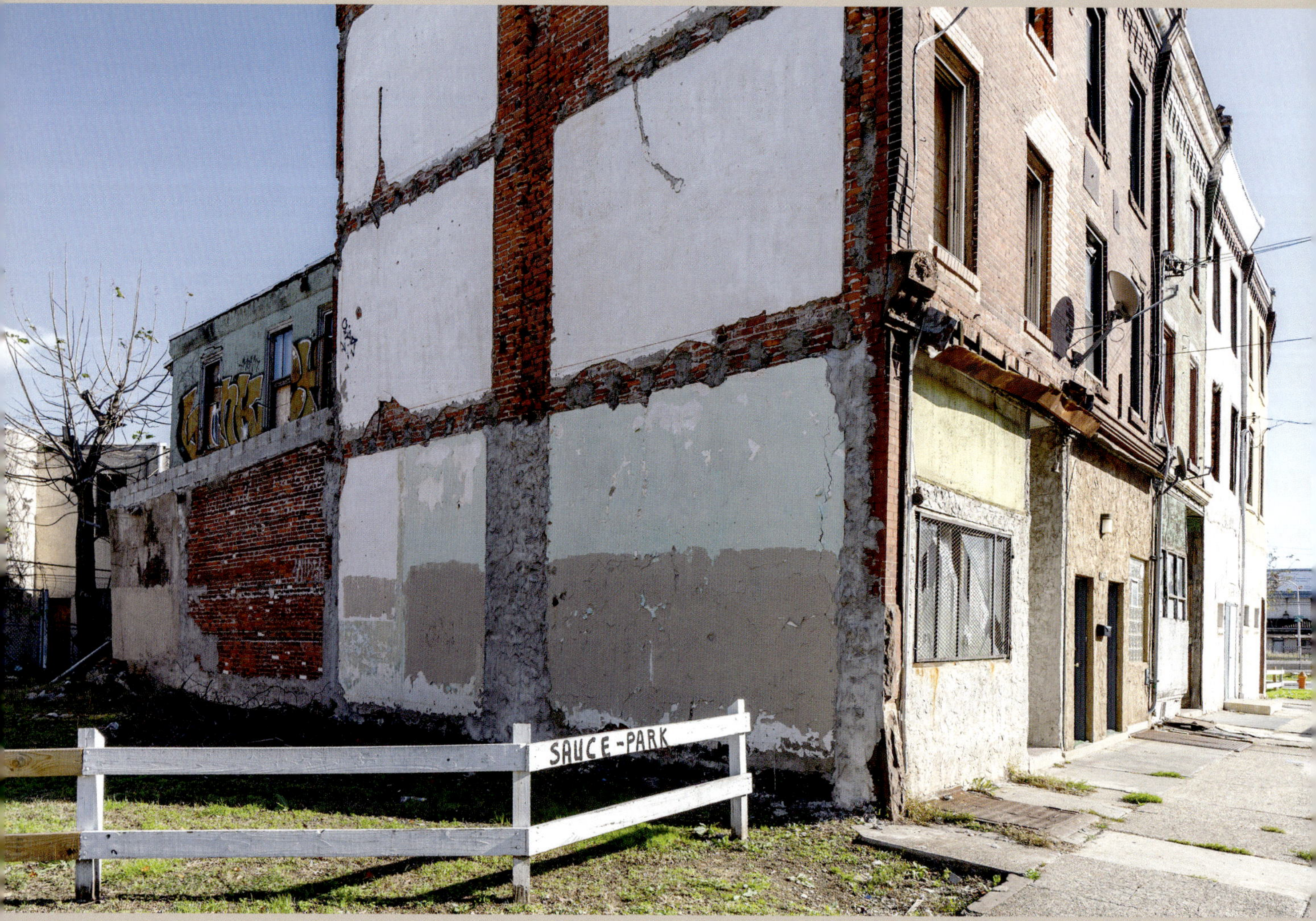

Detail of 3029 Ridge Avenue. (Photographed November 16, 2020.)

629–635 West Girard Avenue

Western section (number 631) constructed ca. 1862 (possibly earlier)
Eastern section (number 629) constructed ca. 1863
Both sections demolished ca. 2009

For a period of about twenty years—the last decade of the nineteenth century and the first decade of the twentieth—629–635 West Girard Avenue functioned as a hotel. The operation changed names several times within that span, beginning as the Farmers and Mechanics Hotel in the 1890s before becoming the Hotel Shepard and then, in 1898, the Hotel Girard. Under new ownership, the inn staffed up—but only on a segregated basis. "Female help wanted: head cook (white), pastry, good appearance"; "Female help wanted: chambermaid, white, must be good"; "Female help wanted: hotel cook, first class, white"; "Male help wanted: bellman and waiter, young man, white"; "Male help wanted: bar, cellar, and can make himself generally useful around hotel; white, and past 21 years," read a series of classified ads in 1900.

Despite the fact that the sixty-room hotel saw "considerable exterior and interior alterations" around this time, carried out for $3,500 by B. Ketcham and Sons, it remained on par with boardinghouses. In fact, its promotional ads compared the Hotel Girard (favorably, of course) to that kind of private rooming house, noting that it offered both transient rates ($1–$1.50 per day) and weekly prices. This class of clientele would seem to explain the misadventures of David P. Miller in 1901.

Miller was a local character and a fixture of the neighborhood, having grown up there. Listed in censuses and directories as everything from a "manufacturer of edged tools" to a "spokemaker," the widowed Miller boarded at the Hotel Girard and worked at times as a waiter there. (Unsurprisingly, he was white.) Staff and patrons of the hotel were fond of him, referring to him as one of the best-known characters on "lower Girard avenue." He had at one time worked for the William Penn Hose Company, a firefighting outfit established in 1830, before pivoting to skilled work as a shuttle maker at a weaving mill in Kensington. He was said to live rather quietly at the hotel, keeping to himself when he wasn't working or visiting with friends.

But in late July 1901, David Miller went missing. At first, hotel staff assumed he had gone to visit a friend, but their concerns grew when he didn't return. It wasn't until several days later that Miller's friends received word—from the New Castle, Delaware, jail. In the custody of police officers, the sixty-nine-year-old Miller could not account for his whereabouts for the preceding days; all he knew was that he had met two strangers on a street in Philadelphia, shared two glasses of beer with them, and woken up dazed, stumbling around a small park in Delaware. He had barely made it to the road before he was arrested, apparently on charges related to public intoxication.

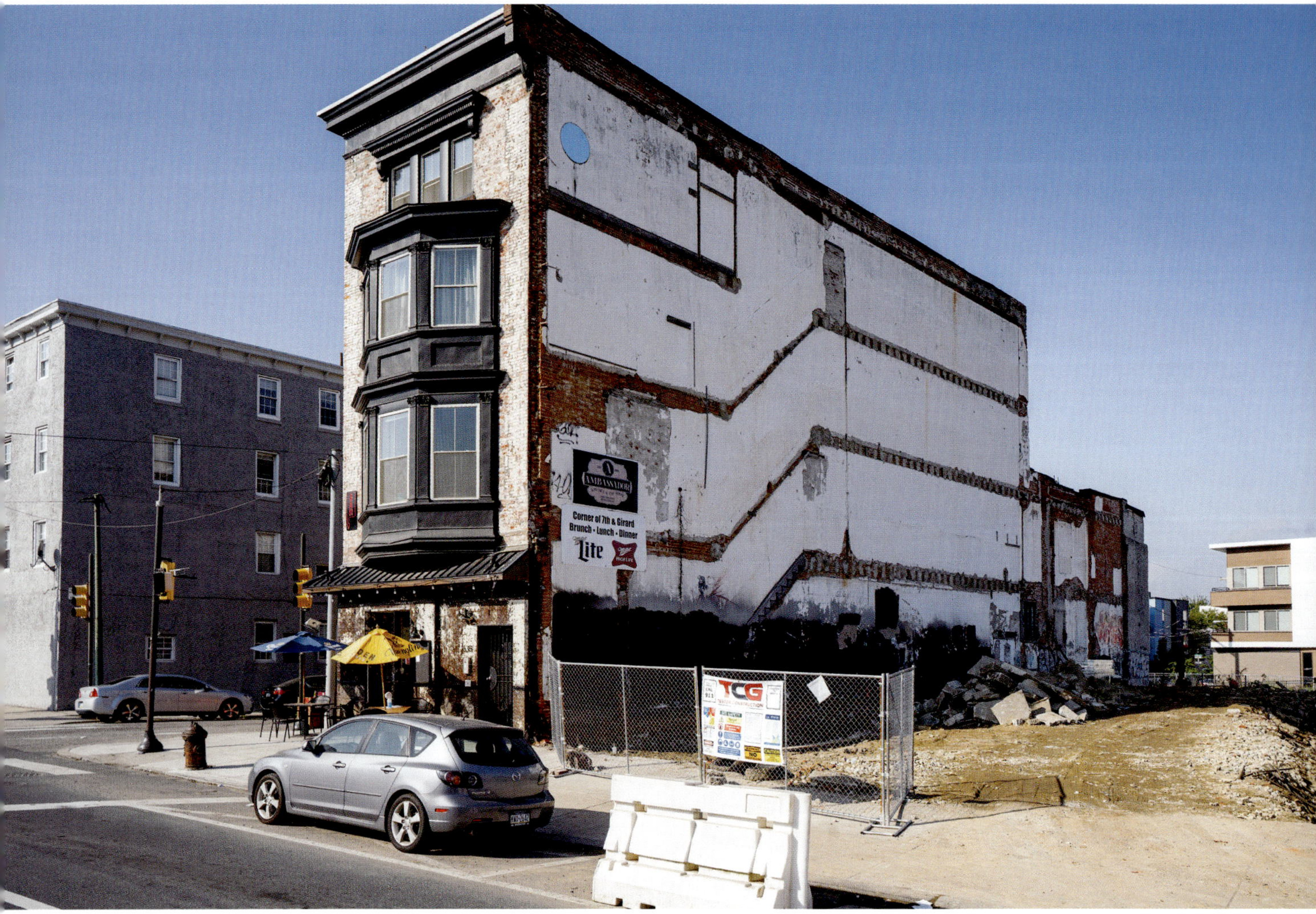

629–635 West Girard Avenue. (Photographed October 22, 2020.)

Miller went on to claim that the strangers had stolen a considerable sum of money from him, but the Hotel Girard employees were skeptical of this (and his entire story?), since they knew him well enough to know that he only ever carried a little bit of money. Still, they warmly received him back at the hotel when two of his friends bailed him out of jail and deposited him at his lodgings on Girard Avenue.

Perhaps the oddest part of the entire story—even stranger than the series of events that David Miller insisted were true—is the fact that the *Philadelphia Inquirer* devoted not one or two but three days of coverage to the saga. It was a dramatic tale, to be sure, but in the end, it was merely a story about a few days in the life of an elderly widower who lived quietly in a hotel in the neighborhood where he was born.

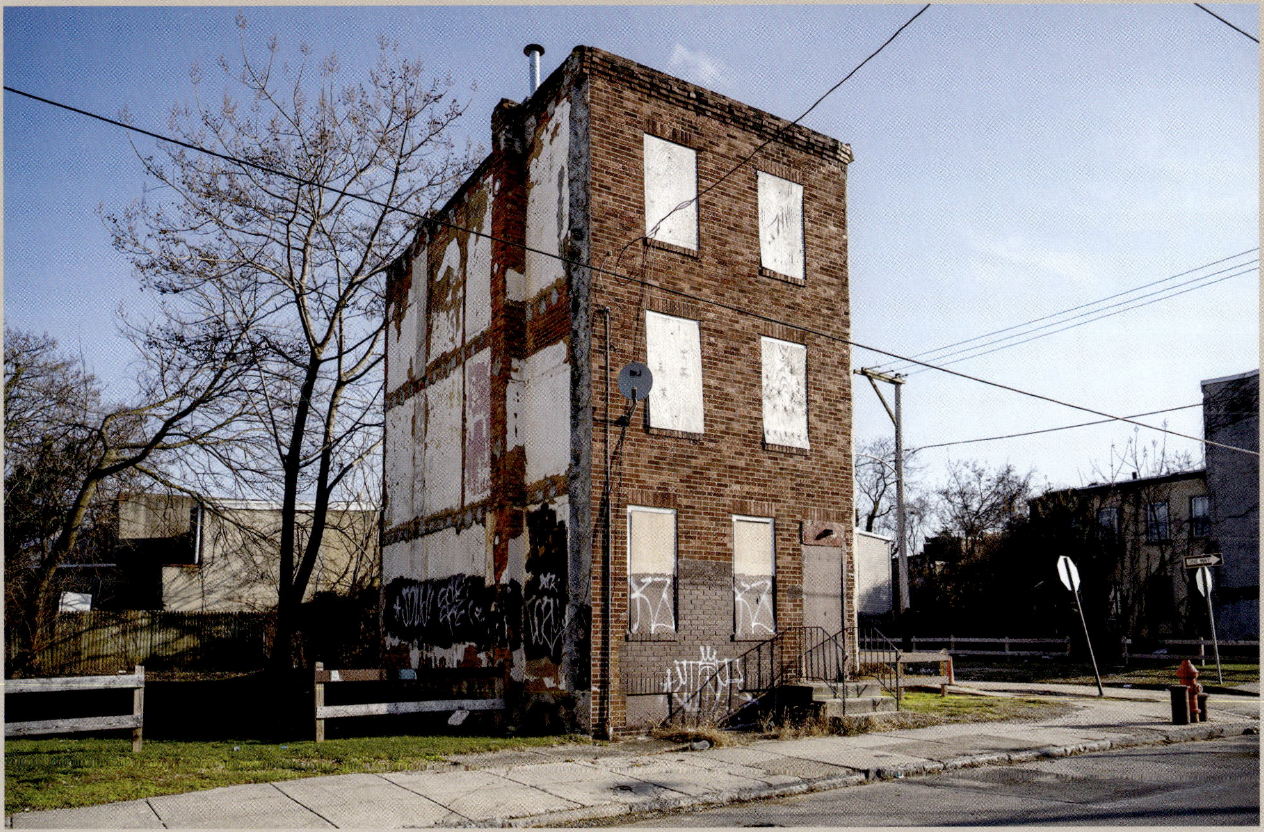

2323 North 10th Street. (Photographed January 13, 2021.)

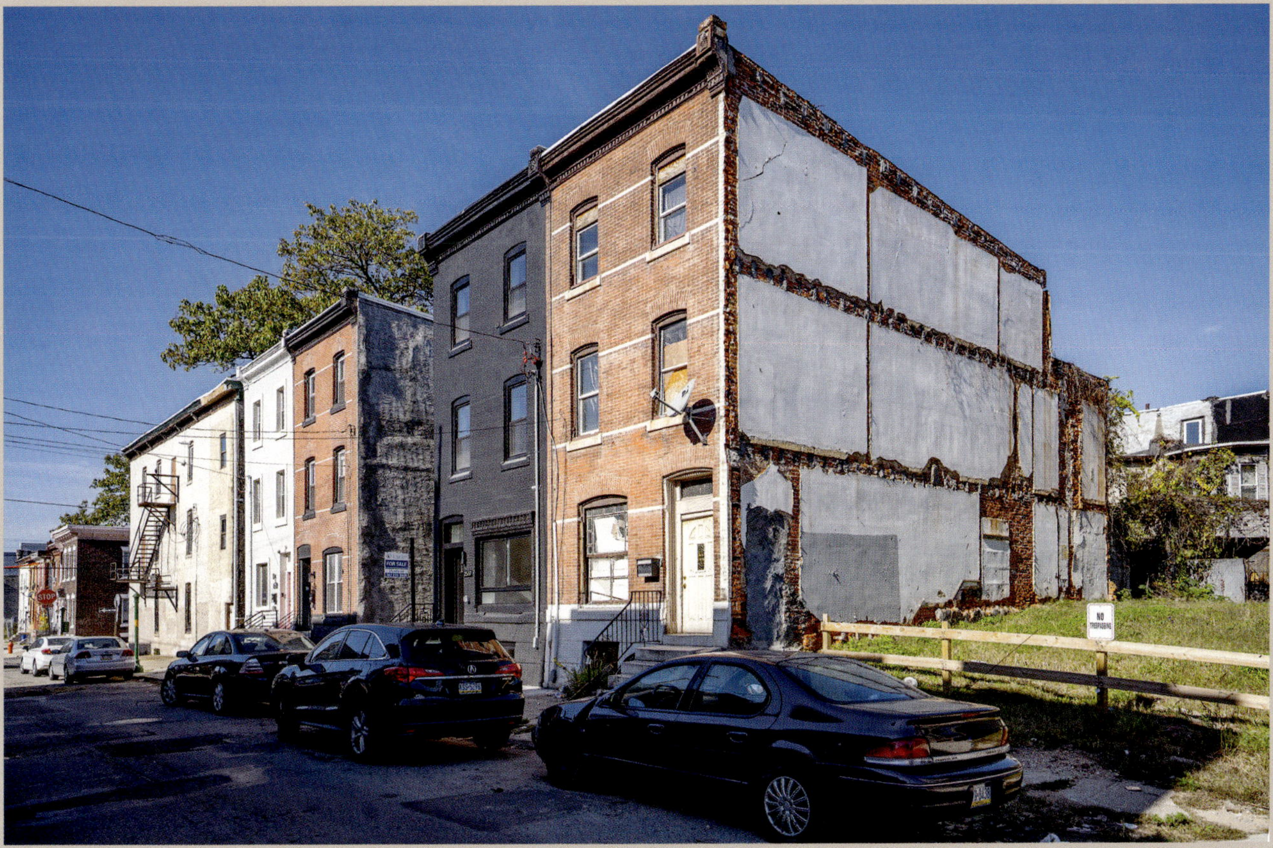

2605 West Oxford Street. (Photographed November 7, 2020.)

2251 North 33rd Street

Constructed in 1906
Demolished in 2012 under the auspices of the L&I Demolition Program

The house at 2251 North 33rd Street had the most magnificent views of Fairmount Park across the street—and three stories of porches to enjoy them. It was the work of architect Carl deMoll, undertaken at the behest of the builder John Stafford, who assembled an entire city block's worth of lots to develop what he called the "33rd Street Boulevard." When they were completed in 1906, the boulevard's homes were "elegantly finished and decorated throughout," summoning a wealthy clientele to the eastern edge of the park.

Compared with some of his contemporaries in the first half of the twentieth century, Carl deMoll was a low-profile architect and engineer, but he trained under and worked alongside some of the city's most prestigious designers of the period, including Horace Trumbauer, William L. Price, Frank Miles Day, and Ballinger and Perot. (He subsequently married Price's daughter, Mary.) A multidisciplinary creative, he took classes at the Pennsylvania Museum and School of Industrial Art and worked for a time as an illustrator in New York before returning to Philadelphia to practice architecture. By the time he died in 1958, he was a partner in the Ballinger Company.

For the 33rd Street houses, deMoll rhythmically arranged the block in pairs, the sole exception being the blocky four-story apartment building at the north end of the block, at number 2253. It fell to 2251 North 33rd Street to be the segue in design between the stout multifamily neighbor to the north and the more reserved single-family homes to the south. The entire block shared a material palette of brick with stone belt courses, and they could all be described as variations on a Colonial Revival style. But it was number 2251 specifically that mediated the broad porches of number 2253—which extended practically to the sidewalks—with the setback bays of the rest of the block.

When number 2251 was torn down a century later, the block's segue was lost. The stocky apartment building remained at 33rd and Dauphin streets, and the lineup of formal twins stood (mostly uninterrupted) along the rest of the street. But the gap between them broke the internal logic of the block. The plaster residue of 2251 North 33rd Street's building ghost was not enough to sustain the embedded transitions in the corridor's design. When number 2251 was demolished, the boulevard's cohesion fragmented and fell, too.

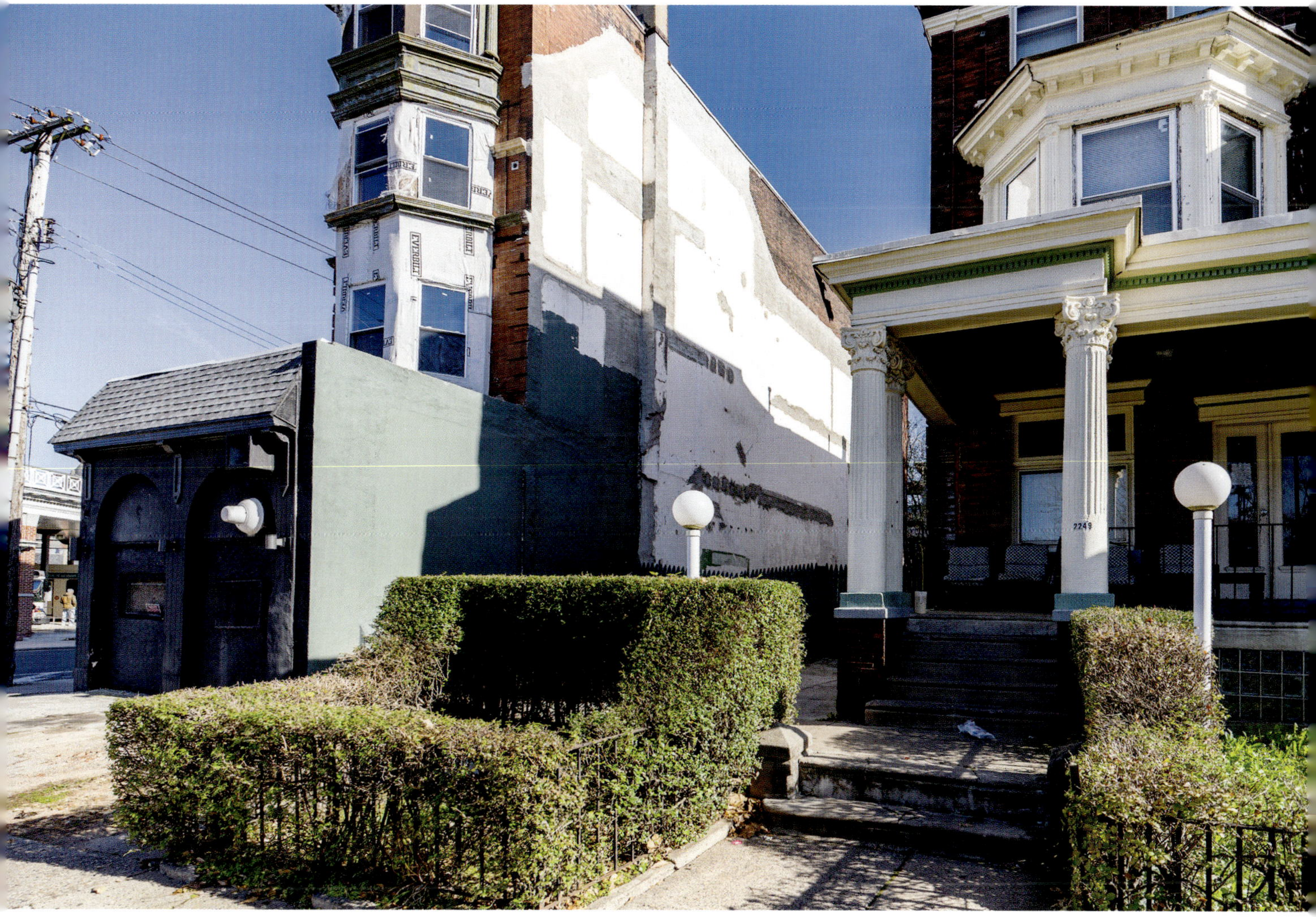

2251 North 33rd Street. (Photographed November 20, 2020.)

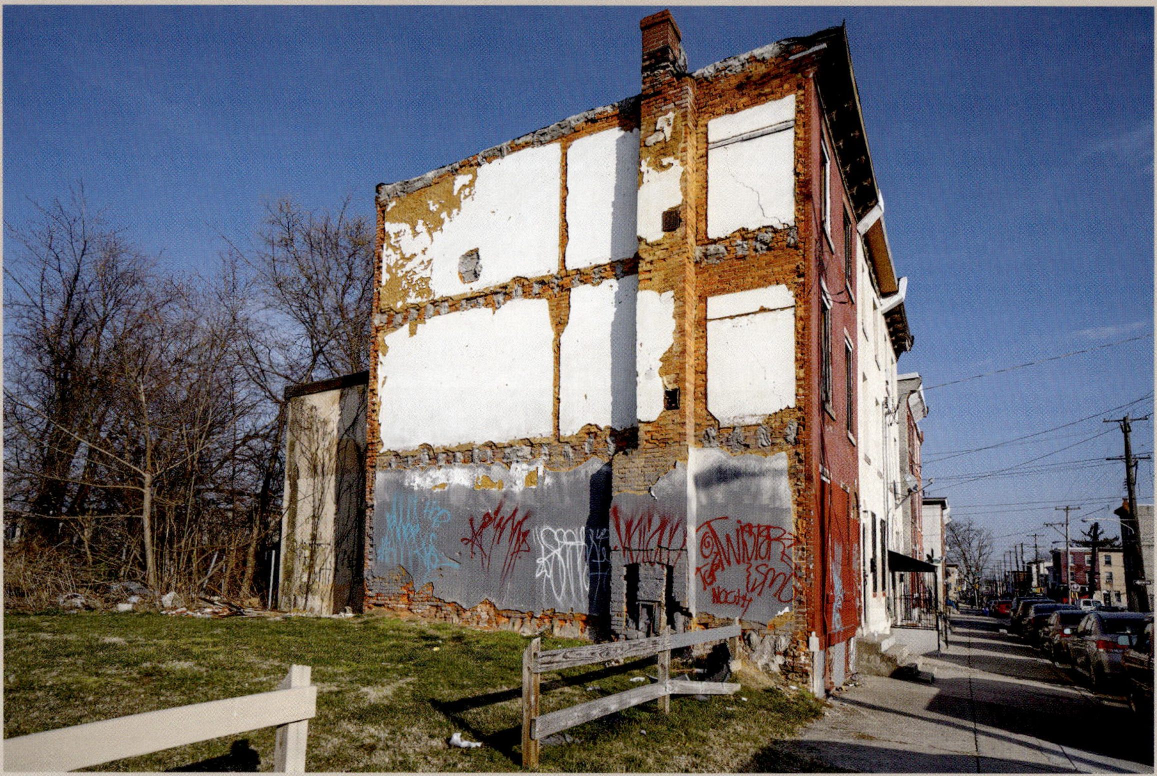

641 West Cumberland Street. (Photographed January 13, 2021.)

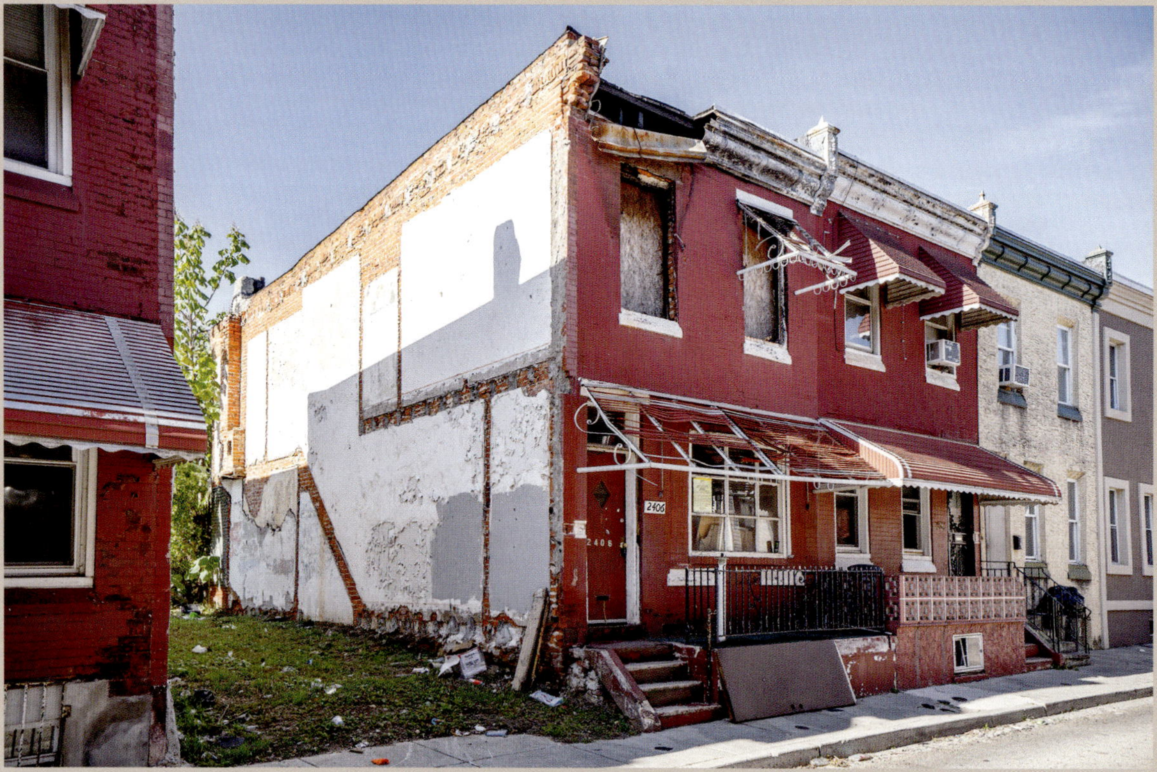

2459 North Chadwick Street. (Photographed November 5, 2020.)

1300 West Erie Avenue

Constructed ca. 1904
Demolished before 2004

Thomas Trefsgar grew up in Northumberland, a town in central Pennsylvania situated at a fork in the Susquehanna River. The town was most famous for its association with the eighteenth-century scientist Joseph Priestley, who was credited with discovering oxygen while living in England before immigrating to the United States. But by the time Thomas Trefsgar was growing up around the turn of the twentieth century, Joseph Priestley was dead, and the town's prosperity had shifted toward decidedly more manual—rather than intellectual—enterprises.

Born in 1893, Thomas was the fourth of Arnold and Catherine Trefsgar's nine children. (Catherine gave birth to a tenth child who did not survive; some decennial censuses recorded such realities, in a remarkable case of statistics intersecting with—and offering glimpses of—painful family histories.) His older brothers Benedict and Lewis labored in a mill and a coal mine, respectively, but Thomas hewed closer to his older sister Stiana's path; born two years before him, she became a dressmaker, and Thomas apprenticed as a tailor.

In 1917, Thomas Trefsgar married Marion Hudock of Mount Carmel, Pennsylvania, and the couple made their way soon after to Philadelphia, where he took a tailoring position at 13th and Arch streets. They had one daughter, Dorothy, creating a decidedly quieter household for themselves than the one Thomas had experienced growing up.

In 1938, the Archdiocese of Philadelphia purchased the three-story, thirteen-room rowhouse at 13th Street and Erie Avenue. The motivation for His Eminence Dennis J. Dougherty, Cardinal Archbishop of Philadelphia, to do so is unclear, although it is worth noting that (1) the archdiocese historically has owned a substantial amount of property in the city (many of the current deeds still bear Archbishop Dougherty's name specifically); and (2) St. Stephen's Roman Catholic Church was located a short distance away at this time, at Broad and Butler streets. Shortly after the archdiocese became the landlord, Thomas Trefsgar became its tenant. Around 1942, he opened a tailoring shop on the ground floor at 1300 West Erie Avenue.[24]

The life path that carried Thomas Trefsgar from central Pennsylvania to North Philadelphia ended abruptly. On September 25, 1943, he had a heart attack and collapsed in his shop at number 1300; he died the next morning at Temple University Hospital, at just fifty years old. It fell, presumably, to Marion and Dorothy to resolve

24. In September 1943, a newspaper article mentioned that Thomas Trefsgar had operated a tailor shop in Tioga for more than twenty years by that point. It is unclear where he was previously based, but evidence suggests that he did not settle at 1300 West Erie Avenue until about 1942.

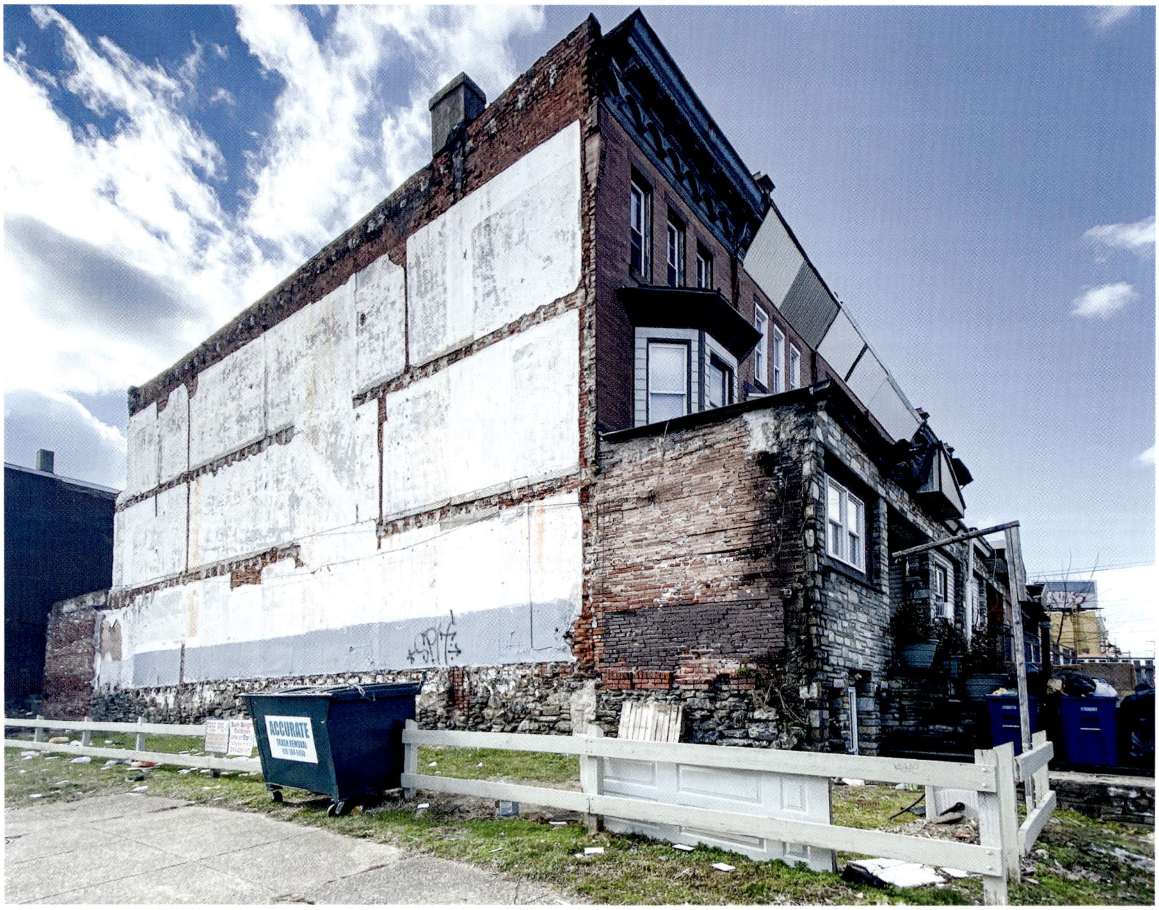

1300 West Erie Avenue. (Photographed January 18, 2021.)

Thomas's unfinished business. On September 30 they placed a brief notice in the *Philadelphia Inquirer*: "Anyone having wearing apparel at Tailor Shop of late Thomas Trefsgar, 1300 W. Erie ave., kindly call for same within 30 days."

The next month must have been an informal wake of sorts for Thomas, as his family or friends received customers at number 1300, minding the store for the sole purpose of emptying it. Eventually, all the clothes were claimed or otherwise disposed of, and the Trefsgar women closed up Thomas's bare shop.

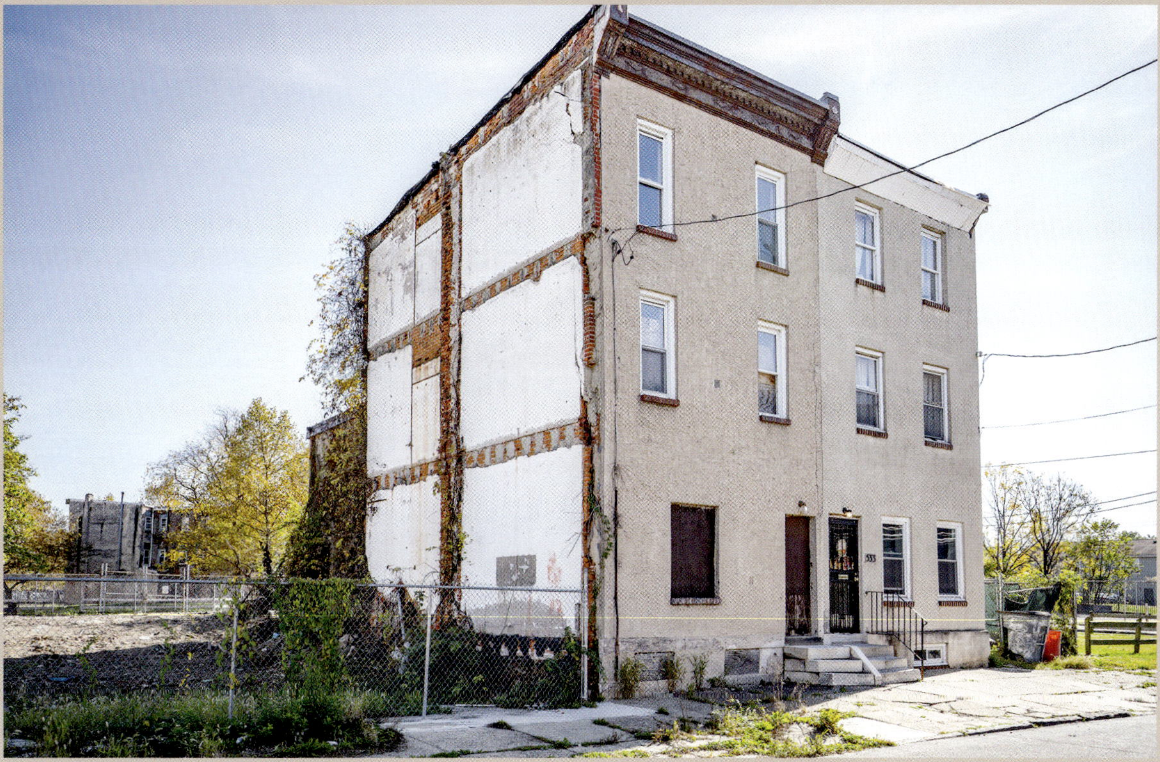

1537 North 22nd Street. (Photographed November 7, 2020.)

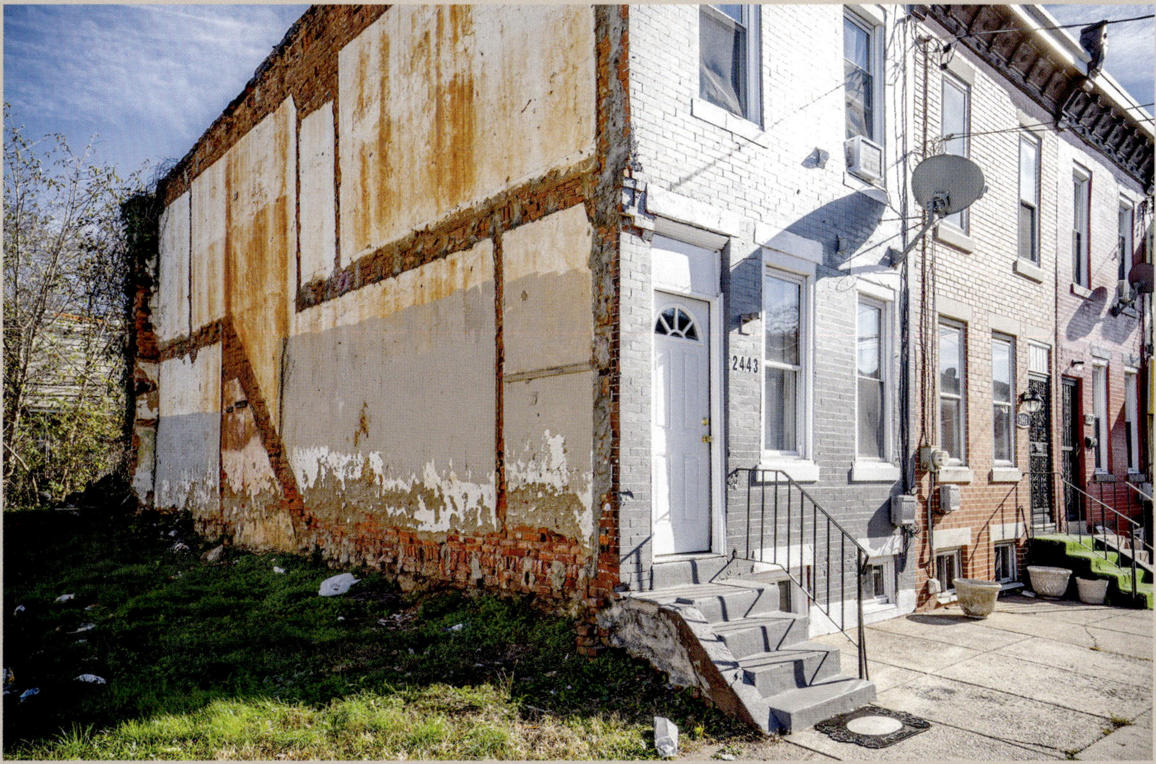

2421 North 28th Street. (Photographed November 20, 2020.)

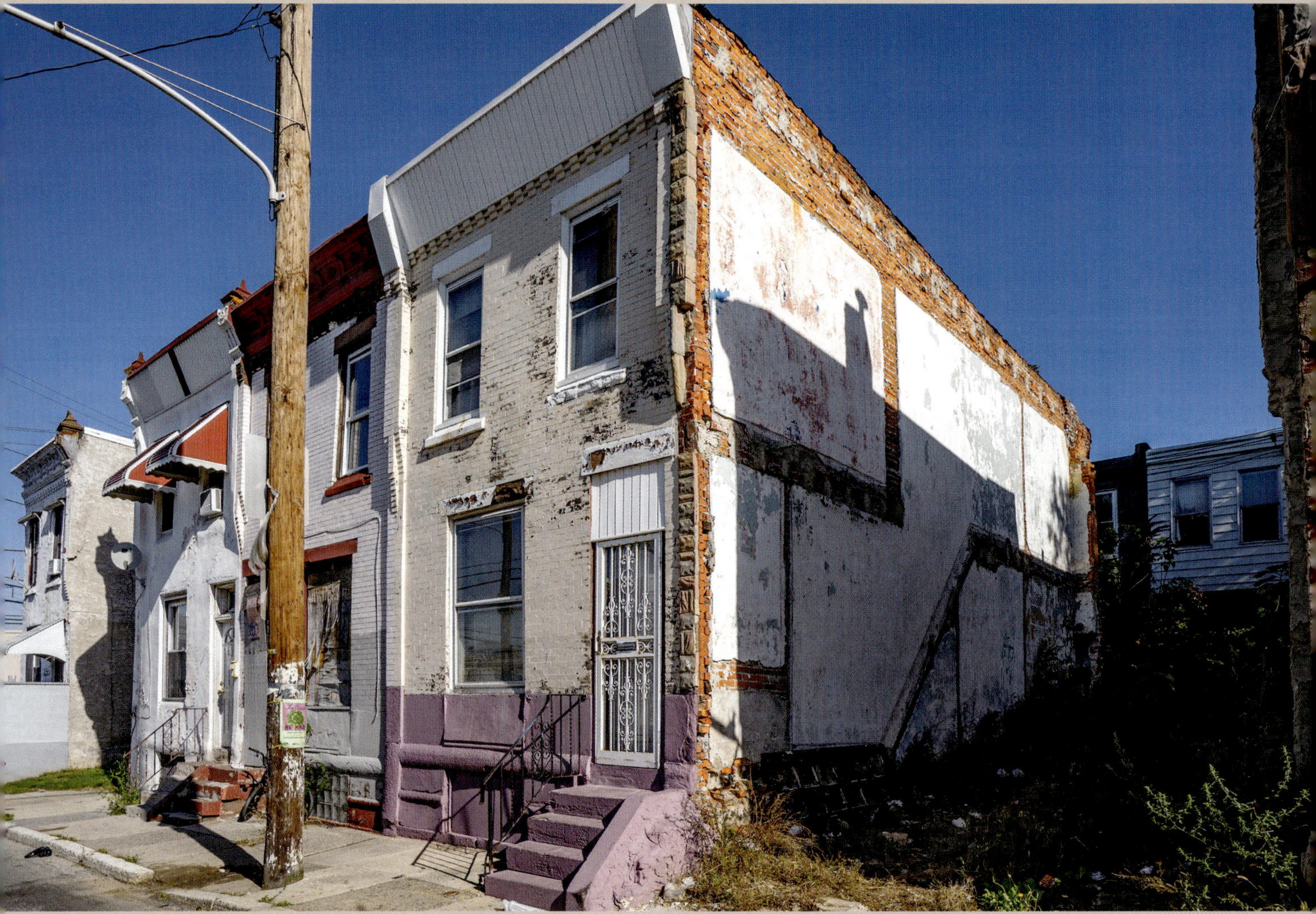

2355 North Beechwood Street. (Photographed November 6, 2020.)

1243 West Lehigh Avenue

Constructed ca. 1901
Demolished ca. 2001

The generous three-story house at 1243 West Lehigh Avenue shared an origin story with 2716 North 12th Street (see page 83). Like its 12th Street counterpart, the land at the northeastern corner of 13th and Lehigh avenues was initially part of the grounds of the Methodist Episcopal Home for the Aged in North Philadelphia. In 1900, though, the builder Frank D. Williams purchased the defunct home and its campus, subdividing the property to construct (among other developments) a series of brick rowhouses on the north side of Lehigh Avenue. Williams set the row of houses back from the sidewalk, creating a buffer of front yards. His laborers accented each house with a pediment that broke through the cornice line and was centered over the bay windows at the second story.

In April 1901, Frank D. Williams traded number 1243 and several other lots with Marshall Knight in a series of back-and-forth transactions; he subsequently sold the house to J. (Joseph) Frederick Greenwood and his wife, Elinor (sometimes misspelled Eleanor). The owner of a dye manufacturing company, J. Frederick Greenwood was active in local politics; eventually, he would wield his influence as a select councilman to gather more than thirty thousand petition signatures opposing a line of elevated rail tracks on Lehigh Avenue. Had these tracks been built (they were not), they would have been right outside his front door.

Around 1897, Elinor Greenwood gave birth to a son, also named J. Frederick Greenwood. The Greenwoods' second child, a daughter named Mary, died in 1903 at just one day old, making it all the more poignant when they placed ads for a servant girl in 1906, stating that they were a "family of three." Elinor would subsequently give birth to two more sons—John (born ca. 1909) and David (born ca. 1912)—although neither survived beyond adolescence.

The Greenwoods lived a comfortable life, splitting their time between their Lehigh Avenue house in the cold months and Ocean City in the summer. They could afford a servant, although they apparently couldn't find or keep one. Between 1910 and 1922, they placed at least fifty-two classified notices for hired help. At first they sought a German girl, despite the fact that neither Frederick nor Elinor had been born in Germany or had German-born parents. They dropped that stipulation in ads placed in 1918 (in the midst of World War I). Regardless of nationality, though, they insisted that their servant be white.

The Greenwoods maintained the Lehigh Avenue house until 1922, when they sold it to Minette Francis. She and her husband, Dr. James Grist, lived in the house until the 1960s, renting out a "bachelor apartment" on the second floor (complete with its own

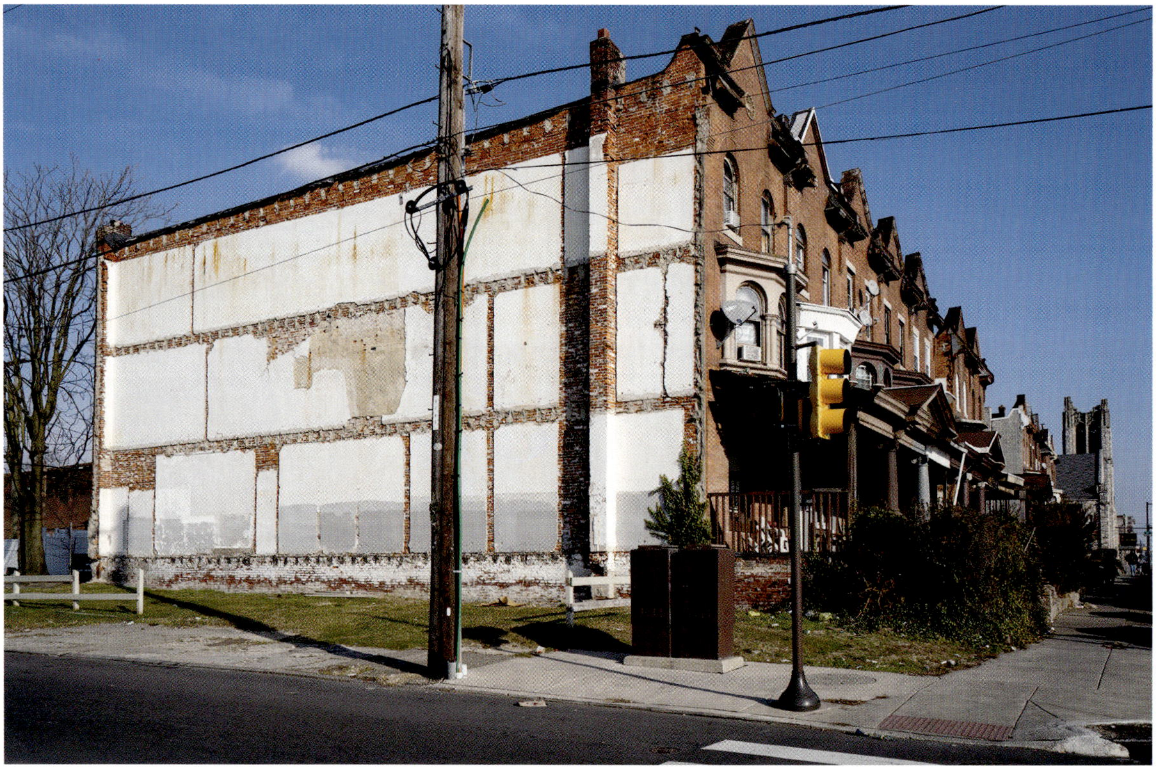

1243 West Lehigh Avenue. (Photographed January 13, 2021.)

kitchenette and bath) to various tenants. When James died in 1962, Minette sold the house and moved to Hunting Park. There she ran an apartment house—an ironic parallel to her old house on Lehigh Avenue, because by 1965 the Lehigh Avenue house had been subdivided into three apartments. (The new owner, David A. Baker, tried several times to get approval to insert a fourth apartment into the building; he was unsuccessful.)

The house on the northeastern corner of 13th and Lehigh remained standing until 2001. With its demolition, Frank D. William's original block of homes was irreversibly truncated, with a hole at its western end. Yet just nine years later, an unexpected coda materialized. On the opposite side of 13th Street, facing the ghost of 1243 West Lehigh Avenue, the artist Ben Volta installed the mural *The Home That Was* in 2010, in partnership with the Mural Arts Program. Inspired by building ghosts such as the one that stretched along the party wall across the street, Volta worked with local students to imagine new layers and patterns for a plaster wall. The finished mural called attention to the same interplay of solid and void, public and private, presence and absence as the ghost of 1243 West Lehigh Avenue across the street. Both ghosts were "created," although under very different circumstances. Now they remain in conversation on opposite sides of the intersection, until either is replaced with something new or they both simply fade away.

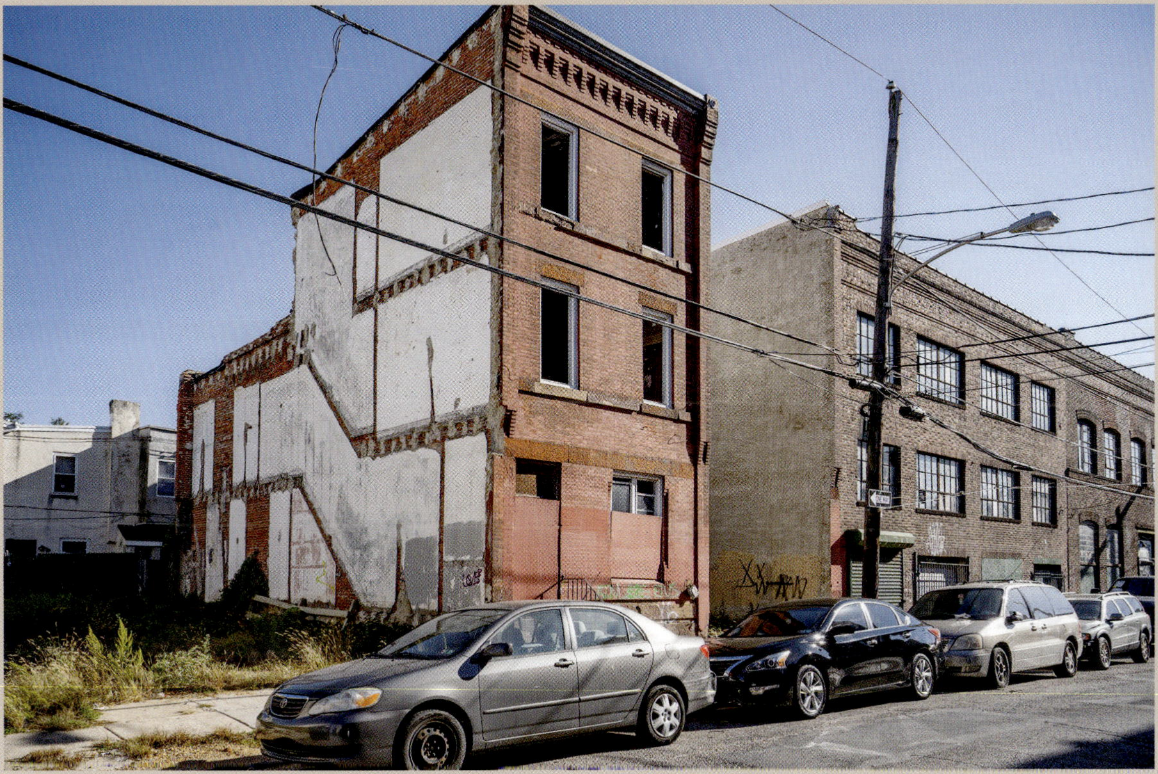

2019 North 19th Street. (Photographed November 5, 2020.)

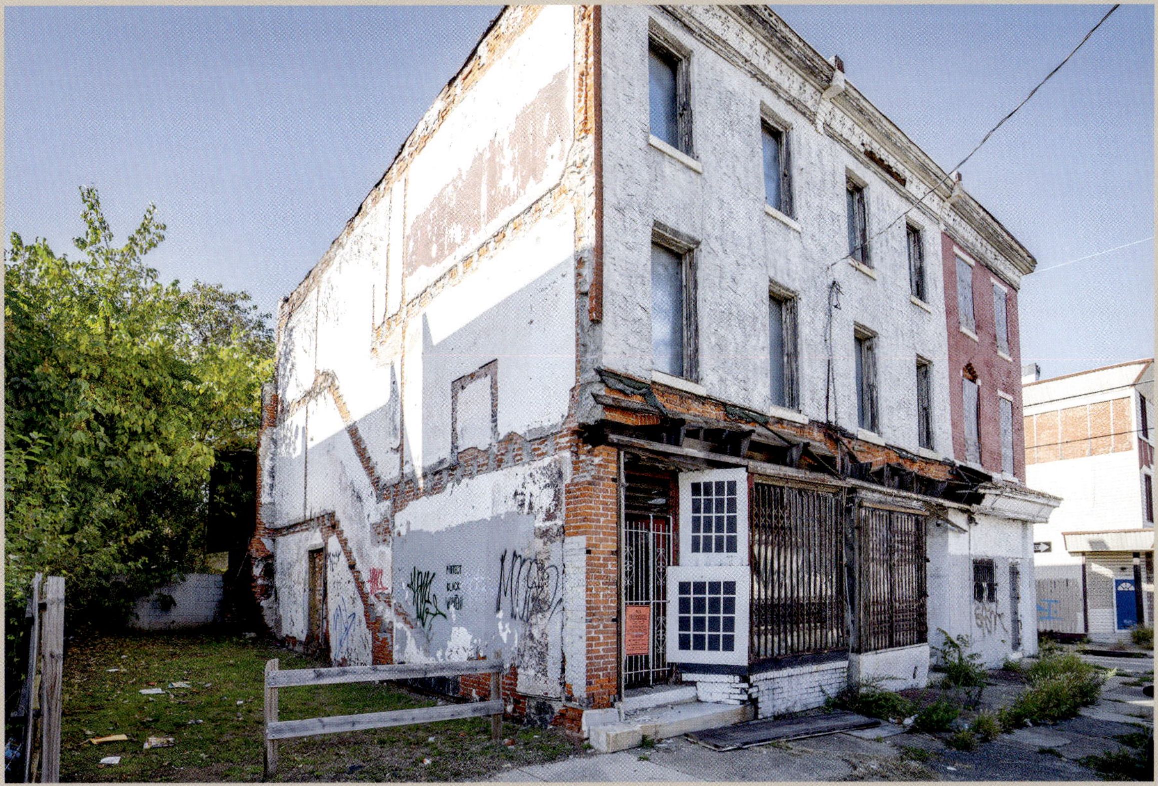

1610 North 20th Street. (Photographed November 6, 2020.)

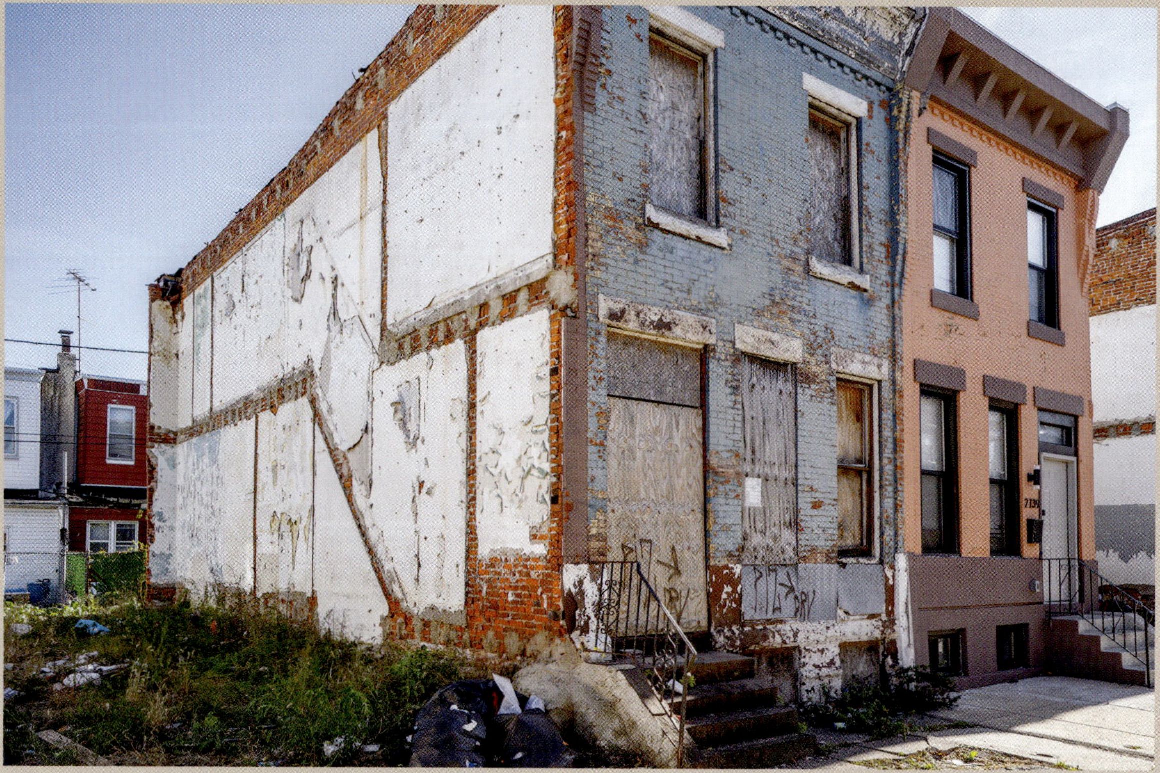

2143 Natrona Street. (Photographed November 20, 2020.)

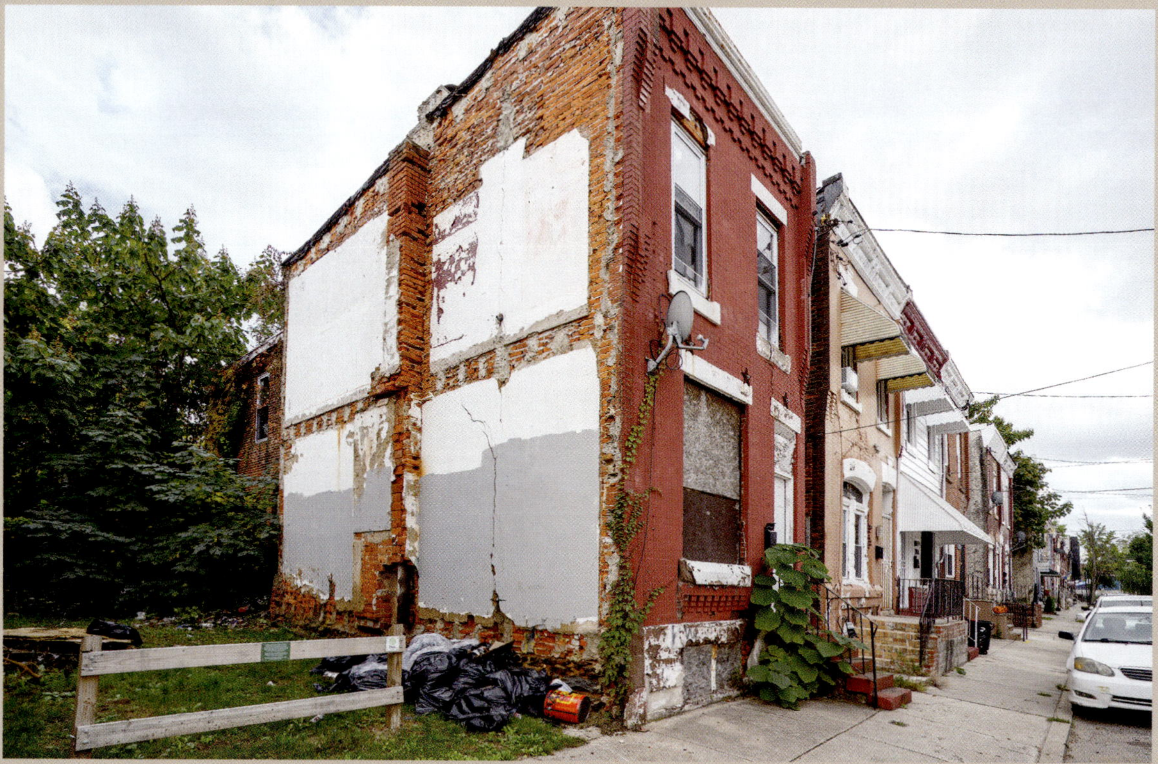

2259 North Sydenham Street. (Photographed October 23, 2020.)

North Philadelphia References

General Resources

Bromley, George. *Atlas of the City of Philadelphia*. Philadelphia: G. W. Bromley, 1895. Athenaeum of Philadelphia, *Greater Philadelphia GeoHistory Network*. http://www.philageohistory.org/tiles/viewer.

Bromley, George W., and Walter S. Bromley. *Atlas of the City of Philadelphia, Complete in One Volume, from Actual Surveys and Official Plans*. Philadelphia: G. W. Bromley, 1901. Map Collection, Free Library of Philadelphia, *Greater Philadelphia GeoHistory Network*. https://www.philageohistory.org/rdic-images/view-image.cfm/BRM1901.Phila.023.Plate19.

———. *Atlas of the City of Philadelphia, Complete in One Volume, from Actual Surveys and Official Plans*. Philadelphia: G. W. Bromley, 1910. Athenaeum of Philadelphia, *Greater Philadelphia GeoHistory Network*. https://www.philageohistory.org/rdic-images/view-image.cfm/237%2DMP%2D022.

Hexamer, Ernest. *Map of the Whole Incorporated City of Philadelphia*. Philadelphia: R. L. Barnes, 1867. Map Collection, Free Library of Philadelphia, *Greater Philadelphia GeoHistory Network*. http://www.philageohistory.org/rdic-images/view-image.cfm/RLB1867.Phila.006.Plate5.

Hopkins, G. M. *City Atlas of Philadelphia by Wards, Complete in Seven Volumes*. (1875). Private collection of Matt Ainslie, *Greater Philadelphia GeoHistory Network*. http://www.philageohistory.org/tiles/viewer.

2327 West Oxford Street

"Club Parties, Birthday Parties, and Other News of Interest to Women." *Philadelphia Tribune*, December 17, 1936. https://www.proquest.com/docview/531446564/A2A7419D4D9B4608PQ/6?accountid=14707.

Department of Records, Philadelphia City Archives. 2327 West Oxford Street deed abstracts (map registry no. 13N100143). Various dates.

"Died." *Philadelphia Inquirer*, May 7, 1890. https://www.newspapers.com/image/168133304.

"Female Help Wanted." *Philadelphia Inquirer*, September 27, 1895. https://www.newspapers.com/image/168249794.

Lynn, Eve. "Rodriques-Hill Wedding Solemnized at Berean." *Philadelphia Tribune*, July 5, 1934. https://www.proquest.com/docview/531351421/A2A7419D4D9B4608PQ/7?accountid=14707.

"Marriages and Deaths: Married." *Philadelphia Times*, March 9, 1891. https://www.newspapers.com/image/52225130.

Penn, Priscilla. "Just Jottings about Folks." *Philadelphia Tribune*, June 3, 1944. https://www.proquest.com/docview/531721517/A2A7419D4D9B4608PQ/5?accountid=14707.

Scribe Video Center. "History Overview." *The Great Migration: A City Transformed, 1916–1930*. Accessed May 26, 2023. https://greatmigrationphl.org/node/24.

"Sheriff's Sale." *Philadelphia Daily News*, June 10, 2014. https://www.newspapers.com/image/198003138.

"Situations Wanted Female." *Philadelphia Inquirer*, October 26, 1921. https://www.newspapers.com/image/171034234.

"Situations Wanted Male." *Philadelphia Inquirer*, October 15, 1923. https://www.newspapers.com/image/170653524.

———. *Philadelphia Inquirer*, November 16, 1923. https://www.newspapers.com/image/170736511.

"Social Glances." *Philadelphia Tribune*, February 27, 1943. https://www.proquest.com/docview/531731387/A2A7419D4D9B4608PQ/4?accountid=14707.

"U.S. Federal Census" (online database). Digital image s.v. "Gourley, Samuel," 1920. *Ancestry.com.* https://www.ancestrylibrary.com/imageviewer/collections/6061/images/4384846_00683?pid=92589054&usePUB=true&_phsrc=VNq389&_phstart=successSource&usePUBJs=true.

———. Digital image s.v. "Montgomery, William," 1930. *Ancestry.com.* https://www.ancestrylibrary.com/imageviewer/collections/6224/images/4639450_00815?pid=55477269&usePUB=true&_phsrc=VNq390&_phstart=successSource&usePUBJs=true.

———. Digital image s.v. "Schoch, Clifford," 1870. *Ancestry.com.* https://www.ancestrylibrary.com/imageviewer/collections/7163/images/4278833_00037?pid=5949797&usePUB=true&_phsrc=VNq375&_phstart=successSource&usePUBJs=true.

"U.S., World War II Draft Registration Cards, 1942" (online database). Digital image s.v. "Montgomery, William." *Ancestry.com.* https://www.ancestrylibrary.com/imageviewer/collections/1002/images/PA-2139093-2830?pid=3506825&usePUB=true&_phsrc=VNq393&_phstart=successSource&usePUBJs=true.

Wolfinger, James. "African American Migration." *Encyclopedia of Greater Philadelphia.* Accessed May 27, 2023. https://philadelphiaencyclopedia.org/essays/african-american-migration.

1522 West Lehigh Avenue

American Institute of Mining Engineers. *Bulletin of the American Institute of Mining Engineers* 85 (January 1914): xxxii.

"Another Big Mill." *Philadelphia Inquirer,* June 28, 1890. https://www.newspapers.com/image/168184885.

"Building and Real Estate Notes." *Philadelphia Real Estate Record and Builders' Guide,* February 5, 1890. *Greater Philadelphia GeoHistory Network.* https://www.philageohistory.org/rdic-images/view-book-uv.cfm/PhilaBuildersGuide_v5_1890.

———. *Philadelphia Real Estate Record and Builders' Guide,* September 12, 1894. *Greater Philadelphia GeoHistory Network.* http://philageohistory.org/rdic-images/view-book-uv.cfm/PhilaBuildersGuide_v9_1894.

———. *Philadelphia Real Estate Record and Builders' Guide,* April 3, 1895. *Greater Philadelphia GeoHistory Network.* http://philageohistory.org/rdic-images/view-book-uv.cfm/PhilaBuildersGuide_v10_1895.

———. *Philadelphia Real Estate Record and Builders' Guide,* April 10, 1895. *Greater Philadelphia GeoHistory Network.* http://philageohistory.org/rdic-images/view-book-uv.cfm/PhilaBuildersGuide_v10_1895.

"Building Permits." *Philadelphia Real Estate Record and Builders' Guide,* April 17, 1895. *Greater Philadelphia GeoHistory Network.* http://philageohistory.org/rdic-images/view-book-uv.cfm/PhilaBuildersGuide_v10_1895.

"Conveyances: Philadelphia." *Philadelphia Real Estate Record and Builders' Guide,* April 29, 1896. *Greater Philadelphia GeoHistory Network.* https://www.philageohistory.org/rdic-images/view-book-uv.cfm/PhilaBuildersGuide_v11_1896.

Department of Records, Philadelphia City Archives. 1522 West Lehigh Avenue deed abstracts (map registry no. 33N140048). Various dates.

"Died: Kohl." *Philadelphia Inquirer,* January 28, 1916. https://www.newspapers.com/image/169017961.

"An Electric Light War." *Philadelphia Times,* January 29, 1895. https://www.newspapers.com/image/52582928.

"1522 W. Lehigh Avenue: Zoning Permit Documents." *City of Philadelphia Atlas.* Accessed May 24, 2021. https://s3.amazonaws.com/lni-zoning-pdfs/219-219087.pdf.

"Improving a Ward's Streets." *Philadelphia Inquirer,* December 7, 1890. https://www.newspapers.com/image/168333049.

King, William Harvey, ed. *History of Homeopathy and Its Institutions in America,* vol. 4. New York: Lewis, 1905. *Google Books.* https://www.google.com/books/edition/History_of_homeopathy_

and_its_institutio/NCkJAAAAIAAJ?hl=en&gbpv=1&dq=frank+nathan+pampinella+philadelphia&pg=PA345&printsec=frontcover.
"Lehigh Avenue, 1522, Mr. and Mrs. August Pfaff." *Boyd's Blue Book.* Philadelphia: C. E. Howe, 1898. https://babel.hathitrust.org/cgi/pt?id=hvd.hxisbn&view=1up&seq=103&q1=1522%20lehigh.
New York Medical College. "Pampinella, Nathan." In *Directory of the Alumni of the New York Homeopathic Medical College and Hospital.* New York: New York Medical College, 1902. *Google Books.* https://www.google.com/books/edition/Directory_of_the_Alumni/fMxLAAAAMAAJ?hl=en&gbpv=1&dq=%221522+w+lehigh%22&pg=PA27&printsec=frontcover.
"No. Philadelphia Apts." *Philadelphia Inquirer,* September 9, 1994. https://www.newspapers.com/image/169511439.
"Pennsylvania, U.S., Wills and Probate Records, 1683–1993" (online database). Digital image s.v. "Pfaff, Anna Maria," 1909. *Ancestry.com.* https://www.ancestrylibrary.com/discoveryui-content/view/2554998:8802?tid=&pid=&queryId=8aecb828a12713b061ccbe0fcb90d6bf&_phsrc=VNq833&_phstart=successSource.
"Philadelphia, Pennsylvania, U.S., Death Certificates Index, 1803–1915" (online database). Digital image s.v. "Pfaff, Augustus," 1896. *Ancestry.com.* https://www.ancestrylibrary.com/discoveryui-content/view/189433:2535?tid=&pid=&queryId=b6ac9888cf934bcd2cdfcf252c47e198&_phsrc=VNq836&_phstart=successSource.
"Philadelphia, Pennsylvania, U.S., Marriage Index, 1885–1951" (online database). Digital image s.v. "Pampinella, Frank N.," 1886. *Ancestry.com.* https://search.ancestrylibrary.com/cgi-bin/sse.dll?indiv=1&dbid=2536&h=968696&tid=&pid=&queryId=9da71b7669ab4e923ada563d2b12bc7a&usePUB=true&_phsrc=NyU106&_phstart=successSource.
"Physicians." In *Physicians' and Dentists' Directory of the States of Pennsylvania, New Jersey and Delaware.* Boston: Galen Gonsier, 1903. *Google Books.* https://www.google.com/books/edition/Physicians_and_Dentists_Directory_of_the/eGcPAAAAYAAJ?hl=en&gbpv=1&dq=%221522+w+lehigh%22&pg=PA220&printsec=frontcover.
"U.S., City Directories, 1822–1995" (online database). Digital image s.v. "Pampinella, F Nathan," 1904. *Ancestry.com.* https://www.ancestrylibrary.com/imageviewer/collections/2469/images/30896_161638-00296?usePUB=true&_phsrc=NyU104&_phstart=successSource&usePUBJs=true&pId=1410470487.
———. Digital image s.v. "Pfaff, Anna," 1899. *Ancestry.com.* https://www.ancestrylibrary.com/imageviewer/collections/2469/images/2859900?usePUB=true&_phsrc=NyU93&_phstart=successSource&usePUBJs=true&pId=145165573.
———. Digital image s.v. "Serrill, Wm G.," 1901. *Ancestry.com.* https://www.ancestrylibrary.com/imageviewer/collections/2469/images/2872011?usePUB=true&_phsrc=NyU88&_phstart=successSource&usePUBJs=true&pId=1188985979.
"U.S., Civil War Draft Registrations Records, 1863–1865" (online database). Digital image s.v. "Pfaff, Augustus." *Ancestry.com.* https://www.ancestrylibrary.com/discoveryui-content/view/3789026:1666?tid=&pid=&queryId=90b18e7bcc8bdb71b01a6bf224c29733&_phsrc=VNq835&_phstart=successSource.
"U.S. Federal Census" (online database). Digital image s.v. "Pampinella, Frank N.," 1900. *Ancestry.com.* https://www.ancestrylibrary.com/discoveryui-content/view/42244229:7602?tid=&pid=&queryId=9da71b7669ab4e923ada563d2b12bc7a&_phsrc=NyU106&_phstart=successSource.
———. Digital image s.v. "Pfaff, Augustus," 1880. *Ancestry.com.* https://www.ancestrylibrary.com/imageviewer/collections/6742/images/4244552-00011?usePUB=true&_phsrc=NyU89&_phstart=successSource&usePUBJs=true&pId=561665.
———. Digital image s.v. "Serrill, John S.," 1870. *Ancestry.com.* https://www.ancestrylibrary.com/discoveryui-content/view/10676527:7163?tid=&pid=&queryId=456be1cabae8396f6d13b7e396665010&_phsrc=NyU87&_phstart=successSource.
———. Digital image s.v. "Serrill, John S.," 1880. *Ancestry.com.* https://www.ancestrylibrary.com/discoveryui-content/view/9782:6742?tid=&pid=&queryId=456be1cabae8396f6d13b7e396665010&_phsrc=NyU87&_phstart=successSource.

———. Digital image s.v. "Serrill, John S.," 1900. *Ancestry.com*. https://www.ancestrylibrary.com/discoveryui-content/view/41973640:7602?tid=&pid=&queryId=456be1cabae8396f6d13b7e396665010&_phsrc=NyU87&_phstart=successSource.

———. Digital image s.v. "Serrill, William G.," 1900. *Ancestry.com*. https://www.ancestrylibrary.com/discoveryui-content/view/42230294:7602?tid=&pid=&queryId=08817f984b1b661e8a354505b37c9aea&_phsrc=NyU84&_phstart=successSource.

"U.S., World War I Draft Registration Cards, 1917–1918" (online database). Digital image s.v. "Pfaff, Jr., Augustus," 1918. *Ancestry.com*. https://www.ancestrylibrary.com/imageviewer/collections/6482/images/005270429_06888?treeid=&personid=&hintid=&queryId=1cbb610e83585db23d560d64fab156ff&usePUB=true&_phsrc=NyU89&_phstart=successSource&usePUBJs=true&pId=25345588.

"U.S., World War II Draft Cards Young Men, 1940–1947" (online database). Digital image s.v. "Haughey, Jesús William." *Ancestry.com*. https://www.ancestrylibrary.com/imageviewer/collections/2238/images/44033_11_00120-01367?usePUB=true&_phsrc=NyU275&_phstart=successSource&usePUBJs=true&pId=9295284.

2546 North 28th Street

"Conveyances." *Philadelphia Real Estate Record and Builders' Guide*, February 7, 1906. *Greater Philadelphia GeoHistory Network*. http://www.philageohistory.org/rdic-images/view-book-uv.cfm/PhilaBuildersGuide_v21_1906#?ft=&q=%22malcolm%20briggs%20jr%22&c=&m=&s=&cv=88&xywh=-148%2C2682%2C2591%2C1637.

———. *Philadelphia Real Estate Record and Builders' Guide*, July 11, 1906. *Greater Philadelphia GeoHistory Network*. http://www.philageohistory.org/rdic-images/view-book-uv.cfm/PhilaBuildersGuide_v21_1906#?ft=&q=%22twenty%2Deighth%22%20AND%202546&c=&m=&s=&cv=457&xywh=-64%2C-1%2C7577%2C4946.

———. *Philadelphia Real Estate Record and Builders' Guide*, October 16, 1907. *Greater Philadelphia GeoHistory Network*. http://www.philageohistory.org/rdic-images/view-book-uv.cfm/PhilaBuildersGuide_v22_1907#?ft=&q=%22twenty%2Deighth%22%20AND%202546&c=&m=&s=&cv=686&xywh=-2053%2C0%2C7804%2C4932.

Department of Records, Philadelphia City Archives. 2546 North 28th Street deed abstracts (map registry no. 32N230216). Various dates.

Federal Reserve Bank of Philadelphia. *A Map of Racially Restrictive Covenants in the City of Philadelphia: Covenants Data*. Accessed May 26, 2023. https://www.philadelphiafed.org/surveys-and-data/consumer-finance-data/racial-covenants.

"Mrs. Hendriks as a Debtor Has Had an Unique Career." *Philadelphia Times*, August 10, 1902. https://www.newspapers.com/image/51614604.

"New York, U.S., Index to Petitions for Naturalization Filed in New York City, 1792–1989" (online database). Digital image s.v. "Gegenheimer, William H.," 1899. *Ancestry.com*. https://www.ancestrylibrary.com/imageviewer/collections/7733/images/INSX_G230S_G260A-2793?pid=491465&usePUB=true&_phsrc=VNq435&_phstart=successSource&usePUBJs=true.

"Pennsylvania, U.S., Death Certificates, 1906–1969" (online database). Digital image s.v. "Kalbach, Rhoda," 1942. *Ancestry.com*. https://www.ancestrylibrary.com/imageviewer/collections/5164/images/42342_622204_0716-01543?pid=3955611&usePUB=true&_phsrc=VNq777&_phstart=successSource&usePUBJs=true.

"Pennsylvania, U.S., Marriages, 1852–1968" (online database). Digital image s.v. "Kalbach, Rhoda B.," 1942. *Ancestry.com*. https://www.ancestrylibrary.com/discoveryui-content/view/901171866:61381?tid=&pid=&queryId=dc50687c163b86b46a2b818031614c97&_phsrc=VNq777&_phstart=successSource.

Rothstein, Richard. *The Color of Law: A Forgotten History of How Our Government Segregated America*. New York: Liveright, 2018.

Santucci, Larry. "How Prevalent Were Racially Restrictive Covenants in Twentieth Century Philadelphia? A New Spatial Data Set Provides Answers." Discussion paper no. 19-05, Federal Reserve Bank of Philadelphia, November 2019.

"U.S., City Directories, 1822–1995" (online database). Digital image s.v. "Gegenheimer, William H.," 1903. *Ancestry.com*. https://www.ancestrylibrary.com/discoveryui-content/view/1194793721:2469?tid=&pid=&queryId=0e93e97bcae4e8ba3551ca85985d74ec&_phsrc=VNq431&_phstart=successSource.

———. Digital image s.v. "Kalbach, Harry M.," 1916. *Ancestry.com*. https://www.ancestrylibrary.com/imageviewer/collections/2469/images/2785374?pid=164746003&usePUB=true&_phsrc=VNq428&_phstart=successSource&usePUBJs=true.

———. Digital image s.v. "Kalbach, Rhoda," 1922. *Ancestry.com*. https://www.ancestrylibrary.com/imageviewer/collections/2469/images/2793248?pid=1494223991&usePUB=true&_phsrc=VNq777&_phstart=successSource&usePUBJs=true.

"U.S. Federal Census" (online database). Digital image s.v. "Gegenheimer, William," 1900. *Ancestry.com*. https://www.ancestrylibrary.com/imageviewer/collections/7602/images/4115220_00750?pid=42259505&usePUB=true&_phsrc=VNq774&_phstart=successSource&usePUBJs=true.

2716 North 12th Street

"Advance Construction News." *Philadelphia Real Estate Record and Builders' Guide*, October 13, 1926. *Greater Philadelphia GeoHistory Network*. http://www.philageohistory.org/rdic-images/view-book-uv.cfm/PhilaBuildersGuide_v41_1926#?ft=&q=%22cookman%20methodist%22&c=&m=&s=&cv=809&xywh=1042%2C269%2C2818%2C1839.

"Building and Real Estate Notes." *Philadelphia Real Estate Record and Builders' Guide*, February 28, 1900. *Greater Philadelphia GeoHistory Network*. http://www.philageohistory.org/rdic-images/view-book-uv.cfm/PhilaBuildersGuide_v15_1900#?ft=&q=%22frank%20d%2E%20williams%22%20AND%20methodist&c=&m=&s=&cv=132&xywh=2868%2C3%2C4547%2C296.

"Church Body Lauds and Rebukes Mayor." *Philadelphia Inquirer*, August 9, 1926. https://www.newspapers.com/image/173334854.

"Church Swept by Fire Will Be Re-built." *Philadelphia Inquirer*, August 10, 1926. https://www.newspapers.com/image/173337356.

Department of Records, Philadelphia City Archives. 2716 North 12th Street deed abstracts (map registry no. 34N130099). Various dates.

"Fire Havoc at Cookman Methodist Episcopal Church." *Philadelphia Inquirer*, August 9, 1926. https://www.newspapers.com/image/173335714.

"Flames Sweep Cookman M.E. Church Edifice." *Philadelphia Inquirer*, August 8, 1926. https://www.newspapers.com/image/173323289.

"Frank D. Williams, Builder, Dies at 79." *Philadelphia Inquirer*, January 12, 1940. https://www.newspapers.com/image/166628589.

"The Latest News in Real Estate." *Philadelphia Inquirer*, July 13, 1901. https://www.newspapers.com/image/168418131.

"Lehighton News." *Morning Call* (Allentown, PA), April 5, 1927. https://www.newspapers.com/image/279424736.

"News and Notes of Real Estate World." *Philadelphia Inquirer*, February 28, 1901. https://www.newspapers.com/image/52581034.

"To Build New Church." *Philadelphia Inquirer*, September 15, 1926. https://www.newspapers.com/image/173348671.

"U.S., City Directories, 1822–1995" (online database). Digital image s.v. "Cornog, Elizabeth H.," 1913. *Ancestry.com*. https://www.ancestrylibrary.com/imageviewer/collections/2469/images/2727179?pid=160041061&usePUB=true&_phsrc=VNq409&_phstart=successSource&usePUBJs=true.

"U.S. Federal Census" (online database). Digital image s.v. "Cornog, Bessie H.," 1900. *Ancestry.com*. https://www.ancestrylibrary.com/imageviewer/collections/7602/images/4115213_00462?pid=68863034&usePUB=true&_phsrc=VNq409&_phstart=successSource&usePUBJs=true.
———. Digital image s.v. "Cornog, Elizabeth H.," 1920. *Ancestry.com*. https://www.ancestrylibrary.com/imageviewer/collections/6061/images/4385040_00626?pid=52249983&usePUB=true&_phsrc=VNq403&_phstart=successSource&usePUBJs=true.
———. Digital image s.v. "Cornog, Elizabeth H.," 1930. *Ancestry.com*. https://www.ancestrylibrary.com/imageviewer/collections/6224/images/4639463_01126?pid=54472798&usePUB=true&_phsrc=VNq403&_phstart=successSource&usePUBJs=true.
"Virginia, U.S., Death Records, 1912–2014" (online database). Digital image s.v. "Fulcher, Elizabeth Cornog," 1974. *Ancestry.com*. https://www.ancestrylibrary.com/imageviewer/collections/9278/images/43006_162028006069_0037-00143?pid=1587696&usePUB=true&_phsrc=VNq409&_phstart=successSource&usePUBJs=true.
"Virginia, U.S., Marriage Records, 1936–2014" (online database). Digital image s.v. "Cornog, Elizabeth Harp," 1939. *Ancestry.com*. https://www.ancestrylibrary.com/imageviewer/collections/9279/images/43067_172028004422_0687-00238?pid=27970935&usePUB=true&_phsrc=VNq409&_phstart=successSource&usePUBJs=true.

2100 Block, North 21st Street

"About Folk You Know." *Philadelphia Tribune*, October 21, 1938. https://www.proquest.com/docview/531511088/1236A6A3E7CD4A95PQ/2?accountid=14707.
"Applications for Marriage Licenses." *Philadelphia Inquirer*, July 6, 1946. https://www.newspapers.com/image/171164336.
"Brother, Sister Hurt When Struck by Car." *Philadelphia Daily News*, June 1, 1964. https://www.newspapers.com/image/184945327.
"Builders' Items." *Philadelphia Real Estate Record and Builders' Guide*, March 21, 1887. *Greater Philadelphia GeoHistory Network*. http://philageohistory.org/rdic-images/view-book-uv.cfm/PhilaBuildersGuide_v2_1887#?ft=&q=%22john%20sharp%22%20AND%20%2221st%22&c=&m=&s=&cv=165&xywh=-602%2C1519%2C4536%2C1536.
"City of Philadelphia Collections Delinquent: Tax Sale." *Philadelphia Daily News*, January 14, 2016. https://www.newspapers.com/image/197865205.
———. *Philadelphia Daily News*, April 14, 2016. https://www.newspapers.com/image/184168253.
Department of Records, Philadelphia City Archives. 2115 North 21st Street deed abstracts (map registry no. 29N040126). Various dates.
———. 2121 North 21st Street deed abstracts (map registry no. 29N040129). Various dates.
———. 2124 North 21st Street deed abstracts (map registry no. 29N050024). Various dates.
———. 2127 North 21st Street deed abstracts (map registry no. 29N040134). Various dates.
———. 2140 North 21st Street deed abstracts (map registry no. 29N050046). Various dates.
"Derailed Trolley Rams Apartment." *Philadelphia Inquirer*, March 26, 1945. https://www.newspapers.com/image/171784509.
"Died." *Philadelphia Inquirer*, February 9, 1899. https://www.newspapers.com/image/168274151.
———. *Philadelphia Inquirer*, May 3, 1919. https://www.newspapers.com/image/171071464.
"Dr. Copeland's Great Aim." *Philadelphia Inquirer*, September 2, 1894. https://www.newspapers.com/image/168104400.
"Female Help Wanted." *Philadelphia Inquirer*, October 26, 1903. https://www.newspapers.com/image/169013945.
"Marriage License Applications." *Philadelphia Inquirer*, September 5, 1959. https://www.newspapers.com/image/178423297.
———. *Philadelphia Inquirer*, January 20, 1960. https://www.newspapers.com/image/178152846.
"Pennsylvania, U.S., Wills and Probate Records, 1683–1993" (online database). Digital image s.v. "Russell, Louisa J.," 1895. *Ancestry.com*. https://www.ancestrylibrary.com/imageviewer/collec

tions/8802/images/004357990_00153?pid=3460061&usePUB=true&_phsrc=VNq470&_phstart=successSource&usePUBJs=true.
Philadelphia Housing Authority. *Moving to Work Annual Plan: Fiscal Year 2021 (April 1, 2020 to March 31, 2021)*, March 18, 2020. https://www.pha.phila.gov/wp-content/uploads/2022/11/pha_mtw_fy_2024_annual_plan_public_comment_version_10282022.pdf.
"Philadelphia, Pennsylvania, U.S., Death Certificates Index, 1803–1915" (online database). Digital image s.v. "Barton, Arthur Victor," 1890. *Ancestry.com*. https://www.ancestrylibrary.com/discoveryui-content/view/1496322:2535?tid=&pid=&queryId=45ed96842fcffedabc0c01aafb52c746&_phsrc=VNq490&_phstart=successSource.
"Philadelphia, Pennsylvania, U.S., Marriage Index, 1885–1951" (online database). Digital image s.v. "Pettingill, Katharine Russell," 1893. *Ancestry.com*. https://www.ancestrylibrary.com/discoveryui-content/view/307888:2536?tid=&pid=&queryId=3d77d848c778e8c98ff99370f4d3e03d&_phsrc=VNq473&_phstart=successSource.
"Real Estate Transfers." *Philadelphia Inquirer*, January 10, 1906. https://www.newspapers.com/image/168396135.
"Slayer Gets Life." *Philadelphia Inquirer*, December 16, 1932. https://www.newspapers.com/image/173218456.
"2115 N. 21st Street: Inspections; Violations; Zoning Permit Documents." *City of Philadelphia Atlas*. Accessed January 10, 2023. https://atlas.phila.gov/2115%20N%2021ST%20ST/li.
"2121 N. 21st Street: Inspections; Violations; Zoning Permit Documents." *City of Philadelphia Atlas*. Accessed January 10, 2023. https://atlas.phila.gov/2121%20N%2021ST%20ST/li.
"2124 N. 21st Street: Inspections; Violations; Zoning Permit Documents." *City of Philadelphia Atlas*. Accessed January 10, 2023. https://atlas.phila.gov/2124%20N%2021ST%20ST/li.
"2127 N. 21st Street: Inspections; Violations; Zoning Permit Documents." *City of Philadelphia Atlas*. Accessed January 10, 2023. https://atlas.phila.gov/2127%20N%2021ST%20ST/li.
"2140 N. 21st Street: Inspections; Violations; Zoning Permit Documents." *City of Philadelphia Atlas*. Accessed January 10, 2023. https://atlas.phila.gov/2140%20N%2021ST%20ST/li.
"2124 N. 21st Street: Zoning Permit Documents." *City of Philadelphia Atlas*. Accessed January 10, 2023. https://s3.amazonaws.com/lni-zoning-pdfs/219-45617.pdf.
"2140 N. 21st Street: Zoning Permit Documents." *City of Philadelphia Atlas*. Accessed January 10, 2023. https://s3.amazonaws.com/lni-zoning-pdfs/219-45557.pdf.
"U.S., City Directories, 1822–1995" (online database). Digital image s.v. "Barton, Edward," 1889. *Ancestry.com*. https://www.ancestrylibrary.com/imageviewer/collections/2469/images/2593727?pid=146148857&usePUB=true&_phsrc=VNq476&_phstart=successSource&usePUBJs=true.
———. Digital image s.v. "Daughaday, Joshua W.," 1895. *Ancestry.com*. https://www.ancestrylibrary.com/imageviewer/collections/2469/images/2591945?pid=145893740&usePUB=true&_phsrc=VNq484&_phstart=successSource&usePUBJs=true.
———. Digital image s.v. "Dickson, Byron C.," 1894. *Ancestry.com*. https://www.ancestrylibrary.com/imageviewer/collections/2469/images/2858056?pid=175281383&usePUB=true&_phsrc=VNq485&_phstart=successSource&usePUBJs=true.
———. Digital image s.v. "Hoff, Jacob," 1891. *Ancestry.com*. https://www.ancestrylibrary.com/imageviewer/collections/2469/images/2590323?pid=145650486&usePUB=true&_phsrc=VNq484&_phstart=successSource&usePUBJs=true.
———. Digital image s.v. "Lavis, Charles H.," 1890. *Ancestry.com*. https://www.ancestrylibrary.com/discoveryui-content/view/160309:3346?tid=&pid=&queryId=924296b5341fdd91ab967f5dc37d5842&_phsrc=VNq479&_phstart=successSource.
———. Digital image s.v. "Milgus, George W.," 1897. *Ancestry.com*. https://www.ancestrylibrary.com/imageviewer/collections/2469/images/2856201?pid=174897383&usePUB=true&_phsrc=VNq488&_phstart=successSource&usePUBJs=true.
———. Digital image s.v. "Myers, William," 1890. *Ancestry.com*. https://www.ancestrylibrary.com/discoveryui-content/view/211367:3346?tid=&pid=&queryId=11c0b163e4fb109af8e861afc39232d9&_phsrc=VNq482&_phstart=successSource.

———. Digital image s.v. "Reid, Sarah J.," 1890. *Ancestry.com*. https://www.ancestrylibrary.com/discoveryui-content/view/236512:3346?tid=&pid=&queryId=0980215a5402f27a11f0d09d13d0fded&_phsrc=VNq488&_phstart=successSource.

———. Digital image s.v. "Vansant, Richard L.," 1895. *Ancestry.com*. https://www.ancestrylibrary.com/discoveryui-content/view/1191566444:2469?tid=&pid=&queryId=3abb8ad984b8fd4dc33ba56d6da8752c&_phsrc=VNq484&_phstart=successSource.

———. Digital image s.v. "Wilgus, Elwood," 1895. *Ancestry.com*. https://www.ancestrylibrary.com/imageviewer/collections/2469/images/2593425?pid=1191566444&usePUB=true&_phsrc=VNq484&_phstart=successSource&usePUBJs=true.

"U.S. Federal Census" (online database). Digital image s.v. "Reid, Sarah J.," 1900. *Ancestry.com*. https://www.ancestrylibrary.com/imageviewer/collections/7602/images/4115214_00346?pid=68899278&usePUB=true&_phsrc=VNq493&_phstart=successSource&usePUBJs=true.

———. Digital image s.v. "Russell, Louisa J.," 1910. *Ancestry.com*. https://www.ancestrylibrary.com/imageviewer/collections/7884/images/4450132_00416?pid=128996031&usePUB=true&_phsrc=VNq468&_phstart=successSource&usePUBJs=true.

1935 Diamond Street

Baron, Randal. *Diamond Street Historic District*. Nomination of Historic District, Philadelphia Register of Historic Places, January 29, 1986.

"Builders' Items." *Philadelphia Real Estate Record and Builders' Guide*, August 30, 1886. *Greater Philadelphia GeoHistory Network*. http://philageohistory.org/rdic-images/view-book-uv.cfm/PhilaBuildersGuide_v1_1886#?ft=&q=diamond%20%2Bwillis%20%2Bhale&c=&m=&s=&cv=536&xywh=1298%2C3089%2C8701%2C1879.

Department of Records, Philadelphia City Archives. 1935 Diamond Street deed abstracts (map registry no. 29N030224). Various dates.

"Eastern Hydraulic-Press Brick Co." *The Brickbuilder*, vol. 2, no. 8, August 1893, vi.

Eaton, Carol. *Willis G. Hale, Architect*. Philadelphia: N.p., ca. 1970.

"Latest News in Real Estate." *Philadelphia Inquirer*, May 4, 1898. https://www.newspapers.com/image/167860240.

Lewis, Michael J. *Philadelphia Builds: Essays on Architecture*. Philadelphia: Paul Dry, 2021.

"1935 Diamond Street: Zoning Permit Documents." *City of Philadelphia Atlas*. Accessed January 10, 2023. http://s3.amazonaws.com/eclipse-docs-pdfs/zoning/ZP-2020-005761.pdf.

Philadelphia Historical Commission. 1935 Diamond Street [PHC files]. Various dates.

Rilling, Donna J. *1416–32 West Girard Avenue Historic District*. Nomination of Historic District, Philadelphia Register of Historic Places, May 11, 2018.

Tatman, Sandra L. "Hale, Willis Gaylord (1848–1907)." *Philadelphia Architects and Buildings*. Accessed May 20, 2023. https://www.philadelphiabuildings.org/pab/app/ar_display.cfm/24990.

1613–1615 Cecil B. Moore Avenue

"All the Latest Novelties in Hair Goods." *Philadelphia Times*, February 24, 1895. https://www.newspapers.com/image/52583523.

"Business Opportunities." *Philadelphia Inquirer*, February 5, 1923. https://www.newspapers.com/image/171049384.

"Charles Smith, Firm Executive." *Philadelphia Inquirer*, December 4, 1967. https://www.newspapers.com/image/179880406.

Department of Records, Philadelphia City Archives. 1613–1615 W. Cecil B. Moore Avenue deed abstracts (map registry no. 14N080068). Various dates.

"Died." *Philadelphia Inquirer*, November 26, 1897. https://www.newspapers.com/image/53392504.

"Female Help Wanted." *Philadelphia Inquirer*, October 7, 1941. https://www.newspapers.com/image/171548013.

Gammage, Jeff. "The Riot That Forever Changed a Neighborhood, and Philadelphia." *Philadelphia Inquirer*, August 23, 2014. https://www.inquirer.com/philly/news/20140824_Fifty_years_ago_in_North_Philadelphia__when_a_rumor_ignited_a_massive_riot.html.

"Laura Virginia Hooper Carpenter." *Find a Grave*. Accessed May 26, 2023. https://www.findagrave.com/memorial/105430370/laura-virginia-carpenter.

"Legal Intelligence." *Philadelphia Inquirer*, October 7, 1943. https://www.newspapers.com/image/171219500.

"Male Help Wanted." *Philadelphia Inquirer*, March 18, 1948. https://www.newspapers.com/image/176236222.

———. *Philadelphia Inquirer*, June 22, 1961. https://www.newspapers.com/image/178343522.

"Miscellaneous." *Philadelphia Inquirer*, January 27, 1895. https://www.newspapers.com/image/168043666.

"Pennsylvania and New Jersey, U.S., Church and Town Records, 1669–2013" (online database). Digital image s.v. "Carpenter, Laura V.," 1897. *Ancestry.com*. https://www.ancestrylibrary.com/imageviewer/collections/2451/images/42154_330007-00066?pid=2021525044&usePUB=true&_phsrc=VNq278&_phstart=successSource&usePUBJs=true.

"Pennsylvania, U.S., Wills and Probate Records, 1683–1993" (online database). Digital image s.v. "Carpenter, Laura V.," 1897. *Ancestry.com*. https://www.ancestrylibrary.com/imageviewer/collections/8802/images/004388443_00208?pid=2396384&usePUB=true&_phsrc=VNq277&_phstart=successSource&usePUBJs=true.

"Personal." *Philadelphia Inquirer*, March 17, 1901. https://www.newspapers.com/image/168148642.

"Personals." *Philadelphia Inquirer*, May 12, 1901. https://www.newspapers.com/image/168334803.

Philadelphia Department of Records. *PhillyHistory.org* (online database). Various dates.

Scheihing, Craig. "Hollywood Shoes," April 14, 2011. Photograph. Temple University Libraries, Special Collections Research Center, Digital Collections. https://digital.library.temple.edu/digital/collection/p16002coll2/id/29/rec/5.

"1613–15 W. Cecil B. Moore Avenue: Zoning Permit Documents." *City of Philadelphia Atlas*. Accessed January 10, 2023. https://s3.amazonaws.com/lni-zoning-pdfs/219-114557.pdf.

"U.S., City Directories, 1822–1995" (online database). Digital image s.v. "Carpenter, William C.," 1887. *Ancestry.com*. https://www.ancestrylibrary.com/imageviewer/collections/2469/images/2587808?pid=145274068&usePUB=true&_phsrc=VNq289&_phstart=successSource&usePUBJs=true.

———. Digital image s.v. "Hooper, Zephora," 1888. *Ancestry.com*. https://www.ancestrylibrary.com/imageviewer/collections/2469/images/2872729?pid=178068428&usePUB=true&_phsrc=VNq295&_phstart=successSource&usePUBJs=true.

"U.S. Federal Census" (online database). Digital image s.v. "Carpenter, Laura V.," 1870. *Ancestry.com*. https://www.ancestrylibrary.com/imageviewer/collections/7163/images/4278570_00226?pid=5416617&usePUB=true&_phsrc=VNq278&_phstart=successSource&usePUBJs=true.

———. Digital image s.v. "Carpenter, Laura V.," 1880. *Ancestry.com*. https://www.ancestrylibrary.com/imageviewer/collections/6742/images/4244553-00286?pid=596370&usePUB=true&_phsrc=VNq277&_phstart=successSource&usePUBJs=true.

———. Digital image s.v. "Hooper, John," 1850. *Ancestry.com*. https://www.ancestrylibrary.com/imageviewer/collections/8054/images/4205385_00022?pid=5193730&usePUB=true&usePUBJs=true.

———. Digital image s.v. "Hooper, Zipporah," 1860. *Ancestry.com*. https://www.ancestrylibrary.com/imageviewer/collections/7667/images/4292170_00474?pid=4333259&usePUB=true&_phsrc=VNq295&_phstart=successSource&usePUBJs=true.

Wallace, Ethan. "Ruminating on Lost Columbia Avenue." *Hidden City Philadelphia*, August 29, 2014. https://hiddencityphila.org/2014/08/ruminating-on-lost-columbia-avenue.

"Wills and Inventories." *Philadelphia Inquirer*, December 15, 1897. https://www.newspapers.com/image/168223027.

"Zipporah Hooper." *Find a Grave.* Accessed May 26, 2023. https://www.findagrave.com/memorial/91495594/zipporah-hooper-carpenter.

3209 W. Arizona Street

Note: The Schockert family's surname was sometimes spelled "Schoeckert" in the records, but the most authoritative records use Schockert, so I use that spelling.

"Activities of Day in Real Estate." *Philadelphia Inquirer,* August 18, 1936. https://www.newspapers.com/image/176079703.

Bonte, C. H. "Story of Noah Is Interpreted in Wood Cuts." *Philadelphia Inquirer,* January 1, 1950. https://www.newspapers.com/image/173721461.

"Building and Real Estate Notes." *Philadelphia Real Estate Record and Builders' Guide,* February 14, 1894. *Greater Philadelphia GeoHistory Network.* http://www.philageohistory.org/rdic-images/view-book-uv.cfm/PhilaBuildersGuide_v9_1894#?ft=&q=%22j%2E%20franklin%20moss%22&c=&m=&s=&cv=98&xywh=2362%2C2186%2C7065%2C2393.

Department of Records, Philadelphia City Archives. 3209 W. Arizona Street deed abstracts (map registry no. 31N050205). Various dates.

"Died." *Philadelphia Inquirer,* January 3, 1902. https://www.newspapers.com/image/168426201.

———. *Philadelphia Inquirer,* March 13, 1958. https://www.newspapers.com/image/177969581.

"G.I. No Money Needed; Bring Discharge or Eligibility." *Philadelphia Tribune,* November 8, 1958. https://www.proquest.com/docview/532324242/221A2F5FC8754A25PQ/1?accountid=14707.

"Ida Schockert." *Find a Grave.* Accessed May 26, 2023. https://www.findagrave.com/memorial/203450016/ida-shockert.

"J. Franklin Moss, Builder, Dies." *Philadelphia Inquirer,* February 19, 1938. https://www.newspapers.com/image/171113859.

"Latest News in Real Estate." *Philadelphia Inquirer,* February 6, 1894. https://www.newspapers.com/image/168268876.

"Obituaries." *Philadelphia Daily News,* July 20, 1961. https://www.newspapers.com/image/184512378.

"Pennsylvania, U.S., Death Certificates, 1803–1915" (online database). Digital image s.v. "[Johnson], Carl," 1899. *Ancestry.com.* https://www.ancestrylibrary.com/discoveryui-content/view/1240735:2535?tid=&pid=&queryId=b8fdfec38a5ffadf9cba4830dcfdd190&_phsrc=VNq436&_phstart=successSource.

———. Digital image s.v. "[Vidlund], Gustav W.," 1900. *Ancestry.com.* https://www.ancestrylibrary.com/discoveryui-content/view/903067:2535?tid=&pid=&queryId=046cd115dc704937395b90066385d1e4&_phsrc=VNq772&_phstart=successSource.

"Pennsylvania, U.S., Death Certificates, 1906–1969" (online database). Digital image s.v. "Schockert, Ida M.," 1958. *Ancestry.com.* https://www.ancestrylibrary.com/imageviewer/collections/5164/images/42410_2421406271_1035-02708?pid=5803647&usePUB=true&_phsrc=VNq438&_phstart=successSource&usePUBJs=true.

———. Digital image s.v. "Schockert, Nathan," 1961. *Ancestry.com.* https://www.ancestrylibrary.com/imageviewer/collections/5164/images/42410_647350_0655-01863?treeid=&personid=&hintid=&queryId=b4608cb9a460ef9c9354a604f4d097f0&usePUB=true&_phsrc=VNq438&_phstart=successSource&usePUBJs=true&pId=756428924.

"U.S., City Directories, 1822–1995" (online database). Digital image s.v. "Danits, Fay," 1950. *Ancestry.com.* https://www.ancestrylibrary.com/imageviewer/collections/2469/images/2606747?pid=147417869&usePUB=true&_phsrc=VNq437&_phstart=successSource&usePUBJs=true.

———. Digital image s.v. "Johnson, A.," 1901. *Ancestry.com.* https://www.ancestrylibrary.com/imageviewer/collections/2469/images/2871549?pid=177822295&usePUB=true&_phsrc=VNq436&_phstart=successSource&usePUBJs=true.

"U.S. Federal Census" (online database). Digital image s.v. "Johnson, Axel," 1900. *Ancestry.com.* https://www.ancestrylibrary.com/imageviewer/collections/7602/images/4115214_00708?pid=68916836&usePUB=true&_phsrc=VNq440&_phstart=successSource&usePUBJs=true.

———. Digital image s.v. "Schockert, Ida," 1930. *Ancestry.com*. https://www.ancestrylibrary.com/imageviewer/collections/6224/images/4639450_00618?pid=55465705&usePUB=true&_phsrc=VNq438&_phstart=successSource&usePUBJs=true.

———. Digital image s.v. "Schockert, Ida," 1950. *Ancestry.com*. https://www.ancestrylibrary.com/imageviewer/collections/62308/images/43290879-Pennsylvania-095903-0014?pid=244091128&usePUB=true&_phsrc=VNq438&_phstart=successSource&usePUBJs=true.

629–635 West Girard Avenue

"Boarding." *Philadelphia Inquirer*, September 11, 1898. https://www.newspapers.com/image/167921637.

———. *Philadelphia Inquirer*, July 8, 1900. https://www.newspapers.com/image/167246962.

"Building and Real Estate Notes." *Philadelphia Real Estate Record and Builders' Guide*, June 29, 1898. *Greater Philadelphia GeoHistory Network*. http://www.philageohistory.org/rdic-images/view-book-uv.cfm/PhilaBuildersGuide_v13_1898#?ft=&q=%22633%20girard%22&c=&m=&s=&cv=402&xywh=3626%2C979%2C5640%2C1218.

"Business Opportunities." *Philadelphia Inquirer*, May 16, 1902. https://www.newspapers.com/image/168129156.

Department of Records, Philadelphia City Archives. 629–635 W. Girard Avenue deed abstracts (map registry nos. 9N150236, 9N150107, 9N150108, 9N150194). Various dates.

"Drugged, Awoke Far from Home." *Philadelphia Inquirer*, July 22, 1901. https://www.newspapers.com/image/168432043.

"Friends Take Miller from New Castle Jail." *Philadelphia Inquirer*, July 23, 1901. https://www.newspapers.com/image/168433001.

"Hotel Girard." *Philadelphia Inquirer*, March 2, 1899. https://www.newspapers.com/image/168210753.

"The News of New Castle." *Philadelphia Inquirer*, July 23, 1901. https://www.newspapers.com/image/161219722.

"U.S., City Directories, 1822–1995" (online database). Digital image s.v. "Miller, David P.," 1882. *Ancestry.com*. https://www.ancestrylibrary.com/imageviewer/collections/2469/images/2875795?pid=178731258&usePUB=true&_phsrc=VNq368&_phstart=successSource&usePUBJs=true.

———. Digital image s.v. "Miller, David P.," 1883. *Ancestry.com*. https://www.ancestrylibrary.com/imageviewer/collections/2469/images/2876728?pid=178942326&usePUB=true&_phsrc=VNq366&_phstart=successSource&usePUBJs=true.

"U.S. Federal Census" (online database). Digital image s.v. "Miller, David P.," 1880. *Ancestry.com*. https://www.ancestrylibrary.com/imageviewer/collections/6742/images/4244465-00469?pid=14292&usePUB=true&_phsrc=VNq368&_phstart=successSource&usePUBJs=true.

———. Digital image s.v. "Miller, David P.," 1900. *Ancestry.com*. https://www.ancestrylibrary.com/imageviewer/collections/7602/images/4115199_00029?pid=90295738&usePUB=true&_phsrc=VNq368&_phstart=successSource&usePUBJs=true.

"Watson Likely to Recover." *Philadelphia Inquirer*, December 19, 1897. https://www.newspapers.com/image/168228629.

2251 North 33rd Street

"Building and Real Estate Notes." *Philadelphia Record and Builders' Guide*, March 14, 1906. *Greater Philadelphia GeoHistory Network*. http://www.philageohistory.org/rdic-images/view-book-uv.cfm/PhilaBuildersGuide_v21_1906#?ft=&q=%22carl%20de%20moll%22&c=&m=&s=&cv=162&xywh=3982%2C874%2C4403%2C1491.

"City Bridges Much Needed." *Philadelphia Times*, June 14, 1898. https://www.newspapers.com/image/53399840.

"DeMoll, 86, Ballinger Engineer." *Delaware County Daily Times*, January 3, 1958. https://www.newspapers.com/image/54104240.
Department of Records, Philadelphia City Archives. 2251 North 33rd Street deed abstracts (map registry no. 30N080034). Various dates.
Minardi, Joseph. *City of Neighborhoods: Philadelphia, 1890–1910*. Atglen, PA: Schiffer, 2020.
Philadelphia Historical Commission. 2200 Block, North 33rd Street [PHC files]. Various dates.
Tatman, Sandra L. "deMoll, Carl (1871–1958)." *Philadelphia Architects and Buildings*. Accessed May 20, 2023. https://www.philadelphiabuildings.org/pab/app/ar_display.cfm/22675.
"Thirty-third Street Boulevard." *Philadelphia Inquirer*, April 21, 1907. https://www.newspapers.com/image/168322525.
———. *Philadelphia Inquirer*, September 22, 1907. https://www.newspapers.com/image/168325990.
"2201–2253 North 33rd Street." *Philadelphia Architects and Buildings*. Accessed May 26, 2023. https://www.philadelphiabuildings.org/pab/app/pj_display.cfm/391566.

1300 West Erie Avenue

"Conveyances: Philadelphia." *Philadelphia Real Estate Record and Builders' Guide*, April 2, 1905. *Greater Philadelphia GeoHistory Network*. http://www.philageohistory.org/rdic-images/view-book-uv.cfm/PhilaBuildersGuide_v20_1905#?ft=&q=snyder%20AND%20macmunn&c=&m=&s=&cv=269&xywh=-3530%2C0%2C14584%2C4940.
Department of Records, Philadelphia City Archives. 1300 W. Erie Avenue deed abstracts (map registry no. 45N240083). Various dates.
"The Latest News in Real Estate." *Philadelphia Inquirer*, March 5, 1904. https://www.newspapers.com/image/168393067.
"Local Couple Married at Wilmington, Del." *Mount Carmel Item*, January 22, 1912. https://www.newspapers.com/image/76745568.
Northumberland Historic District. National Register of Historic Places Registration Form, NR no. 88002313. November 18, 1988.
"Obituary." *Philadelphia Inquirer*, September 30, 1943. https://www.newspapers.com/image/171436993.
"Pennsylvania, U.S., Death Certificates, 1906–1969" (online database). Digital image s.v. "Trefsgar, Thomas J.," 1943. *Ancestry.com*. https://www.ancestrylibrary.com/imageviewer/collections/5164/images/42342_2421406272_0812-02999?pid=4325454&usePUB=true&_phsrc=VNq420&_phstart=successSource&usePUBJs=true.
"Personals." *Philadelphia Inquirer*, September 30, 1943. https://www.newspapers.com/image/171438318.
"Philadelphia, Pennsylvania, U.S., Marriage Index, 1885–1951" (online database). Digital image s.v. "Trefsgar, Thomas," 1917. *Ancestry.com*. https://www.ancestrylibrary.com/discoveryui-content/view/1133314:2536?tid=&pid=&queryId=cc467ebb96ac94359fe825cffe8d15dc&_phsrc=VNq420&_phstart=successSource.
"Real Estate for Rent: Tioga." *Philadelphia Inquirer*, September 8, 1915. https://www.newspapers.com/image/76745568.
"Thomas Trefsgar Dies in Hospital in Philadelphia." *Mount Carmel Item*, September 28, 1943. https://www.newspapers.com/image/75970944.
"U.S. Federal Census" (online database). Digital image s.v. "Trefsgar, Thomas," 1910. *Ancestry.com*. https://www.ancestrylibrary.com/imageviewer/collections/7884/images/4449656_00973?pid=109207396&usePUB=true&_phsrc=VNq420&_phstart=successSource&usePUBJs=true.
———. Digital image s.v. "Trefsgar, Thomas J.," 1920. *Ancestry.com*. https://www.ancestrylibrary.com/imageviewer/collections/6061/images/4384802_00753?pid=99706144&usePUB=true&_phsrc=VNq420&_phstart=successSource&usePUBJs=true.
"U.S., World War I Draft Registration Cards, 1917–1918" (online database). Digital image s.v. "Trefsgar, Thomas J.," 1918. *Ancestry.com*. https://www.ancestrylibrary.com/imageviewer/collections

/6482/images/005270440_00609?pid=25382589&usePUB=true&_phsrc=VNq420&_phstart=successSource&usePUBJs=true.

"U.S., World War II Draft Registration Cards, 1942" (online database). Digital image s.v. "Trefsgar, Thomas John." *Ancestry.com*. https://www.ancestrylibrary.com/imageviewer/collections/1002/images/PA-2281555-3287?pid=894834&usePUB=true&_phsrc=VNq420&_phstart=successSource&usePUBJs=true.

1243 West Lehigh Avenue

Note: *Minette Francis's first name was alternatively recorded as Minetta, and her surname varied among Francis (as used in the vignette, based on the spelling on the deed), Frances, and Grist (her husband's surname).*

"Apartments." *Philadelphia Inquire*r, September 13, 1923. https://www.newspapers.com/image/171062153.

"Building and Real Estate Notes." *Philadelphia Real Estate Record and Builders' Guide*, February 28, 1900. *Greater Philadelphia GeoHistory Network*. http://www.philageohistory.org/rdic-images/view-book-uv.cfm/PhilaBuildersGuide_v15_1900#?ft=&q=%22frank%20d%2E%20williams%22%20AND%20methodist&c=&m=&s=&cv=132&xywh=2868%2C3%2C4547%2C2968.

"Councils Receive Subway Measure from the Mayor." *Philadelphia Inquirer*, March 1, 1912. https://www.newspapers.com/image/169035460.

Department of Records, Philadelphia City Archives. 1243 W. Lehigh Avenue deed abstracts (map registry no. 34N130083). Various dates.

"Female Help Wanted." *Philadelphia Inquirer*, October 7, 1906. https://www.newspapers.com/image/168205076.

———. *Philadelphia Inquirer*, September 29, 1912. https://www.newspapers.com/image/169065727.

———. *Philadelphia Inquirer*, April 26, 1914. https://www.newspapers.com/image/169071145.

"Frank D. Williams, Builder, Dies at 79." *Philadelphia Inquirer*, January 12, 1940. https://www.newspapers.com/image/166628589.

"Just Gossip about People." *Evening Public Ledger* (Philadelphia), June 15, 1920. https://www.newspapers.com/image/162311091.

———. *Evening Public Ledger* (Philadelphia), September 29, 1920. https://www.newspapers.com/image/162315058.

"Pennsylvania, U.S., Death Certificates, 1803–1915" (online database). Digital image s.v. "Greenwood, Mary," 1903. *Ancestry.com*. https://www.ancestrylibrary.com/discoveryui-content/view/895477:2535?tid=&pid=&queryId=970543da49712b0ed7fa44eb57f59ec3&_phsrc=VNq451&_phstart=successSource.

"Pennsylvania, U.S., Death Certificates, 1906–1969" (online database). Digital image s.v. "Grist, James Miner," 1962. *Ancestry.com*. https://www.ancestrylibrary.com/imageviewer/collections/5164/images/42410_647350_0656-00929?pid=5443689&usePUB=true&_phsrc=VNq467&_phstart=successSource&usePUBJs=true.

"Purse Thief Gets $1000." *Philadelphia Daily News*, February 24, 1971. https://www.newspapers.com/image/184954668.

"R. Penn Smith, Sr., Dies at Age of 61." *Philadelphia Inquirer*, February 21, 1926. https://www.newspapers.com/image/173539640.

"Today's Marriage Licenses." *Philadelphia Inquirer*, June 1, 1917. https://www.newspapers.com/image/162308940.

"1243 W. Lehigh Avenue: Zoning Permit Documents." *City of Philadelphia Atlas*. Accessed January 10, 2023. https://s3.amazonaws.com/lni-zoning-pdfs/219-218847.pdf.

"U.S., City Directories, 1822–1995" (online database). Digital image s.v. "Greenwood, J. Frederick," 1907. *Ancestry.com*. https://www.ancestrylibrary.com/imageviewer/collections/2469/images

/2868929?pid=177355709&usePUB=true&_phsrc=VNq452&_phstart=successSource&usePUBJs=true.
"U.S. Federal Census" (online database). Digital image s.v. "Greenwood, J. Frederick," 1910. *Ancestry.com*. https://www.ancestrylibrary.com/imageviewer/collections/7884/images/4449316_01053?pid=25654643&usePUB=true&_phsrc=VNq458&_phstart=successSource&usePUBJs=true.
——. Digital image s.v. "Greenwood, Fred," 1920. *Ancestry.com*. https://www.ancestrylibrary.com/imageviewer/collections/6061/images/4384803_00204?pid=105519234&usePUB=true&_phsrc=VNq458&_phstart=successSource&usePUBJs=true.
——. Digital image s.v. "Grist, Frances," 1940. *Ancestry.com*. https://www.ancestrylibrary.com/imageviewer/collections/2442/images/M-T0627-03731-00223?pid=27497300&usePUB=true&_phsrc=VNq464&_phstart=successSource&usePUBJs=true.
——. Digital image s.v. "Grist, Minette G.," 1950. *Ancestry.com*. https://www.ancestrylibrary.com/imageviewer/collections/62308/images/43290879-Pennsylvania-221660-0020?pid=245247728&usePUB=true&_phsrc=VNq464&_phstart=successSource&usePUBJs=true.
——. Digital image s.v. "Grist, M. James," 1930. *Ancestry.com*. https://www.ancestrylibrary.com/imageviewer/collections/6224/images/4639461_00850?pid=55566558&usePUB=true&_phsrc=VNq467&_phstart=successSource&usePUBJs=true.
"U.S., World War II Draft Registration Cards, 1942" (online database). Digital image s.v. "Grist, James M." *Ancestry.com*. https://www.ancestrylibrary.com/imageviewer/collections/1002/images/PA-2240341-3212?pid=1701818&usePUB=true&_phsrc=VNq467&_phstart=successSource&usePUBJs=true.

SOUTH PHILADELPHIA

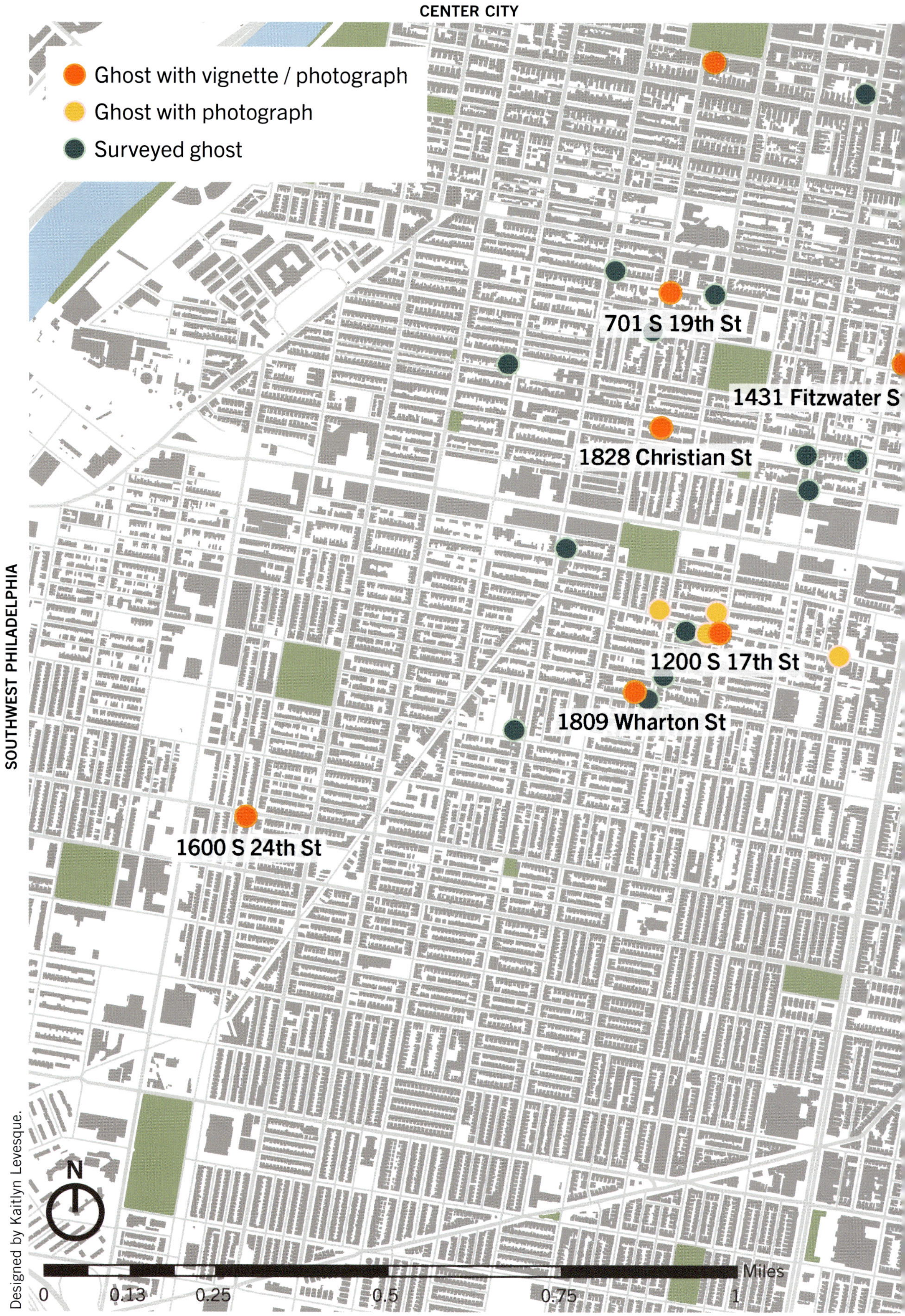

Designed by Kaitlyn Levesque.

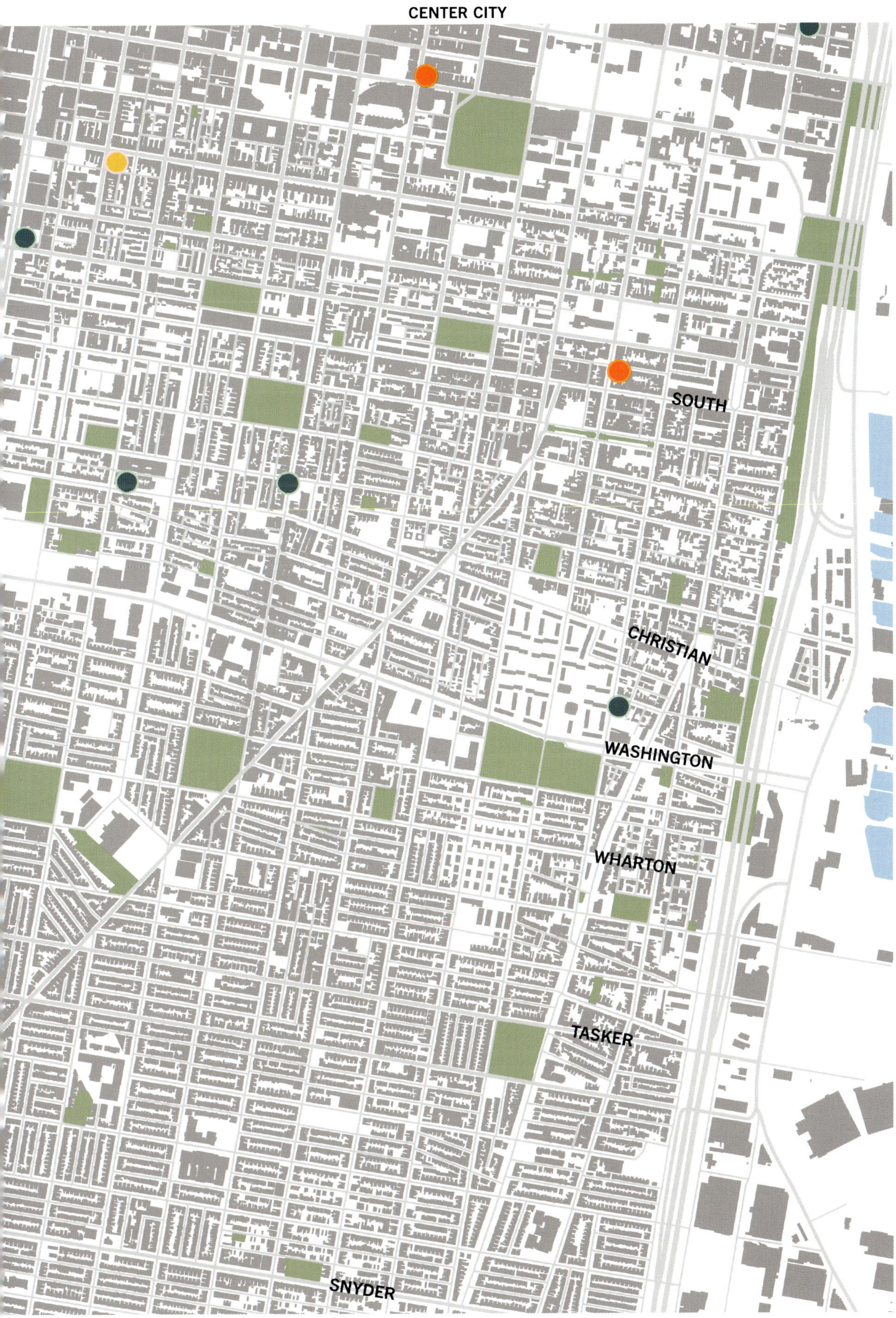
CENTER CITY
SOUTH
CHRISTIAN
WASHINGTON
WHARTON
TASKER
SNYDER

Deep in South Philadelphia, someone made a coy addition to the building ghost at 1600 South 24th Street (see page 147): a small, tidy bistro table and chairs off to the side of the ghost, where the demolished building's dining room might have been. We stumbled on the tongue-in-cheek artistic flourish at this ghost—and then several others in South Philadelphia and around the city, all clearly the work of the same street artist. (We've tried to locate the artist, to no avail.) A table and chairs here, a scrawled faucet and sink there—each tag an invitation into a house that no longer exists and a gesture that links the city's building ghosts with Philadelphia's strong tradition of public art.

Although it has none of the officiality (or permission) of a formal mural, the ghost in South Philadelphia has deep roots in the city's broader legacy of murals and other public art, quietly invoking and improvising alongside a long-standing civic tradition. Some of the most distinctive sprawling pieces of public art in Philadelphia date to the early twentieth century, attributed to Violet Oakley or various New Deal artists. Individual artists have long made their mark on the city's walls—perhaps most notably, Isaiah Zagar's famed mosaic murals, scattered around various neighborhoods. But the city's present-day reputation for public art unquestionably picked up momentum with the establishment of the Philadelphia Anti-Graffiti Network (PAGN) in the 1980s, the Mural Arts Program in the 1990s, and Conrad Benner's Streets Dept in the 2010s. With each successive (and still extant) initiative, the city celebrated its investment in the creative landscape as splashy and thoughtful murals took up residence on the side walls of the city's buildings. Today, Philadelphia features more than four thousand such murals.[1] Some are so striking that they give you pause every time you encounter them; others are so familiar that they're a gracious companion to your daily commute.

---

1. Johnna Rizzo, "This City Has More than 4,000 Murals—and Counting," *National Geographic*, April 20, 2022, https://www.nationalgeographic.com/travel/article/this-city-has-more-than-4000-murals.

The city prides itself on its public art—perhaps not so much on its propensity for demolition. But Philadelphia's montage of building ghosts, including the one with playful art at 24th and Tasker streets, pierces the liminal space between the city's creativity and its destructiveness. With these party walls—which, much like their mural counterparts, can be arresting or muted—the city has inadvertently fostered public art of a different sort, a series of accidental creative works interspersed with more deliberate canvases.

Philadelphia's prolific murals share several qualities with their ghostly cousins (and not just their intersections, although there are several instances where murals and building ghosts sit across from each other). In their physicality, they both depend on a relationship between solid and void, the perforations in the urban fabric that allow for the art to exist, and for people to see it. They share similar risks of loss—murals can be covered over, too—even if they typically exist at different moments on the trajectory toward erasure.[2] And in their subject matter, they are often grounded in the same sense of community, whether that hyperlocalism is embedded within the wall's (and building's) history or shaped by more recent artists and interpretations.

Indeed, building ghosts have been fodder for many creatives over the years, including muralists, photographers, and other installation artists in Philadelphia and around the world. I suspect these artists are captivated by ghosts for many of the reasons we were in this project: their vividness, their ephemerality, their combination of anonymity and specificity of place. They offer an opportunity to make something generative out of loss, to be creative in the face of destruction.

Benjamin Volta's *The Home That Was* (2010–present), created as part of the Mural Arts Program, is situated at 13th and Lehigh, in conversation with the ghost at 1243 West Lehigh Avenue (page 121).[3] Created with Mural Arts' Restorative Justice Guild, the project began with the thin plaster remains of a previous building but added its own accretions to those traces. The artists crafted "wallpaper" with intricate and knowing patterns (in one example, what seems at first to be a florid Victorian pattern eventually reveals itself to be a whimsical series of paneled doors), demonstrating the same ghost-centered awareness as the street artist tagging 1600 South 24th Street.

Meanwhile, Shira Walinsky and Ernel Martinez's mural *Journey to Home* (2014), created in the 4100 block of Lancaster Avenue with the Mural Arts Program, is not as literal in its inspiration and interpretation.[4] Yet its painted abstractions on the theme of

2. Eric Dale, "Philly: It's Time to Rethink Mural Ownership," *Streets Dept*, April 10, 2023, https://streetsdept.com/2023/04/10/philly-its-time-to-rethink-mural-ownership.

3. Ben Volta, "Home That Was, 2010–Present," accessed May 28, 2023, http://www.benvolta.com/home-that-was.

4. Mural Arts Philadelphia, "Journey2Home," accessed May 28, 2023, https://www.muralarts.org/artworks/journey2home.

housing insecurity and homelessness are nested under the very clear outline of a pitched roof. The project, then, is not about an actual building ghost (real or imagined), but it speaks to the same structural absences and search for place. Unsurprisingly, an actual building ghost is a mere block away, at 4138–4140 Lancaster Avenue (page 190).

Beyond Philadelphia, there is a long tradition of artists tapping into the same resonances, reinterpreting building ghosts in any number of media and connotations.[5] Building ghosts seem to summon creative interventions, perhaps because they are a form of art unto themselves. Of course, the demolished buildings were themselves often works of art (whether molded by an architect or a builder), so the public realm is already diminished without those compositions, even when other artistic works take their place. But on a more intimate scale, building ghosts often reveal the deliberative creative choices and interior lives of their residents, including paint selections, tile details, wallpaper (traditional? trendy? utterly quirky?), and entire reconfigurations of rooms to adapt to changing lives. Not every ghost is so vocal—maybe the owner was too cash-strapped or a tenant had little creative freedom to transform the interior of their home—but on the whole, these ghosts are a palimpsest of artistry, an accumulation of finishes that lasted the entire life of the building and others introduced mere months before the demolition.

Still, what was intentional creative work for those residents is accidental art for us, the passersby. Each building ghost is a private jewel box that has spilled into public view in a way that was never intended. Even the simplest ghosts may offer uncomfortably personal glimpses of those carefully crafted lives, excavating what had been the deepest recesses of the house and making a public display of those archaeological finds.

Maybe this is to be expected of urban life, where we live shoulder to shoulder; the same adjacencies that produce building ghosts can also give rise to disconcerting discoveries. We hear muffled chatter through party walls, share adjoining alleyways, and relax by open windows as pedestrians walk by on narrow streets. We make peace with these complications of city living because of the sense of community they bring with them. With this understanding, then, we might hope that building ghosts remain a meaningful part of the creative and physical landscape of Philadelphia (and, indeed, any city that produces them), since they can be as vital as any mural in helping us make sense of ourselves.

---

5. See, e.g., Thierry Mandon's *Tableau Vivant* (2007–2008) and *Inside-Outside* (2015), at https://www.thisiscolossal.com/2021/09/thierry-mandon-performance-art and https://www.instagram.com/p/CT4d3cSMXqs/?hl=en, respectively; Rachel Whiteread's *Ghost* (1990), at https://www.nga.gov/collection/art-object-page.131285.html; Carlie Trosclair's work at https://carlietrosclair.com/section/129213.html; Jay Simple's *Extension over Demolition* (2020), at https://www.artsy.net/artwork/jay-simple-extension-over-demolition; Tim Portlock's *Ghost City* (2008–2010), at https://www.timportlock.net/ghostcity; Marika's work in Barcelona (2005), photographed by Jose Antonio Millan, at http://jamillan.com/medianeraw.htm; and Luis Marsan's *La casa desparecida* (1997), at https://www.claude-bernard.com/index.php?option=com_content&view=article&id=353&Itemid=543&lang=fr#gid=gallery plugin4879516087b4101f2619de9d19198f29&pid=212.

Yet what are the limits of such communal ownership when it comes to building ghosts? The residents have gone, but their lives remain exposed. At what point does the curiosity veer into prying, and when does the generative muse of a building ghost prey on loss and decay? On which side of those lines does this very book exist?

Building ghosts are works of art that we were never meant to see. Whether embellished or not, temporary or long-standing, their vividness appeals to our imaginations and our consciences. The fundamental question, then, is this: Is a building ghost a canvas for something new to be created or a finished work unto itself? And in either case, for whom?

1600 South 24th Street

Constructed in 1909
Demolished in 2020

The graffiti artist who tagged 1600 South 24th Street with a table and chairs would not have known it, but food was central to the history of this building. The inadvertent motif began with Frank Gelman and Samuel Doak, who began peddling produce and meat (respectively) out of the building in 1914; at one address, neighbors could account for most of their shopping needs. The following year, two Yiddish-speaking Russian immigrants, Joseph Susman and Abraham Bronfman, peddled the same provisions.

In 1922, Giuseppe Giorgio would purchase the property in the first of several sales that kept the building within the Giorgio family. Born in Italy in 1873, Giorgio was a "non-declared alien" as of 1918 when he registered for the World War I draft on behalf of his adopted country. He and his wife, Maria, had five children. Most of their four sons worked in a laundry, but their only daughter, Theresa, was a "saleslady" at Giuseppe's butcher shop—and later, an assistant butcher herself. The Giorgios created a multigenerational home and shop at 1600 South 24th Street, picking up where Joseph Susman and Abraham Bronfman left off.

In 1940, Theresa Giorgio (now Ranalli, after her marriage to Harry Ranalli) purchased the building from her parents. She continued to work as a butcher in the brick building while her husband was a bricklayer elsewhere. (Harry would later follow his wife into business, and they would run several meat markets together in Pennsylvania and New Jersey.) She sold the building to her brother Vincent in 1947; when Vincent and his wife, Helen, sold it in 1951, it passed out of the Giorgio family for the first time in a quarter-century.

Sosangelis Brothers and Company purchased number 1600 from the Giorgios. Composed of Saterios, Savas, and Constantine Sosangelis, as well as Soterios Doucas, the partnership operated a wholesale grocery business, with storefronts at 11th and Locust streets, 45th and Walnut streets, and elsewhere. The property on South 24th Street was likely a back-of-house warehouse for them, since it didn't feature in their public advertisements or notices. Nevertheless, it was part of their growing success as they built on the roots of their father's store on South 9th Street, where they had all gotten their start. (Another formative start for the brothers: they were key founders of St. George Greek Orthodox Cathedral at 8th and Locust Streets, cultivating a religious community for fellow Philadelphians of Greek descent.)

Sosangelis Brothers and Company catered primarily to independent mom-and-pop markets—just the sort that 1600 South 24th Street had long hosted—carving out a niche opposite the major supermarket chains. The strategy paid off, as the company remained in business until 1986, although it did not hold on to number 1600 that entire

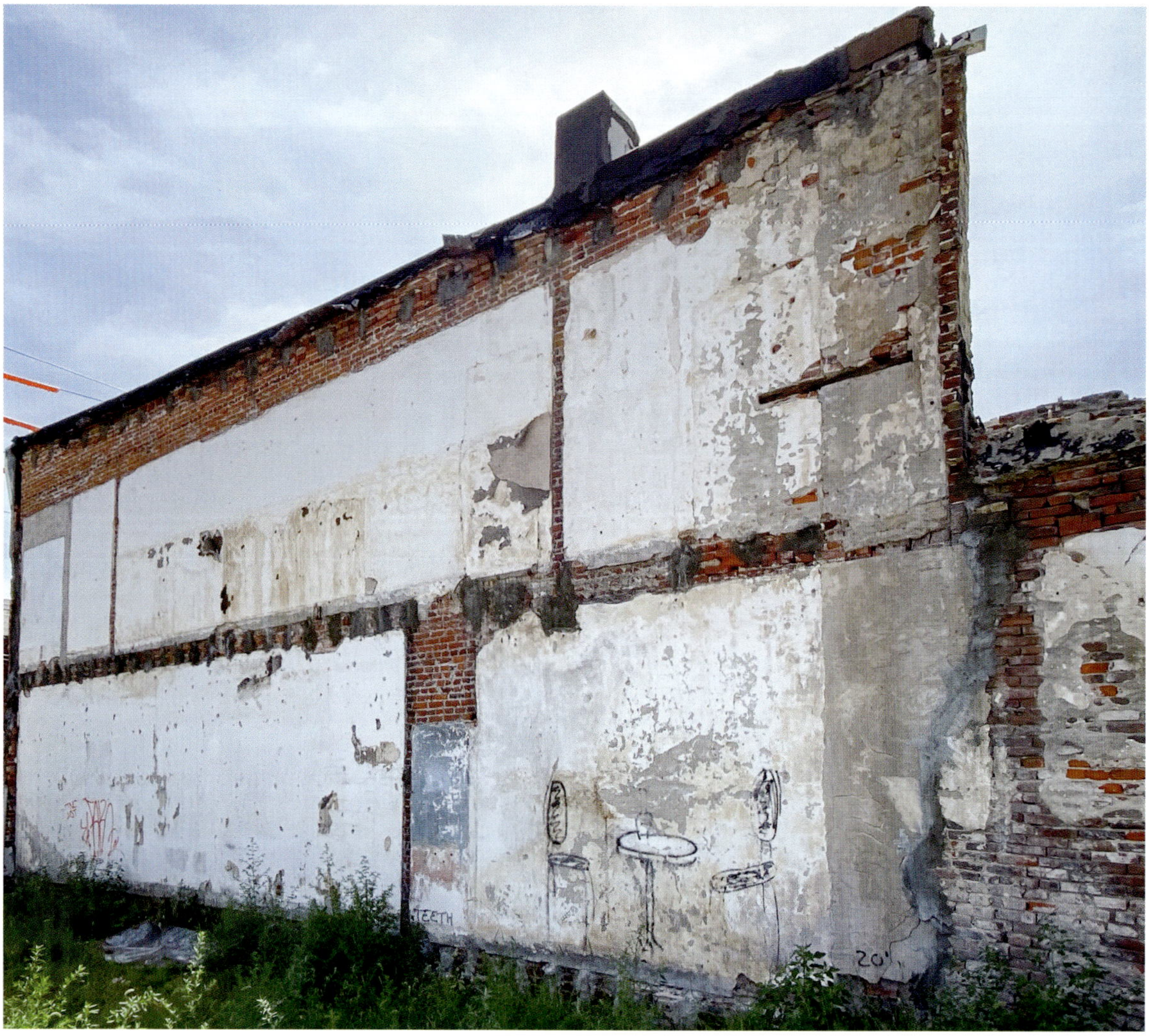

1600 South 24th Street. (Photographed November 3, 2020.)

time. Rather, in more recent decades the address was linked with DiBruno Brothers (as of 1959) and an unnamed deli (in the 1970s). By 2005, the storefront was considered a nuisance and designated unsafe. In 2016, a sheriff's sale loomed, and in 2020, the building was demolished.

Within months of the demolition, the graffiti artist had tagged a "room" at the rear of the property, adding a wry touch to the otherwise blank walls. In any other rowhouse, this would have been the kitchen; the artist was clever enough to know this and mark this portion of plaster in particular. Yet the distinct history of 1600 South 24th Street, and its long association with food distribution rather than domesticity, means that for most of the building's existence, there likely wasn't a traditional kitchen on the first floor. The building's history, then, renders its present state even more ironic and accidentally subversive.

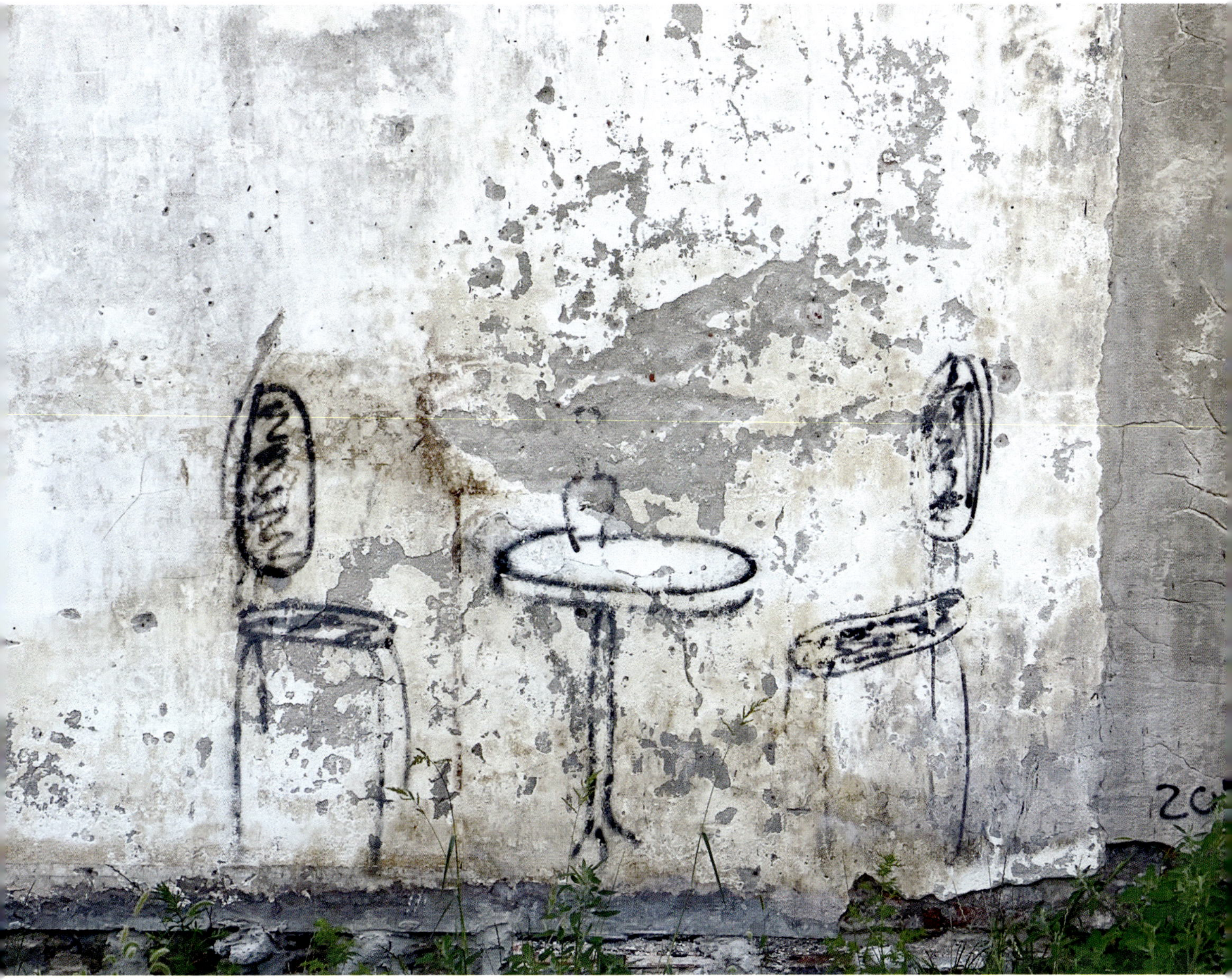

Detail of 1600 South 24th Street. (Photographed November 3, 2020.)

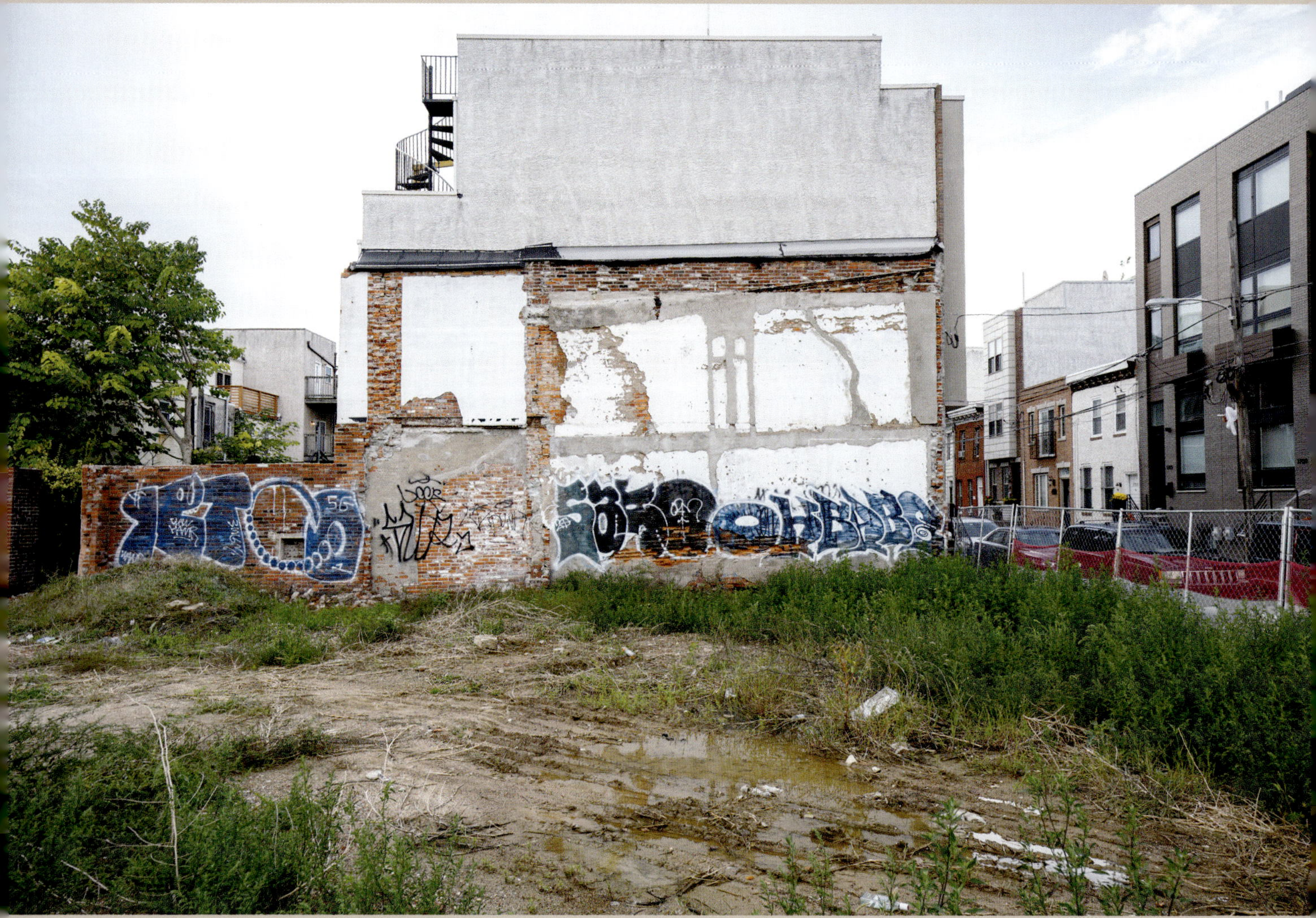

1700–1704 Annin Street. (Photographed November 3, 2020.)

1254–1256 South 18th Street

Constructed between 1862 and 1882
Rear section demolished in 2019–2020

The dual rowhouse at 1254–1256 South 18th Street was a latecomer to the party of religious institutions in South Philadelphia. Converted into a house of worship (with five apartments on the upper stories) as recently as 1964, the True Way Church of Christ Jesus, Apostolic Faith, Inc., was a rowhouse church in a neighborhood full of rowhouses and churches.

The tradition began early in the Point Breeze area of South Philadelphia. As of 1895, shortly after number 1254–1256 was constructed, there were no fewer than five churches within a single block of the brick rowhouse. For the Methodists, there was the 18th Street Methodist Episcopal Church on the southeastern corner of 18th and Wharton streets, opposite the house at number 1254–1256, on the northwestern corner. The Lutherans could walk to 19th and Lawrence (today, Earp) streets. The Church of the Holy Comforter had a large plant at 19th and Titan streets, and the Reformed congregation of St. Paul's gathered on the 1800 block of Wharton Street. (This doesn't even account for the sacred places that required all of two blocks' walk.) Sundays must have been the most boisterous day of the week for the residents of number 1254–1256 (given that the nearby institutions were all Christian), witnessing all that to-ing and fro-ing and perhaps joining in themselves.

The population of Philadelphia reached a crescendo in the first half of the twentieth century, contemporaneous with cresting trends of religious participation in America. It is unsurprising, then, that one small segment of South Philadelphia could sustain so many congregations at once. The four large purpose-built churches remained intact through the early 1940s; by then, they had been joined by a rowhouse church at 1731 Reed Street, and the Church of the Holy Comforter had become the 19th Street Baptist Church. All the while, 1254–1256 South 18th Street (and its rear section at 1809 Wharton Street, which was absorbed into the property's ownership in the late nineteenth century) remained residential, living alongside the sacred rituals of its holy neighbors.

In 1964, the rowhouse at 1254–1256 South 18th Street became its own church—just as shifts were underway in both the city's population (dwindling) and the country's religiosity (declining in many mainline Christian traditions). The mere presence of the True Way Church of Christ Jesus, Apostolic Faith, in South Philadelphia spoke to shifting forces among faith traditions at this time. As attendance at Methodist, Lutheran, Episcopal, and Reformed congregations started waning in the 1960s—including, quite possibly, at all of the churches within a block of True Way Church—Pentecostal congregations and practices rose in popularity.

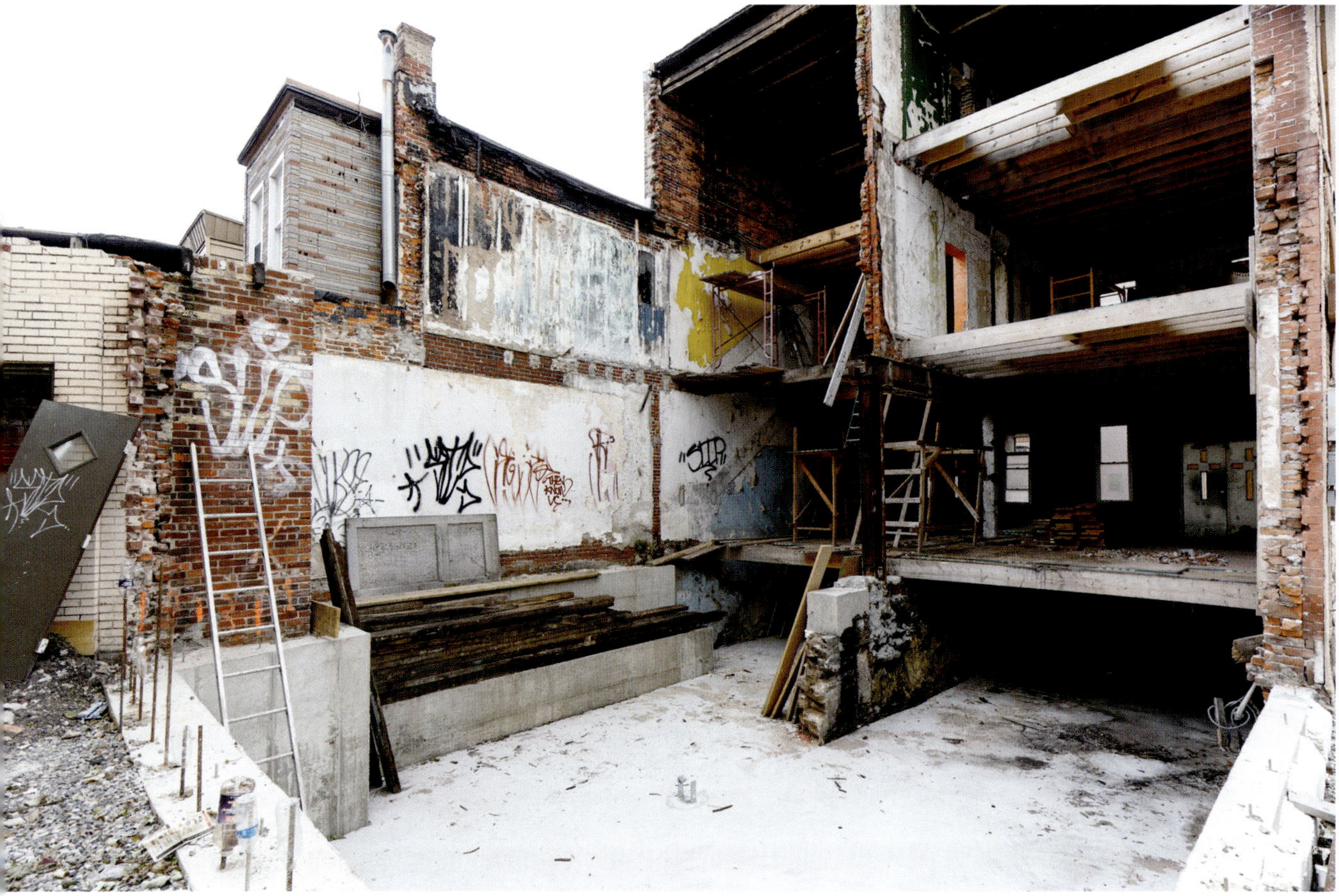

1254–1256 South 18th Street. (Photographed November 3, 2020.)

Eventually, though, 1254–1256 South 18th Street fell back in line with its neighbors, receding from its religious use when True Way Church sold the building in 2018 and moved to Chester. Construction workers peeled away the rear walls of the house, creating a building ghost en route to a rehabbed multifamily home—a restoration of the building's original residential function. Number 1254–1256 progressed through deconsecration and conversion in a sequence that was subsequently repeated at the rowhouse church on Reed Street and is currently underway (as of 2023) at the former 18th Street Methodist Episcopal Church, on the corner opposite number 1254–1256. Of the six houses of worship that existed within a one-block radius in the mid-1960s, only half remain in religious use today. Sundays have a different rhythm in South Philadelphia now.

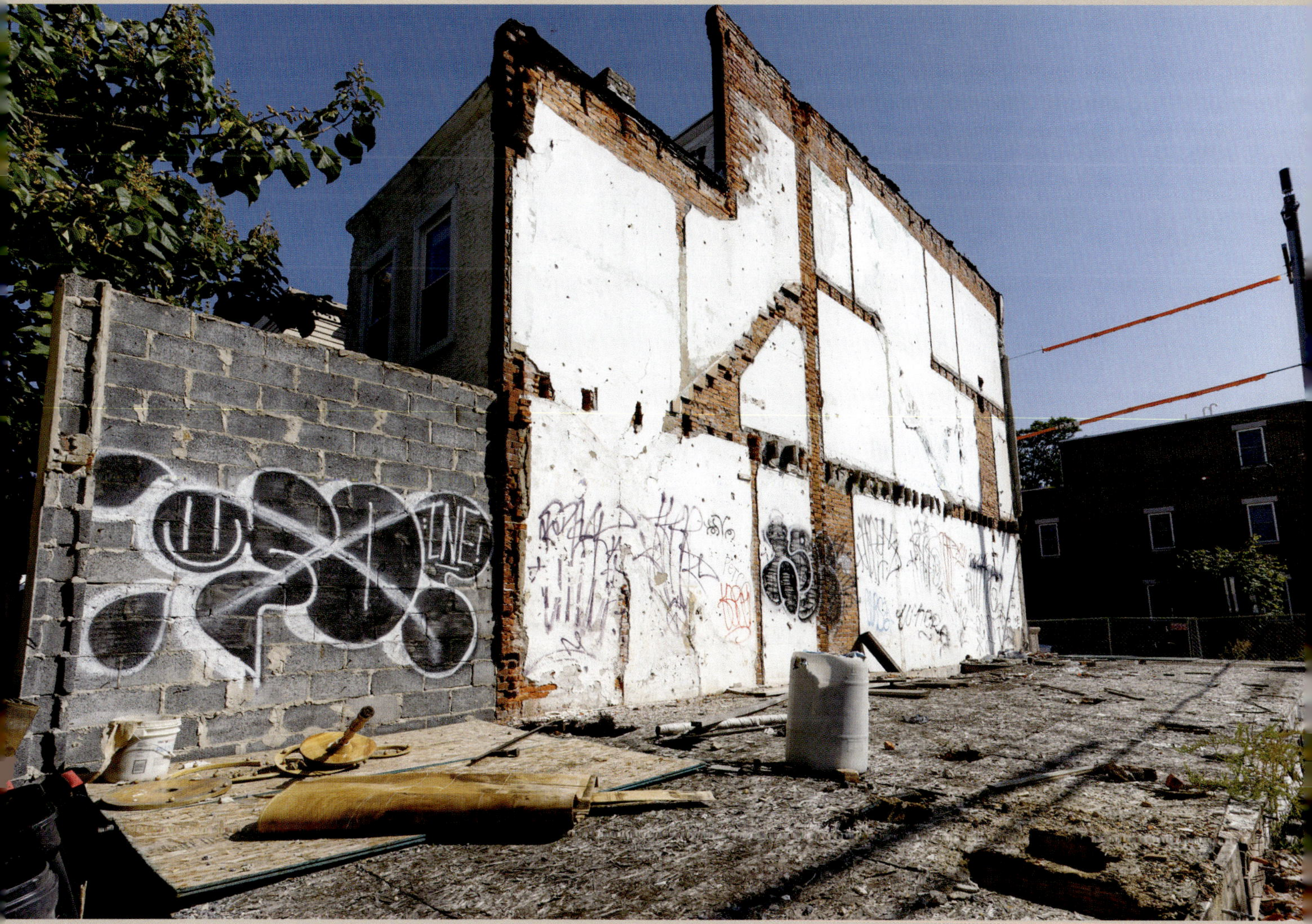

1164 South 18th Street. (Photographed November 3, 2020.)

1728 Federal Street

Constructed ca. 1868 (rear addition constructed in 1891)
Demolished ca. 2007

Between 1878 and 1941, a lot of people said goodbye to their loved ones in 1728 Federal Street. In the care of undertaker Samuel Foster (and later his son Samuel Foster Jr.), scores of people passed through the mid-block funeral home to memorialize someone. Business boomed sufficiently to justify a rear addition, constructed in 1891. (That same year, Samuel Foster Sr. received multiple health board violations; it is unclear whether the two events were related.) In these early years of the at-home funeral home, the Foster family lived upstairs, including Samuel Sr., Samuel Jr., and Samuel Sr.'s wife, Wilhelmine (Minnie, for short). They maintained a residential vigil of sorts for those lying in repose below.

The Foster men prepared burials for deceased as young as eleven years old (C. Frank Trought, who died in 1912) and as old as eighty-two (Captain William P. Davis, a veteran of the Union Army in the Civil War, who lived a full forty-two years beyond his wounding experience at the Battle of Gettysburg). The Fosters tended to the remains of a train brakeman who died a gruesome, dismembering death in an 1889 train accident and to Marion (Mary) Carr, who drowned in a boating accident on the Schuylkill River in 1891. But there were dozens of other people who died quieter deaths, departing from number 1728 to Mount Moriah Cemetery or Fernwood or the Woodlands. When Samuel Foster Sr. himself died in 1894, he was prepared for burial at—where else?—1728 Federal Street.

His son took over the business after his death, although Samuel Jr. tended to live off-site, maintaining number 1728 (and, by this time, number 1726) as a funeral home without making it his *actual* home. He found other ways to extend beyond his father's shadow, maintaining a very active sideline of work breeding puppies. In that he could tend to births, not deaths.

Samuel Foster Jr. died in 1943, and in 1946 the trail of wills and probates ultimately sold the house out of the family for the first time in nearly seventy years. The building would stand for sixty-one more years before meeting the wrecking ball. In the final accounting, the building spent half of its existence as a funeral home. We do not know how many people were mourned in 1728 Federal Street, yet we must presume (and hope) that for every human being who lingered in the house for burial, at least one other person set foot inside to remember them. In the ledger of a building ghost, then, 1728 Federal Street held a lot of death—but even more life.

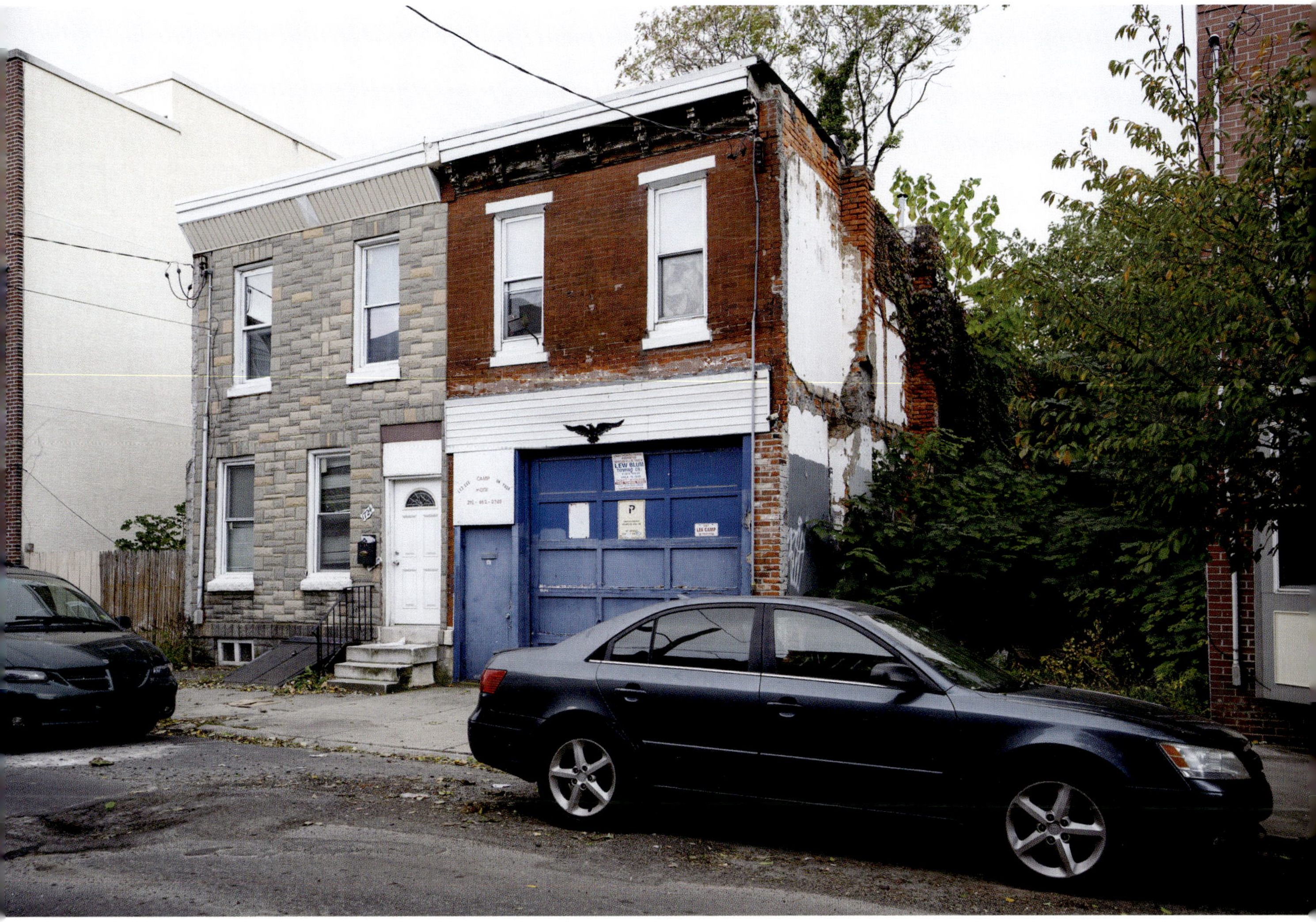

1728 Federal Street. (Photographed November 3, 2020.)

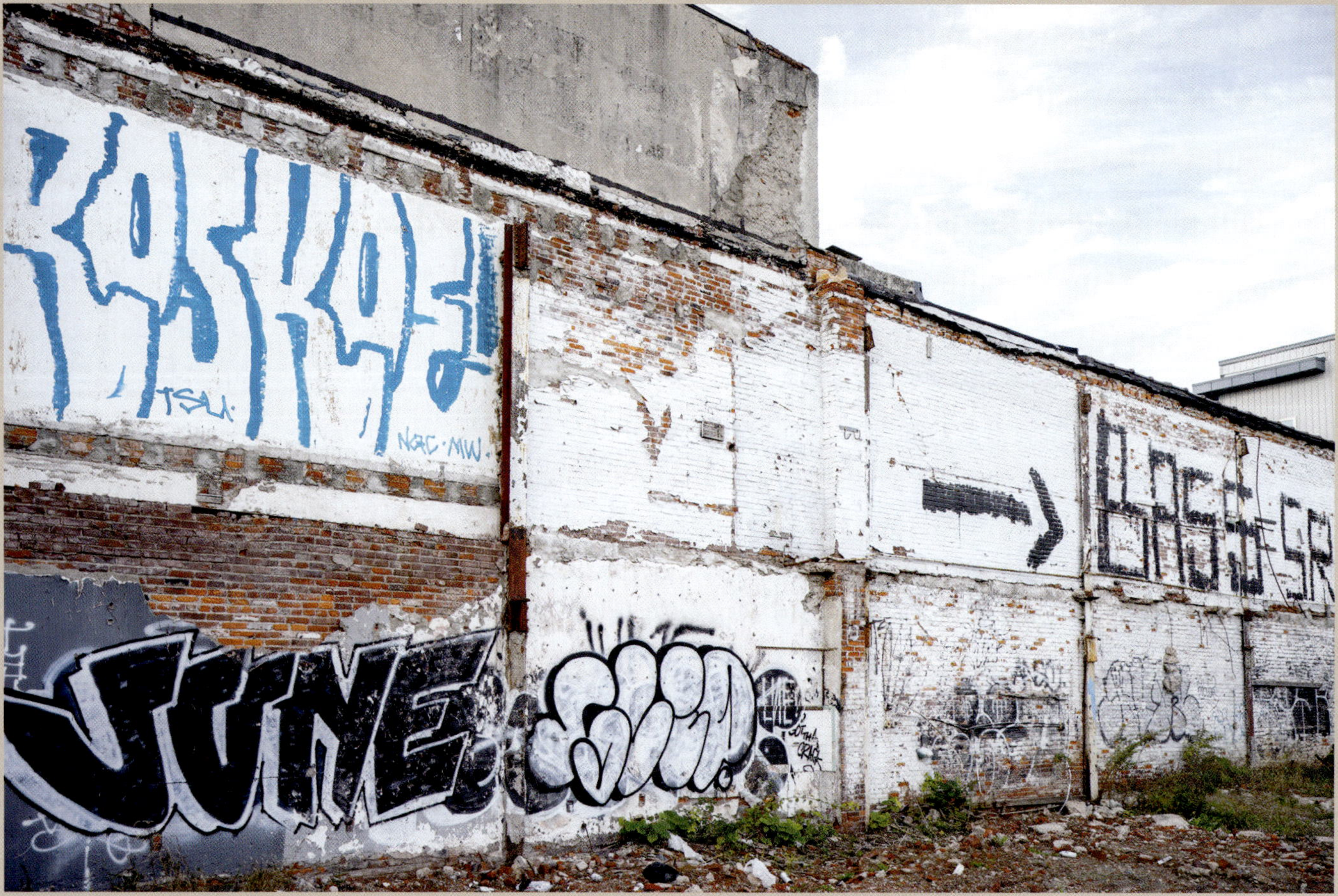

1439 Federal Street. (Photographed November 3, 2020.)

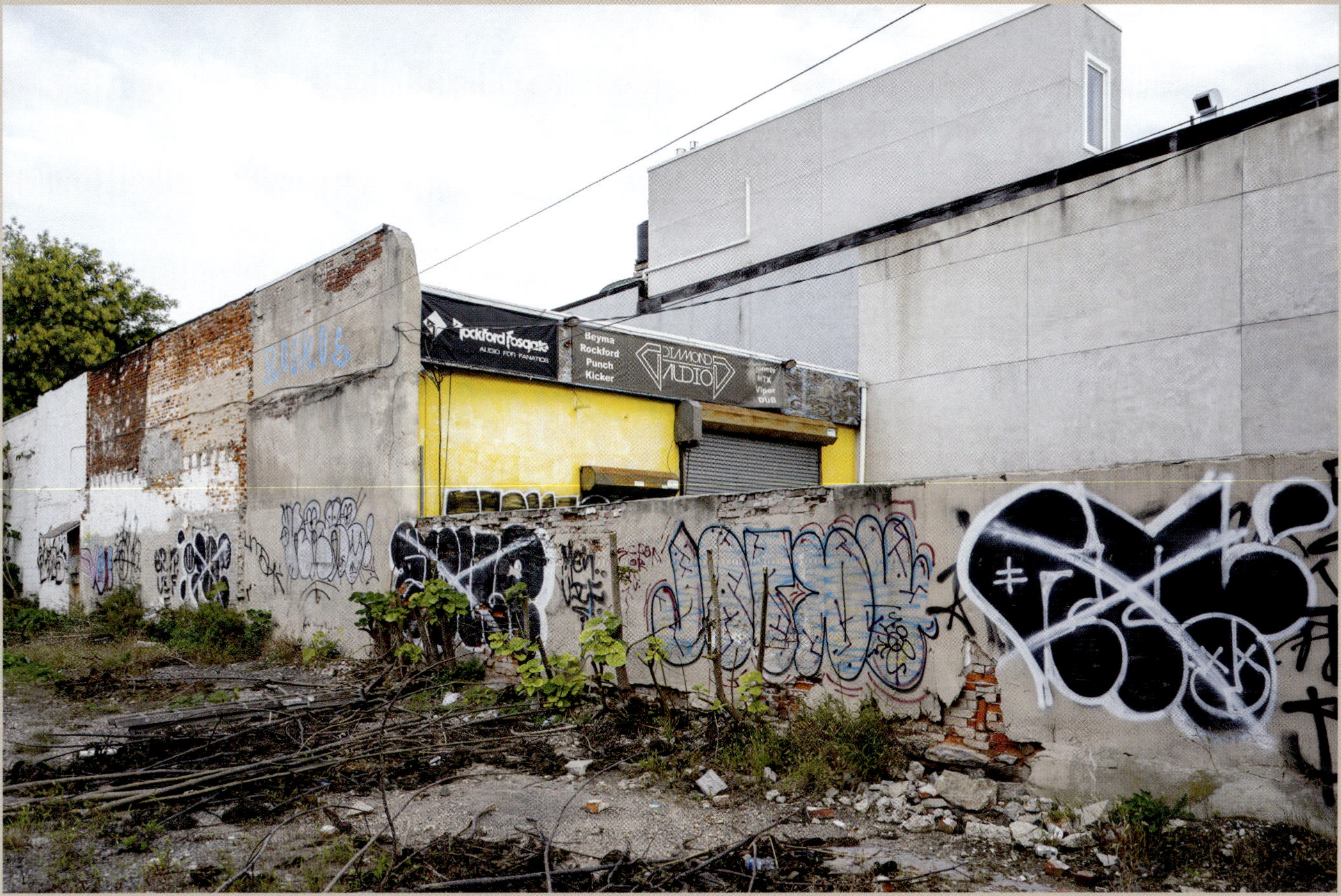

1439 Federal Street. (Photographed November 3, 2020.)

701 South 19th Street

Constructed ca. 1866
Demolished in 2020

In its first few decades, the rowhouse at the southeastern corner of 19th and Bainbridge streets sent the smell of bread and baked goods wafting into the air in South Philadelphia. Charles Young ran a bakery at the address for several years, perhaps even until his death in 1912. His son Alexander was a bit of a local terror (he was arrested in 1881 at age twelve for some hooliganism), but with three bakers on hand, Charles's shop was otherwise a popular neighborhood spot.

Meanwhile, on a parallel path that would eventually find its way to number 701, a Baptist minister named Reverend Lewis G. Jordan was elected in 1896 to be the third executive secretary of the Foreign Mission Board of the National Baptist Convention (NBC). The predominantly Black NBC, and its Foreign Mission Board, traced its roots to a meeting in Montgomery, Alabama, in 1880, when more than 150 people gathered around a shared hope to deploy Christian missions to Africa. The organization launched its first mission just three years later, when six people representing the board traveled to West Africa in 1883.

While many of its white missionary counterparts approached evangelism in Africa with the same ingrained sense of supremacy that was dominant in Jim Crow–era America, the Black-led Foreign Mission Board's work combined proselytization with a sense of self-determination and social justice. "It must not be forgotten that the colored American needs to be a missionary to help change the spirit of many of the missionaries who are carrying a perverted gospel of humiliation to the darker races," one of the board's publications stated in 1919. "We must have foreign missionaries who will insist that the black people of Africa and the whole world be given what is given others to make them fit for citizenship in the Kingdom of God on earth." To achieve its vision for that kingdom on Earth, the board paired its religious instruction with more material investments in these communities, constructing hospitals and establishing "industrial missions" to employ local residents in the countries where its missionaries worked.

In the years before Reverend Jordan's election as executive secretary, the board's headquarters were in Richmond, Virginia. Once elected, Jordan—who was also the pastor of the Union Baptist Church in Philadelphia—relocated the Foreign Mission Board's operations to the city so that he could juggle the two roles in one place. (The move angered board members from North Carolina and Virginia, who needed to travel much greater distances now for board meetings.) For its first nineteen years in Philadelphia, the board operated elsewhere (likely out of the NBC's offices at 18th and Bainbridge), but in 1915 it purchased 701 South 19th Street. Having acquired the property

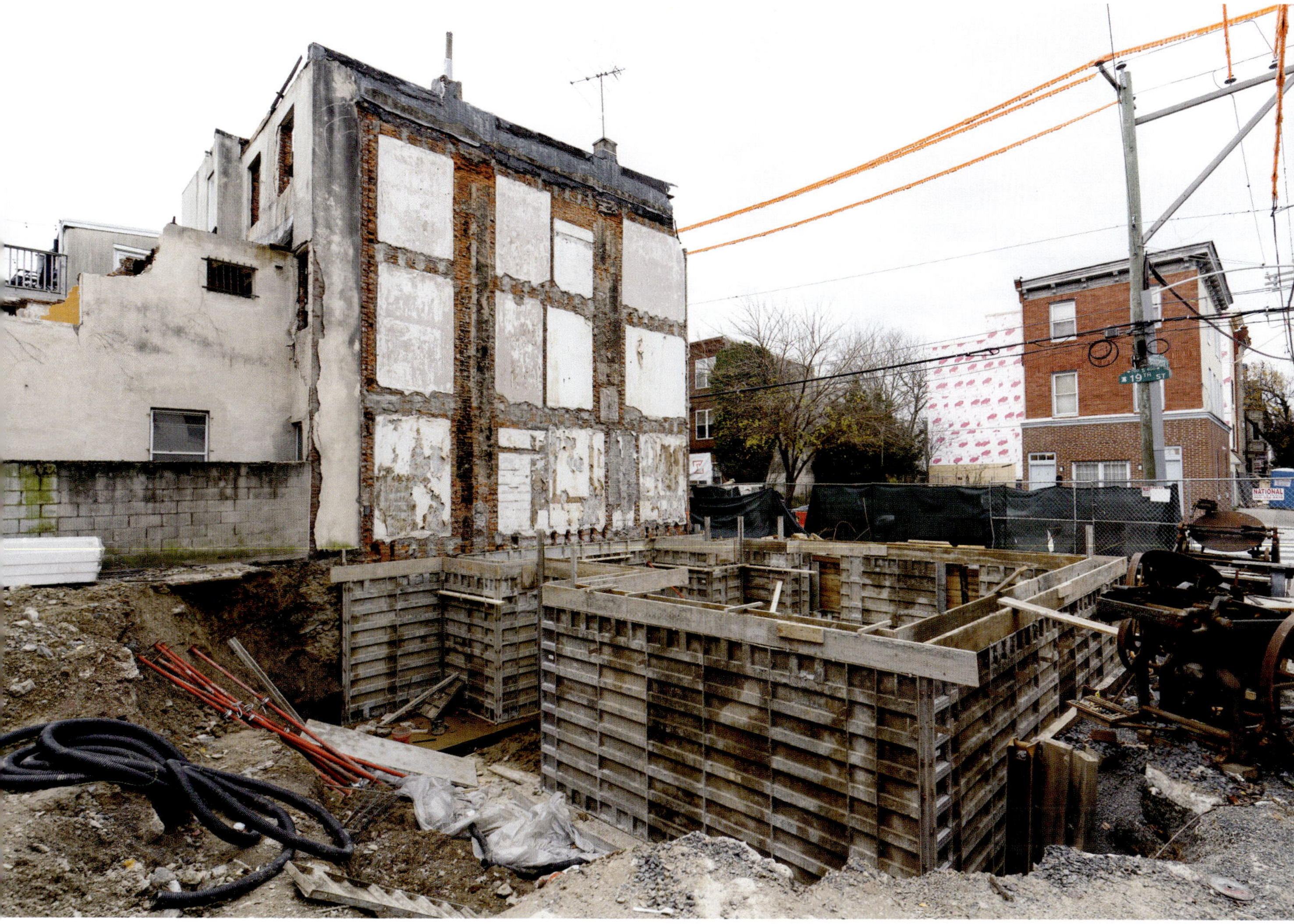

701 South 19th Street. (Photographed December 2, 2020.)

in August, the organization in September contracted $1,225 worth of alterations to fit out the building for its work.

The Foreign Mission Board operated out of the building for 105 years, deploying missions to the Canary Islands, Bermuda Islands, Senegal, Sierra Leone, and Liberia. The board's roots in Liberia went so deep that the country would eventually knight Reverend Jordan. "Spend Christmas in Liberia," read a typical board advertisement in Baptist publications. "Join the African cruise of 1921, endorsed by President King and the Liberian Plenary Commission."

The board issued its own publications, too, establishing a print shop at the rear of number 701 to promote its missions to Baptist audiences. (The building also included apartments off and on during the board's tenure.) Two of its printing presses—manufactured circa 1914, around the same time the board purchased the building—were exhumed when the building was demolished in 2020. For a time, the presses languished on the sidewalk next to the building ghost and its new construction in a sort of purgatory of their own. Their bulk and visible heft might explain why in 1940 the Foreign Mission Board had replaced the frame walls at the rear of the building with more substantial brick ones.

In 1955, the board expanded its operations next door, into 703 South 19th Street; it would make use of both properties for sixty-five more years, cultivating long-standing mission relationships that linked Philadelphia with communities in Africa, the Caribbean, and Central America—many of which the organization continues to maintain today. In 2019, having constructed countless buildings in developing countries, the board ceded its own building to a different sort of development. Faced with the Graduate Hospital neighborhood's insatiable appetite for new condominiums and townhouses, the Foreign Mission Board sold the building to a developer and decamped to West Philadelphia. On 19th Street, multifamily housing replaced its missions.

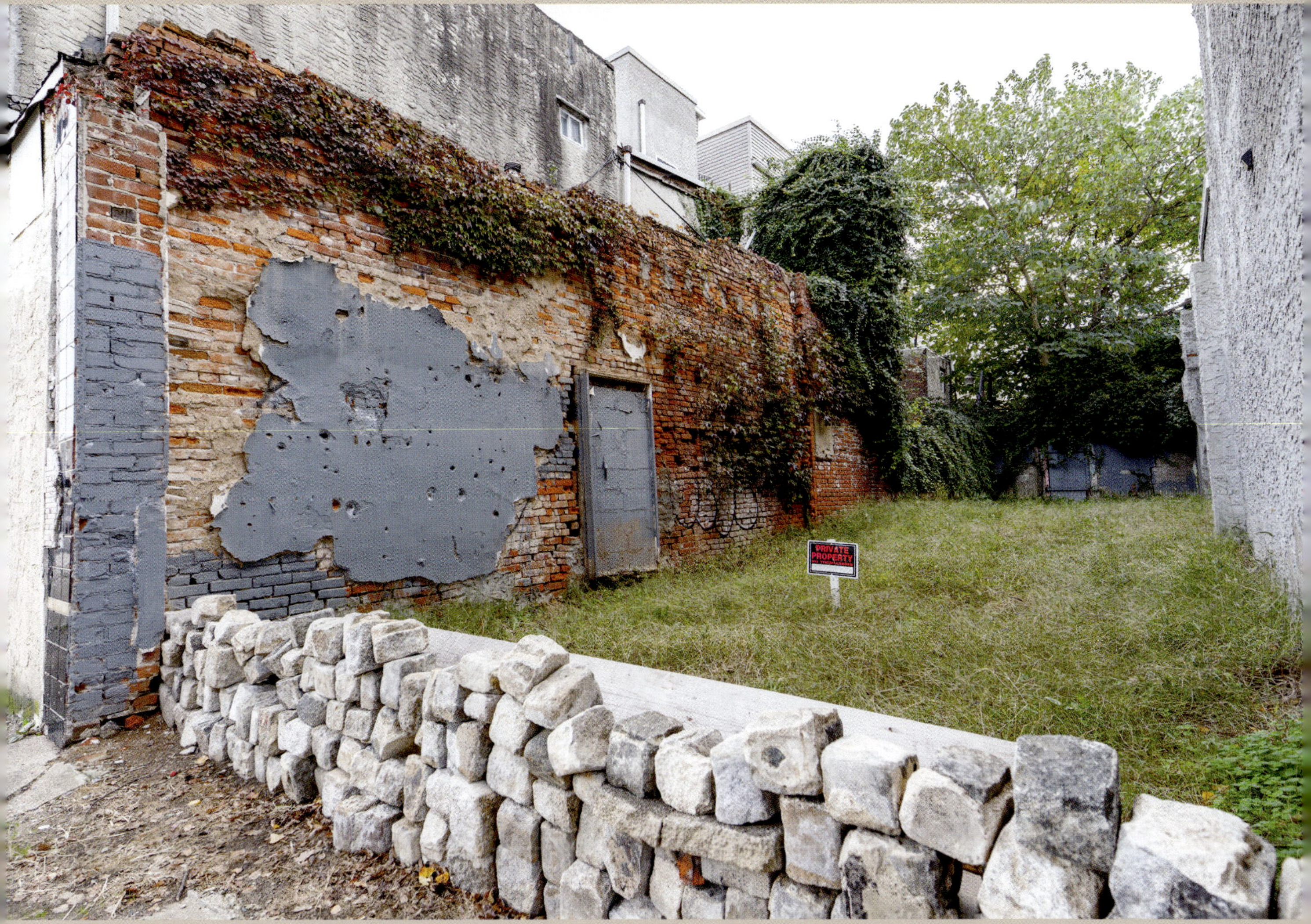

1702 Federal Street. (Photographed November 3, 2020.)

1431 Fitzwater Street

Constructed by 1862
Demolished in 2020

The story of the Curry women and their lives at 1431 Fitzwater Street requires a lot of speculation. Such is the nature of researching vernacular buildings and everyday Philadelphians—and women such as Susan, Isabelle, and Mary Curry in particular.

Susan Curry purchased the house in 1875, by which point it had been standing for a little more than a decade. She was a dressmaker, but beyond her occupation the record is sparse. What is known is that she sold the house again in 1877, to a woman named Jane Long, yet remained as a tenant. In 1881, a relation named Mary Curry joined her. Mary was a widow, having buried a husband named Samuel, but as with Susan's larger life story, the narrative of Mary's life before Fitzwater Street, and what brought her to number 1431, is ambiguous.

What was the relationship between the two women? They shared a last name, suggesting that somewhere in their family trees they shared a male relation, but the usual censuses, city directories, and other records have all been unhelpful, mostly because they barely include either woman. It seems likely that Susan was either Mary's mother-in-law or her sister-in-law—both of which would mean that Mary's husband Samuel was the common relation—or that Susan was Mary's daughter. Further tangling this family tree, a woman named Isabella Curry briefly joined Susan and Mary in 1876. Her age, relations, and occupation are all unknown (and seemingly unknowable).

For at least a few years, Susan and Mary shared the house (along with a handful of other tenants) and shared their work: Mary was also a dressmaker. Number 1431 Fitzwater Street must have had a constant stream of visitors, bringing piecework and patterns for the Curry women, and their rented rooms must have been heaped with fabric at all times.

Susan's time in the house trails off in contemporary records around 1880. Mary, meanwhile, lived there until her death in 1915. The house continued on without them, with plenty of other owners and tenants to fill their places. If the archival record were the sole narrator of 1431 Fitzwater Street, it would seem that the Curry women had hardly been there at all. But they were.

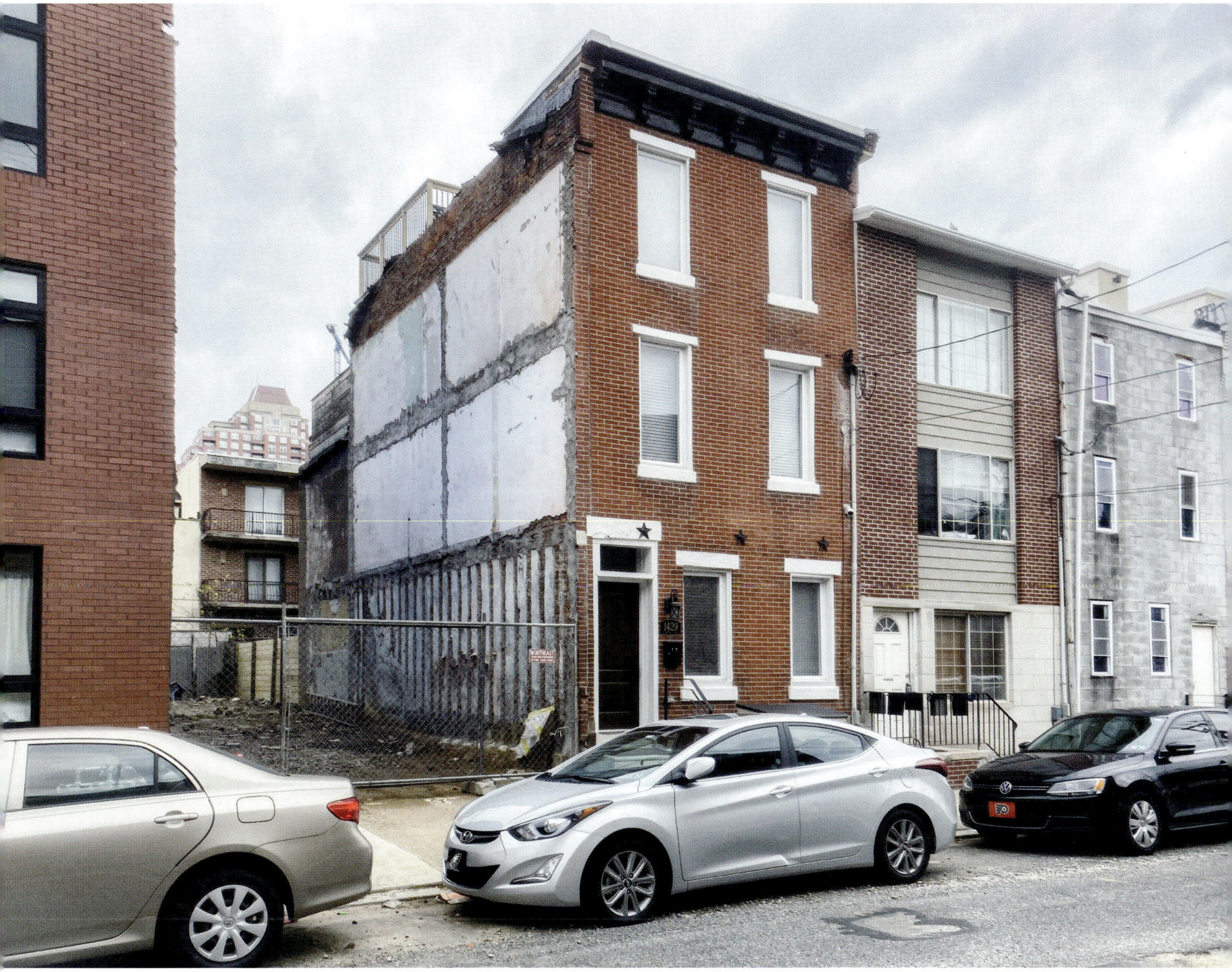

1431 Fitzwater Street. (Photographed December 2, 2020.)

1828 Christian Street

Constructed ca. 1864
Demolished in 2020

When twenty-one-year-old William Malloch left his house at 1828 Christian Street for the theater on April 27, 1892, he must have been expecting a carefree night of spectacle. Two nights before, the *Philadelphia Inquirer* had raved about the new production of *The Devil's Auction* at the Central Theatre on Walnut Street, calling it a "magnificent presentation [with] well deserved popularity":

> For a number of seasons, "The Devil's Auction" has been one of the most prominent spectacular productions of the country, and every season has seen it altered and improved, until it has reached such a state of perfection that further improvement seems entirely out of the question.

The newspaper went on to praise the show's stage sets ("magnificent works of the scenic artist's brush"), costumes ("as handsome as it is possible to make them"), and performers ("the dances and marches are of the most intricate nature"). The night Malloch attended, though, a devastating fire broke out, sparked and spread by those same sets, costumes, and choreographies, killing at least thirteen people and altering Malloch's own life trajectory.

Malloch would have been watching from the audience as the orchestra warmed up and a piece of scenery descended from the rafters onstage in preparation for the performance. As it was lowered, however, the backdrop bumped into a gaslight fixture, igniting an inferno of paint and canvas. Within minutes, the building was in flames up to its roof; the fire would eventually spread to the building next door, and the smoke would be visible from Trenton, New Jersey, thirty miles away.

William Malloch and the rest of the theater's occupants fled in panic. (It cannot have escaped them that this very same site had already seen three other major fires in the nineteenth century.) Audience members tried to flee through stairwells next to the stage, only to find themselves even closer to the fire. At least seven theatergoers and six cast members died in the blaze, while scores of other attendees and performers were injured by the flames, smoke inhalation, and ensuing stampede. William Malloch was among the injured; it is unclear whether he knew any of the dead.

Malloch was treated at Pennsylvania Hospital for burns on his hands and released to return home to Christian Street. He would live there for a few more years, taking in his mother, Sarah, when his father died in 1894. By 1898, at the latest, he had moved out of number 1828, starting fresh with a new address and, the following year, a new bride.

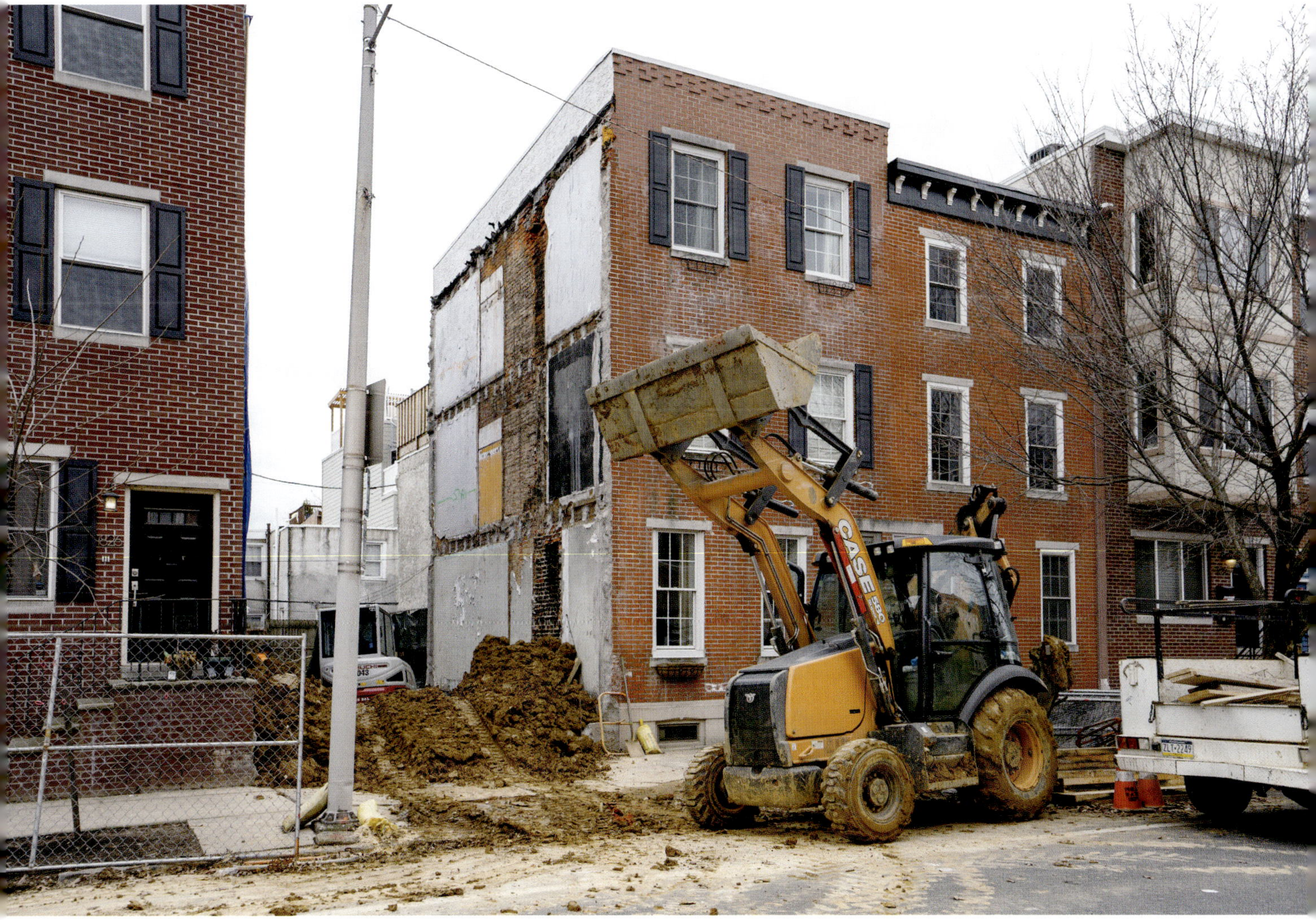

1828 Christian Street. (Photographed December 2, 2020.)

A machinist at the time of the Central Theatre fire, Malloch became an electrician in the years after it. Was this a relatively minor pivot among the trades? Or did the fire damage his hands so badly that he could no longer operate machinery? Of course, it's also darkly ironic to consider that a man who survived one of the worst theater fires in Philadelphia history—an inferno sparked by a lighting fixture—would ultimately take up work as an electrician.

South Philadelphia References

General Resources

Baist, G. Wm. *Baist's Atlas of the City of Philadelphia, Complete in One Volume*. Philadelphia: G. Wm. Baist, 1888. Athenaeum of Philadelphia, *Greater Philadelphia GeoHistory Network*. https://www.philageohistory.org/rdic-images/view-image.cfm/BST1888.Phila.040.Plate33.

Bromley, George. *Atlas of the City of Philadelphia*. Philadelphia: G. W. Bromley, 1895. Athenaeum of Philadelphia, *Greater Philadelphia GeoHistory Network*. http://www.philageohistory.org/tiles/viewer.

Bromley, George W., and Walter S. Bromley. *Atlas of the City of Philadelphia, Complete in One Volume, from Actual Surveys and Official Plans*. Philadelphia: G. W. Bromley, 1910. Athenaeum of Philadelphia, *Greater Philadelphia GeoHistory Network*. https://www.philageohistory.org/rdic-images/view-image.cfm/237%2DMP%2D022.

City Plans Division, Bureau of Surveys and Design, Department of Streets. *Philadelphia Land Use Map*. Philadelphia: Federal Works Progress Administration for Pennsylvania, 1962. Map Collection, Free Library of Philadelphia, *Greater Philadelphia GeoHistory Network*. http://www.philageohistory.org/rdic-images/view-image.cfm/LUM1962.Title.

Hopkins, G. M. *City Atlas of Philadelphia by Wards, Complete in Seven Volumes* (1875). Private collection of Matt Ainslie, *Greater Philadelphia GeoHistory Network*. http://www.philageohistory.org/tiles/viewer.

"Insurance Maps of Philadelphia, Pennsylvania, Volume 6" (online database). Sanborn Map Company, New York, 1916. *ProQuest Digital Sanborn Maps, 1867–1970*. https://digitalsanbornmaps.proquest.com/browse_maps/39/7881/38451/40225/536378?accountid=10977.

Plans and Registry Division, Bureau of Engineering Surveys and Zoning, Department of Public Works. *Philadelphia Land Use Map*. Philadelphia: Federal Works Progress Administration for Pennsylvania, 1942. Map Collection, Free Library of Philadelphia, *Greater Philadelphia GeoHistory Network*. http://www.philageohistory.org/rdic-images/view-image.cfm/LUM1942.Title.

"Sanborn Fire Insurance Map from Philadelphia, Philadelphia County, Pennsylvania, Volume 6" (online database). Sanborn Map Company, New York, [1916–1950]. *Library of Congress*. http://hdl.loc.gov/loc.gmd/g3824pm.g3824pm_g07905195001.

Smedley, Samuel. *Atlas of the City of Philadelphia*. Philadelphia: J. B. Lippincott, 1862. Map Collection, Free Library of Philadelphia, *Greater Philadelphia GeoHistory Network*. http://www.philageohistory.org/tiles/viewer.

Smith, Elvino V. *Atlas of the 2nd, 3rd, 4th, and 30th Wards of the City of Philadelphia* (1917). Athenaeum of Philadelphia, *Greater Philadelphia GeoHistory Network*. https://www.philageohistory.org/rdic-images/view-image.cfm/EVS1917.PhilaWards2_3_4_30.017.Plate14.

——. *Atlas of the 26th and 36th Wards of the City of Philadelphia* (1903). Athenaeum of Philadelphia, *Greater Philadelphia GeoHistory Network*, https://www.philageohistory.org/rdic-images/view-image.cfm/JLS1903.PhilaWards26_36.019.Plate15.

1600 South 24th Street

"Death Notices." *Philadelphia Inquirer*, August 11, 1981. https://www.newspapers.com/image/173917714.

"Deaths Elsewhere." *Philadelphia Inquirer*, May 1, 1955. https://www.newspapers.com/image/176162367.

Department of Records, Philadelphia City Archives. 1600 South 24th Street deed abstracts (map registry no. 12S190036). Various dates.

"For Sale." *Philadelphia Inquirer*, January 31, 1925. https://www.newspapers.com/image/171084909.

"Funeral Announcements." *Philadelphia Inquirer,* July 15, 2004. https://www.newspapers.com/image/200069872.
Nicholson, Jim. "Deaths: 'Gus' Sosangelis, 73, Grocer and Churchman." *Philadelphia Daily News,* August 9, 1996. https://www.newspapers.com/image/187192685.
"Obituary." *Philadelphia Inquirer,* July 17, 1962. https://www.newspapers.com/image/179076344.
"Oscar Mayer Smokie Links and Wieners at These Stores in Delaware Valley." *Philadelphia Inquirer,* October 1, 1959. https://www.newspapers.com/image/178436881.
"S. E. Sosangelis Dies, Food Chain Head, 83." *Philadelphia Inquirer,* May 16, 1972. https://www.newspapers.com/image/180032524.
"Settlement Effected for Sale of 1028 Chestnut St[reet]; $140,000 Dwelling Operation." *Philadelphia Inquirer,* July 28, 1909. https://www.newspapers.com/image/169069733.
"1600 S. 24th Street: Zoning Permit Documents." *City of Philadelphia Atlas.* Accessed January 10, 2023. https://s3.amazonaws.com/lni-zoning-pdfs/219-50245.pdf.
"Swift's Premium Dealers: Central Philadelphia." *Philadelphia Inquirer,* April 6, 1950. https://www.newspapers.com/image/173763872.
"U.S., City Directories, 1822–1995" (online database). Digital image s.v. "Bronfman, Abraham," 1915. *Ancestry.com.* https://www.ancestrylibrary.com/imageviewer/collections/2469/images/2725622?pid=1195566008&usePUB=true&_phsrc=VNq572&_phstart=successSource&usePUBJs=true.
———. Digital image s.v. "Doak, Samuel," 1914. *Ancestry.com.* https://www.ancestrylibrary.com/imageviewer/collections/2469/images/30896_161644-00101?pid=1436326087&usePUB=true&_phsrc=VNq572&_phstart=successSource&usePUBJs=true.
———. Digital image s.v. "Gelman, Frank," 1914. *Ancestry.com.* https://www.ancestrylibrary.com/discoveryui-content/view/1436318602:2469?tid=&pid=&queryId=322f36bf900cb05a524e8604e749025b&_phsrc=VNq572&_phstart=successSource.
———. Digital image s.v. "Susman, Joseph," 1915. *Ancestry.com.* https://www.ancestrylibrary.com/imageviewer/collections/2469/images/2725712?pid=1195610746&usePUB=true&_phsrc=VNq572&_phstart=successSource&usePUBJs=true.
"U.S. Federal Census" (online database). "Giorgio, Joseph," 1930. *Ancestry.com.* https://www.ancestrylibrary.com/imageviewer/collections/6224/images/4639460_01103?pid=54440493&usePUB=true&_phsrc=VNq577&_phstart=successSource&usePUBJs=true.
———. Digital image s.v. "Giorgio, Joseph," 1940. *Ancestry.com.* https://www.ancestrylibrary.com/imageviewer/collections/2442/images/M-T0627-03729-00912?pid=19936072&usePUB=true&_phsrc=VNq577&_phstart=successSource&usePUBJs=true.
———. Digital image s.v. "Marcolongo, Madalena," 1920. *Ancestry.com.* https://www.ancestrylibrary.com/imageviewer/collections/6061/images/4383803_00865?pid=52206836&usePUB=true&_phsrc=VNq581&_phstart=successSource&usePUBJs=true.
"U.S., World War I Draft Registration Cards, 1917–1918" (online database). Digital image s.v. "Giorgio, Guiseppe." *Ancestry.com.* https://www.ancestrylibrary.com/imageviewer/collections/6482/images/005270025_04251?pid=10240594&usePUB=true&_phsrc=VNq573&_phstart=successSource&usePUBJs=true.

1254–1256 South 18th Street

Department of Records, Philadelphia City Archives. 1254–1256 deed abstracts (map registry no. 8S190386). Various dates.
Shapiro, Howard S. "Giveaway of American Cheese Will Begin Tomorrow in Phila[delphia]." *Philadelphia Inquirer,* March 7, 1982. https://www.newspapers.com/image/174514627.
Sundberg, Walter. "Religious Trends in Twentieth-Century America." *Word and World* 20, no. 1 (Winter 2000): 22–31.
"1254–56 S. 18th Street: Zoning Permit Documents." *City of Philadelphia Atlas.* Accessed January 10, 2023. https://s3.amazonaws.com/lni-zoning-pdfs/219-37768.pdf.

1728 Federal Street

"Deaths." *Philadelphia Evening Ledger*, February 27, 1917. https://www.newspapers.com/image/162305723.

Department of Records, Philadelphia City Archives. 1728 Federal Street deed abstracts (map registry no. 8S180415). Various dates.

"Died." *Philadelphia Inquirer*, September 9, 1901. https://www.newspapers.com/image/168387643.

———. *Philadelphia Inquirer*, March 27, 1905. https://www.newspapers.com/image/168017000.

———. *Philadelphia Inquirer*, December 29, 1912. https://www.newspapers.com/image/168565293.

"Happy Builders." *Philadelphia Times*, June 10, 1891. https://www.newspapers.com/image/52227538.

"He Died like a Hero." *Philadelphia Inquirer*, January 26, 1889. https://www.newspapers.com/image/167247992.

"Mary Carr's Body Found." *Philadelphia Times*, May 23, 1891. https://www.newspapers.com/image/52227200.

Miller, Herman P., ed. "State Board of Undertakers." *Smull's Legislative Hand Book and Manual of the State of Pennsylvania*. Harrisburg: Wm. Stanley Ray, 1916. *Google Books*. https://www.google.com/books/edition/The_Pennsylvania_Manual/9Lo-AQAAMAAJ?hl=en&gbpv=1&dq=%22samuel+r.+foster%22+philadelphia&pg=PA85&printsec=frontcover.

"Pennsylvania, U.S., Death Certificates, 1803–1915" (online database). Digital image s.v. "Davis, Wm.," 1905. *Ancestry.com*. https://www.ancestrylibrary.com/discoveryui-content/view/824912:2535?tid=&pid=&queryId=1496064566da06aa41b00e42eaed400e&_phsrc=VNq570&_phstart=successSource.

"Pennsylvania, U.S., Death Certificates, 1906–1969" (online database). Digital image s.v. "Foster, Samuel R.," 1943. *Ancestry.com*. https://www.ancestrylibrary.com/imageviewer/collections/5164/images/42342_2421401696_0643-02680?ssrc=pt&treeid=16428480&personid=1741006402&hintid=&usePUB=true&usePUBJs=true&pId=4132193.

"Samuel R. Foster, Undertaker." *Catholic Charities Review* 5, no. 10 (December 1921): n.p. *Google Books*. https://www.google.com/books/edition/The_Catholic_Charities_Review/-3QXAAAAYAAJ?hl=en&gbpv=1&dq=%22samuel+r.+foster%22+philadelphia&pg=PA317-IA5&printsec=frontcover.

"Undertakers Lectured or Fined for Violating Health Rules—Urging Action on the Boulevard." *Philadelphia Inquirer*, November 18, 1891. https://www.newspapers.com/image/168406017.

"U.S., City Directories, 1822–1995" (online database). Digital image s.v. "Foster, Samuel R.," 1878. *Ancestry.com*. https://www.ancestrylibrary.com/discoveryui-content/view/176035357:2469?tid=&pid=&queryId=89ac1ea8fb4aca579dddde4d83c273bd&_phsrc=VNq566&_phstart=successSource.

———. Digital image s.v. "Foster, Samuel R.," 1880. *Ancestry.com*. https://www.ancestrylibrary.com/discoveryui-content/view/178460313:2469?tid=&pid=&queryId=89ac1ea8fb4aca579dddde4d83c273bd&_phsrc=VNq566&_phstart=successSource.

———. Digital image s.v. "Foster, Samuel R.," 1888. *Ancestry.com*. https://www.ancestrylibrary.com/imageviewer/collections/2469/images/2872612?pId=178038194.

"U.S. Federal Census" (online database). Digital image s.v. "Foster, Samuel R," 1920. *Ancestry.com*. https://www.ancestrylibrary.com/discoveryui-content/view/52195452:6061?ssrc=pt&tid=16428480&pid=1741006402.

———. Digital image s.v. "Foster, Samuel R.," 1930. *Ancestry.com*. https://www.ancestrylibrary.com/discoveryui-content/view/124426788:6224?ssrc=pt&tid=16428480&pid=1741006402.

701 South 19th Street

"Advance Construction News." *Philadelphia Real Estate Record and Builders' Guide*, June 7, 1939. *Greater Philadelphia GeoHistory Network*. http://www.philageohistory.org/rdic-images/view-book-uv.cfm/PhilaBuildersGuide_v54_1939#?ft=&q=%22se%20cor%22%20%2B%2219th%20and%20bainbridge%22&c=&m=&s=&cv=88&xywh=5077%2C269%2C2497%2C1688.

“Alterations and Additions.” *Philadelphia Real Estate Record and Builders’ Guide*, September 29, 1915. *Greater Philadelphia GeoHistory Network*. http://www.philageohistory.org/rdic-images/view-book-uv.cfm/PhilaBuildersGuide_v30_1915#?ft=&q=%22701%20south%20nineteenth%22&c=&m=&s=&cv=784&xywh=3767%2C2182%2C2186%2C1314.
Department of Records, Philadelphia City Archives. 701 South 19th Street deed abstracts (map registry nos. 5S070352, 5S070055). Various dates.
“Died.” *Philadelphia Inquirer*, October 19, 1908. https://www.newspapers.com/image/168426283.
———. *Philadelphia Inquirer*, August 30, 1912. https://www.newspapers.com/image/169071050.
“Directory, Prepared by the Bureau of Statistics and Research; Baptist National Convention, 24—Foreign Mission Board of the National Baptist Convention.” In *Foreign Missions Year Book of North America*, edited by Burton St. John. New York: Committee of Reference and Counsel of the Foreign Missions Conference of North America, 1919. *Google Books*. https://www.google.com/books/edition/Foreign_Missions_Year_Book_of_North_Amer/mUFQAQAAMAAJ?hl=en&gbpv=1&dq=%22701+s+19th%22+philadelphia&pg=PA93&printsec=frontcover.
“Easter Is Coming.” *The Crisis* 11, no. 6 (April 1916): 282. *Google Books*. https://www.google.com/books/edition/The_Crisis/MAIcSWRw5ggC?hl=en&gbpv=1&bsq=%22701%20s%2019th%22.
Foreign Mission Board, National Baptist Convention. “About Us.” Accessed May 23, 2023. https://www.nbcforeignmissions.org/about-us.
Haas, Kimberly. “A Building Demolished, but the Mission Continues.” *Hidden City Philadelphia*, February 8, 2021. https://hiddencityphila.org/2021/02/a-building-demolished-but-the-mission-continues.
Jordan, Lewis G. “The National Baptist Convention.” *Negro Baptist History U.S.A.* Nashville: Sunday School Publishing Board, 1930. *HathiTrust*. https://hdl.handle.net/2027/wu.89064059140.
“Male Help Wanted.” *Philadelphia Inquirer*, August 13, 1898. https://www.newspapers.com/image/167934130.
“Missions Gain, Baptists Are Told.” *Philadelphia Inquirer*, September 10, 1950. https://www.newspapers.com/image/173310038.
Moses, W. H. *The White Peril*. Philadelphia: Lisle-Carey, [1919]. *HathiTrust*. https://hdl.handle.net/2027/emu.010000212007.
National Baptist Convention. “History of the National Baptist Convention, USA, Inc.” Accessed May 23, 2023. https://www.nationalbaptist.com/about-nbc/our-history.
“Points from the Police.” *Philadelphia Inquirer*, April 11, 1884. https://www.newspapers.com/image/167592151.
“701 S. 19th Street: Zoning Permit Documents.” *City of Philadelphia Atlas*. Accessed January 10, 2023. https://s3.amazonaws.com/lni-zoning-pdfs/219-39674.pdf.
“Spend Christmas in Liberia.” *The Crisis* 22, no. 4 (August 1921): 231. *Google Books*. https://www.google.com/books/edition/Crisis/FgtFAQAAMAAJ?hl=en&gbpv=1&bsq=%22701%20s%2019th%22%20.
“U.S., City Directories, 1822–1995” (online database). Digital image s.v. “Young, Charles,” 1870. *Ancestry.com*. https://www.ancestrylibrary.com/discoveryui-content/view/197543249:2469?tid=&pid=&queryId=8d606399f977aedda2776435a608687d&_phsrc=VNq516&_phstart=successSource.

1431 Fitzwater Street

Department of Records, Philadelphia City Archives. 1431 Fitzwater Street deed abstracts (map registry no. 5S050238). Various dates.
“Died.” *Philadelphia Inquirer*, November 9, 1915. https://www.newspapers.com/image/169005204.
“U.S., City Directories, 1822–1995” (online database). Digital image s.v. “Curry, Isabella,” 1876. *Ancestry.com*. https://www.ancestrylibrary.com/discoveryui-content/view/176694230:2469?tid=&pid=&queryId=4abfa8e2d009fb36a8420e2625dddfde&_phsrc=VNq523&_phstart=successSource.

———. Digital image s.v. "Curry, Mary," 1881. *Ancestry.com*. https://www.ancestrylibrary.com/discoveryui-content/view/145037491:2469?tid=&pid=&queryId=4abfa8e2d009fb36a8420e2625dddfde&_phsrc=VNq523&_phstart=successSource.

———. Digital image s.v. "Curry, Mary," 1886. *Ancestry.com*. https://www.ancestrylibrary.com/discoveryui-content/view/172804579:2469?tid=&pid=&queryId=4abfa8e2d009fb36a8420e2625dddfde&_phsrc=VNq523&_phstart=successSource.

———. Digital image s.v. "Curry, Mary," 1887. *Ancestry.com*. https://www.ancestrylibrary.com/discoveryui-content/view/145290417:2469?tid=&pid=&queryId=4abfa8e2d009fb36a8420e2625dddfde&_phsrc=VNq523&_phstart=successSource.

———. Digital image s.v. "Curry, Susan," 1877. *Ancestry.com*. https://www.ancestrylibrary.com/discoveryui-content/view/176844216:2469?tid=&pid=&queryId=4abfa8e2d009fb36a8420e2625dddfde&_phsrc=VNq523&_phstart=successSource.

———. Digital image s.v. "Long, John," 1878. *Ancestry.com*. https://www.ancestrylibrary.com/discoveryui-content/view/176082618:2469?tid=&pid=&queryId=4abfa8e2d009fb36a8420e2625dddfde&_phsrc=VNq523&_phstart=successSource.

1828 Christian Street

Note: *William Malloch's name is alternatively spelled in the records as Mallach, Mallack, and Malloch. I use Malloch, as that is the spelling used on his death certificate.*

"The Central." *Philadelphia Inquirer*, April 26, 1892. https://www.newspapers.com/image/168458837.

"Chest St. Opera House Special." *Philadelphia Inquirer*, May 1, 1892. https://www.newspapers.com/image/168274054.

"Dead in the Ruins." *Philadelphia Times*, April 30, 1892. https://www.newspapers.com/image/52832548.

Department of Records, Philadelphia City Archives. 1828 Christian Street deed abstracts (map registry no. 7S050041). Various dates.

"Echoes of the Central Theatre Fire." *Philadelphia Inquirer*, May 1, 1892. https://www.newspapers.com/image/168273703.

"1828 Christian Street: Zoning Permit Documents." *City of Philadelphia Atlas*. Accessed January 10, 2023. http://s3.amazonaws.com/eclipse-docs-pdfs/zoning/ZP-2020-004465.pdf.

"Flames Ravage a Very Notable Neighborhood." *Philadelphia Inquirer*, April 28, 1892. https://www.newspapers.com/image/168459227.

"Flames Spread Ruin." *Philadelphia Times*, April 28, 1892. https://www.newspapers.com/image/52832458.

"Jersey News of All Sorts." *Philadelphia Inquirer*, May 1, 1892. https://www.newspapers.com/image/168273818.

Kyriakodis, Harry. "Blazing Ballerinas and a Rampaging Elephant at 807 Walnut Street." *Hidden City Philadelphia*, May 7, 2013. https://hiddencityphila.org/2013/05/blazing-ballerinas-and-a-rampaging-elephant-at-807-walnut-street.

"Pennsylvania, U.S., Death Certificates, 1906–1969" (online database). Digital image s.v. "Malloch, William H.," 1962. *Ancestry.com*. https://www.ancestrylibrary.com/imageviewer/collections/5164/images/42410_2421401696_0739-04607?treeid=&personid=&hintid=&queryId=be893ab1d8f97fea79aa34273235334e&usePUB=true&_phsrc=VNq552&_phstart=successSource&usePUBJs=true&pId=5755018.

"Philadelphia, Pennsylvania, U.S., Marriage Index, 1885–1951" (online database). Digital image s.v. "Malloch, William H.," 1899. *Ancestry.com*. https://www.ancestrylibrary.com/discoveryui-content/view/634703:2536?tid=&pid=&queryId=be893ab1d8f97fea79aa34273235334e&_phsrc=VNq552&_phstart=successSource.

"Seven Dead or Missing." *New York Times*, April 29, 1892. https://timesmachine.nytimes.com/timesmachine/1892/04/29/104126713.html?pageNumber=6.

"U.S., City Directories, 1822–1995" (online database). Digital image s.v. "Mallach, William," 1894.

Ancestry.com. https://www.ancestrylibrary.com/discoveryui-content/view/175387508:2469?tid=&pid=&queryId=0584fa3b8f8400f9c28379e55518d75c&_phsrc=VNq553&_phstart=successSource.
———. Digital image s.v. "Mallock, William H.," 1893. *Ancestry.com.* https://www.ancestrylibrary.com/discoveryui-content/view/174097567:2469?tid=&pid=&queryId=823688c0c61bca8cdf81ff18f926972a&_phsrc=VNq564&_phstart=successSource.
"U.S. Federal Census" (online database). Digital image s.v. "Mallack, William," 1900. *Ancestry.com.* https://www.ancestrylibrary.com/discoveryui-content/view/68842005:7602?tid=&pid=&queryId=be893ab1d8f97fea79aa34273235334e&_phsrc=VNq552&_phstart=successSource.
———. Digital image s.v. "Malloch, William H.," 1930. *Ancestry.com.* https://www.ancestrylibrary.com/discoveryui-content/view/124427065:6224?tid=&pid=&queryId=65c4dfa3ec4edfc38b340bd70001f8a5&_phsrc=VNq557&_phstart=successSource.
———. Digital image s.v. "Mallock, William H," 1920. *Ancestry.com.* https://www.ancestrylibrary.com/discoveryui-content/view/52469003:6061?tid=&pid=&queryId=be893ab1d8f97fea79aa34273235334e&_phsrc=VNq552&_phstart=successSource.

WEST PHILADELPHIA

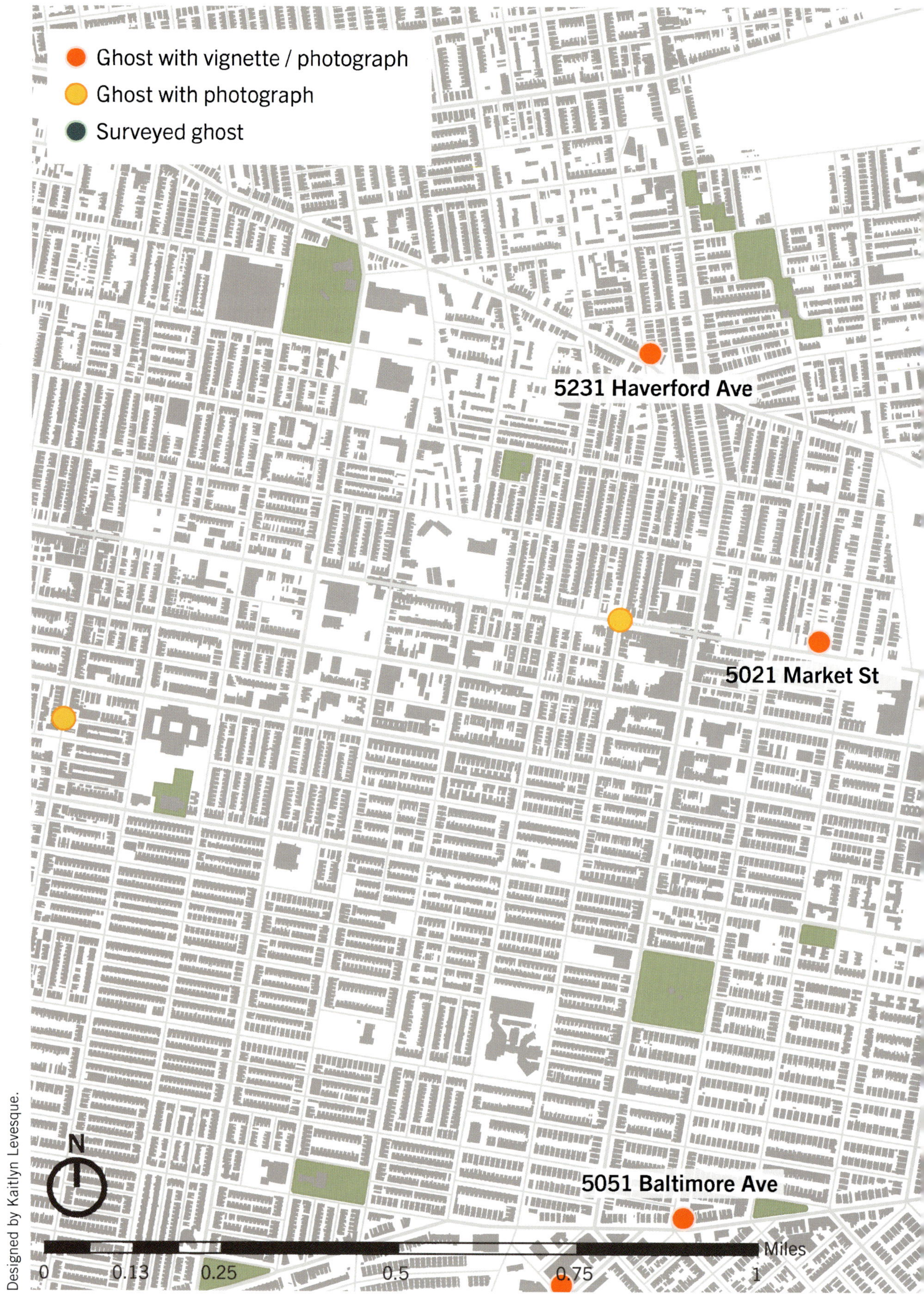

SOUTHWEST PHILADELPHIA

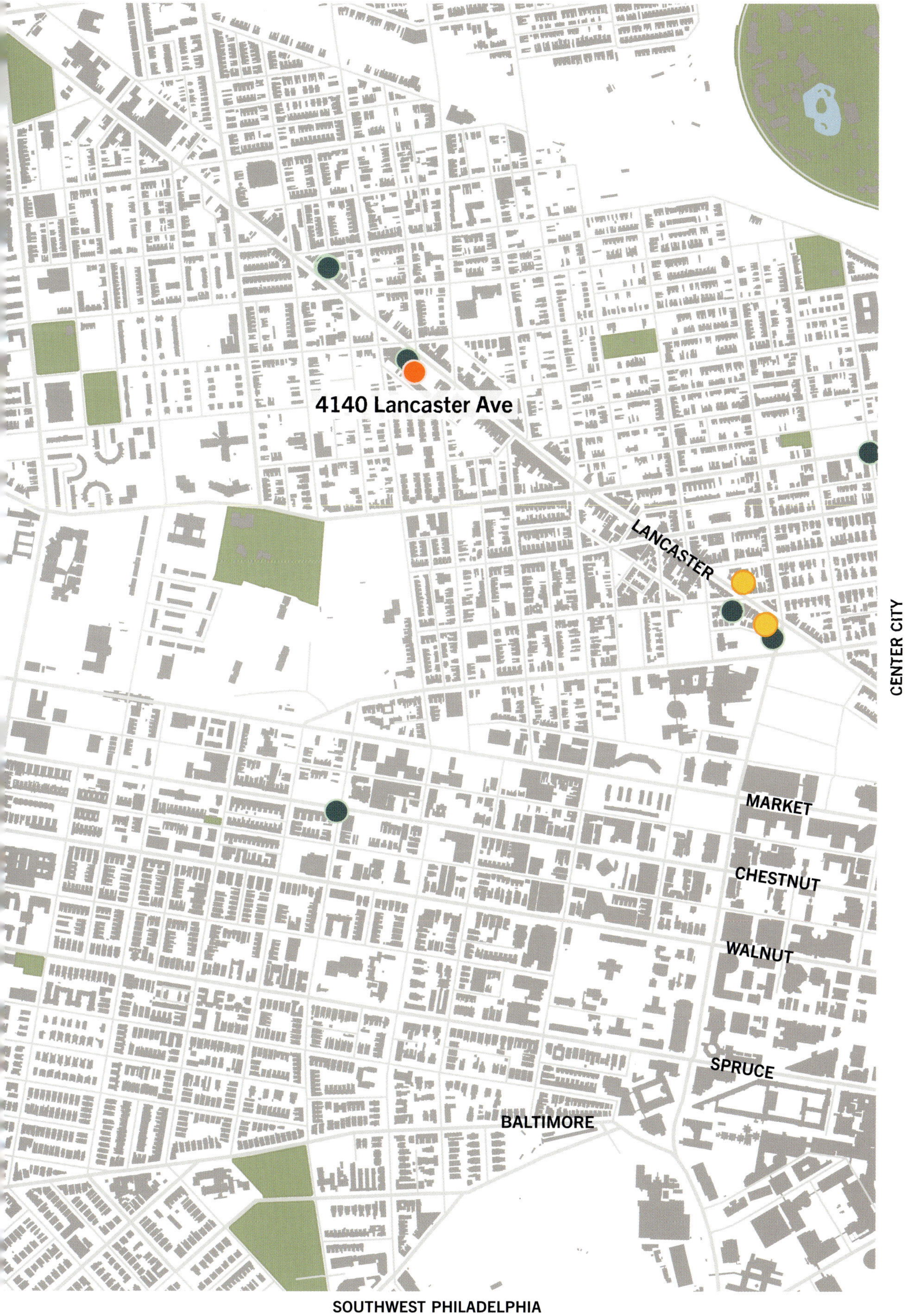
4140 Lancaster Ave
LANCASTER
MARKET
CHESTNUT
WALNUT
SPRUCE
BALTIMORE
CENTER CITY
SOUTHWEST PHILADELPHIA

West Philadelphia's building ghosts are easy to get to, and easy to spot. At any given moment, they tend to be arrayed along the major corridors that fan out from 30th and Market streets, readily accessible via subway, bus, or trolley. All too often, they reveal themselves on the truncated side of a former twin, coming into view as one rounds a corner and realizes that a home's roofline was not always so oddly cropped. Within the atlas of the city's building ghosts, it is this interplay between transit and twins that characterizes West Philadelphia in particular.

Until the early nineteenth century, West Philadelphia had neither the dense population nor the overlapping land uses to justify entire blocks of houses. It had none of the conditions, then, to produce building ghosts. Houses were generally too large, and lot sizes too generous, to result in the party walls that generate ghosts.

With the advent of the omnibus and the subsequent introduction of streetcars in the first half of the twentieth century, the population of Center City saw a release valve to the west, spilling over the Schuylkill River to build out what had been, to that point, mostly villages and farmland.[1] Sensing an opportunity, transit companies established routes throughout West Philadelphia, angling them out from the Schuylkill like hands on a clock that began at the river's bridge crossings and ended wherever the real estate demand petered out (boundaries that kept shifting in the nineteenth and early twentieth centuries, until they eventually reached the city's western limits). With the commuter lines in place, West Philadelphia's population increased tenfold in the second half of the nineteenth century, exploding from 13,265 residents in 1850 to 129,110 in 1900.[2]

1. Cynthia Rose Hamilton, *West Philadelphia Streetcar Suburb Historic District*, National Register of Historic Places Nomination, National Park Service, Washington, DC, 1998, 8-3.

2. West Philadelphia Community History Center, "West Philadelphia: The History," University Archives and Records Center, University of Pennsylvania, Philadelphia, 2008, https://westphillyhistory.archives.upenn.edu/history/chapter-2.

The boom was made possible by profound changes in transportation and was popularized by contemporary American movements that envisioned an ideal suburban lifestyle just beyond the reach of industrialized downtowns. (The consolidation of the city's original extents and its surrounding county in 1854 also helped, extending municipal services to the annexed sections such as West Philadelphia.[3]) Initially, the transformation from farmland to city was led, ironically, by horses; beginning in the 1830s, omnibuses replaced earlier coaches as a new form of transportation, but like their predecessors, they were pulled by horses. Later, in the 1850s, railroad companies introduced streetcars, which shuttled commuters around on tracks (a more efficient option than simply driving the omnibuses on rutted dirt roads), but once again, horses drew the vehicles. Eventually, the electric trolley was developed in the 1880s, giving the horses a break, and the Market Street elevated rail line opened in 1907, adding subway service to the network of public transportation that linked West Philadelphia with Center City.[4]

With each successive transit option, residential development lined up along the routes; the proximity was the point. First, the tracks reached Haverford Avenue, then Woodland, Lancaster, Baltimore, and other thoroughfares.[5] Developers staked out new homes, leaning on the twin house plan in particular.[6] Not as large and wealthy as the single-family detached houses constructed earlier in the nineteenth century, and not as modest and compressed as a typical rowhouse, the transit-adjacent twin house was a sales pitch for middle-class buyers, seeming to say: "This home is dense enough to be affordable in the city, but spaced out enough to give you a nice suburban life. We know you need a job (you're not wealthy enough not to), but this house's streetcar connections will get you to work quickly." West Philadelphia was thus a model of transit-oriented development in the late nineteenth and early twentieth centuries, defined by the trolley lines and twins that depended on each other.

In the decades since the neighborhood's explosive growth, it has seen plenty of transit-oriented demolition, too. In wave after wave of "renewal"—including the whitewashing that cleared out the community of Black Bottom to make way for University City, and countless other examples of segregated erasure and replacement—West Philadelphia redevelopers capitalized on those same trolley connections. It is unsurprising, then, that West Philadelphia's building ghosts bear out the same historical throughlines that have characterized its neighborhood fabric since the mid-nineteenth century: inevitably close to a streetcar or subway track, these ghosts are disproportionately associated with lopped-off twins made into singles.

3. Ibid.

4. Hamilton, *West Philadelphia Streetcar Suburb Historic District*, 8-10–8-13.

5. West Philadelphia Community History Center, "West Philadelphia."

6. Anne E. Krulikowski, "Twin Houses," *Encyclopedia of Greater Philadelphia*, accessed May 4, 2023, https://philadelphiaencyclopedia.org/essays/twin-houses.

Each ghost of a twin (can it still be called a twin?) is odd and omissive, left with just half of its original form. Its roofline ends suddenly; its floor plan looks unfinished (because it is). These building ghosts are unambiguous symbols of loss—even more potent than the simpler ghosts of boxy rowhouses.

Yet for all the missing structures that West Philadelphia's ghosts make visible, they are also a reminder of what remains. If we didn't have these ghosts—if their twins hadn't been spared from the wrecking ball—we would lack key evidence of the infrastructure, architectural character, social ties, and sheer potential that drove the growth of West Philadelphia in the past and continue to direct its present and future. Yes, these ghosts betray that fact that something has been dismantled, but they also flaunt the opportunities that are still intact. Moreover, the mere presence of these ghosts demands some measure of responsibility when it comes to future development, since the ghosts and their associated buildings (however asymmetrical they may be) stand in the way of wholesale clearance and erasure of what came before. Maybe West Philadelphia's ghosts offer a provocation, then: How can we—how *should* we—build on our building ghosts?

5021 Market Street

Constructed ca. 1896
Demolished in 2020

Number 5021 Market Street was the last place Lillie Wager saw her husband, Harry. Theirs was a rough marriage, and once he walked out the front door one day around 1937, Lillie lost all trace of him. So one day she walked out the door, too. She boarded the elevated train that stopped a block from the house and rode it five stops down to City Hall. There, she told Sheriff William Hamilton Jr. about Harry and how he'd hurt her long before deserting her. She didn't know where Harry was, but she knew she wanted a divorce.

The first announcement ran in the newspaper on January 7, 1938: "To Harry Taylor Wager, late of 5021 Market Street, Philadelphia, Pennsylvania." The notice ran three more times that year, clinging each time to 5021 Market Street as the last known place where Harry had lived. (Perhaps if Harry had returned home, she wouldn't have had to bide so much time. But did she really want him to turn up on the doorstep?) By February 1939, after thirteen months of waiting for her abusive husband, Lillie and her attorney published one last announcement:

> FINAL RULE FOR DIVORCE
>
> To Harry Taylor Wager, present residence is unknown, but the last known residence was 5021 Market Street, Philadelphia, Pa. You are hereby notified that a final rule for divorce . . . has been granted against you at the suit of Lillie M. Wager, your wife, which will be heard . . . on Friday, the 17th day of March, A.D. 1939.

The notice garnered as little response as the others, and on March 19, 1939, a fragment of an update ran on page 10 of the Sunday morning paper: "The following decrees of divorce were handed down yesterday: Lillie M. from Harry Taylor Wager; David M. from Elizabeth Clements; Emily Morelli from . . ." It was done, and Lillie moved on.

Three years later, Harry Taylor Wager registered for the draft at the onset of World War II. At forty-seven, he was unlikely to be called for service, but he filled out the registration card, as required. Halfway down the card, question number 7 asked for "a person who will always know your address." Harry wrote his father's name. Where the form asked for his own address, he printed in large, clear lettering: "5021 Market Street."

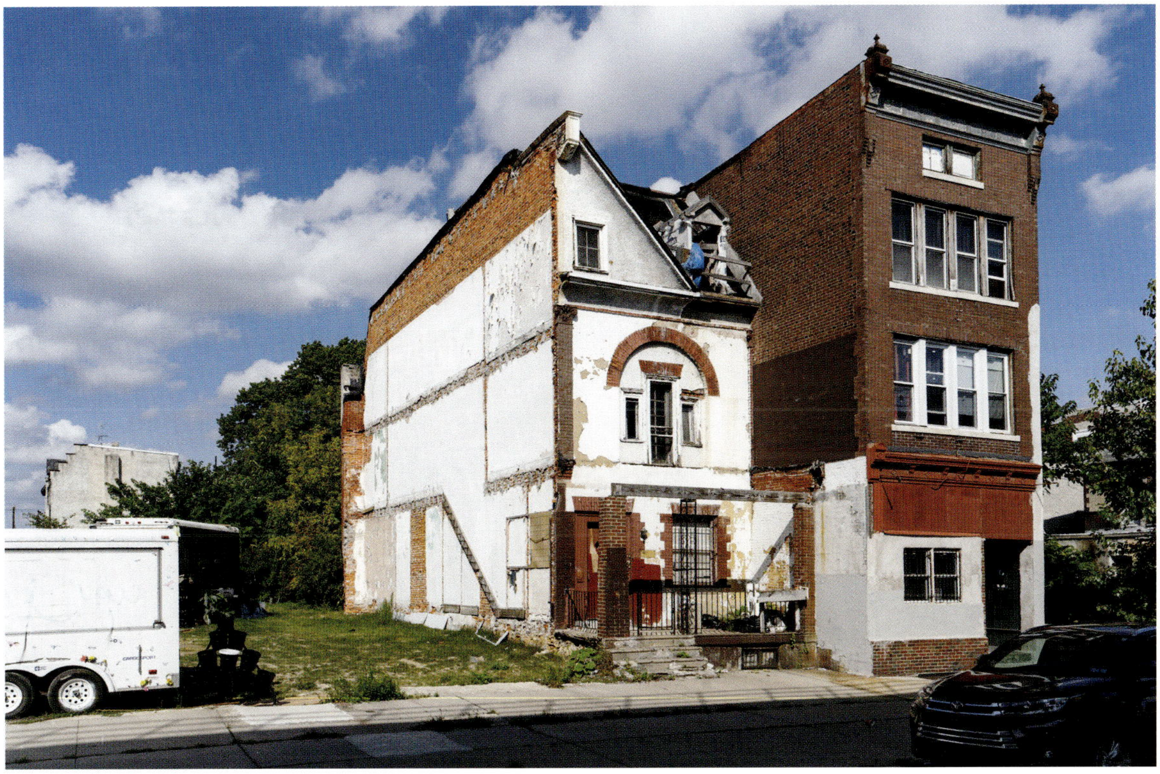

5021 Market Street. (Photographed September 28, 2020.)

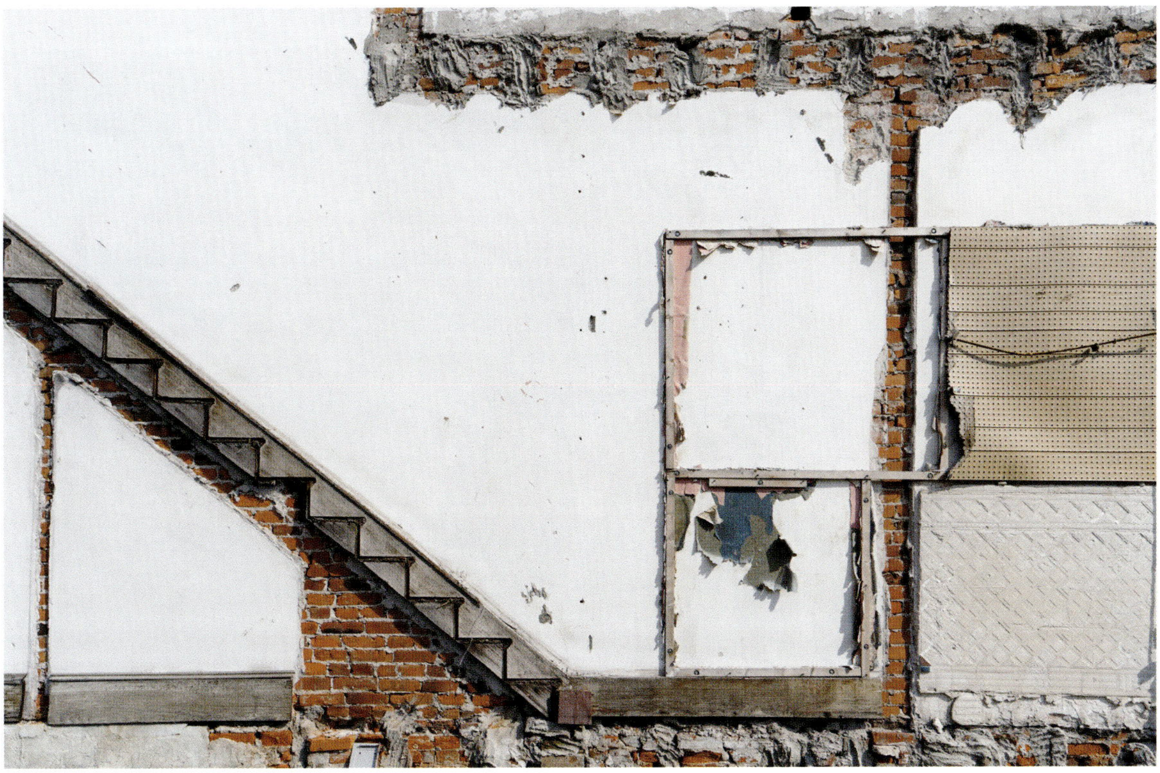

Detail of 5021 Market Street. (Photographed September 28, 2020.)

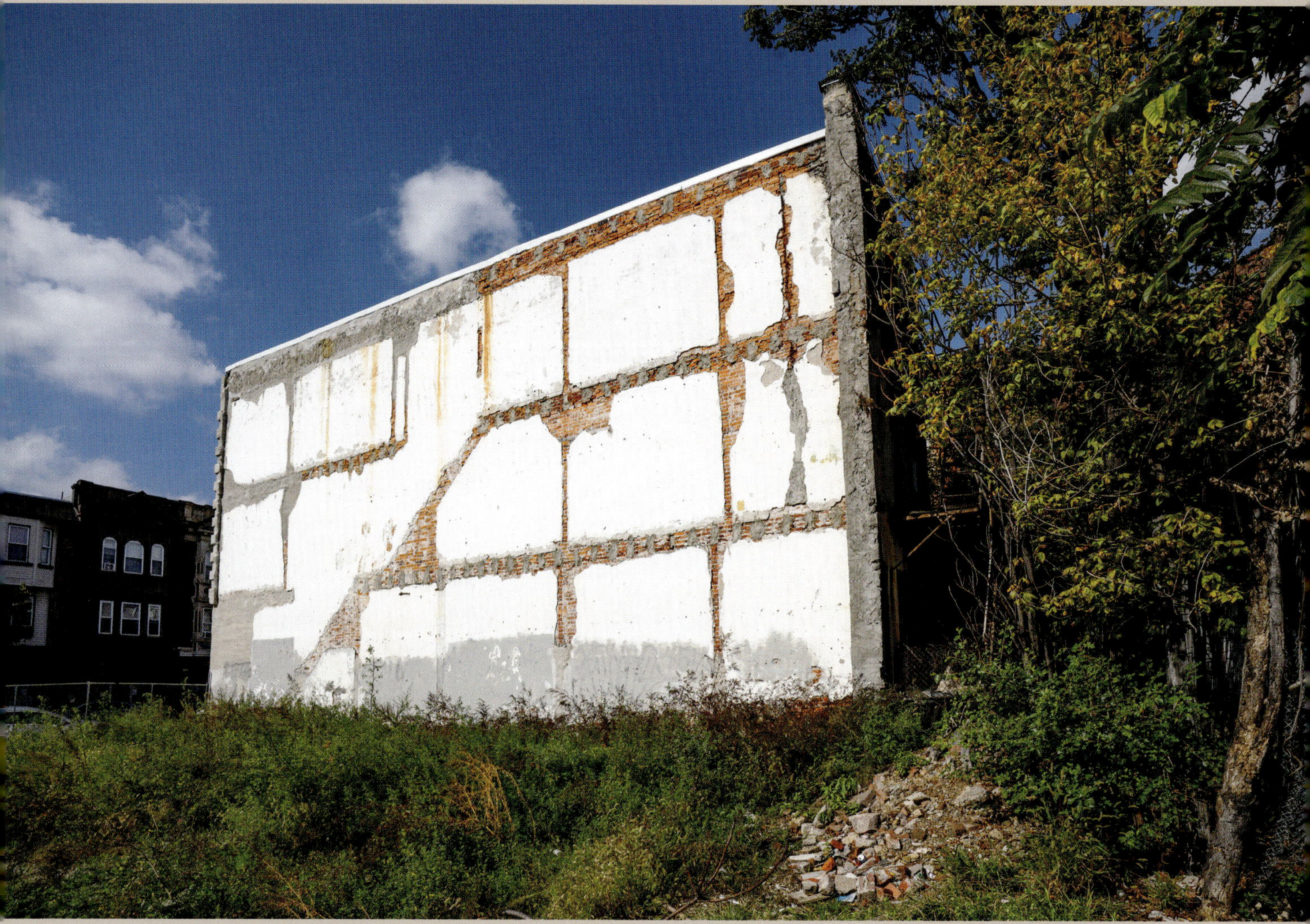

225 South 60th Street. (Photographed September 28, 2020.)

5051 Baltimore Avenue

Constructed ca. 1901
Demolished in 2012

Rose Pollon and her family first settled into the gambrel-roofed rowhouse at 5051 Baltimore Avenue around 1915. The building's distinctive design—mirrored in its brick neighbors, all constructed at the turn of the twentieth century—must have served the Pollons well, calling attention to their dry goods business on the first floor. With seven living children (of the nine to whom she had given birth), Rose and her husband, Louis, needed their business to fare well. The Yiddish-speaking family had journeyed all the way from Russia (or some unnamed Russian territory) in 1903 in hopes of such prospects.

Between 1915 and 1920, the city directories reflected a simple orbit to the Pollons' lives at 5051: the parents maintained the store, and their children became adults; some worked in the family business, while others gravitated toward trades elsewhere in the city. Their son Alex, for instance, was an electrician on Hog Island when he wasn't serving in World War I. Joseph, meanwhile, worked for Bell Telephone. Throughout these years, several of the Pollon children migrated in and out of the upper floors of 5051, taking up residence with their parents until (as was true for a few of them) they married and moved out.

The Pollons were renters for these first five years, leasing the store and house from Aaron and Rosa Sabel. But by 1920, Rose had saved enough money to purchase the building from her landlords. (Hers was the only name on the deed, for some reason; Louis's name did not appear.) She held on to the property and the storefront even after her family moved in the mid-1920s to Catharine Street nearby.

In 1928, Louis died. Coupled with the stock market crash the following year and the onset of the Great Depression, the loss of Louis apparently spurred a downfall of sorts for the Pollons. In 1932, Rose lost the property in a sheriff's sale. The Famous Building and Loan Association took ownership, and Rose was forced to run her store as a tenant once again.

Over the next five years, however, Rose clawed her way back to financial stability. With the help of her son Alex, she managed to repurchase 5051 Baltimore Avenue from the Famous Building and Loan Association in 1937, reclaiming the title from the same institution to which she'd lost it just a few years earlier.

Once again, though, life was unkind to Rose. Just two years after he had helped his mother buy back their property, Alex Pollon died suddenly in 1939 of a coronary thrombosis. It's little wonder, then, that by 1950 Rose had sold 5051 Baltimore Avenue and quit Philadelphia, following one of her other children to California.

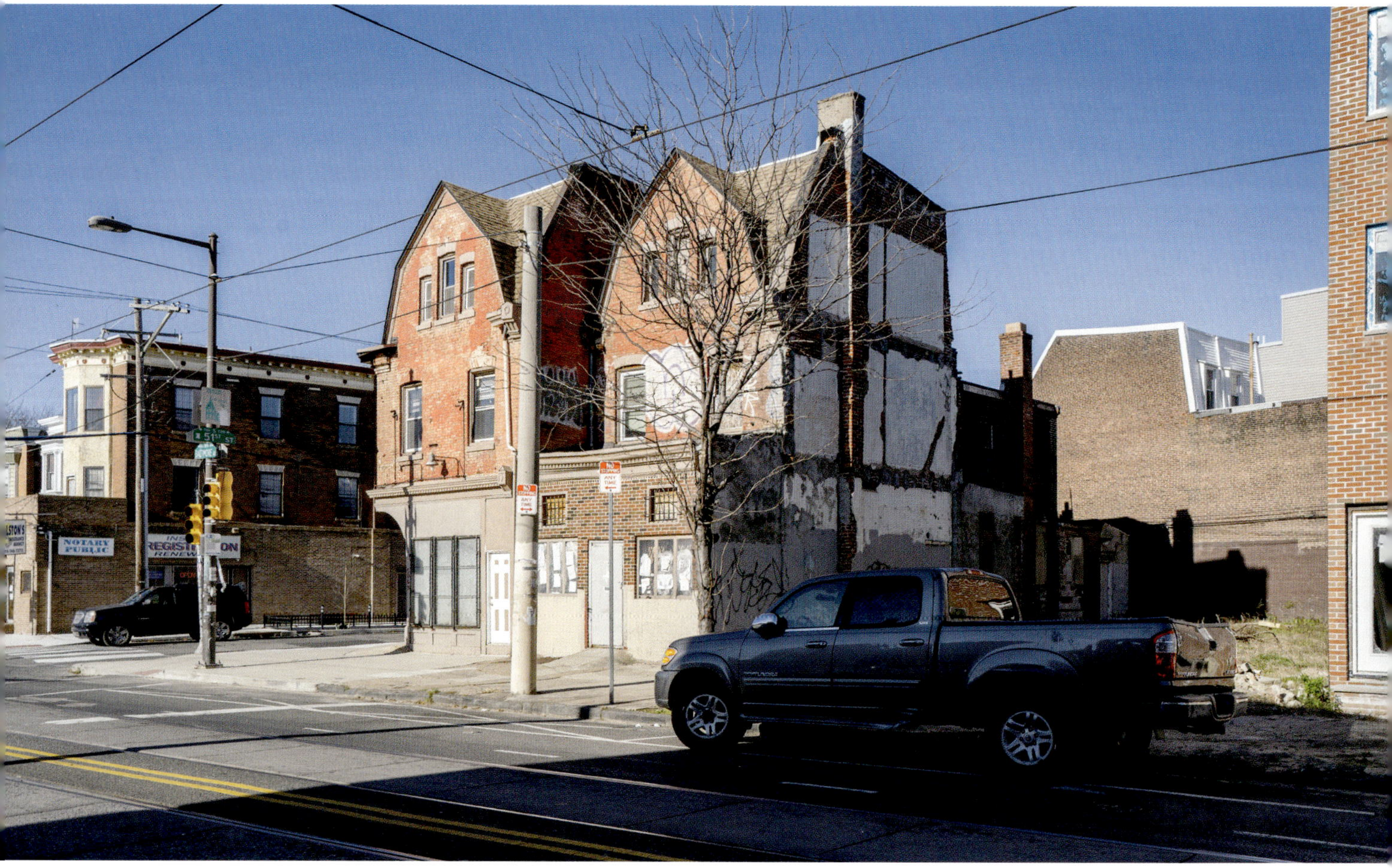

5051 Baltimore Avenue. (Photographed December 10, 2020.)

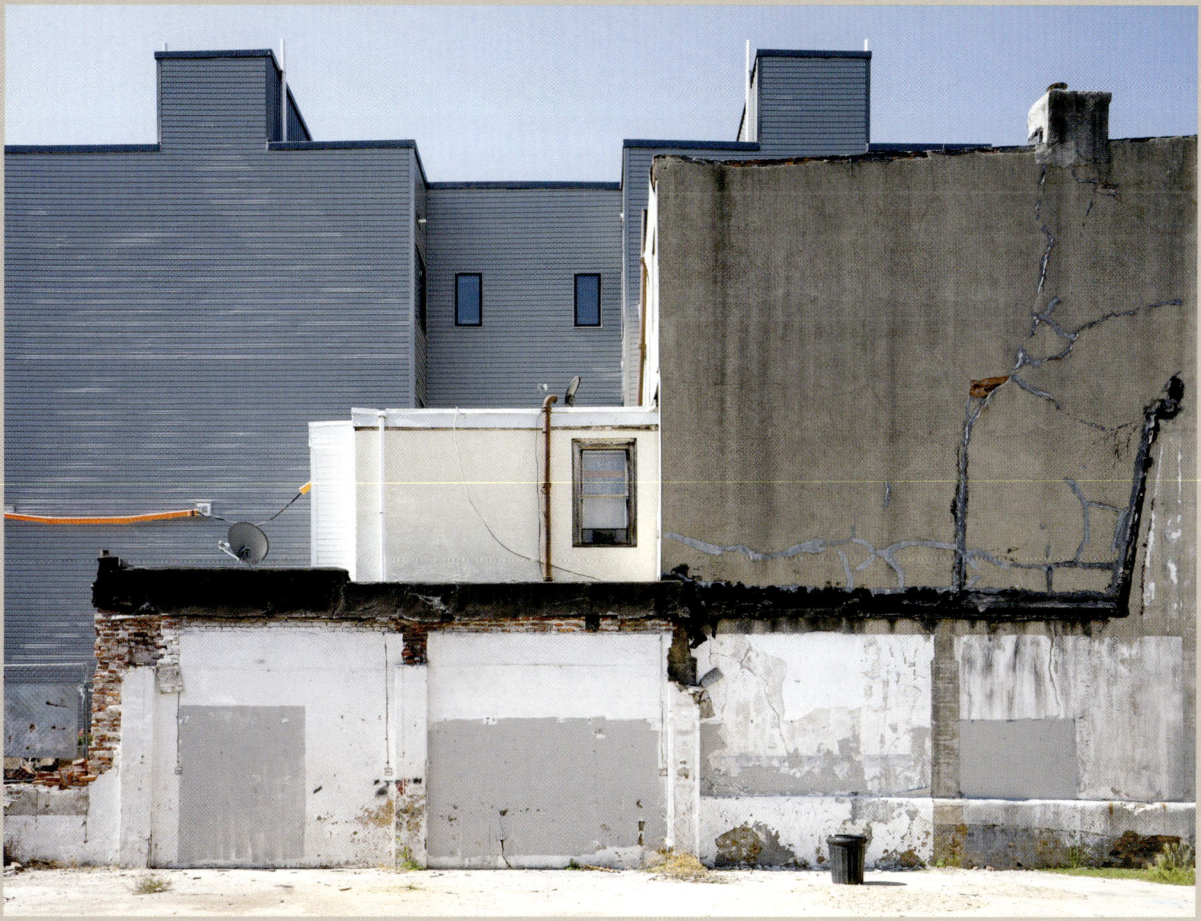

3804 Lancaster Avenue. (Photographed September 23, 2020.)

5231 Haverford Avenue

Constructed in 1897
Demolished in 2013 under the auspices of the L&I Demolition Program

Number 5231 Haverford Avenue was half of a pair, with a gambrel roof that jutted up and over the party wall, linking it with its twin at number 5229. The houses were just a fraction of what was considered the largest building operation in the area in early 1897, when the developer Edward Roney constructed seventy-two two- and three-story brick and stone residences at a total cost of a quarter-million dollars. It certainly kept architect William J. McCauley busy, together with several other large-scale residential projects in the 1890s. But for all his productivity, McCauley was a relatively low-profile designer in Philadelphia at the turn of the twentieth century.

For the duplex at numbers 5229–5231, McCauley confronted an odd wedge-shaped parcel; he dealt with it with an equally odd design. Leaning on the architectural language of the Colonial Revival style—including tripartite windows, lintels with central keystones, and yes, that segmented gambrel roof—McCauley nevertheless broke convention, upending the typical symmetry of the style. Rather than unifying the twins behind a shared, mirrored façade, he staggered their front walls, recessing the footprint of number 5231 slightly behind its neighbor, which seemed to outmuscle it toward the sidewalk on Haverford Avenue. These twins were the fraternal kind.

When the building operation was complete in late 1897, Roney issued a provocation in local newspapers: "Practical builders have told us we have built too good a house. We would like your opinion." For all Roney's marketing swagger, though, it took thirteen months for him to sell 5231 Haverford Avenue for the first time. In February 1899, he packaged number 5231 in a sale of several lots, off-loading the bunch to Frank J. Sullivan. The house changed hands a few more times in the ensuing years until the Gefrorer siblings purchased it in 1904.

Charles, Louisa, Mary, and Annie Gefrorer were four of the seven children born to Charles Gefrorer and Mary Haedrich Gefrorer. Charles Jr. (forty-six when the siblings purchased the house) was the eldest of the clan. Louisa (forty-one) was the fourth child, smack dab in the middle of the birth order, followed by her younger sisters Mary (thirty-six) and Annie (thirty-four). None of them would ever marry or have children. (Indeed, only their brother Henry appears to have done so.) Two of them would eventually die at 5231 Haverford Avenue.

When the Gefrorers purchased the house, it was an elegant eight-room abode with a side yard, referred to in sales advertisements as in "good order"—an "exceptional bargain" overall. It was made all the more appealing in 1907, when one of the Gefrorer women hired a laborer to add a two-story bay window that spanned the upper stories of the house.

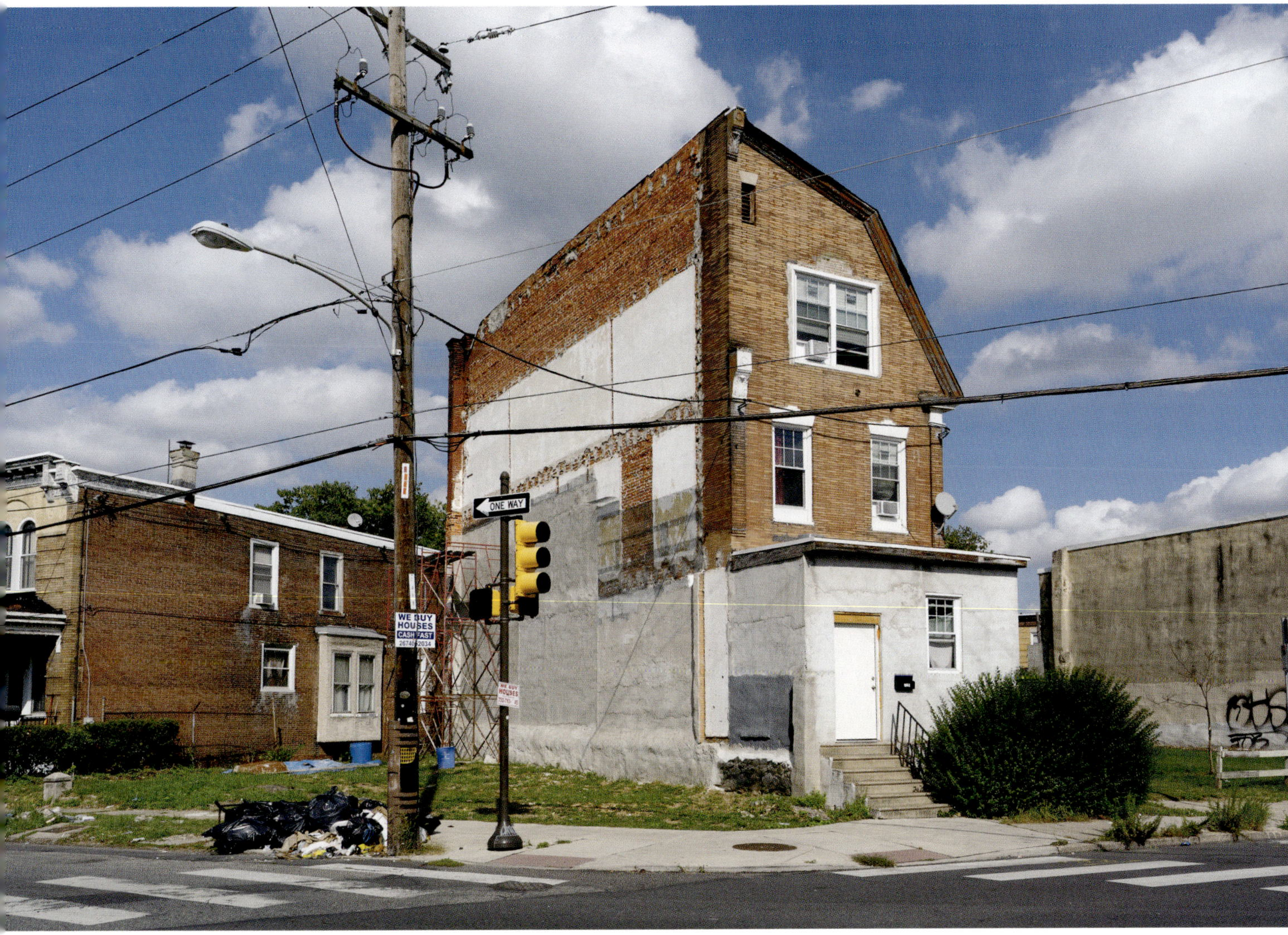

5231 Haverford Avenue. (Photographed September 28, 2020.)

Number 5231 Haverford Avenue also featured a storefront, capitalizing on the corner lot to catch passersby on both 53rd Street and Haverford Avenue. Initially, the Gefrorers rented the retail space out as a barbershop (this use might have predated their time in the house), but by 1908 they were running their own dry goods business out of the storefront. In addition to working in the retail outfit themselves, the four Gefrorer owners also occasionally employed two of their other siblings, Gustave and John. (Once again, Henry was the only exception, as he seems to have been the only one of the seven siblings who never had an association with number 5231.)

Louisa in particular seems to have spearheaded the store: it was known as L. D. Gefrorer and Company Dry Goods, and she and her sister Mary were listed in a U.S. Federal Census from this time as "merchants of notions." (Notions!) Louisa was clearly an educated woman, inheriting her father's books and bookcase when he died and moonlighting at times as a teacher. (What she taught, or where, is unclear.) Among her siblings she had the longest-lasting ties to the house—and was the longest-living of all of them. Her sister Annie would die in 1916; brother John, in 1919 (he had only just survived World War I as a naval machinist); and the eldest Gefrorer, Charles, in 1924. By 1926, the losses had compounded too much, and Louisa sold the house to Janet and Claude Lyon. (After the sale, she moved to 5123 Baltimore Avenue, shuffling the same address digits around a little bit. She would live until 1951.)

The Lyons did not hold on to the house for long. In 1934, during the bleakest years of the Great Depression, the Thirty-fourth Ward Building and Loan Association acquired the property in a sheriff's sale. In the 1940s, the notions and dry goods of the Gefrorer era were gone, replaced in the commercial space by a luncheonette; in 1948, the diner was hiring a Black "fountain girl," an archival hint at the changing demographics (or, at least, the Jim Crow–era employment classes) of the neighborhood by this time.

The luncheonette remained on the site for a couple decades, owned variously by Edna Brown, Nannie Brown, and Mary Knowles. When Mary Knowles was robbed in her own store by two men in 1963, at least one of the assailants was sent to Eastern State Penitentiary in the waning years of its operations as a prison. Eventually, Haverford Avenue's storefront segued to a barbecue joint, and then a sandwich shop. Meanwhile, the floors above the food establishment were subdivided into three apartments at some point in the mid-twentieth century.

In recent decades, the condition of the building declined. By 2010, it had started to receive violations from the Department of Licenses and Inspections (L&I), spiraling into an imminently dangerous situation as the roof caved in. On February 1, 2013, L&I issued a demolition order, and the building was torn down within a few months. Its twin remained standing at 5229 Haverford Avenue, left to feint at a symmetry that the twins had never actually shared.

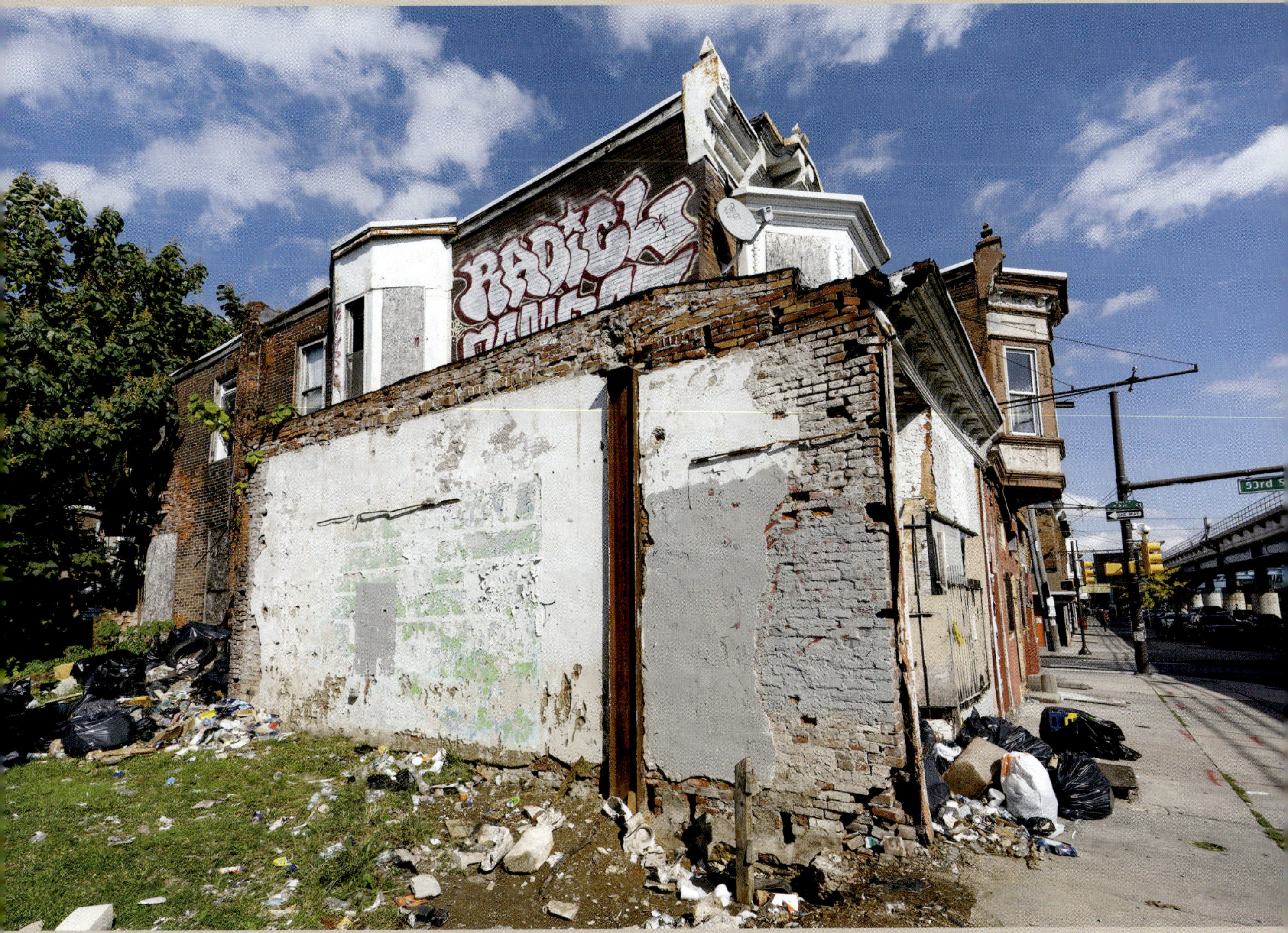

5307 Market Street. (Photographed September 28, 2020.)

4138–4140 Lancaster Avenue

Eastern section (number 4138) constructed ca. 1865; expanded into western parcel (number 4140) in 1904
Demolished in 2017

The 150-year history of 4138–4140 Lancaster Avenue had two running themes: German immigrants and beer. The eastern half of the building was constructed around 1865, when John Crouse and Frederick W. C. Reidenbach sold the property to Charles Müller, who opened Müller's Hall in the "sixth house above 41st" just a few years after arriving in the United States in 1861. While the tavern operated on the first floor, the rooms on the upper floors were rented by tenants who included a machinist, a butcher, a carpenter, and a cigar dealer. John Steckline and Theodore Finke were noticeable exceptions from the generally rugged types of tenants living over the social hall: confectioners by trade, they both lived at number 4138 in the 1880s.

Charles Müller ran his eponymous hall for about thirty years. By the start of the twentieth century, he was in his sixties and likely ready to retire. In 1898, he transferred his liquor license to Joseph Folk, another immigrant from the old country. Folk kept the cultural thread alive, preferring to hire bartenders who could speak his native tongue.

Joseph Folk was married to Katherine Folk, who was also German-born. It was her second marriage, having been widowed (with four children) when her first husband, William Wegman (or Weightman), died in 1891. She and Joseph married in 1895, and they moved to West Philadelphia to run the tavern on Lancaster Avenue. In 1904, they expanded the bar into the adjacent parcel at number 4140.

In 1907, Katherine was widowed once more: Joseph died of consumption, leaving the Lancaster Avenue property to Katherine in his will. She held on to the property for thirty more years, making improvements along the way, such as lowering the first floor and hiring a builder to reconstruct the front wall on its upper stories. She seems to have outsourced the running of the bar to others, including Lucien Fellbrath (in a departure, he was an immigrant of Swiss-French birth) and Peter Lynch (a natural-born citizen, a rarity for this property). But the income no doubt sustained Katherine in her later decades, even in the early years of the Great Depression. (After all, taverns can thrive even in—especially in—the bleakest of economies.) In 1937, however, a trust company acquired it in a sheriff's sale.

In 1958, the owners chipped away at the front wall, installing a veneer, removing a bulk window, and infilling the opening with solid block. A taproom still operated in the interior, but it would receive less daylight now. By the 1960s, the tavern that had been Müller's Hall was known as the Spotlite Bar.

By 2007—if not earlier—the storefront was boarded up, curtailing what had been a remarkably continuous use for a century and a half. Even so, a projecting sign for the Spotlite Bar would linger on the building until its demolition in 2017.

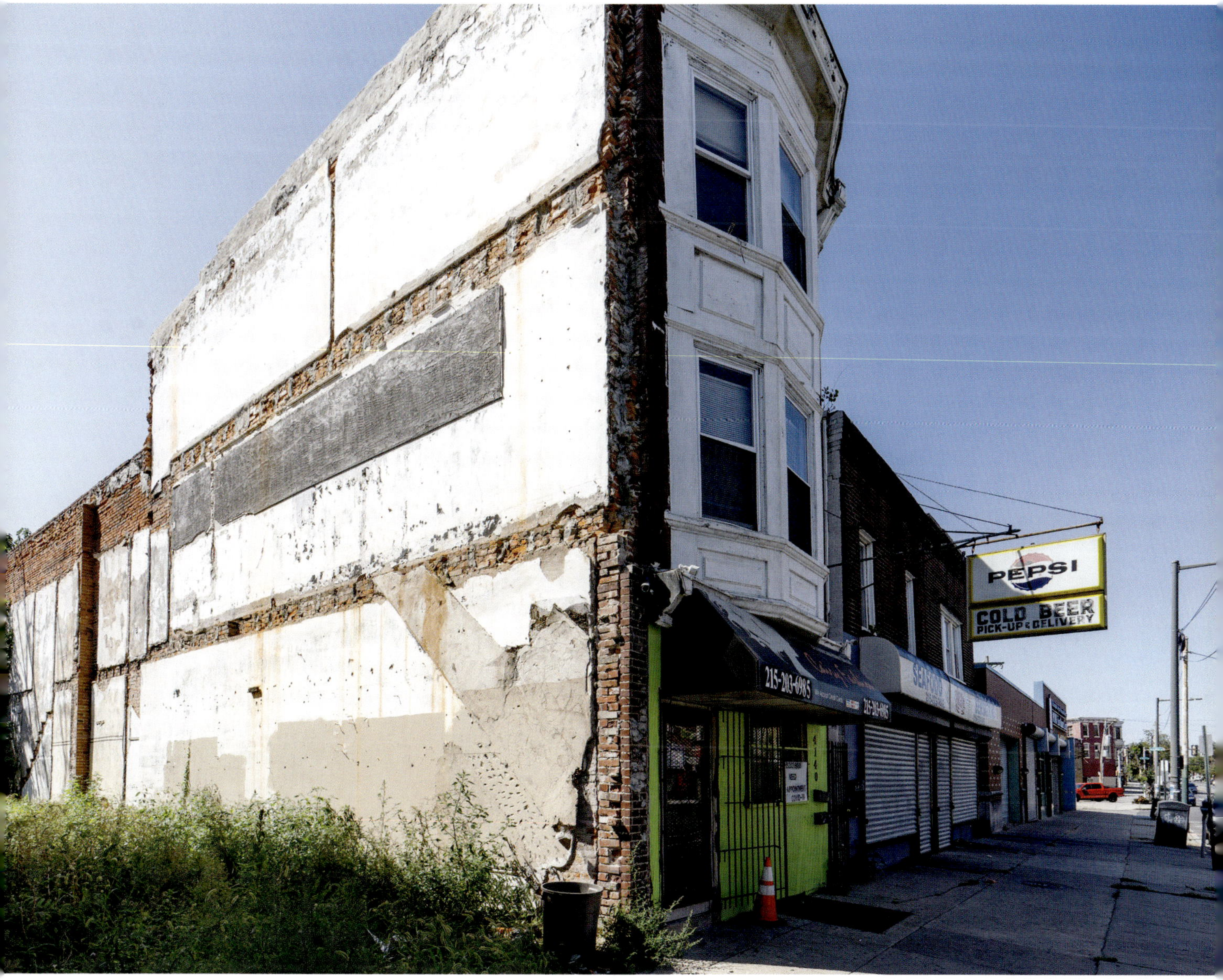

4138–4140 Lancaster Avenue. (Photographed September 28, 2020.)

West Philadelphia References

General Resources

Bromley, George. *Atlas of the City of Philadelphia*. Philadelphia: G. W. Bromley, 1895. Athenaeum of Philadelphia, *Greater Philadelphia GeoHistory Network*. http://www.philageohistory.org/tiles/viewer.

Bromley, George W., and Walter S. Bromley. *Atlas of the City of Philadelphia, Complete in One Volume, from Actual Surveys and Official Plans*. Philadelphia: G. W. Bromley, 1910. Athenaeum of Philadelphia, *Greater Philadelphia GeoHistory Network*. https://www.philageohistory.org/rdic-images/view-image.cfm/237%2DMP%2D022.

———. *Atlas of the City of Philadelphia (West Philadelphia)*. Philadelphia: G. W. Bromley, 1918. Athenaeum of Philadelphia, *Greater Philadelphia GeoHistory Network*. https://www.philageohistory.org/rdic-images/view-image.cfm/BRM1918.WestPhiladelphia.010.Plate6.

———. *Atlas of the City of Philadelphia (West Philadelphia)*. Philadelphia: G. W. Bromley, 1927. Athenaeum of Philadelphia, *Greater Philadelphia GeoHistory Network*. https://www.philageohistory.org/rdic-images/view-image.cfm/BRM1927.WestPhila.009.Plate_6.

5021 Market Street

"Annual Report of the Solicitor of the City of Philadelphia for the Year 1897." In *Third Annual Message of Charles F. Warwick, Mayor of Philadelphia*, volume 4. Philadelphia: Dunlap, 1898. *Google Books*. https://www.google.com/books/edition/Annual_Message_of_the_Mayor_of_the_City/rLtEAQAAMAAJ?hl=en&gbpv=1&dq=%22bischoff+%26+campbell%22+philadelphia&pg=PA19&printsec=frontcover.

"Building and Real Estate Notes." *Philadelphia Real Estate Record and Builders' Guide*, January 23, 1895. *Greater Philadelphia GeoHistory Network*. http://philageohistory.org/rdic-images/view-book-uv.cfm/PhilaBuildersGuide_v10_1895.

———. *Philadelphia Real Estate Record and Builders' Guide*, February 13, 1895. *Greater Philadelphia GeoHistory Network*. http://philageohistory.org/rdic-images/view-book-uv.cfm/PhilaBuildersGuide_v10_1895.

———. *Philadelphia Real Estate Record and Builders' Guide*, July 17, 1895. *Greater Philadelphia GeoHistory Network*. PhilaGeoHistory.org, http://philageohistory.org/rdic-images/view-book-uv.cfm/PhilaBuildersGuide_v10_1895.

———. *Philadelphia Real Estate Record and Builders' Guide*, August 14, 1895. *Greater Philadelphia GeoHistory Network*. http://philageohistory.org/rdic-images/view-book-uv.cfm/PhilaBuildersGuide_v10_1895.

Department of Records, Philadelphia City Archives. 5021 Market Street deeds (map registry no. 60N140201). Various dates.

"Divorce Notices: Court of Common Pleas No. 7 for the County of Philadelphia." *Philadelphia Inquirer*, January 7, 1938. https://www.newspapers.com/image/171446067.

"Divorce Notices: Master's Notice in Divorce." *Philadelphia Inquirer*, May 4, 1938. https://www.newspapers.com/image/171215452.

"Divorces Granted." *Philadelphia Inquirer*, March 19, 1939. https://www.newspapers.com/image/171419912.

"Final Rule for Divorce." *Philadelphia Inquirer*, February 14, 1939. https://www.newspapers.com/image/171395381.

———. *Philadelphia Inquirer*, February 28, 1939. https://www.newspapers.com/image/171433299.

"Property History: 5021–25 Market St[reet]: Demolition Permit: 1040891." *City of Philadelphia At-*

las, January 11, 2020. https://li.phila.gov/Property-History/search/Permit-Detail?address=5021-25%20MARKET%20ST&Id=1040891.

"U.S., City Directories, 1822–1995" (online database). Digital image s.v. "Weger, Frank [*sic*]," 1919. *Ancestry.com*. https://www.ancestrylibrary.com/imageviewer/collections/2469/images/2792832?usePUB=true&_phsrc=NyU153&_phstart=successSource&usePUBJs=true&pId=1197003230.

"U.S. Federal Census" (online database). Digital image s.v. "Wager, Harry," 1910. *Ancestry.com*. https://www.ancestrylibrary.com/imageviewer/collections/7884/images/4449569_00034?usePUB=true&_phsrc=NyU218&_phstart=successSource&usePUBJs=true&pId=25411940.

———. Digital image s.v. "Wager, Harry," 1920. *Ancestry.com*. https://www.ancestrylibrary.com/imageviewer/collections/6061/images/4384844_00756?usePUB=true&_phsrc=NyU218&_phstart=successSource&usePUBJs=true&pId=89057253.

"U.S., World War II Draft Registration Cards, 1942" (online database). Digital image s.v. "Wager, Harry Taylor." *Ancestry.com*. https://www.ancestrylibrary.com/imageviewer/collections/1002/images/PA-2281612-2073?usePUB=true&_phsrc=NyU151&_phstart=successSource&usePUBJs=true&pId=2667023.

5051 Baltimore Avenue

"Contracts Waiving Lien Laws." *Philadelphia Real Estate Record and Builders' Guide*, June 12, 1901. *Greater Philadelphia GeoHistory Network*. https://www.philageohistory.org/rdic-images/view-book-uv.cfm/PhilaBuildersGuide_v16_1901#?ft=&q=%22francis%20j%2E%20purdy%22&c=&m=&s=&cv=378&xywh=3587%2C3134%2C5097%2C1727.

"Conveyances: Philadelphia." *Philadelphia Real Estate Record and Builders' Guide*, June 5, 1901. *Greater Philadelphia GeoHistory Network*. https://www.philageohistory.org/rdic-images/view-book-uv.cfm/PhilaBuildersGuide_v16_1901#?ft=&q=%22fifty%2Dfirst%20st%20and%20baltimore%22&c=&m=&s=&cv=364&xywh=-110%2C-68%2C8772%2C2972.

Department of Records, Philadelphia City Archives. 5051 Baltimore Avenue deeds (map registry no. 22S020009). Various dates.

"Died." *Philadelphia Inquirer*, August 28, 1939. https://www.newspapers.com/image/171106180.

"5051 Baltimore Avenue: Zoning Permit Documents." *City of Philadelphia Atlas*. Accessed January 10, 2023. https://s3.amazonaws.com/lni-zoning-pdfs/219-82698.pdf.

Minardi, Joseph. *City of Neighborhoods: Philadelphia, 1890–1910*. Atglen, PA: Schiffer Publishing, 2020.

"Obituary." *Philadelphia Inquirer*, January 15, 1960. https://www.newspapers.com/image/178026579.

Pennsylvania Department of Banking. *Pennsylvania Building and Loan Associations*. Harrisburg[?]: Department of Banking, 1930.

"Pennsylvania, U.S., Death Certificates, 1906–1969" (online database). Digital image s.v. "Pollon, Alexander." *Ancestry.com*. https://www.ancestrylibrary.com/imageviewer/collections/5164/images/42342_647661_0649-01858?ssrc=pt&treeid=11207160&personid=220045211804&hintid=&usePUB=true&usePUBJs=true&pId=3999918.

"Pennsylvania, U.S., World War I Veterans Service and Compensation Files, 1917–1919, 1934–1948" (online database). Digital image s.v. "Pollon, Alexander." *Ancestry.com*. https://www.ancestrylibrary.com/imageviewer/collections/60884/images/41744_1521003235_0900-02626?pid=1352144&treeid=11207160&personid=220045211804&usePUB=true&usePUBJs=true.

"Real Estate for Rent." *Philadelphia Inquirer*, May 13, 1906. https://www.newspapers.com/image/168421091.

"Soon to Be Married." *Philadelphia Evening Public Ledger*, May 24, 1922. https://www.newspapers.com/image/50638875.

"U.S., City Directories, 1822–1995" (online database). Digital image s.v. "Pollon, Jas.," 1915. *Ancestry.com*. https://www.ancestrylibrary.com/imageviewer/collections/2469/images/2725138?ssrc=&backlabel=Return.

———. Digital image s.v. "Pollon, Louis," 1916. *Ancestry.com.* https://www.ancestrylibrary.com/imageviewer/collections/2469/images/2785594?pid=1491714062&treeid=11207160&personid=220045211695&usePUB=true&usePUBJs=true.

———. Digital image s.v. "Pollon, Rose," 1917. *Ancestry.com.* https://www.ancestrylibrary.com/imageviewer/collections/2469/images/2728301?pid=160202175&usePUB=true&_phsrc=VNq603&_phstart=successSource&usePUBJs=true.

———. Digital image s.v. "Pollon, Rose," 1923. *Ancestry.com.* https://www.ancestrylibrary.com/imageviewer/collections/2469/images/2808359?ssrc=&backlabel=Return.

———. Digital image s.v. "Pollon, Rose," 1925. *Ancestry.com.* https://www.ancestrylibrary.com/imageviewer/collections/2469/images/3036541?ssrc=&backlabel=Return.

———. Digital image s.v. "Pollon, Rose," 1935. *Ancestry.com.* https://www.ancestrylibrary.com/discoveryui-content/view/1195507920:2469?tid=&pid=&queryId=983c4b6350a952a8fa4f1b8bee0dabab&_phsrc=VNq603&_phstart=successSource.

"U.S. Federal Census" (online database). Digital image s.v. "Pollan [*sic*], Rose," 1910. *Ancestry.com.* https://www.ancestrylibrary.com/imageviewer/collections/7884/images/4449858_00148?pid=168496144&usePUB=true&_phsrc=VNq603&_phstart=successSource&usePUBJs=true.

———. Digital image s.v. "Pollon, Rose," 1920. *Ancestry.com.* https://www.ancestrylibrary.com/discoveryui-content/view/86559807:6061?tid=&pid=&queryId=983c4b6350a952a8fa4f1b8bee0dabab&_phsrc=VNq603&_phstart=successSource.

———. Digital image s.v. "Pollon, Rose," 1930. *Ancestry.com.* https://www.ancestrylibrary.com/imageviewer/collections/6224/images/4639478_00586?pid=55176740&usePUB=true&_phsrc=VNq603&_phstart=successSource&usePUBJs=true.

———. Digital image s.v. "Pollon, Rose," 1950. *Ancestry.com.* https://www.ancestrylibrary.com/imageviewer/collections/62308/images/43290879-California-040140-0018?pid=258148915&usePUB=true&_phsrc=VNq618&_phstart=successSource&usePUBJs=true.

"U.S., World War I Draft Registration Cards, 1917–1918" (online database). Digital image s.v. "Pollon, Alexander." *Ancestry.com.* https://www.ancestrylibrary.com/imageviewer/collections/6482/images/005270452_04833?pid=10545892&treeid=11207160&personid=220045211804&usePUB=true&usePUBJs=true.

5231 Haverford Avenue

"Architect Notes." *Philadelphia Real Estate Record and Builders' Guide*, February 3, 1897. *Greater Philadelphia GeoHistory Network.* http://www.philageohistory.org/rdic-images/view-book-uv.cfm/PhilaBuildersGuide_v12_1897#?ft=&q=%22fifty%2Dthird%20and%20haverford%22&c=&m=&s=&cv=64&xywh=2761%2C1358%2C4241%2C916.

Department of Records, Philadelphia City Archives. 5231 Haverford Avenue deeds (map registry no. 61N030076). Various dates.

"Died." *Philadelphia Inquirer*, March 1, 1924. https://www.newspapers.com/image/171029252.

"Female Help Wanted." *Philadelphia Inquirer*, March 2, 1948. https://www.newspapers.com/image/176316163.

"5231 Haverford Avenue: Zoning Permit Documents." *City of Philadelphia Atlas*. Accessed January 10, 2023. https://s3.amazonaws.com/lni-zoning-pdfs/219-187557.pdf.

"Grocer's Two Shots Foil Holdup; Three Seized in Bizarre Sequence." *Philadelphia Inquirer*, March 18, 1963. https://www.newspapers.com/image/179187479.

"Judge Spurns Alibi, Jails Rob Suspect." *Philadelphia Daily News*, May 16, 1963. https://www.newspapers.com/image/184810946.

"Louisa Dorothy Gefrorer." *Find a Grave*. Accessed May 23, 2023. https://www.findagrave.com/memorial/139575592/louisa-dorothy-gefrorer.

"Male Help Wanted." *Philadelphia Inquirer*, April 27, 1906. https://www.newspapers.com/image/168459949.

"More Points of Merit." *Philadelphia Inquirer*, November 28, 1897. https://www.newspapers.com/image/168116515.
"Pennsylvania, U.S., Wills and Probate Records, 1683–1993" (online database). Digital image s.v. "Gefrorer, Louisa D." *Ancestry.com*. https://www.ancestrylibrary.com/imageviewer/collections/8802/images/004436656_00282?pid=3526126&usePUB=true&_phsrc=VNq600&_phstart=successSource&usePUBJs=true.
"Real Estate for Sale: In the City." *Philadelphia Inquirer*, March 28, 1905. https://www.newspapers.com/image/168017173.
"Real Estate for Sale: West Philadelphia, Particular Houses for Particular People." *Philadelphia Times*, November 20, 1897. https://www.newspapers.com/image/53392416.
"Real Estate News." *Philadelphia Inquirer*, May 4, 1897. https://www.newspapers.com/image/168124532.
"U.S., City Directories, 1822–1995" (online database). Digital image s.v. "Gefrorer, Charles L.," 1895. *Ancestry.com*. https://www.ancestrylibrary.com/imageviewer/collections/2469/images/2592186?pid=145930175&usePUB=true&_phsrc=VNq599&_phstart=successSource&usePUBJs=true.
———. Digital image s.v. "Gefrorer, Charles L.," 1908. *Ancestry.com*. https://www.ancestrylibrary.com/imageviewer/collections/2469/images/2790404?pid=166199252&usePUB=true&_phsrc=VNq600&_phstart=successSource&usePUBJs=true.
———. Digital image s.v. "Gefrorer, Louisa," 1911. *Ancestry.com*. https://www.ancestrylibrary.com/imageviewer/collections/2469/images/2788397?pid=1197564932&usePUB=true&_phsrc=VNq599&_phstart=successSource&usePUBJs=true.
———. Digital image s.v. "Gefrorer, Louisa," 1917. *Ancestry.com*. https://www.ancestrylibrary.com/imageviewer/collections/2469/images/2727861?pid=1195169588&usePUB=true&_phsrc=VNq599&_phstart=successSource&usePUBJs=true.
"U.S. Federal Census" (online database). Digital image s.v. "Gefrorer, Charles L," 1910. *Ancestry.com*. https://www.ancestrylibrary.com/imageviewer/collections/7884/images/4449662_01030?pid=25747345&usePUB=true&_phsrc=VNq601&_phstart=successSource&usePUBJs=true.
———. Digital image s.v. "Gefrorer, Louisa," 1900. *Ancestry.com*. https://www.ancestrylibrary.com/imageviewer/collections/7602/images/4115212_00364?pid=52811850&usePUB=true&_phsrc=VNq599&_phstart=successSource&usePUBJs=true.
———. Digital image s.v. "Gefrorer, Louisa," 1930. *Ancestry.com*. https://www.ancestrylibrary.com/imageviewer/collections/6224/images/4639478_00600?pid=55177214&usePUB=true&_phsrc=VNq598&_phstart=successSource&usePUBJs=true.
"U.S., World War I Draft Registration Cards, 1917–1918" (online database). Digital image s.v. "Gefrorer, John Levy." *Ancestry.com*. https://www.ancestrylibrary.com/imageviewer/collections/6482/images/005270448_04365?treeid=&personid=&hintid=&queryId=5b2f0e9527c53f44a6689545f0a0d609&usePUB=true&_phsrc=NyU222&_phstart=successSource&usePUBJs=true&pId=25393941.
"We Have." *Philadelphia Times*, November 7, 1897. https://www.newspapers.com/image/53392240.
"West Philadelphia: Model Two-Story Houses." *Philadelphia Times*, November 10, 1897. https://www.newspapers.com/image/53392278.
"West Philadelphia: Some Men." *Philadelphia Inquirer*, December 15, 1897. https://www.newspapers.com/image/168222727.

4138–4140 Lancaster Avenue

"Applications for Retail Liquor License." *Philadelphia Times*, February 16, 1899. https://www.newspapers.com/image/52585629.
"Building Permits." *Philadelphia Real Estate Record and Builders' Guide*, October 12, 1904. *Greater Philadelphia GeoHistory Network*. http://www.philageohistory.org/rdic-images/view-book-uv

.cfm/PhilaBuildersGuide_v19_1904#?ft=&q=%224138%20lancaster%22&c=&m=&s=&cv=666&xywh=-753%2C3066%2C7652%2C1652.

Department of Records. Philadelphia City Archives. 4138–4140 Lancaster Avenue deeds (map registry nos. 57N010423, 57N010340). Various dates.

"Died." *Philadelphia Inquirer,* October 2, 1913. https://www.newspapers.com/image/168761045.

"4138–40 Lancaster Avenue: Zoning Permit Documents." *City of Philadelphia Atlas.* Accessed January 10, 2023. https://s3.amazonaws.com/lni-zoning-pdfs/219-211957.pdf.

Hexamer and Locher. *Maps of the City of Philadelphia* (1858–1860). Map Collection, Free Library of Philadelphia, *Greater Philadelphia GeoHistory Network.* http://www.philageohistory.org/tiles/viewer.

"The License Court." *Philadelphia Inquirer,* May 15, 1895. https://www.newspapers.com/image/168186384.

"License Transfers." *Philadelphia Inquirer,* June 18, 1897. https://www.newspapers.com/image/168126812.

"Male Help Wanted." *Philadelphia Inquirer,* June 29, 1903. https://www.newspapers.com/image/168573956.

"Many Indignant Depositors." *Philadelphia Times,* May 2, 1890. https://www.newspapers.com/image/52187522.

"Pennsylvania, U.S., Death Certificates, 1906–1969" (online database). Digital image s.v. "Folk, Joseph." *Ancestry.com.* https://www.ancestrylibrary.com/imageviewer/collections/5164/images/41381_645856_0485-03529?treeid=&personid=&hintid=&queryId=e48b7521f6e6065e5929bcada2b2135b&usePUB=true&_phsrc=VNq594&_phstart=successSource&usePUBJs=true&pId=2401095.

"Pennsylvania, U.S., Wills and Probate Records, 1683–1993" (online database). Digital image s.v. "Folk, Joseph." *Ancestry.com.* https://www.ancestrylibrary.com/imageviewer/collections/8802/images/004441101_00199?pid=2205914&usePUB=true&_phsrc=VNq594&_phstart=successSource&usePUBJs=true.

———. Digital image s.v. "Wegman, William." *Ancestry.com.* https://www.ancestrylibrary.com/imageviewer/collections/8802/images/004297698_00075?pid=2496043&usePUB=true&_phsrc=VNq593&_phstart=successSource&usePUBJs=true.

"Philadelphia Contracts Awarded." *Philadelphia Real Estate Record and Builders' Guide,* July 5, 1933. *Greater Philadelphia GeoHistory Network.* http://www.philageohistory.org/rdic-images/view-book-uv.cfm/PhilaBuildersGuide_v48_1933#?ft=&q=%224138%20lancaster%22&c=&m=&s=&cv=209&xywh=-3398%2C0%2C14162%2C4797.

"Public Sales." *Philadelphia Daily News,* September 18, 1970. https://www.newspapers.com/image/184953278.

"Serenaded." *Philadelphia Inquirer,* May 4, 1871. https://www.newspapers.com/image/169284951.

"Sheriff's Sales." *Philadelphia Inquirer,* November 30, 1936. https://www.newspapers.com/image/178349189.

Smedley, Samuel. *Atlas of the City of Philadelphia.* Philadelphia: J. B. Lippincott, 1862. Map Collection, Free Library of Philadelphia, *Greater Philadelphia GeoHistory Network.* http://www.philageohistory.org/tiles/viewer.

"Taverns: Spotlite Bar." *Philadelphia Inquirer,* September 10, 1961. https://www.newspapers.com/image/178349189.

"Twenty-Fourth Ward." *Philadelphia Inquirer,* April 15, 1890. https://www.newspapers.com/image/168108917.

"U.S., City Directories, 1822–1995" (online database). Digital image s.v. "Carber, Edward R.," 1874. *Ancestry.com.* https://www.ancestrylibrary.com/imageviewer/collections/2469/images/2863593?pid=176366365&usePUB=true&_phsrc=VNq596&_phstart=successSource&usePUBJs=true.

———. Digital image s.v. "Colflesh, Jeremiah," 1875. *Ancestry.com.* https://www.ancestrylibrary.com/imageviewer/collections/2469/images/2864404?pid=176538815&usePUB=true&_phsrc=VNq596&_phstart=successSource&usePUBJs=true.

———. Digital image s.v. "Colflesh, Jeremiah Jr.," 1875. *Ancestry.com*. https://www.ancestrylibrary.com/imageviewer/collections/2469/images/2864404?pid=176538815&usePUB=true&_phsrc=VNq596&_phstart=successSource&usePUBJs=true.
———. Digital image s.v. "Finke, Theodore E.," 1887. *Ancestry.com*. https://www.ancestrylibrary.com/imageviewer/collections/2469/images/2588067?pid=145314701&usePUB=true&_phsrc=VNq596&_phstart=successSource&usePUBJs=true.
———. Digital image s.v. "Houser, Samuel," 1874. *Ancestry.com*. https://www.ancestrylibrary.com/imageviewer/collections/2469/images/2863793?pid=176416059&usePUB=true&_phsrc=VNq596&_phstart=successSource&usePUBJs=true.
———. Digital image s.v. "Meier, August," 1894. *Ancestry.com*. https://www.ancestrylibrary.com/imageviewer/collections/2469/images/2858504?pid=1189850068&usePUB=true&_phsrc=VNq596&_phstart=successSource&usePUBJs=true.
———. Digital image s.v. "Spang, William," 1891. *Ancestry.com*. https://www.ancestrylibrary.com/imageviewer/collections/2469/images/2591223?pid=145791591&usePUB=true&_phsrc=VNq596&_phstart=successSource&usePUBJs=true.
———. Digital image s.v. "Steckline, John C.," 1883. *Ancestry.com*. https://www.ancestrylibrary.com/imageviewer/collections/2469/images/2876926?pid=178988914&usePUB=true&_phsrc=VNq596&_phstart=successSource&usePUBJs=true.
———. Digital image s.v. "Wegman, William," 1898. *Ancestry.com*. https://www.ancestrylibrary.com/imageviewer/collections/2469/images/2861483?pid=175969699&usePUB=true&_phsrc=VNq596&_phstart=successSource&usePUBJs=true.
"U.S. Federal Census" (online database). Digital image s.v. "Folk, Catherine [*sic*]," 1920. *Ancestry.com*. https://www.ancestrylibrary.com/imageviewer/collections/6061/images/4385037_00872?pid=52152530&usePUB=true&_phsrc=VNq589&_phstart=successSource&usePUBJs=true.
———. Digital image s.v. "Folk, Katherine," 1880. *Ancestry.com*. https://www.ancestrylibrary.com/imageviewer/collections/7602/images/4115210_00361?pid=52769408&usePUB=true&_phsrc=VNq590&_phstart=successSource&usePUBJs=true.
———. Digital image s.v. "Folk, Katherine," 1910. *Ancestry.com*. https://www.ancestrylibrary.com/imageviewer/collections/7884/images/4449859_00186?pid=25473828&usePUB=true&_phsrc=VNq589&_phstart=successSource&usePUBJs=true.
———. Digital image s.v. "Muller, Charles," 1870. *Ancestry.com*. https://www.ancestrylibrary.com/imageviewer/collections/7163/images/4278834_00370?pid=10719919&usePUB=true&_phsrc=VNq739&_phstart=successSource&usePUBJs=true.
———. Digital image s.v. "Muller, Charles," 1880. *Ancestry.com*. https://www.ancestrylibrary.com/imageviewer/collections/6742/images/4244548-00388?pid=461798&usePUB=true&_phsrc=VNq741&_phstart=successSource&usePUBJs=true.

SOUTHWEST PHILADELPHIA

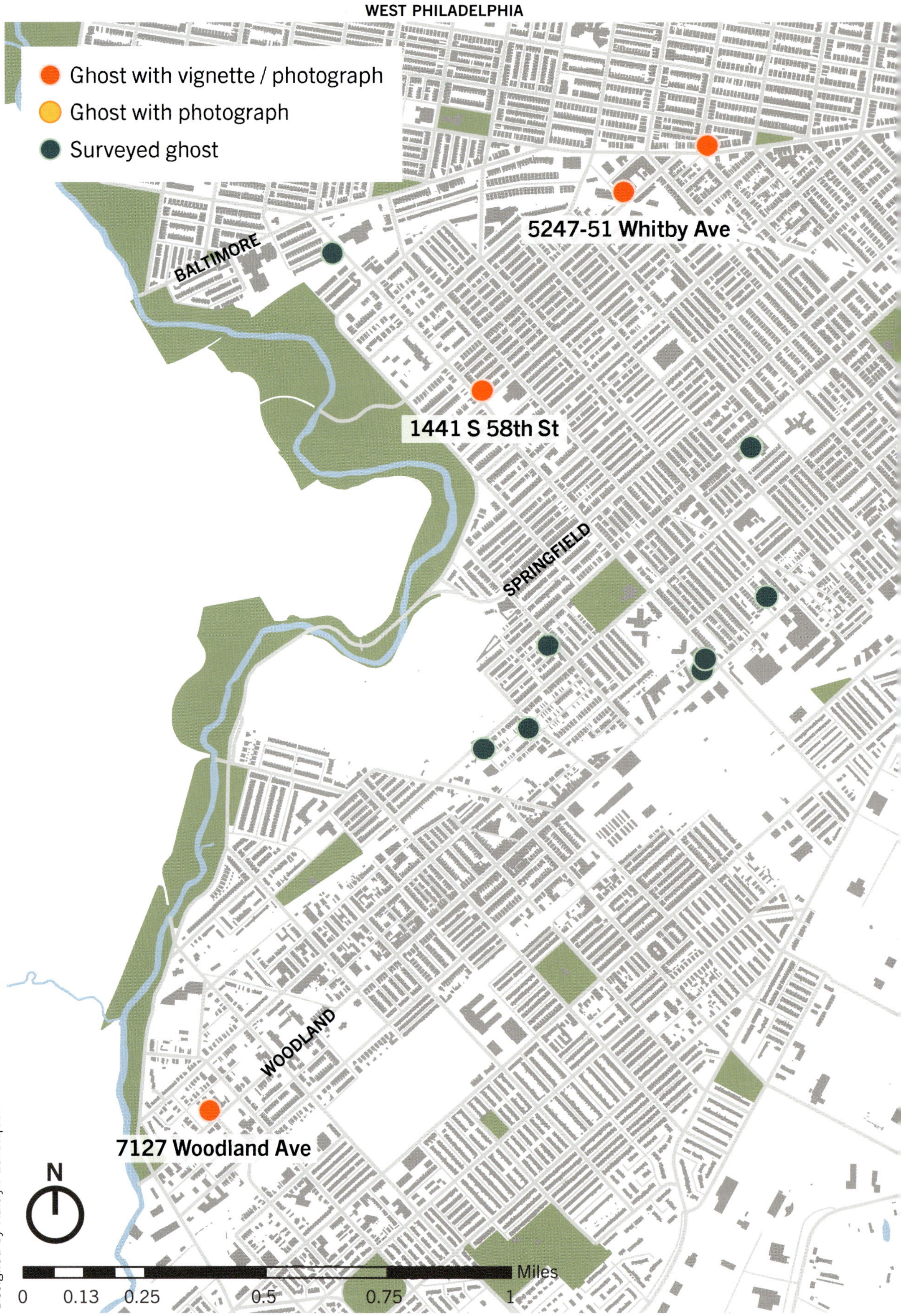

Designed by Kaitlyn Levesque.

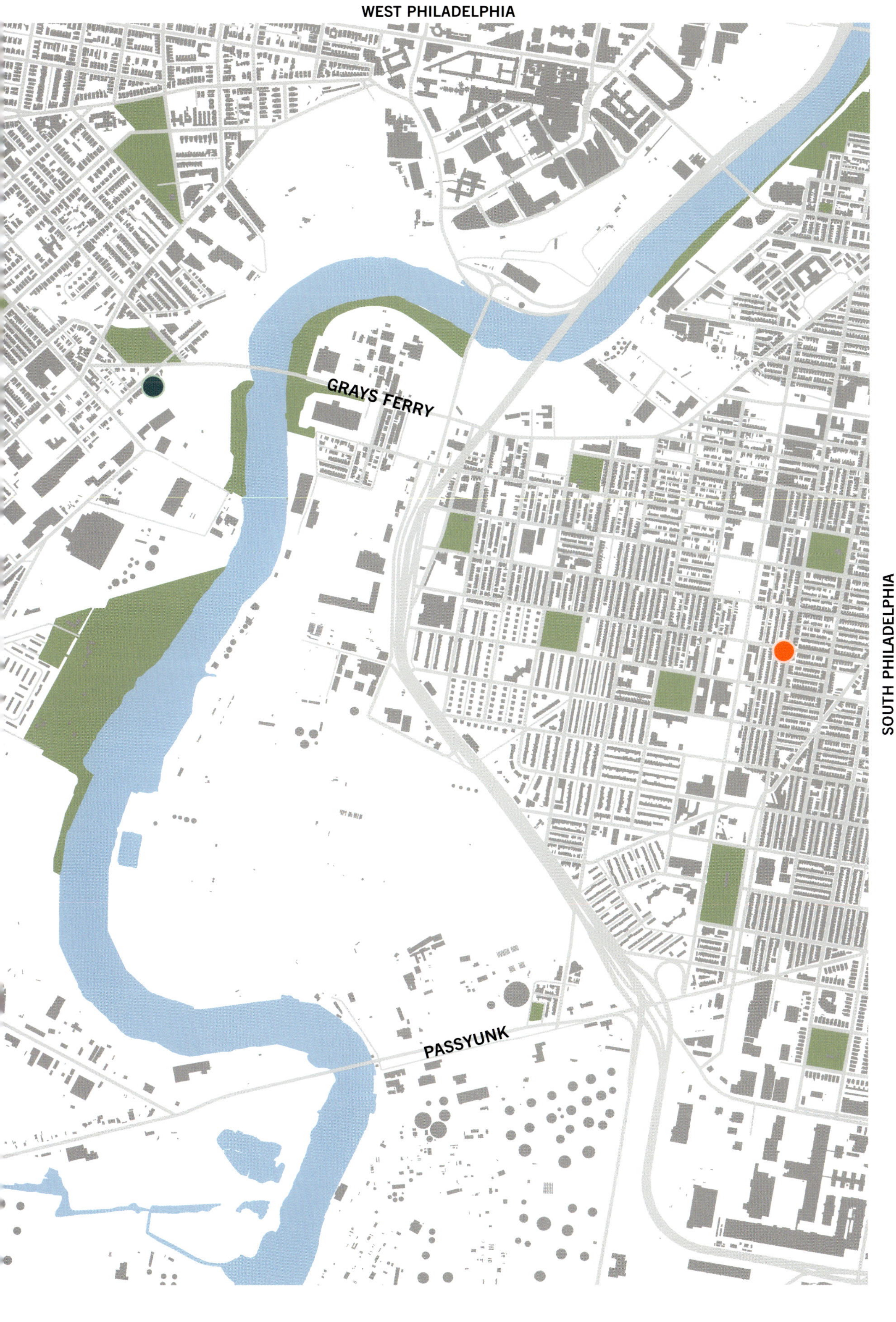
WEST PHILADELPHIA
GRAYS FERRY
SOUTH PHILADELPHIA
PASSYUNK

Building ghosts typically memorialize a residential structure, but Southwest Philadelphia features one of the few examples otherwise.[1] It's only fitting that this area of the city would have a ghost of an industrial building: despite many pockets of charming, close-knit neighborhoods and the proximity of natural assets such as Cobbs Creek Park and the John Heinz National Wildlife Refuge, Southwest Philadelphia and its residents have long been forced to bear a disproportionate burden of the city's dirtier land uses. Since the nineteenth century, Philadelphia has imposed many of its industrial demands on the Southwest, as sprawling manufactories and refineries needed to be far from the population center but close to the railroad and the rivers. In the context of dramatic environmental impacts such as Superfund sites and toxic plants, a smattering of building ghosts would seem insignificant. Yet even here—maybe even especially here—building ghosts offer a measure of tangibility for the decades of intangible, unjust forces and environmental racism that have targeted Southwest Philadelphia.

The Southwest's villages—now neighborhoods—date back to the earliest European colonization in Philadelphia. Even after their consolidation with the City of Philadelphia in 1854, the villages remained at a remove from the metropolis. John Bartram established a major botanical garden; John Dick founded the Helendale Nurseries; and other residents were drawn to the flora, fauna, and flowing water that still characterize the area today.[2] (The area is bounded by Cobbs Creek, Darby Creek, and the Schuylkill River.)

1. Among the ghosts featured in this book, 5247–5251 Whitby Avenue in Southwest Philadelphia is matched only by the ghost of the former industrial building at 2101 North American Street, in the River Wards (see page 217). Other ghosts have hosted light-manufacturing uses (e.g., food production), but the examples in the Southwest and the River Wards stand out for their association with heavier industry.

2. Anne E. Krulikowski, "Southwest Philadelphia," *Encyclopedia of Greater Philadelphia*, accessed May 5, 2023, https://philadelphiaencyclopedia.org/locations/southwest-philadelphia.

By the later decades of the nineteenth century, though, many within Philadelphia took note of those same natural assets—and their distance from the city center—and seized an opportunity. It began slowly at first, with a few mills constructed along the waterways that frame the Southwest, and the Philadelphia, Wilmington and Baltimore Railroad constructed through Kingsessing.[3] As Philadelphia became the "Workshop of the World," though, the Southwest was especially appealing for heavy industry. Kensington and other neighborhoods along the Delaware River became hotbeds of manufacturing, too, but in Southwest Philadelphia operators could cluster many of the dirtiest processing plants, with the understanding that they were too far downstream to affect many Philadelphians. The industrialization of the Southwest only increased when World War I broke out and the world's largest shipyard was constructed on Hog Island. A decade later, an early version of the airport opened, dispatching planes into the sky while transportation networks simultaneously intensified on the ground below.[4]

Amid these developments, Southwest Philadelphia saw waves of residential construction in the 1920s, '30s, and '40s, creating an integrated community of primarily Black and immigrant working-class residents.[5] They built close-knit communities and enjoyed the natural scenery of the Southwest, with more elbow room and greenery than many other Philadelphians enjoyed. Yet they also coped with insufficient sewer and water infrastructure (due in part to the disenfranchisement of such predominantly Black neighborhoods), recurrent floods in the adjacent marshland, and the heavy industry that surrounded them. In the early 1950s, the Redevelopment Authority of Philadelphia (RDA) pointed to all of these factors (as if the residents could be blamed for them) when it deemed the area "blighted." With that designation, and the associated Eastwick Redevelopment Area Plan, the RDA moved to seize more than 2,100 acres of land and displace more than eight thousand people, in what would be one of the largest urban renewal projects in the country.[6]

One would think that the upside of such a traumatic clearance strategy would be long-term environmental gains for the Southwest, replacing industrial pollution with investment. Yet as the intervening decades and unfulfilled policies have demonstrated, that has not been the case. Instead, the neighborhoods of Southwest Philadelphia have endured generations of ongoing environmental threats and hazards.

Individual catastrophes have poisoned the Southwest, including, in recent years, a two-alarm fire at a junkyard in 2023 and an explosion and three-alarm fire that burned

3. Anne E. Krulikowski, "'Farms Don't Pay': The Transformation of the Philadelphia Metropolitan Landscape, 1880–1930," *Pennsylvania History* 72, no. 2 (Spring 2005): 196.

4. Krulikowski, "Southwest Philadelphia."

5. Amy Laura Cahn, "What Eastwick Wants: Transforming the Environmental Justice Legacy of Urban Renewal," *Strategies for Health Justice: Lessons from the Field* (2018): 71, www.jstor.org/stable/resrep27198.11.

6. Ibid.; Amy Laura Cahn, "On Retiring Blight as Policy and Making Eastwick Whole," *Harvard Civil Rights-Civil Liberties Law Review* 49 (June 2014): 451; Interface Studio, "Lower Eastwick Public Land Strategy," accessed May 5, 2023, http://interface-studio.com/projects/lower-eastwick-public-land-strategy.

for more than twenty-four hours at the Philadelphia Energy Solutions (PES) refinery in 2019.[7] The latter event was so devastating, it was detected by infrared imagery on a satellite in space.[8] The Chemical Safety and Hazard Investigation Board would eventually calculate that the PES refinery blast released more than five thousand pounds of hydrofluoric acid into the air (for context, the *New York Times* noted that "even a thimbleful can prove deadly"), cloaking the Southwest (and Grays Ferry, on the opposite bank of the Schuylkill) with toxins, day in and day out.

Meanwhile, Southwest Philadelphia already *was* shouldering environmental harms day in and day out. Indeed, this incremental damage—to health and well-being, first and foremost, but also to the properties that eventually become building ghosts—is most often born from familiar, routine circumstances: the airplanes that fly overhead every day; the two interstate highways that carry countless vehicles, belching exhaust; the many distribution centers taking advantage of those planes and highways; the landfill (now part of the fifth-largest Superfund site in the country) that operated without a permit for several decades and was used unwittingly by local children as a massive play mound; and the scores of zoning variances that allow auto body shops to overrun the neighborhood with car parts, discarded oil, and noxious spray fumes.[9] Even before the catastrophe at PES in 2019, investigative journalists calculated that the refinery had routinely emitted the chemical benzene (which is known to cause cancer) at twenty-one times the federal limit, exceeding the legal threshold in all but twelve weeks between January 2018 and September 2019 and racking up more than a half-million dollars in fines.[10]

Not often listed in the litany of environmental threats in the Southwest, but relevant nonetheless, is the toll of demolition. As in North Philadelphia, much of the Southwest's demolition track record can be attributed to public agencies—the urban renewal clearance program then and the Department of Licenses and Inspections' (L&I) demolition program now. The effects are felt both at the community level—the social psychiatrist Dr. Mindy Fullilove refers to the "root shock" of urban renewal's displacement

7. Nick Vadala, "Southwest Philly Junkyard Fire Is under Control," *Philadelphia Inquirer*, May 26, 2023, https://www.inquirer.com/news/philadelphia/junkyard-fire-southwest-philadelphia-20230526.html.

8. Linda Villarosa, "Pollution Is Killing Black Americans: This Community Fought Back," *New York Times Magazine*, July 28, 2020, https://www.nytimes.com/2020/07/28/magazine/pollution-philadelphia-black-americans.html.

9. On the landfill, see Hadas Kuznits, "Southwest Philly Site Picked for Nationwide Environmental Cleanup," KYW NewsRadio, December 17, 2021, https://www.audacy.com/kywnewsradio/news/local/southwest-philadelphia-site-epa-environmental-cleanup. On the play mound, see U.S. Environmental Protection Agency, "Lower Darby Creek Area—Clearview Landfill," accessed May 5, 2023, https://response.epa.gov/site/site_profile.aspx?site_id=5864; Zein Nakhoda, Alexa Ross, and Milena Velis, dirs., *Eastwick in the Middle: Organizing for Environmental Justice*, video, Movement Alliance Project, https://vimeo.com/141186932. On auto body shops, see Sophia Schmidt, "Lawsuit Filed against Southwest Philly Auto Repair Shop Is Just One Example of a 'Common Problem,' Advocates Argue," *PlanPhilly*, May 2, 2023, https://whyy.org/articles/southwest-philly-battles-life-in-an-auto-zone.

10. Villarosa, "Pollution Is Killing Black Americans."

effects—and by individuals as they deal with daily asthma and worse.[11] The U.S. Environmental Protection Agency has documented the health risks of residential demolition, noting that harmful materials can seep into the air, ground, and water in the course of the destruction.[12] (Even when the express purpose of demolition is to remove hazardous materials, the process can still exact an environmental toll.) Residents of Eastwick (or the Meadows, as many locals call it) already deal with enough flooding issues (made worse by climate change) without the added concern of floodwater bringing toxic materials into their homes. Moreover, although those hazardous construction materials theoretically are carted away to a landfill, in the case of Southwest Philadelphia's demolition debris, some of those landfills are in its own backyard. Demolition, then, merely adds to neighbors' pile of concern.

In the face of such daunting issues—which local organizers such as the Eastwick Action Committee, Philly Thrive, and others are fighting to redress—building ghosts would seem to be minor players.[13] Their circumstances are certainly less dramatic than events such as the PES explosion. But environmental racism works at scales large and small, and residents' health conditions certainly don't distinguish between specific disasters and ongoing, debilitating weathering.[14] In that light, then, if building ghosts are tangible evidence of intangible forces at work, then how do they represent the invisible, visceral injustices that Southwest Philadelphia has had to withstand?

---

11. Cahn, "What Eastwick Wants," 71; Sophia Schmidt, "'Poison Is in the Dose': Philly Aims to Limit Environmental Hazards with New Legislation," *PlanPhilly*, February 2, 2022, https://whyy.org/articles/poison-is-in-the-dose-philly-aims-to-limit-environmental-hazards-with-new-legislation.

12. U.S. Environmental Protection Agency, "Harmful Materials and Residential Demolition," accessed May 5, 2023, https://www.epa.gov/large-scale-residential-demolition/harmful-materials-and-residential-demolition; U.S. Environmental Protection Agency, "Managing Stormwater and Dust at Demolition Sites," accessed May 5, 2023, https://www.epa.gov/large-scale-residential-demolition/managing-stormwater-and-dust-demolition-sites.

13. Indeed, proportionate to the number of building ghosts in the city overall, the Southwest has a smaller share. However, this is likely more attributable to the area's detached building stock than to an actual lack of demolitions.

14. Alisha Haridasani Gupta, "How 'Weathering' Contributes to Racial Health Disparities," *New York Times*, April 12, 2023, https://www.nytimes.com/2023/04/12/well/live/weathering-health-racism-discrimination.html.

5247–5251 Whitby Avenue

Constructed in 1924–1925
Demolished in 2011

When Florence Stockton purchased the property at 5247–5251 Whitby Avenue from Isaac Wood Massey in 1925, it was hardly of use to her in its existing state: marketed for sale as a two-story garage with a capacity of nearly eighty cars, the brick building, in reality, was unfinished. "Owner will build," Massey's real estate notice mentioned in its last sentence, almost as an afterthought. Undaunted by the prospect, Stockton completed the sale in February 1925 and quickly transferred it a month later to her business enterprise, F. E. Stockton and Company. By late March, the "Stockton Garage" was already looking to hire an "experienced garage man," even as construction remained underway. On May 24, her business announced that its new seventy-five-car garage at the northeastern corner of 53rd Street and Whitby Avenue was ready to open.

In fact, much of Florence Stockton's life was apparently in (re)building mode in the early 1920s. The daughter of a German-born father and an American mother, Florence Friesleben was born around 1892 in Pennsylvania. She married Robert G. Stockton in 1908, and the couple moved into a house on Osage Avenue in West Philadelphia. Robert worked initially as a ticket agent for the Pullman Company, then as a brakeman for Westinghouse; his wife had no apparent job outside the home in the early years of their marriage and particularly after their first (and only?) child was born sometime in the 1910s. Florence was listed in the 1910 U.S. Federal Census, alongside Robert and sans formal occupation, but she was not mentioned at all in several city directories around that time, as her husband represented the household in the listings. Around 1918, however, things evidently shifted in their marriage: Florence *was* listed in the directory now, living on Market Street while Robert lived on Greenway Avenue. As of 1920, Robert was divorced and boarding (alone) in a house on Front Street; his apparent ex-wife, Florence, remained in West Philadelphia.

It is unclear what propelled Florence Stockton to purchase the property on Whitby Avenue or what financial resources she mustered to do so. But it was a venture, in more ways than one: having purchased an active construction site, she first hired builders to complete the structure, then her "experienced garage man" to help run it, then (as of June 7, 1925), "young Jewish men to take charge of [the] new garage, not afraid of hard work and long hours."

Southwest Philadelphia was rife with similar garages by this point in the 1920s, as the automobile increased in popularity (and decreased in cost). But Florence Stockton's garage was not just any auto shop. In hiring salesmen and mechanics, she advertised an "unusual opportunity" for her employees: the chance to sell and apply Duco finishing, a groundbreaking new paint for cars, fresh off the auto show floor.

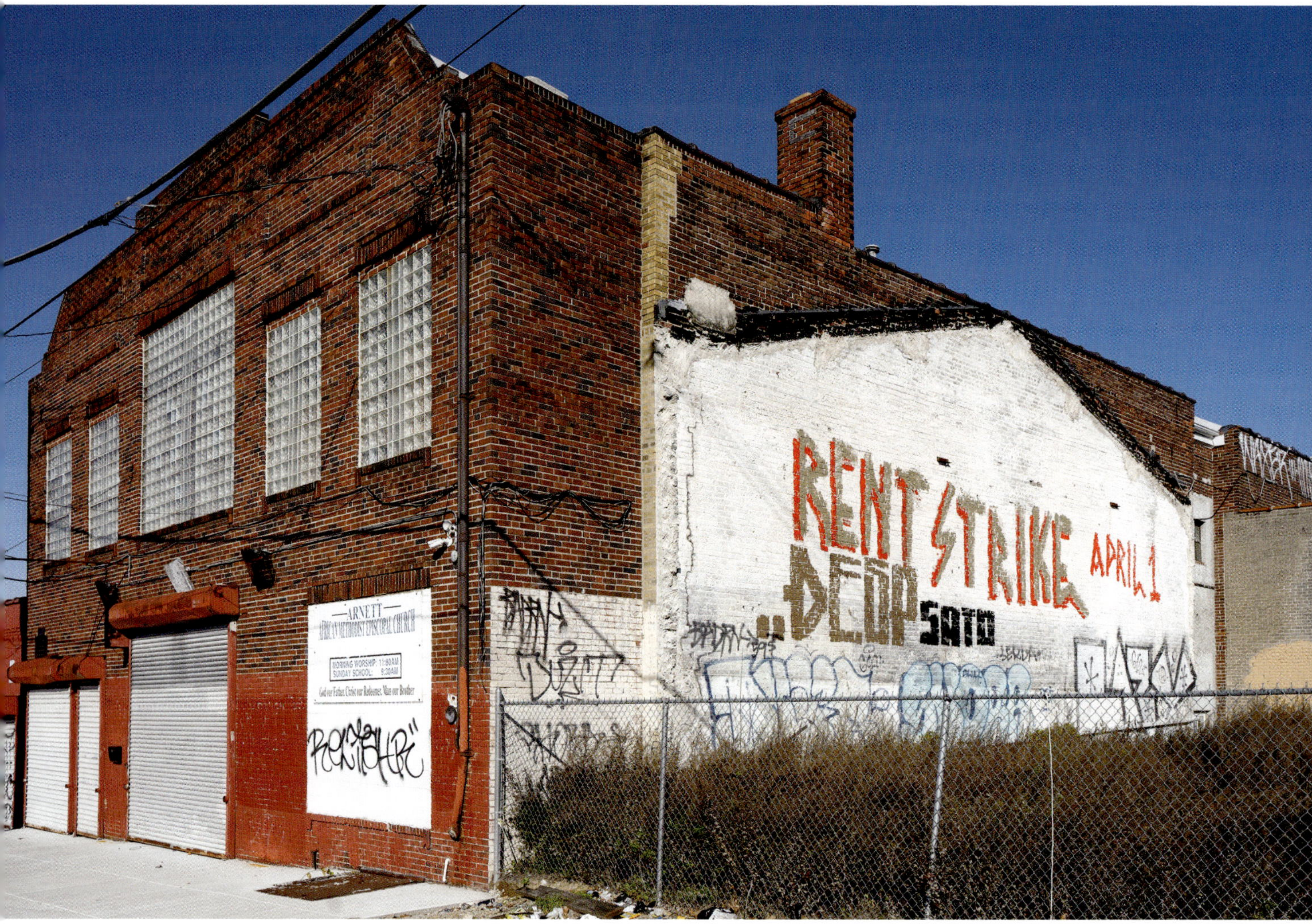

5247–5251 Whitby Avenue. (Photographed December 10, 2020.)

Introduced in New York in 1923—just two years before Stockton bought the Whitby Avenue property—Duco paint was developed by General Motors (GM) and DuPont and was available in a range of colors. The breakthrough paint offered GM a competitive edge over Ford Motor, where Henry Ford once famously said, "Any customer can have a car painted any color that he wants, so long as it is black." Hampered by the complications of different drying times for different pigments, Ford had prioritized mass production over a complex color palette. But Duco paints managed to achieve both ends: they were more durable than earlier finishes and could dry in minutes (not hours or days), *and* they offered customers the option to choose among shades as exotic as "Vert Atlantique," "Jaune de Murcie," and "Bleu Salvador." Much as she had with her unfinished garage, then, Florence Stockton saw a promising prospect with Duco paint and seized it early on.

Curiously, though, her venture was short-lived, even if the building in which it was housed was not. Having purchased the property from Isaac Wood Massey for $65,000 in 1925, she sold the completed building in 1926 for $90,000. There is no further trace of her dabbling in automotive finishes at her other properties. (She bought and sold various parcels, in the area of 61st and Vine streets especially.) Perhaps her real estate ventures were sufficiently profitable on their own. But the Stockton Garage remained standing until 2011, with few alterations from the version that Florence Stockton saw to completion.

1441 South 58th Street

Constructed in 1915
Demolished in 2011 under the auspices of the L&I Demolition Program

When Daniel Crawford Jr. and his laborers finished construction on the block of houses at 58th Street and Willows Avenue in late 1915, he marketed them as "an exceptional opportunity" to purchase. In fact, Crawford himself had recognized an exceptional opportunity first: to buy and build in this area, located just a few blocks south of Baltimore Avenue and its trolley. From Center City, his rowhouses would be readily accessible via "any car running west," as he trumpeted in his ads for these "Crawford Homes." Now that the streetcar tracks segued into the subway-surface lines (a connection established a decade earlier, in 1906), the city could continue to expand westward (and southwestward), offering outlying residential properties to downtown employees.

To appeal to these potential residents, Crawford catered to their perceived tastes by incorporating "every modern appointment" and "the very latest in artistic chandeliers and decorations," all situated behind "beautifully terraced fronts, with colonial columns producing an imposing exterior." (The exteriors of these homes were made all the more imposing when many owners enclosed the frame porches in the ensuing years, extending the masonry walls to the sidewalk to capture the square footage of the formerly terraced fronts.)

This was the same marketing language Crawford would hone nearly a decade later for the Hotel Pennsylvania (now, Chestnut Hall) at 39th and Chestnut streets. But where that sales pitch was heightened to correspond with the grand multifamily apartment building (the "hotel" in the name was a misnomer), here at 58th and Willows he promoted an intimate scale of living that was more appropriate for the proportions of these houses. In this block—each a *real* home, according to Crawford's language—each structure comprised eight rooms. With the building ghost as a guide, that likely meant a foyer, living room, dining room, and kitchen on the first floor; three bedrooms upstairs; and a bathroom. Some houses even boasted built-in bathtubs, "recognized by the trade as the most sanitary and highest class plumbing fixtures."

All told, the sales pitch was enough to entice Gustav and Florence Breustle, who purchased number 1441 in November 1915, just a few months after it was completed. Within just eight months, however, the Breustles resold the house; like Daniel Crawford before them, the Breustles could recognize an exceptional opportunity.

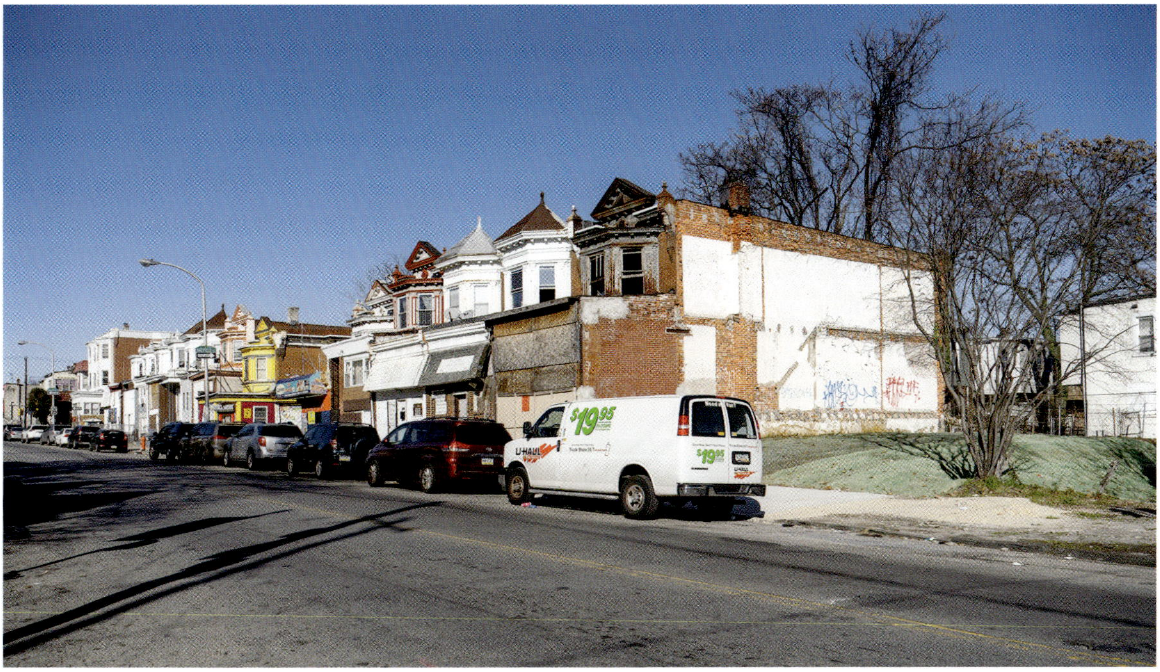

1441 South 58th Street. (Photographed December 10, 2020.)

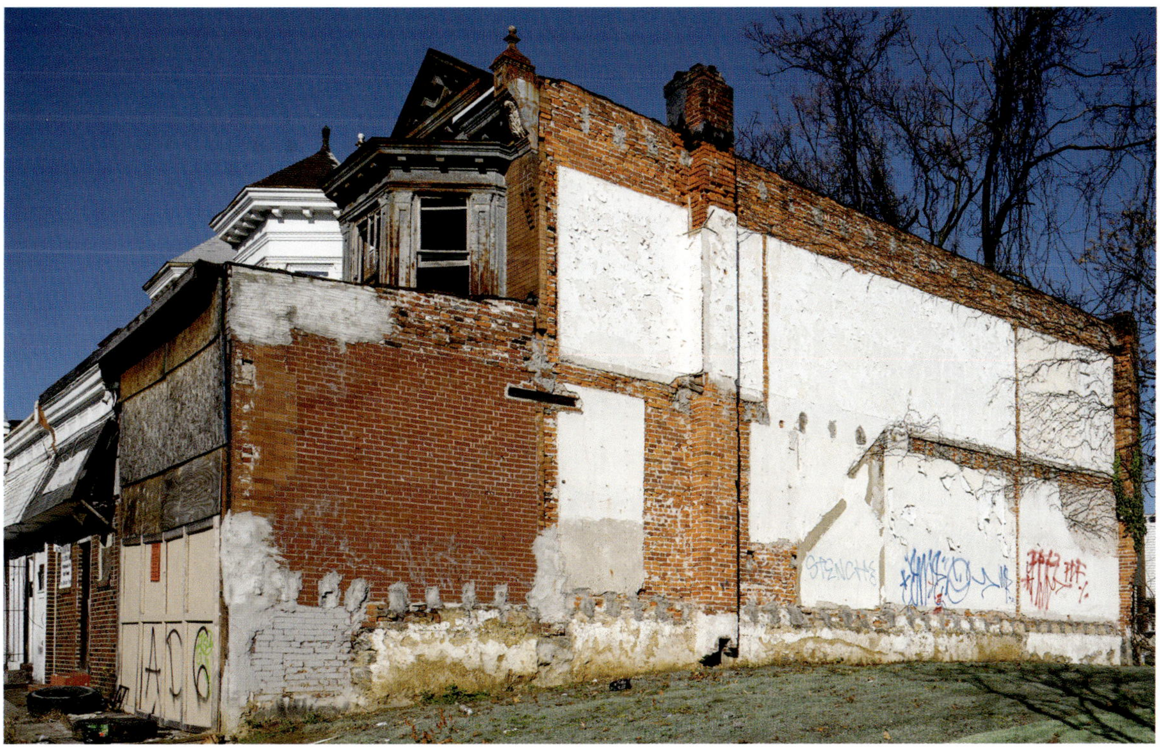

1441 South 58th Street. (Photographed December 10, 2020.)

7127 Woodland Avenue

Constructed in 1897
Demolished in 2019 under the auspices of the L&I Demolition Program

When grocer Robert Beith (who moonlighted occasionally as a real estate developer) erected five houses on the 7100 block of Woodland Avenue in May 1897, there was already a house assigned the address of number 7127. Located in the parcel immediately west of Beith's rowhouses, the old number 7127 ceded its number to one of its new neighbors just in time for Eugene Leech to purchase it in December of that year and welcome his bride, Mary, to the house the following year. (Some maps of the area apparently lagged a bit, as they don't reflect the reassigned numbers until more than a decade later.)

Eugene Leech was an undertaker. In his early years on Woodland Avenue, he would walk or take the avenue's streetcar a mile and a half east, to a funeral parlor in the 5700 block of Woodland Avenue. In 1908, however, he hired a builder to complete $300 worth of alterations on his and Mary's house; the following year, newspapers began using the Woodland Avenue address in reference to the burial services he offered.

Leech ran his funeral parlor at number 7127 for at least forty years. By the time World War II broke out, he therefore spoke with a certain measure of authority on the subject of death when he wrote—often—to the editors of the *Philadelphia Inquirer*, lamenting the conditions of war and its devastating costs for all involved. "In these days of bombing scares (which we hope will not materialize)," he wrote in January 1942, just a few weeks after the attack on Pearl Harbor, "wouldn't it be a good idea to anticipate suffering in the case of unwanted stray animals?"

Leech was much more scathing when the nation's War Production Board (WPB) ruled in March 1943 that all standard caskets should reduce their use of essential materials—going as far as to mandate a maximum coffin length of six feet. The undertaker (who, not coincidentally, was noted as "tall" on his registration card for the previous world war) heaped derision on this directive:

> So, according to your article in today's paper, some bright baby of the WPB is going to limit the length of caskets to six feet. That's going to be tough on the feelings of my family (I will neither know nor care), for they may object to my suggestion that they can solve it by cutting off a few inches from my possibly too long legs.
>
> Seriously, anyone with brains enough to get a headache knows that such a ruling is ridiculous. Rulings of that kind, repeated too often, will not help the general morale of our people in these times.

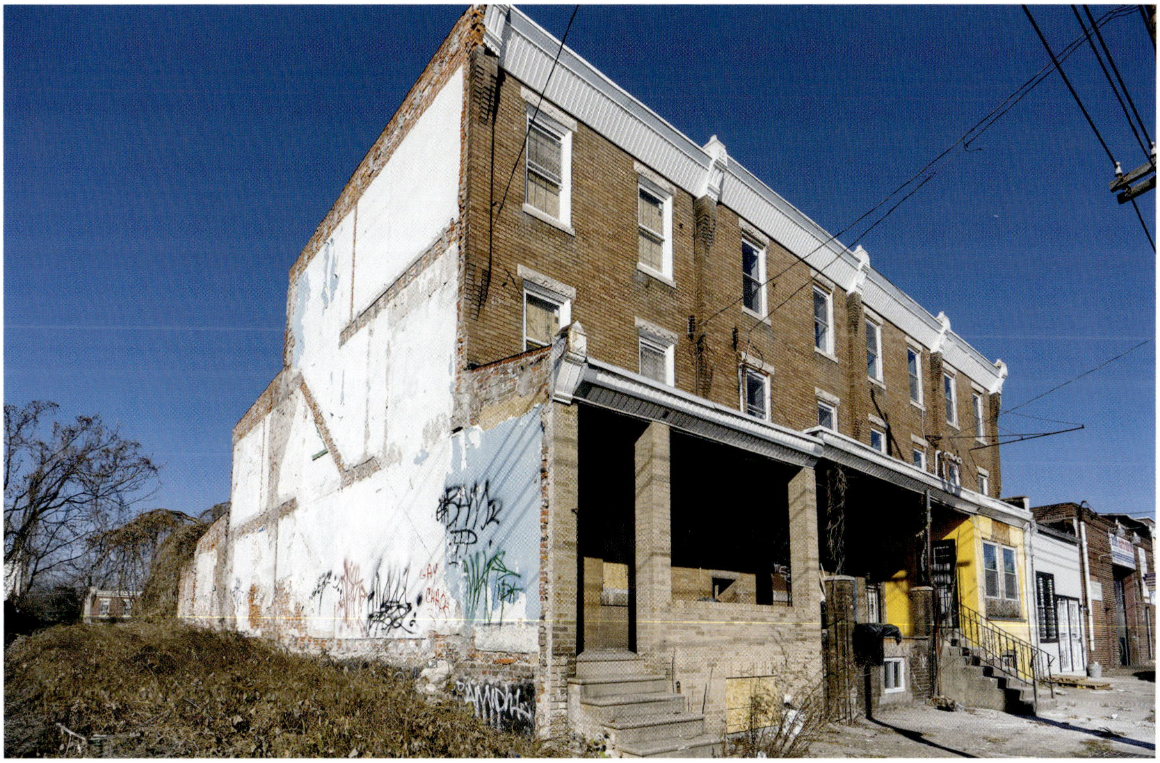

7127 Woodland Avenue. (Photographed December 10, 2020.)

By May, the WPB had loosened its restrictions on the dimensions of caskets, bowing to vocal pressure from—who else?—the nation's funeral directors, such as Leech.

Eugene and Mary Leech sold 7127 Woodland Avenue in September 1949. For the remaining seven decades of its existence, the building would host apartments for the living rather than memorial services for the dead.

Southwest Philadelphia References

General Resources

Bromley, George. *Atlas of the City of Philadelphia*. Philadelphia: G. W. Bromley, 1895. Athenaeum of Philadelphia, *Greater Philadelphia GeoHistory Network*. http://www.philageohistory.org/tiles/viewer.

Bromley, George W., and Walter S. Bromley. *Atlas of the City of Philadelphia, Complete in One Volume, from Actual Surveys and Official Plans*. Philadelphia: G. W. Bromley, 1910. Athenaeum of Philadelphia, *Greater Philadelphia GeoHistory Network*. https://www.philageohistory.org/rdic-images/view-image.cfm/237%2DMP%2D022.

——. *Atlas of the City of Philadelphia (West Philadelphia)*. Philadelphia: G. W. Bromley, 1916. Athenaeum of Philadelphia, *Greater Philadelphia GeoHistory Network*. https://www.philageohistory.org/rdic-images/view-image.cfm/BRM1918.WestPhiladelphia.010.Plate6.

——. *Atlas of the City of Philadelphia (West Philadelphia)*. Philadelphia: G. W. Bromley, 1918. Athenaeum of Philadelphia, *Greater Philadelphia GeoHistory Network*. https://www.philageohistory.org/rdic-images/view-image.cfm/BRM1918.WestPhiladelphia.033.Plate29.

"Insurance Maps of Philadelphia, Pennsylvania, Volume 18" (online database). Sanborn Map Company, New York, [1916–1950]. *ProQuest Digital Sanborn Maps, 1867–1970*. https://digitalsanbornmaps.proquest.com/browse_maps/39/7881/38451/40224/536312?accountid=10977.

5247–5251 Whitby Avenue

"Activities of Day in Real Estate." *Philadelphia Inquirer*, March 1, 1925. https://www.newspapers.com/image/171061415.

——. *Philadelphia Inquirer*, April 9, 1925. https://www.newspapers.com/image/171079613.

——. *Philadelphia Inquirer*, January 21, 1926. https://www.newspapers.com/image/173343189.

"Advance Construction News." *Philadelphia Real Estate Record and Builders' Guide*, October 8, 1924. *Greater Philadelphia GeoHistory Network*. http://philageohistory.org/rdic-images/view-book-uv.cfm/PhilaBuildersGuide_v39_1924#?ft=&q=whitby&c=&m=&s=&cv=802&xywh=-5054%2C-186%2C17420%2C4694.

"Business Opportunities." *Philadelphia Inquirer*, June 4, 1924. https://www.newspapers.com/image/171047449.

Department of Records, Philadelphia City Archives. 5247–5251 Whitby Avenue deeds (map registry nos. 26S030049, 26S030012, 26S030060, 26S030068). Various dates.

Hoover, Gary. "Why Cars Don't Have to Be Black." *American Business History Center*, October 8, 2021. https://americanbusinesshistory.org/why-cars-dont-have-to-be-black.

"Male Help Wanted." *Philadelphia Inquirer*, February 8, 1925. https://www.newspapers.com/image/171072555.

——. *Philadelphia Inquirer*, March 27, 1925. https://www.newspapers.com/image/171080943.

——. *Philadelphia Inquirer*, May 6, 1925. https://www.newspapers.com/image/170797384.

——. *Philadelphia Inquirer*, May 10, 1925. https://www.newspapers.com/image/170798984.

——. *Philadelphia Inquirer*, May 24, 1925. https://www.newspapers.com/image/171077816.

——. *Philadelphia Inquirer*, June 7, 1925. https://www.newspapers.com/image/171073861.

"Philadelphia, Pennsylvania, U.S., Marriage Index, 1885–1951" (online database). Digital image s.v. "Stockton, Robert G; Friesleben, Florence." *Ancestry.com*. https://www.ancestrylibrary.com/discoveryui-content/view/1443706:2536?tid=&pid=&queryId=ddd2dfb8a63ce887e4af604cc5c30e1a&_phsrc=VNq631&_phstart=successSource.

Quirk, Mary Beth. "A Brief History of Car Colors—And Why Are We So Boring Now?" *Consumer Reports*, October 10, 2014. https://www.consumerreports.org/consumerist/a-brief-history-of-car-colors-and-why-are-we-so-boring-now.
"Real Estate for Rent: Floor Space." *Philadelphia Inquirer*, June 2, 1928. https://www.newspapers.com/image/176286708.
"Real Estate for Sale: Garages." *Philadelphia Inquirer*, February 8, 1925. https://www.newspapers.com/image/171072809.
———. *Philadelphia Inquirer*, May 24, 1925. https://www.newspapers.com/image/171077058.
"Sheriff's Sales." *Philadelphia Inquirer*, June 28, 1926. https://www.newspapers.com/image/173361585.
"U.S., City Directories, 1822–1995" (online database). Digital image s.v. "Stockton, Florence," 1918. *Ancestry.com*. https://www.ancestrylibrary.com/imageviewer/collections/2469/images/2789934?ssrc=&backlabel=Return.
———. Digital image s.v. "Stockton, Florence," 1919. *Ancestry.com*. https://www.ancestrylibrary.com/imageviewer/collections/2469/images/2792789?ssrc=&backlabel=Return.
———. Digital image s.v. "Stockton, Florence," 1921. *Ancestry.com*. https://www.ancestrylibrary.com/imageviewer/collections/2469/images/2785727?pid=164840846&usePUB=true&_phsrc=VNq631&_phstart=successSource&usePUBJs=true.
———. Digital image s.v. "Stockton, Robert," 1916. *Ancestry.com*. https://www.ancestrylibrary.com/imageviewer/collections/2469/images/2802047?ssrc=&backlabel=Return&pId=1491876222.
"Used Automobiles." *Philadelphia Inquirer*, February 7, 1939. https://www.newspapers.com/image/176137442.
"U.S. Federal Census" (online database). Digital image s.v. "Stockton, Robert G.," 1910. *Ancestry.com*. https://www.ancestrylibrary.com/imageviewer/collections/7884/images/4449969_00778?pid=25761490&usePUB=true&usePUBJs=true.
"U.S., World War I Draft Registration Cards, 1917–1918" (online database). "Stockton, Robert Graham." *Ancestry.com*. https://www.ancestrylibrary.com/imageviewer/collections/6482/images/005270443_03927?pid=27391188&usePUB=true&usePUBJs=true.

1441 South 58th Street

"Crawford Homes." *Philadelphia Inquirer*, May 7, 1916. https://www.newspapers.com/image/169001408.
———. *Philadelphia Inquirer*, June 11, 1916. https://www.newspapers.com/image/168416454.
Department of Records, Philadelphia City Archives. 1441 South 58th Street deeds (map registry no. 26S110222). Various dates.
"Philadelphia's Finest Apartments." *Philadelphia Inquirer*, September 21, 1924. https://www.newspapers.com/image/171064651.
"Real Estate for Sale: West Philadelphia." *Philadelphia Inquirer*, June 25, 1916. https://www.newspapers.com/image/168442027.
———. *Philadelphia Inquirer*, July 12, 1922. https://www.newspapers.com/image/170692877.
"U.S. Federal Census" (online database). Digital image s.v. "Crawford, Daniel," 1910. *Ancestry.com*. https://www.ancestrylibrary.com/imageviewer/collections/7884/images/4449572_00808?pid=25616787&usePUB=true&_phsrc=VNq666&_phstart=successSource&usePUBJs=true.
———. Digital image s.v. "Crawford, Daniel," 1920. *Ancestry.com*. https://www.ancestrylibrary.com/imageviewer/collections/6061/images/4385040_00014?pid=52221037&usePUB=true&_phsrc=VNq666&_phstart=successSource&usePUBJs=true.
"West Philadelphia: Crawford Homes." *Philadelphia Inquirer*, July 9, 1916. https://www.newspapers.com/image/169130898.

7127 Woodland Avenue

"Alterations and Additions." *Philadelphia Real Estate Record and Builders' Guide*, July 2, 1913. *Greater Philadelphia GeoHistory Network*. http://www.philageohistory.org/rdic-images/view-book-uv.cfm/PhilaBuildersGuide_v28_1913#?ft=&q=woodland%20AND%207127&c=&m=&s=&cv=534&xywh=3521%2C510%2C3133%2C1963.

"Building Permits." *Philadelphia Real Estate Record and Builders' Guide*, May 26, 1897. *Greater Philadelphia GeoHistory Network*. http://www.philageohistory.org/rdic-images/view-book-uv.cfm/PhilaBuildersGuide_v12_1897#?ft=&q=woodland%20AND%20%2271st%22&c=&m=&s=&cv=328&xywh=3957%2C2776%2C1879%2C1177.

"'Casketeers' Happy; So Are Tall People." *Oakland Tribune*, May 30, 1943. https://www.newspapers.com/image/149653398.

"Conveyances: Philadelphia." *Philadelphia Real Estate Record and Builders' Guide*, December 29, 1897. *Greater Philadelphia GeoHistory Network*. http://www.philageohistory.org/rdic-images/view-book-uv.cfm/PhilaBuildersGuide_v12_1897#?ft=&q=woodland%20AND%207127&c=&m=&s=&cv=852&xywh=2339%2C1602%2C1885%2C1181.

Department of Records, Philadelphia City Archives. 7127 Woodland Avenue deeds (map registry no. 30S090062). Various dates.

"Died." *Philadelphia Inquirer*, June 7, 1909. https://www.newspapers.com/image/169047156.

"The Home Front: Morticians, WPB Feud over Caskets' Length." *Evening Sun* (Baltimore), April 2, 1943. https://www.newspapers.com/image/369682687.

"Latest News in Real Estate." *Philadelphia Inquirer*, April 21, 1908. https://www.newspapers.com/image/168334421.

"Length of Coffins Limited." *Philadelphia Inquirer*, March 5, 1943. https://www.newspapers.com/image/171395106.

"Letters to the Editor: Help Stray Animals." *Philadelphia Inquirer*, January 9, 1942. https://www.newspapers.com/image/171787383.

"Letters to the Editor: Not the Only Ones." *Philadelphia Inquirer*, December 23, 1941. https://www.newspapers.com/image/171740861.

"Undertakers Here to Discuss New WLB Casket Order." *Dayton Herald*, April 10, 1943. https://www.newspapers.com/image/391558625.

"U.S., City Directories, 1822–1995" (online database). Digital image s.v. "Beith, Robert B.," 1887. *Ancestry.com*. https://www.ancestrylibrary.com/imageviewer/collections/2469/images/2587666?pid=145252662&usePUB=true&_phsrc=VNq673&_phstart=successSource&usePUBJs=true.

———. Digital image s.v. "Beith, Robert B.," 1897. *Ancestry.com*. https://www.ancestrylibrary.com/imageviewer/collections/2469/images/2855567?pid=174748403&usePUB=true&_phsrc=VNq673&_phstart=successSource&usePUBJs=true.

———. Digital image s.v. "Leech, Eugene," 1900. *Ancestry.com*. https://www.ancestrylibrary.com/imageviewer/collections/2469/images/2870233?pid=177568189&usePUB=true&_phsrc=VNq678&_phstart=successSource&usePUBJs=true.

"U.S., World War I Draft Registration Cards, 1917–1918" (online database). "Leech, Eugene." *Ancestry.com*. https://www.ancestrylibrary.com/imageviewer/collections/6482/images/005270444_01801?pid=27396659&usePUB=true&_phsrc=VNq677&_phstart=successSource&usePUBJs=true.

"The Voice of the People: How to Get a Headache." *Philadelphia Inquirer*, March 9, 1943. https://www.newspapers.com/image/171414512.

RIVER WARDS

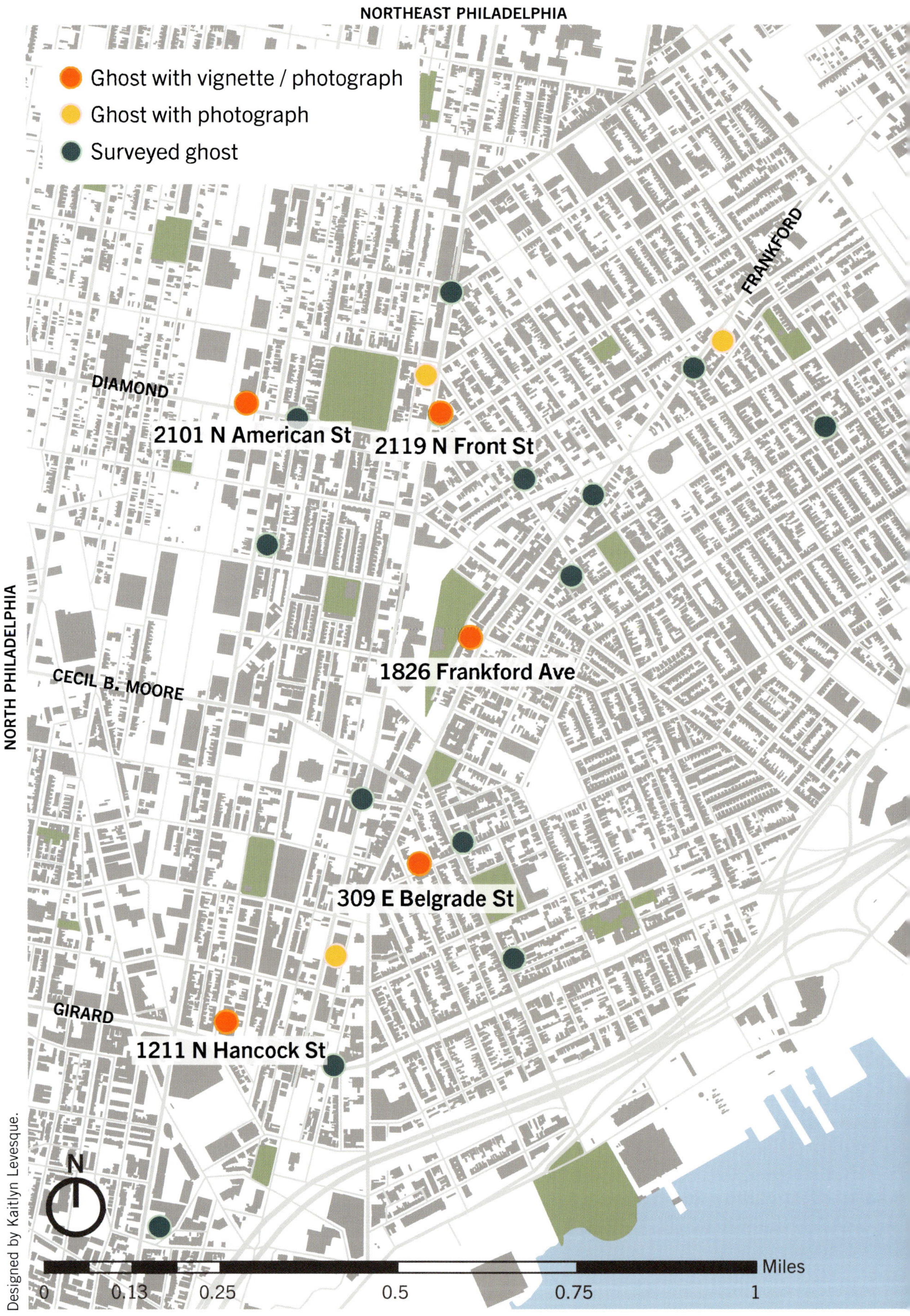
NORTHEAST PHILADELPHIA
Ghost with vignette / photograph
Ghost with photograph
Surveyed ghost
FRANKFORD
DIAMOND
2101 N American St
2119 N Front St
NORTH PHILADELPHIA
1826 Frankford Ave
CECIL B. MOORE
309 E Belgrade St
GIRARD
1211 N Hancock St
N
Miles
0
0.13
0.25
0.5
0.75
1
Designed by Kaitlyn Levesque.

NORTHEAST PHILADELPHIA

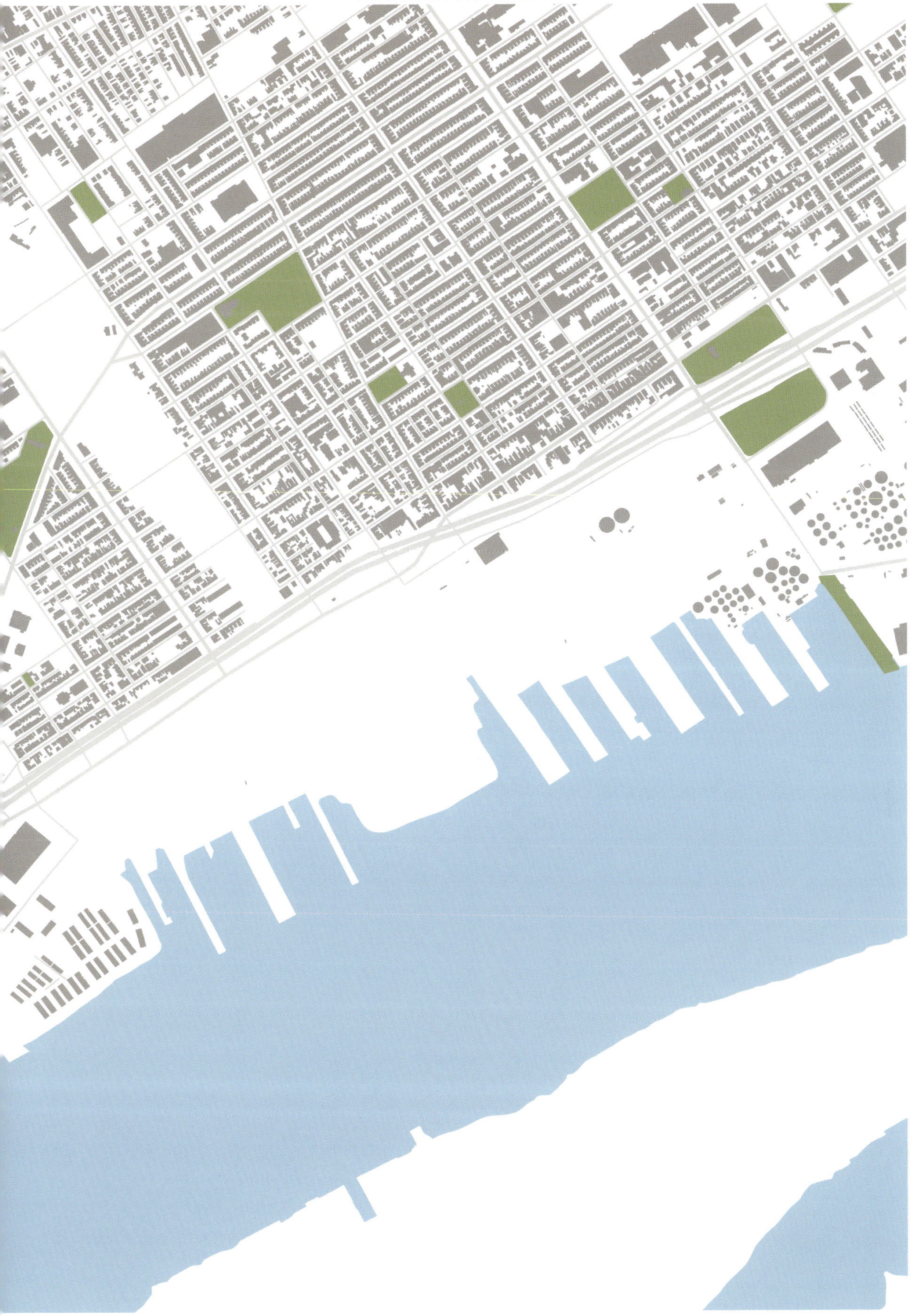

The River Wards' building ghosts tend to show up in the southern area of this part of the city, so this perspective is admittedly focused on communities such as Fishtown and South Kensington, which are experiencing churn and change on pace with Center City. Their ghosts include a mix of residential, industrial, and institutional buildings, befitting the community's long history as a social ecosystem of waterfront life. There is a memorable specificity, then, in the building ghosts of the River Wards, but after they're gone (and, given the insatiable appetite for new construction, the neighborhood inevitably loses these ghosts quickly), they are replaced with something considerably more forgettable.

Historically, the River Wards were a working-class place, resonant with immigrant communities clustered close to the same water that had brought many of them to Philadelphia. They lived alongside local industry—zoning codes would not exist to pry them apart until the early twentieth century—and constructed houses of worship for their brief windows of ritual and rest. These laborers and laypeople certainly created beautiful places, but on the whole it was an everyday beauty that epitomized a vernacular.

In the 1920s, the Frankford section of the Market-Frankford Elevated Line opened for service in the River Wards, establishing new connections to the rest of the city. The construction of Interstate 95 in the 1960s and '70s had the opposite effect. Now, many of the neighborhoods that had grown up near the Delaware River waterfront could no longer reach it. Coupled with the deindustrialization that drained their factories of life and labor, the River Wards spent the later decades of the twentieth century in some stagnation, seeing little to no change.

No longer. Perhaps no part of the city has transformed more in the past two decades than Northern Liberties, Fishtown, and parts of Kensington. Transformed by private investments and public planning initiatives, these neighborhoods have surged in population. But in a community that has always been characterized by recent arrivals, these latest newcomers have inflected the vernacular of the River Wards.

Few other places in the city have been more illustrative of the sort of displacement and dislocation that comes with new construction. The River Wards still include pockets of working-class and immigrant communities, but on the whole the everyday character of the community has become one of teardowns and bloated townhouses. Luxury housing is becoming the prevailing standard—although that "luxury" does not always extend to the building materials. The ubiquitous brick veneers and metal cladding may dominate now, but they'll be disposable later, thus ensuring that these sorts of permutations will repeat every few decades rather than centuries.

The gluttonous demand for construction that is newer, bigger, and shinier (literally, with all that metal sheathing and glass) is not limited to the residential blocks. It has also whittled away at the industrial mammoths and institutional anchors that were once interspersed with all that housing, leaving behind rare instances of building ghosts for something other than rowhouses. And why wouldn't such development seek out those pieces of the ecosystem? They offer the largest possible sites and purportedly blank slates.

Although there are distinctive building ghosts within the River Wards, they speak to losses that are not about any one particular building. Rather, they are about a cumulative tipping point between neighborhood history and identity. Surrounded by so much anonymous design that makes little gesture to community and context, these building ghosts are the remaining link to a particular sense of place. No one would wish for the same torpor that haunted the River Wards in the past, but one would hope that such change could be managed and more thoughtfully considered. Building ghosts can offer both signposts and warning signs for that process. In the pressing case study of the River Wards, how do building ghosts contribute to, and chip away at, a community's sense of self?

1826 Frankford Avenue

Constructed ca. 1880
Demolished in 2019

Number 1826 Frankford Avenue was the latecomer on its block. While most of the neighboring properties to the south were built up before 1875, the undeveloped parcels at numbers 1824–1828 left the block unfinished at its northern end. Until around 1880, the open lots were part of the Cobb and Sheets lumberyard that stretched from Frankford Avenue to Warder (now Blair) Street. At some point between 1875 and 1884, though, the lumberyard left the site, and the last remaining lots received three-story brick buildings to match their neighbors.

The first confirmation of a building on the site at 1826 Frankford Avenue, and people making a home there, is the public notice of the death of ten-month-old George Madden in April 1884. (It was presumably placed by George's parents, Thomas and Carolina Madden.) In the years that followed, the house's tenants included Henry Ingham, who sold cigars, and George Tay, a foreman of some sort. In the ensuing 130-plus years, number 1826 would house as many as nine people at a time.

Around 1889, Julian Jozefowski moved in, along with Caspar Crozier. Both men were tailors, and both may have been Polish immigrants—Jozefowski definitely was. Born circa 1854, Jozefowski settled in Philadelphia by the 1880s. In 1881, he married Bibijanne Kraszewska at St. Peter's Church, at 5th and Girard; they had their first child, Stanislaus "Cheswar," the following year. By the time they moved into 1826 Frankford Avenue, Bibijanne had given birth to four surviving children; two more would be born during their years at number 1826. Filling out the house during this period, a few other tailors of Polish descent moved in and out: Gottlieb, Caspar, and Jacob Krause each lived at number 1826 for a time, although the relationship (if any) among them is unclear.

As number 1826's residents make clear, the area around Frankford Avenue had become a Polish American enclave by the late nineteenth century. It was a community knit together by waves of immigrants driven out of Poland in search of economic opportunity or, all too often, by occupying forces that invaded their country from the east or west. In Philadelphia, they established their own business ventures and mutual aid organizations; the John Sobieski Building and Loan Association, for which Julian Jozefowski served as treasurer, was a blend of both.

Named for a seventeenth-century Polish king, the John Sobieski Building and Loan Association was established in 1889 by a Polish émigré named Vincent Domanski. After struggling upon arrival in Philadelphia, Domanski developed his English skills and carved out a multilingual niche catering to immigrants with their own language barriers. At first, he acted as a sort of banking representative for them, assisting them with forms or fi-

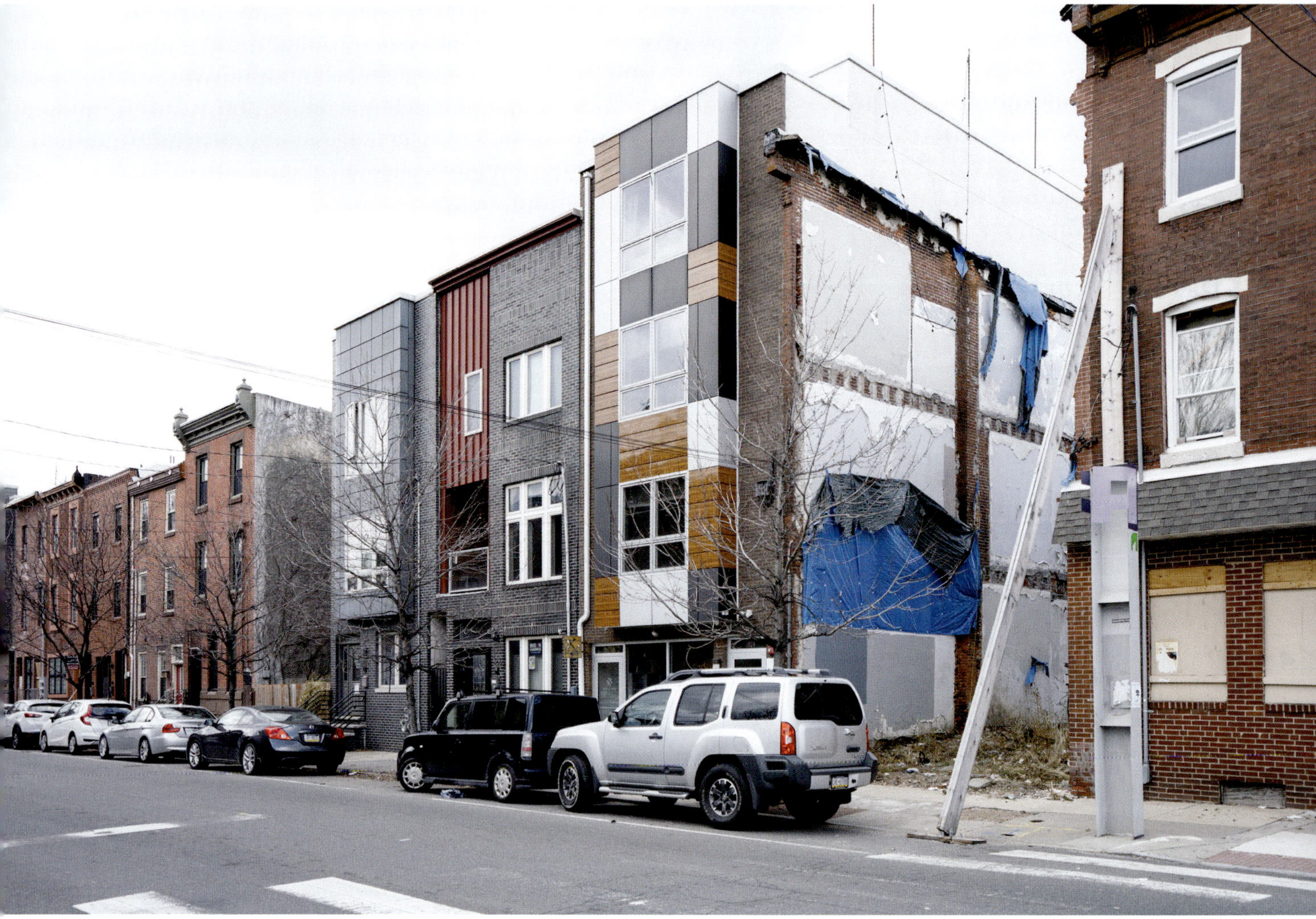

1826 Frankford Avenue. (Photographed January 18, 2021.)

nancial transactions. Later, as he established a foothold and position of trust among them, he became one of the founders of the Polish National Alliance in 1880 and of the Building and Loan Association in 1889. Where traditional banks ignored—or were hostile to—Polish-speaking potential clients, Domanski's organization helped recent immigrants buy housing and insurance.

Although Julian Jozefowski was a treasurer for the association, the organization did not actually help the Jozefowskis purchase the Frankford Avenue property. They were renters for the duration of their time there. Nevertheless, when Julian died in 1896, it was Vincent Domanski himself who accompanied Bibijanne to the City Register's office to act as a witness for the probate process.

After Julian's death, Bibijanne and her six children (the youngest was just two) moved out of 1826 Frankford Avenue to some unknown subsequent address. In place of the tailor's family, a milliner's family moved in. Margaret Hannon had much in common with Bibijanne Jozefowski: a widow herself, Hannon had six or seven grown children in tow when she moved into number 1826. (She had buried three other children.) Hannon, though, was born in Scotland, not Poland, to an Irish father and a Scottish mother. Her family represented a different sort of immigrant enclave in the city's riverfront communities.

As soon as they were old enough to work, most of Margaret Hannon's children took some sort of textile job. Two of her daughters were listed in city directories with the eyebrow-raising job of "underwear operator"; in actuality, these were sewing positions. James Hannon, Margaret's oldest son, was a hat sizer, while the next-oldest child, Owen, was a cloth finisher and dyer. Michael Hannon and a younger Margaret Hannon (the matriarch's daughter) swerved from the professions of their family members. According to the 1900 U.S. Federal Census, Michael was a baseball maker (although the city directory from that same year concurrently listed him as a plumber), while Margaret began working a few years later as a candymaker. At least a few members of the Hannon family would live on Frankford Avenue until 1910 or shortly after.

The building lived an unrecorded existence from 1910 until the late 1930s, when its immigrant associations shifted again. In 1939, Teresa J. Wojenski, the daughter of a Czech immigrant, purchased 1826 and 1828 Frankford Avenue. She quickly resold the properties.

In 1940, the properties were purchased by Anthony Ziemba and Jozefina, his Polish-born wife. Unlike several other owners in the history of number 1826, the Ziembas lived on-site. In 1945, they constructed a new addition at the rear of the building, supplementing the available space for what was by this point five apartments: two on the first story, two on the second story, and one on the third. This multifamily arrangement would remain in place until the building's demolition. In its final five decades, it would be home to people with surnames as varied as Minarik, Murray, Velasquez, Rodriguez, and Marshall.

When the churn of neighborhood change (well, this particular round of neighborhood change, after many preceding generations of it) reached the River Wards in the early twenty-first century, 1826 Frankford Avenue was once again one of the few stragglers on the block. The 2010s saw most of the neighboring properties to the south cleared of their nineteenth-century buildings, making way for modern townhouses, with all the familiar hallmarks: gray exterior finishes; boxy geometric configurations of the primary elevation; sleek metal railings that look as if they were transposed straight from a ship; and metal bump-out bays that jut out from the façade. For several years, number 1826 was a holdout at the north end of the block, insisting on remaining solid while the lots to the south became temporary voids. (It was a reversal of the 1870s, when 1826 Frankford Avenue was one of the few empty lots on the block.) In 2019, though, development marched northward, and the bulldozers reached number 1826.

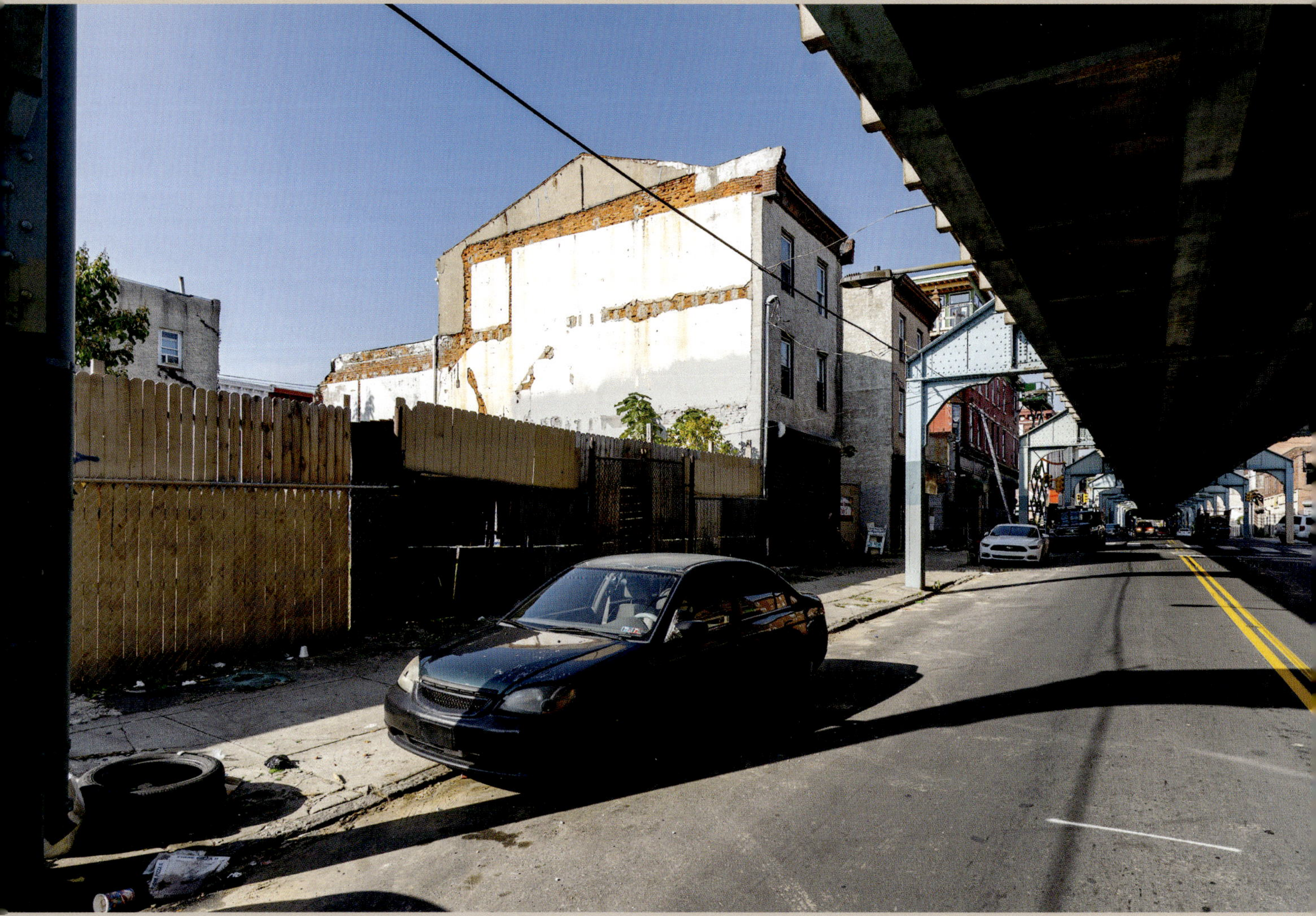

2150 North Front Street. (Photographed October 22, 2020.)

2119 North Front Street

Constructed ca. 1870
Demolished in 2020

For its first forty years, 2119 North Front Street dabbled in other uses: a dry goods store under Henry Kline; a dyeing and scouring operation under R. Rothkugel; J. Cavanaugh's branch store, which sold "baby coaches and go-carts exclusively" (the company's ads emphasized that the store did not bother with dry goods or furniture). By 1917 at the latest, though, the brick building had landed on its longest-term trade: wallpaper.

At first, the building's occupants handled the wallpapering themselves. Someone with the surname Goldberg placed ads offering their services in "first class papering" for $1.75 per room, a fee that somehow included both the material paper itself and the labor of scraping and sizing. By 1932, Samuel Schultz Inc. had purchased the building and begun using it to print and assemble wallpaper books. It maintained this use for more than half a century, although the industrial functions weren't actually sanctioned by the city until 1969, when Samuel Schultz Inc. filed the paperwork to legalize a use that had been in place for more than fifty years by that point. The Front Street property was the company's back-of-house facility, nestled under the Frankford Elevated Line that loomed over Front Street by the 1920s. The company's public-facing shops were at first down the block at 2102 North Front Street, then later on Frankford Avenue, putting a little more distance between its customers and the rumble of the elevated railcars. Number 2119, then, was the utilitarian workhorse that made it possible for the other buildings to be more polished.

Samuel Schultz died at seventy-three in 1967, nearly a year to the day after his wife, Ada, died. His company remained in business after his death but apparently migrated to South Philadelphia, near Passyunk Avenue. Number 2119, meanwhile, declined in condition. In 1986, the front wall was stuccoed to comply with a violation from the city's Department of Licenses and Inspections. When the entire structure was ultimately torn down in 2020 to make way for a new mixed-use building, the demolition revealed—fittingly enough—an entire ghost's worth of painted, peeling wallpaper.

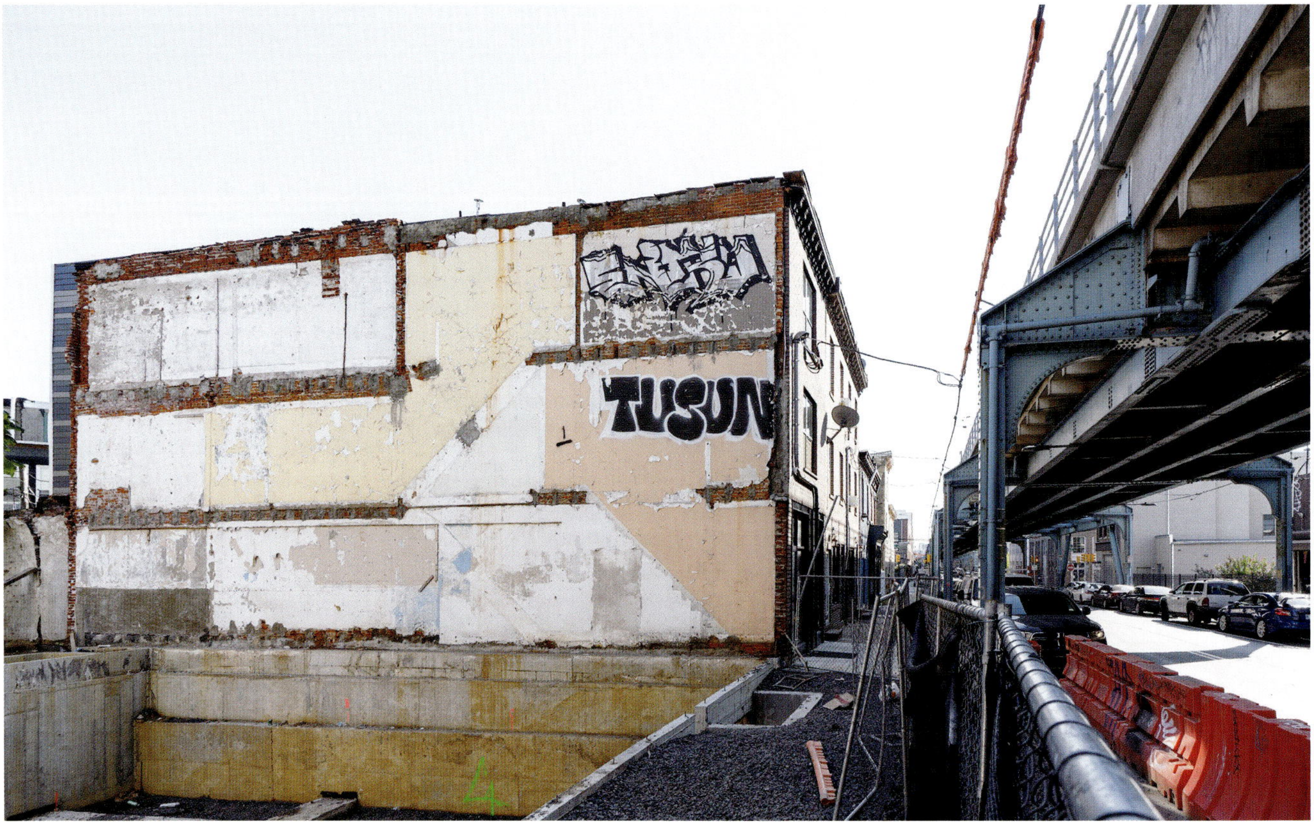

2119 North Front Street. (Photographed October 22, 2020.)

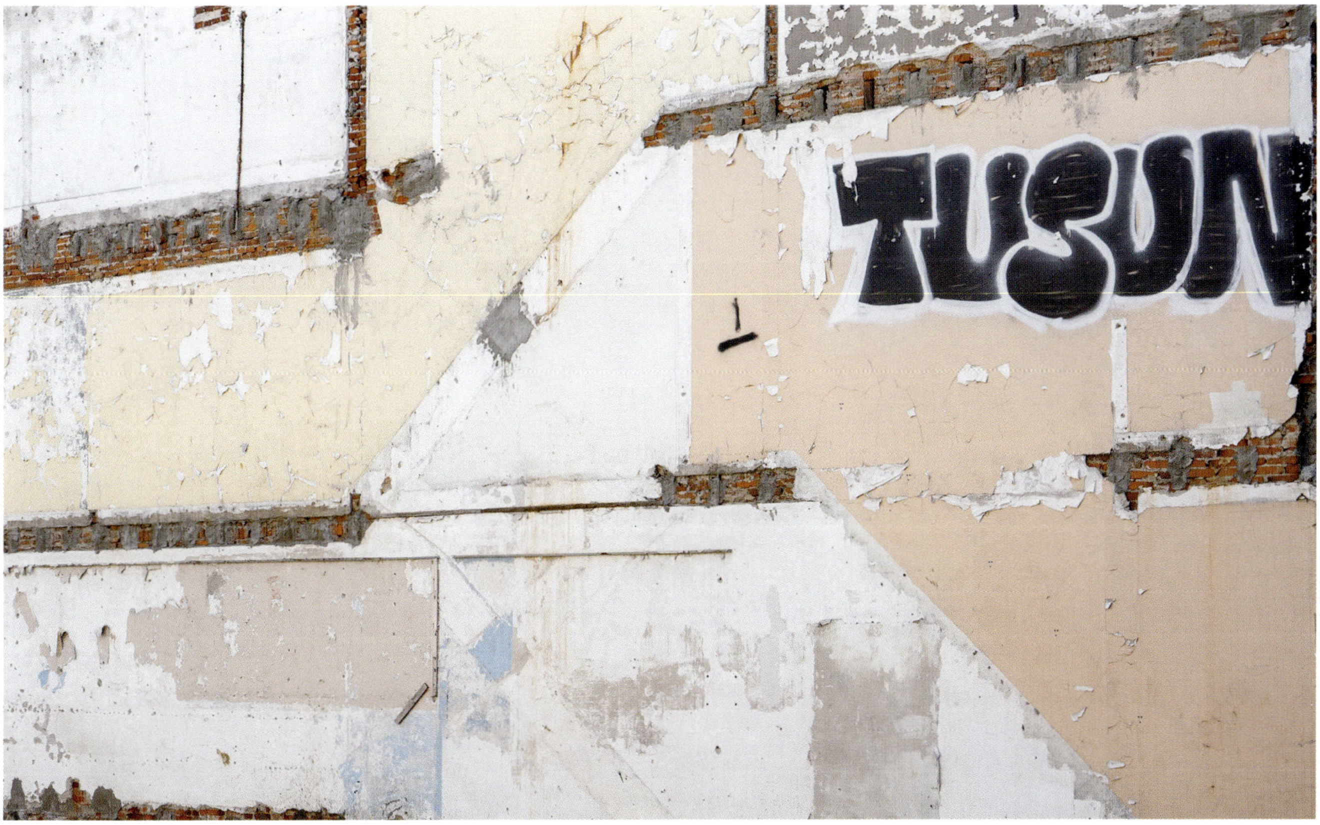

2119 North Front Street. (Photographed October 22, 2020.)

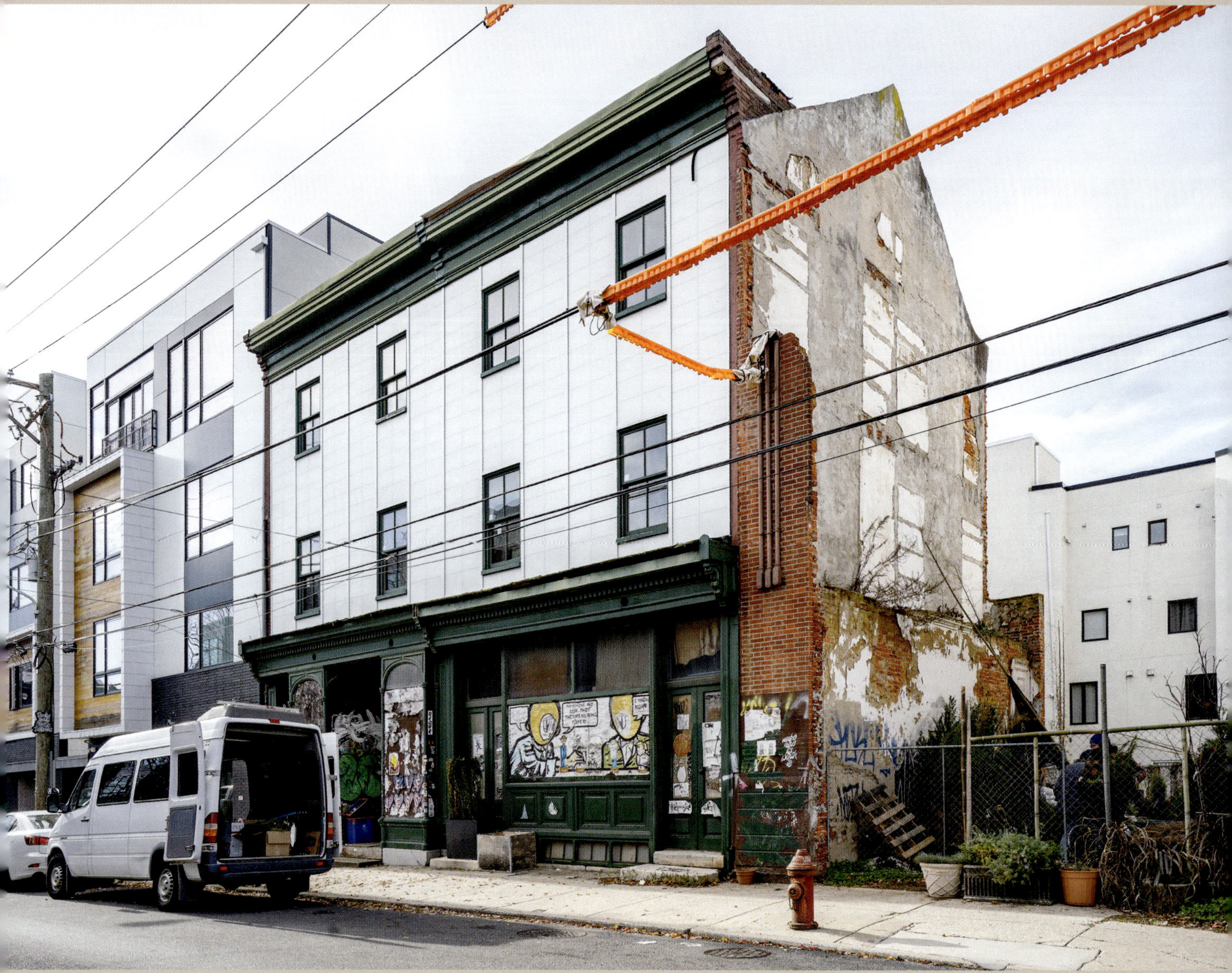

830 North 4th Street. (Photographed December 3, 2020.)

2101 North American Street

Constructed in sections: oldest sections (at southwestern and southeastern corners of the block) constructed ca. 1862; remaining Diamond Street frontage added in 1905; additional American Street frontage constructed in 1915

Demolished ca. 2002

It was hard to pinpoint the appropriate address to research for 2101 North American Street, because by the time it was demolished, the sprawling building (or, more accurately, buildings) spanned most of a city block, fronting Diamond, Philip, and American streets all at once. Yet for all its heft by the time it came down, one of the complex's earliest sections—located at the southeastern corner of the site—began as a simple stable. This utilitarian structure, along with another one on the southwestern corner of the block, was constructed sometime between 1859 and 1862.

In October 1869, Albert E. Eldridge and Ezekiel Stewart purchased the property with robust ambitions for its development. Operating as a real estate outfit known as Eldridge and Stewart, the two men were linked with many acquisitions and sales during this period. At American and Diamond streets, they clearly thought they'd scored a highly desirable tract, given the bordering thoroughfares; in addition to the roads themselves, a branch of the Pennsylvania Railroad stretched north on American Street, heightening the lot's industrial connections. In 1878, Eldridge and Stewart aggressively marketed the lot for use as a fire truck facility, assuming that the municipal government would be motivated to purchase such a well-placed lot in the city's developing River Wards. The sale never went through, though, and the men pivoted to developing it themselves.

Their starting points were the two existing structures: a two-story house at the corner of American and Diamond streets and a two-story stable at Diamond and Philip streets. With those brackets at each end of the site, they commissioned a new building in August 1882. The new structure would extend from American Street to Philip Street, linking the preexisting buildings at their northern ends. The resulting footprint of all three structures formed a horseshoe-shaped building (befitting its earliest section), leaving an opening on Diamond Street. It was this U-shaped structure that was likely responsible for the remarkably persistent outline of a stair on the building ghost.

By 1887, Eldridge and Stewart amplified the industrial capacity (and bankability) of the site: no longer content to watch the train merely pass by their property, the developers constructed spur tracks leading from the American Street railroad branch directly into their buildings. Thus, any industrial operator in the complex could import raw materials directly onto the manufacturing floors and ship the finished products directly out again. Sure enough, by 1900 the American Stone and Builders' Supply Company, as well as a coal outfit known as Bromley and Wittmaier, were both based at the site.

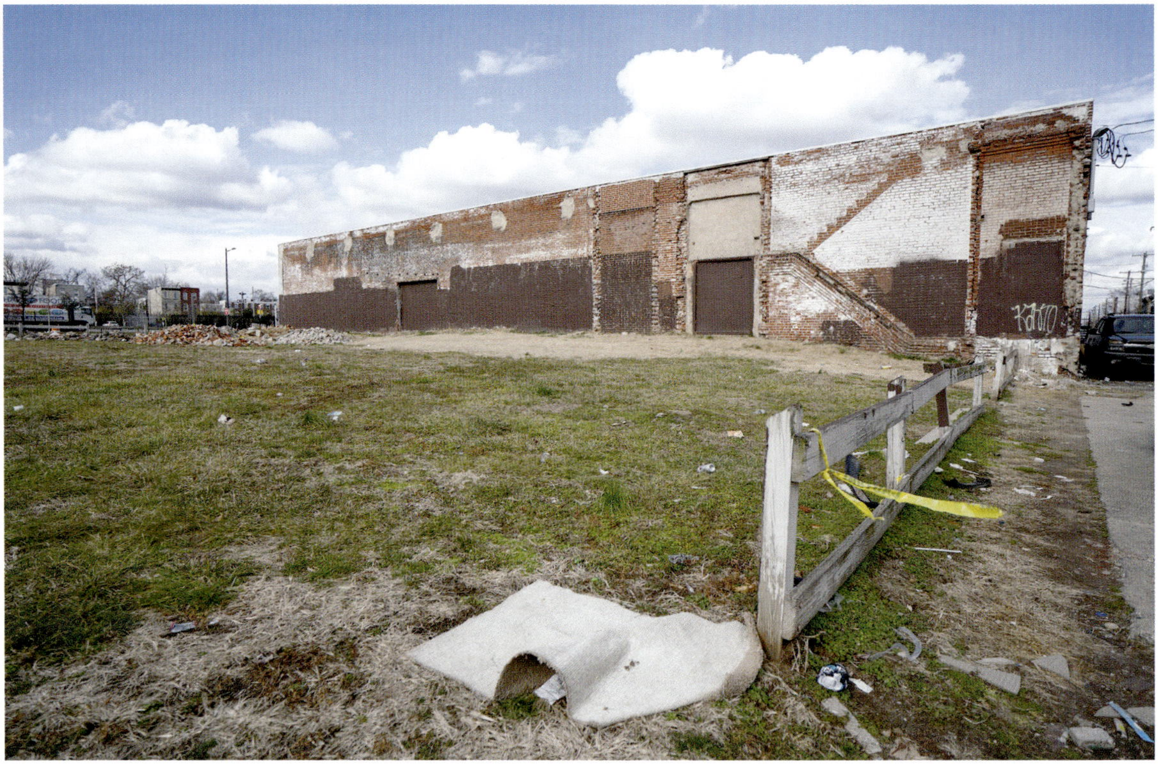

2101 North American Street. (Photographed October 22, 2020.)

The companies no doubt selected this location based on the ease of transport for their heavy, messy materials and products.

Sometime between 1901 and 1904, John Scott and Company purchased the property at an assessed value of $20,000. As a grocery distributor, the company purchased what amounted to a two-story brick office (the former house at the southwestern corner), a two-story brick stable, and the large two-story brick storehouse that connected them, along with an assortment of coal sheds. (The trains needed to be powered somehow!) All together, the lot measured 100 feet by nearly 122 feet.

In 1905, John Scott and Company commissioned the renowned local builders William Steele and Sons to construct a four-story store and warehouse, measuring 50 feet by 120 feet, to complete the Diamond Street frontage. William Steele and Sons drew up the plans themselves, designing a structure to be built of "brick and slow burning construction"—a necessary precaution, given that the site summoned in volatile train engines on a regular basis. In 1915, John Scott and Company doubled down on its investment, constructing another four-story warehouse on the site, this time apparently on the American Street side. The local architect M. Ward Easby was responsible for those expansion plans.

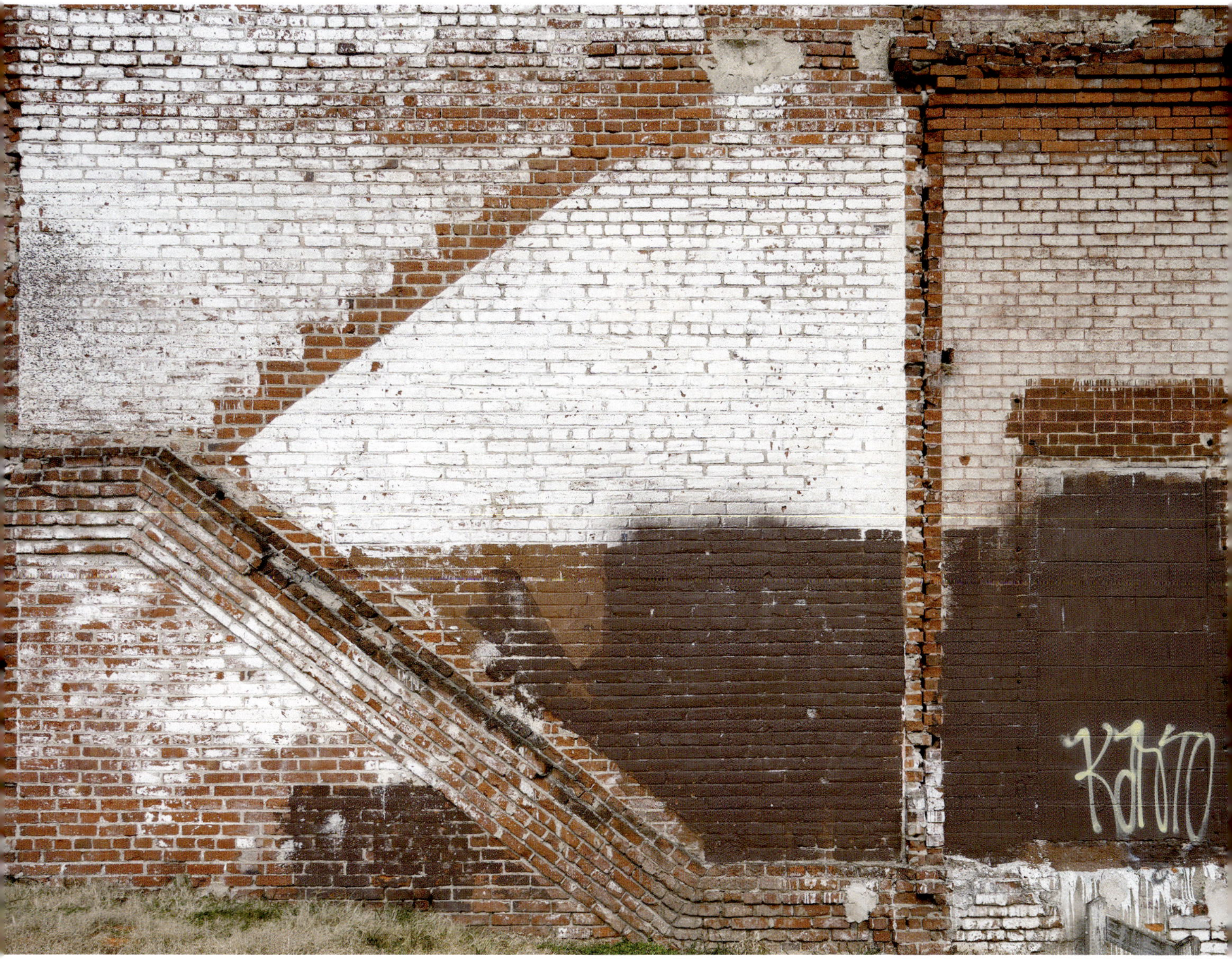

Detail of 2101 North American Street. (Photographed October 22, 2020.)

The grocers continued to operate at Diamond and American streets until 1934, when John Scott and Company sold the parcel to E. Winfield Scott and his wife, Margaret. It is unclear whether the two Scott men were related, but Winfield does not appear to have shared the grocery business with John: as of 1936, he was president of the North Star Building and Loan Association. In 1941, he sold 2101 North American Street (and the many frontages that constituted that parcel address) to Budget Food Markets Inc., reintroducing the grocery business to the site.

In 1957, the property pivoted from foodstuffs to tires when the Hoffman Tire Service Company purchased the building. Capitalizing on the wide openings created for the railroad connections and other shipping bays, and the large industrial windows that lit the service bays on the interior, the company imported and exported car parts. It painted the building exterior at the first story, with bold vertical lettering applied to the brick spandrels between the windows. The three upper stories were much more muted, in keeping with the apparent office functions within.

In October 1966, Hoffman Tire Service Company announced plans to construct a new fifty thousand-square-foot warehouse on a six-acre tract in Spring House, Pennsylvania. Although the announcement did not mention the company's American Street site, it seems likely that Hoffman's move to the suburbs also meant a retreat from the city. It was not the only industrial operation to bid farewell to the neighborhood around this time. Indeed, Hoffman's departure was but one in a much larger pattern of deindustrialization that marked this period in the River Wards, in Philadelphia, and in the country as a whole.

The building was demolished in the first few years of the twenty-first century. As the neighborhood around it accelerated toward demographic change, the property cycled through various city agencies (including the Redevelopment Authority and the Philadelphia Authority for Industrial Development) before landing in private ownership again after the 2008 financial crisis. As of 2023, construction is underway on a new building to host a day-care center—complete, unsubtle proof that this site isn't for heavy industry anymore.

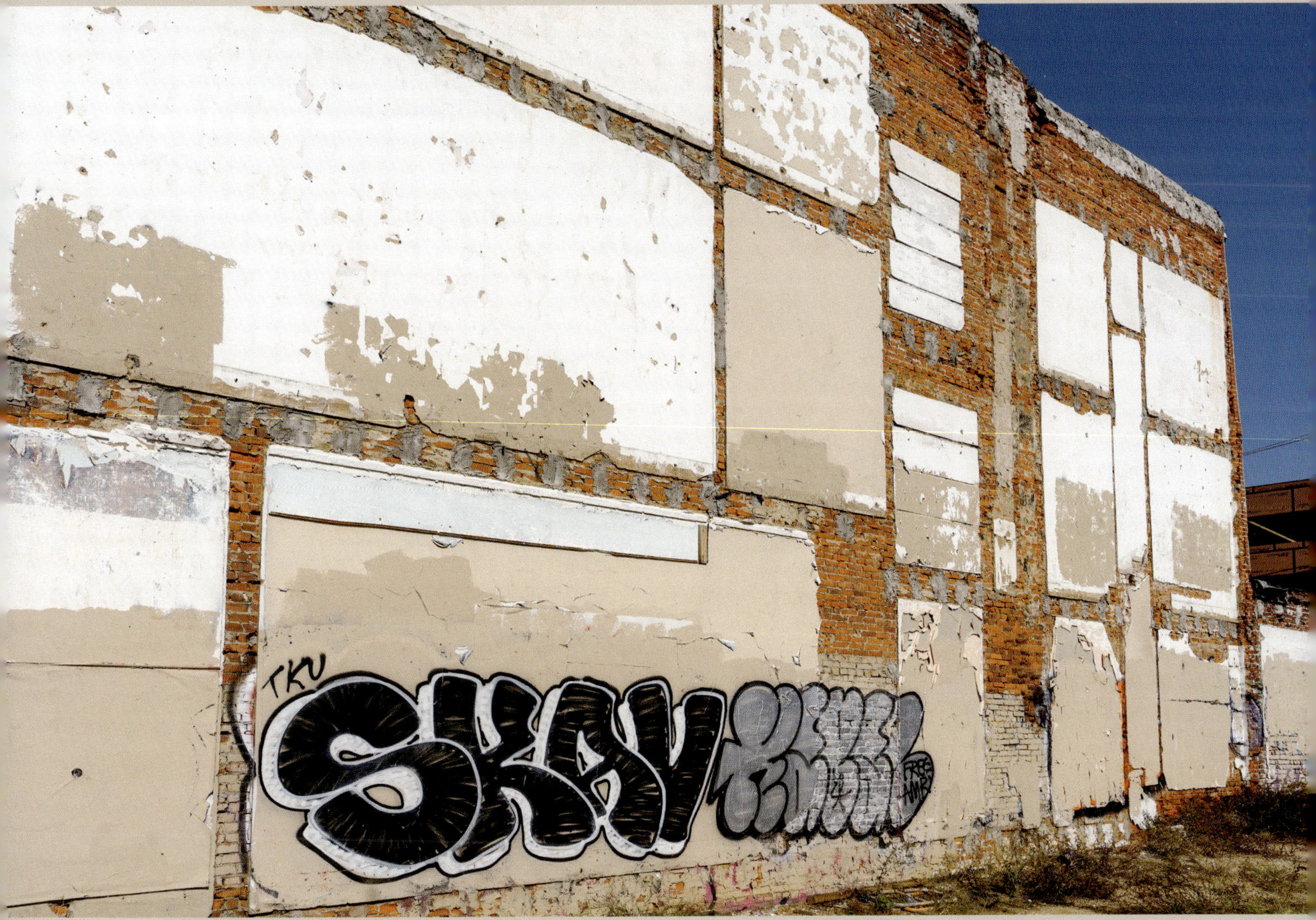

1329 North Front Street. (Photographed October 22, 2020.)

1209–1211 North Hancock Street

Constructed ca. 1862
Demolished in 2017

Philip Hammerschlag was born in Hanover, Germany; his wife, Henrietta Gardner, was born in Savannah, Georgia. Yet somehow they met, married, and built a life in Philadelphia—at 1209–1211 North Hancock Street specifically. Philip was seventeen years older than Henrietta; he was thirty-four to her seventeen when they got married in 1875. By that time, he had owned the building on Hancock Street for more than a decade; his butcher shop (which he started alongside his father, Solomon) was likely one of the first uses of the three-story rowhouse.

In the 1880s, Philip Hammerschlag traded the building back and forth with his business partner, Werner Amran. Together, the two sold kosher meat and goose cheese for a few years, placing ads in the *Jewish Exponent* to "respectfully solicit the patronage of a Matzo-loving community." From 1209–1211 North Hancock Street, Philip maintained a web of trade connections around the world, particularly in the Scandinavian countries. Meanwhile, at home (side by side with the business), Henrietta gave birth to nine surviving children in thirteen years. Minnie was the oldest, born circa 1879, and Beulah was the youngest, born circa 1892.

In September 1901, Philip Hammerschlag died suddenly; his illness gave only three days' warning. Shortly after his death, the Mickve Israel Congregation passed a resolution to pay tribute to him as a pillar of the Jewish community in Philadelphia, memorializing his "fidelity and whole-hearted zeal." In closing, the resolution issued its condolences to Philip's family.

Philip Hammerschlag's loss may have been deeply felt in many circles, but at Hammerschlag's butcher shop there was hardly a noticeable gap between his death and Henrietta's succession. He bequeathed to her all of his real estate, including numbers 1209–1211, and she stepped quickly into the breach of his business interests, even with several of her children still young and at home. She was soon listed in city directories as "Henrietta Hammerschlag, [of] P. Hammerschlag & Co." The company's newspaper ads continued unabated in the *Jewish Exponent*, making sure that readers knew that Hammerschlag's Sausage still prospered and was available for sale at local delicatessen dealers or directly from 1209–1211 North Hancock Street.

Three years after her husband's death, in 1904, Henrietta commissioned Matthew Schmidt to erect a two-story brick addition (measuring 23 feet by 38 feet) to the property. At a cost of $3,590, the project was substantial. Then, as if she weren't already juggling enough with her business, family, and construction project, Henrietta announced the betrothal of her daughter the following year: Rachel Hammerschlag would be marrying Arthur B. Wertheim of Toronto.

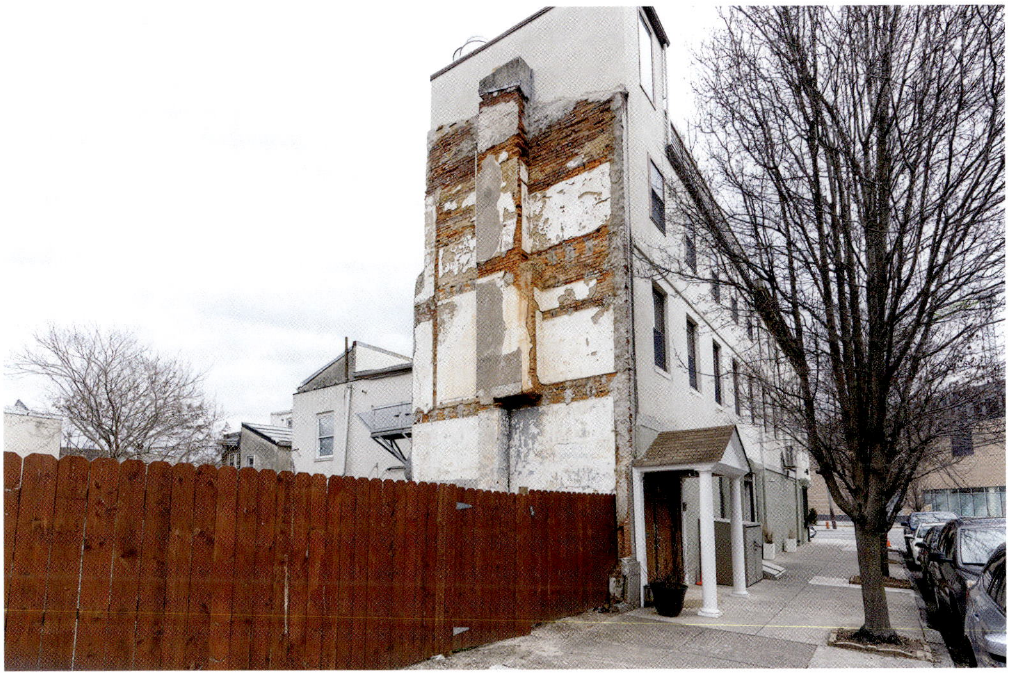

1209–1211 North Hancock Street. (Photographed January 18, 2021.)

In 1910, as her youngest daughter, Beulah, reached eighteen, Henrietta placed ads in the real estate section of the newspapers listing the property in both the "For Sale" and "For Rent" columns on the same day. She marketed 1209–1211 North Hancock as both a "large . . . factory that can be used as machine, blacksmith, [or] rag shop" and a "double dwelling, 14 rooms, suitable for apartments." When those sales pitches didn't work in March, she tried again in June: "1211 North Hancock Street, store and 2-story concrete factory in rear, suitable for ice cream manufacturer." It was not until 1920 that Henrietta was able to offload the property, nearly sixty years after Philip had purchased it.

Despite all of Henrietta's creative ideas for other building uses, the sausage factory operations in the building were persistent. After the Hammerschlags, the building housed first the Sinai Kosher Sausage Factory, then the Philadelphia Kosher Meat and Provision Company, the Hallstead Provision Company, and the Girard Provision Company. Shortly before the building was demolished in 2017, it still bore the signage of Jon Breslow Deli Products. In all, 1209–1211 North Hancock Street saw nearly universal use as a butcher shop from the time it was constructed in the mid-nineteenth century until its demolition in the early twenty-first century. Without Henrietta Hammerschlag, though, and her doggedness at the helm after her husband's death, such a continuous story might not have been possible.

1407 Marlborough Street/309 Belgrade Street

Constructed in 1851 (expanded in 1870)
Demolished in 2015

The building ghost is so muted, it's almost banal—a backdrop for a quiet private parking lot for the three-story townhouses on Marlborough Street (banal in their own right). But when it stood, from 1851 to 2015, the ghosted building was anything but muted; a former church, it owed its very existence to the boisterous clamor of the Second Great Awakening in the nineteenth century. The building was enlarged at least once, and it changed affiliations many times over the course of its history, with seemingly as many names then as it has parking spaces now. For each of its incarnations, though, the building ghost's wall framed the chancel, orienting worshipers toward the east, as Christian ecclesiastical architecture has tried to arrange itself for millennia.

When it was demolished, the building was the home of Pilgrim Congregational Church. (That congregation merged with St. Michael's Lutheran Church of Kensington as part of the sale and demolition of the site.) The building began in 1851, though, as the First Independent Christian Church of Kensington, an offshoot of the Union Wesleyan Church of Kensington (also known at some points as the First Associated Methodist Church of Kensington and Ebenezer Associated Methodist Episcopal Church). One of just two independent churches in the city at that time, the congregation split from its predecessor under the leadership of a charismatic preacher named Reverend J. (John) G. Wilson. As one newspaper described the split:

> The history of all independent church organizations is very much the same. The ecclesiastical garment is found too tight in some part, and is exchanged for a fuller robe. . . . The people of the Marlborough Street Church were originally Methodist Protestants, but in 1851, they withdrew with their pastor, the Rev. J.G. Wilson, taking . . . the Bible alone as their creed.

The move (in both address and affiliation) marked a rejection of sectarianism as the congregation renounced its ties to the Methodist Protestant Church. Its members purchased the lot in April 1851 and started construction on a new building soon after to host their revivalist services.

By 1870, the congregation had grown enough to merit (and fund) a new building campaign, enlarging the earlier brick structure and adding a serpentine stone façade on its western elevation. Known for its green tint, serpentine stone was popular through the late nineteenth century until it also became known for its notoriously porous, deteriorating quality, which probably explains why the church parged and painted its serpentine stone in the twentieth century.

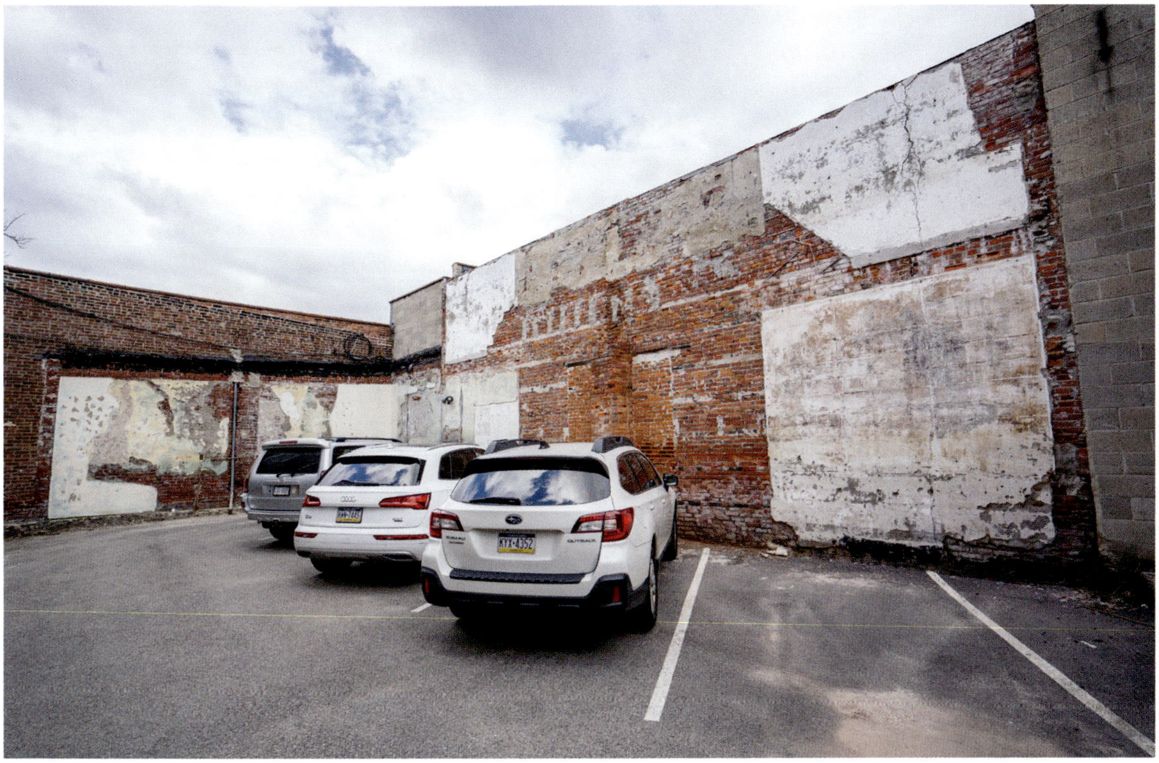

1407 Marlborough Street/309 Belgrade Street. (Photographed January 18, 2021.)

In 1897, the First Independent Christian Church of Kensington became Pilgrim Congregational Church and then, in the 1950s, the Pilgrim Community United Church of Christ (UCC). Despite the transformations in name and liturgy, though, the building beckoned congregation members with the same procession for more than a century and a half: approaching the church on Marlborough Street, they crossed the threshold from the west and moved toward the east—an ecclesiastical orientation linked from the earliest Christian churches with the symbolism of Christ as the rising sun (or Son). There, the congregation would worship, pray, and sing, turning toward the wall that would become a building ghost, and then turning away from it to leave the church and disperse back into the Kensington neighborhood.

Eventually, these rituals ceased as the congregation shrank and decided to merge with a Lutheran church nearby. The sacred symbols were pared from the building, and the building was cleared to make way for private residences. Now it's the homeowners' cars that enter and face east.

River Wards References

General Resources

Bromley, George. *Atlas of the City of Philadelphia*. Philadelphia: G. W. Bromley, 1895. Athenaeum of Philadelphia, *Greater Philadelphia GeoHistory Network*. http://www.philageohistory.org/tiles/viewer.

Bromley, George W., and Walter S. Bromley. *Atlas of the City of Philadelphia, Complete in One Volume, from Actual Surveys and Official Plans*. Philadelphia: G. W. Bromley, 1910. Athenaeum of Philadelphia, *Greater Philadelphia GeoHistory Network*. https://www.philageohistory.org/rdic-images/view-image.cfm/237%2DMP%2D022.

——. *Atlas of the City of Philadelphia, 18th, 19th, and 31st Wards*. Philadelphia: G. W. Bromley, 1887. Philadelphia Water Department, *Greater Philadelphia GeoHistory Network*. http://www.philageohistory.org/rdic-images/view-image.cfm/BRM1887.PhilaWards18_19_31.013.Plate_K.

Hopkins, G. M. *City Atlas of Philadelphia by Wards, Complete in Seven Volumes* (1875). Private collection of Matt Ainslie, *Greater Philadelphia GeoHistory Network*, http://www.philageohistory.org/tiles/viewer.

"Insurance Maps of Philadelphia, Pennsylvania, Volume 8" (online database). Sanborn Map Company, New York, 1917. *Penn State University Libraries, Digital Collections*. https://digital.libraries.psu.edu/digital/collection/maps1/id/18045/rec/1.

Smedley, Samuel. *Atlas of the City of Philadelphia*. Philadelphia: J. B. Lippincott, 1862. Map Collection, Free Library of Philadelphia, *Greater Philadelphia GeoHistory Network*. http://www.philageohistory.org/tiles/viewer.

Smith, J. L. *Atlas of the 18th, 19th, and 31st Wards of the City of Philadelphia*. Athenaeum of Philadelphia, *Greater Philadelphia GeoHistory Network*. https://www.philageohistory.org/rdic-images/view-image.cfm/JLS1904.PhilaWards18_19_31.009.Plate_5.

1826 Frankford Avenue

Note: Julian Jozefowski's first name was at times mistakenly recorded as Julius, and his surname was alternately transcribed as Jozewowski or Jozefhwski. "Julian Jozefowski" is used on his final will and probate, so I use it as the authoritative spelling.

"Applications for Marriage Licenses Issued in Philadelphia." *Philadelphia Inquirer*, April 24, 1949. https://www.newspapers.com/image/172034377.

Commonwealth of Pennsylvania. *Official Documents Comprising the Department and Other Reports Made to the Governor, Senate and House of Representatives of Pennsylvania*, vol. 5. Harrisburg[?]: Clarence M. Busch, 1897. *Google Books*. https://www.google.com/books/edition/Official_Documents_Comprising_the_Depart/jGZDAQAAMAAJ?hl=en&gbpv=1.

Department of Records, Philadelphia City Archives. 1826 Frankford Avenue deeds (map registry no. 14N210069). Various dates.

"Died." *Philadelphia Inquirer*, December 19, 1896. https://www.newspapers.com/image/168410127.

"1826 Frankford Avenue: Zoning Permit Documents." *City of Philadelphia Atlas*. Accessed January 10, 2023. https://s3.amazonaws.com/lni-zoning-pdfs/219-158299.pdf.

General Assembly of the Commonwealth of Pennsylvania. *Laws of the General Assembly of the Commonwealth of Pennsylvania, Passed at the Session of 1889, in the One Hundred and Thirteenth Year of Independence*. Harrisburg: Edwin K. Meyers, 1889. *Google Books*. https://www.google.com/books/edition/Laws_of_the_General_Assembly_of_the_Comm/rh1AAAAAYAAJ?hl=en&gbpv=1&dq=%22john+sobieski+building+and+loan+association%22&pg=SL1-PA155&printsec=frontcover.

Kuzniewski, Anthony J. "The Catholic Church in the Life of the Polish Americans." In *Poles in America: Bicentennial Essays*, edited by Frank Mocha, 399–422. Stevens Point, WI: Worzalla, 1978.

Magda, Matthew S. *Polish Presence in Pennsylvania*. Pennsylvania History Studies no. 24. University Park: Pennsylvania Historical Association, 1992.

[Pennsylvania] Department of Banking. *Pennsylvania Building and Loan Associations*. [Harrisburg]: Department of Banking, 1930.

"Pennsylvania, U.S., Death Certificates, 1803–1915" (online database). Digital image s.v. "Jozefowski, Julius." *Ancestry.com*. https://www.ancestrylibrary.com/discoveryui-content/view/1380411:2535?tid=&pid=&queryId=554fd4e6c426ee154f423c8c45492ef4&_phsrc=VNq688&_phstart=successSource.

———. Digital image s.v. "Madden, Geo. Wm." *Ancestry.com*. https://www.ancestrylibrary.com/discoveryui-content/view/2223046:2535?tid=&pid=&queryId=554fd4e6c426ee154f423c8c45492ef4&_phsrc=VNq692&_phstart=successSource.

"Pennsylvania, U.S., Death Certificates, 1906–1969" (online database). Digital image s.v. "Ziemba, Josephine." *Ancestry.com*. https://www.ancestrylibrary.com/imageviewer/collections/5164/images/42410_1521003238_0943-02249?pid=7037753&usePUB=true&_phsrc=VNq763&_phstart=successSource&usePUBJs=true.

"Pennsylvania, U.S., Wills and Probate Records, 1683–1993" (online database). Digital image s.v. "Jozefowski, Julian." *Ancestry.com*. https://www.ancestrylibrary.com/imageviewer/collections/8802/images/004378468_00224?pId=2440137.

"Philadelphia Real Estate Transactions." *Philadelphia Inquirer*, May 9, 1999. https://www.newspapers.com/image/179625602.

———. *Philadelphia Inquirer*, January 16, 2005. https://www.newspapers.com/image/199289691.

Pinkowski, Edward. "The Great Influx of Polish Immigrants and the Industries They Entered." In *Poles in America: Bicentennial Essays*, edited by Frank Mocha, 303–370. Stevens Point, WI: Worzalla, 1978.

"Polish Roman Catholics." *Philadelphia Times*, September 18, 1896. https://www.newspapers.com/image/52848749.

"U.S., City Directories, 1822–1995" (online database). Digital image s.v. "Cobb & Sheetz," 1874. *Ancestry.com*. https://www.ancestrylibrary.com/discoveryui-content/view/176371177:2469?tid=&pid=&queryId=d4de440b77264e1c96ca8cac21e8646c&_phsrc=VNq687&_phstart=successSource.

———. Digital image s.v. "Crozier, Caspar," 1889. *Ancestry.com*. https://www.ancestrylibrary.com/imageviewer/collections/2469/images/2594002?pid=146190488&usePUB=true&_phsrc=VNq693&_phstart=successSource&usePUBJs=true.

———. Digital image s.v. "Hannon, Margaret," 1901. *Ancestry.com*. https://www.ancestrylibrary.com/imageviewer/collections/2469/images/2871447?pid=1188973096&usePUB=true&_phsrc=VNq693&_phstart=successSource&usePUBJs=true.

———. Digital image s.v. "Hannon, Margaret," 1908. *Ancestry.com*. https://www.ancestrylibrary.com/imageviewer/collections/2469/images/2790468?pid=166220256&usePUB=true&_phsrc=VNq687&_phstart=successSource&usePUBJs=true.

———. Digital image s.v. "Hannon, Michael," 1900. *Ancestry.com*. https://www.ancestrylibrary.com/imageviewer/collections/2469/images/2870045?pid=177527032&usePUB=true&_phsrc=VNq694&_phstart=successSource&usePUBJs=true.

———. Digital image s.v. "Ingham, Henry R.," 1887. *Ancestry.com*. https://www.ancestrylibrary.com/imageviewer/collections/2469/images/2588350?pid=145358735&usePUB=true&_phsrc=VNq693&_phstart=successSource&usePUBJs=true.

———. Digital image s.v. "Jozefowski, Julian," 1889. *Ancestry.com*. https://www.ancestrylibrary.com/imageviewer/collections/2469/images/2594512?pid=146269752&usePUB=true&_phsrc=VNq693&_phstart=successSource&usePUBJs=true.

———. Digital image s.v. "Jozefowski, Julius," 1893. *Ancestry.com*. https://www.ancestrylibrary.com/imageviewer/collections/2469/images/2852627?pid=174055667&usePUB=true&_phsrc=VNq694&_phstart=successSource&usePUBJs=true.

———. Digital image s.v. "Krause, Caspar," 1890. *Ancestry.com*. https://www.ancestrylibrary.com/imageviewer/collections/2469/images/2854934?pid=174599150&usePUB=true&_phsrc=VNq694&_phstart=successSource&usePUBJs=true.

———. Digital image s.v. "Krouse, Gottlieb," 1890. *Ancestry.com*. https://www.ancestrylibrary.com/imageviewer/collections/2469/images/2590497?pid=145677599&usePUB=true&_phsrc=VNq693&_phstart=successSource&usePUBJs=true.

———. Digital image s.v. "Tay, George W.," 1888. *Ancestry.com*. https://www.ancestrylibrary.com/imageviewer/collections/2469/images/2873167?pid=178175468&usePUB=true&_phsrc=VNq694&_phstart=successSource&usePUBJs=true.

"U.S. Federal Census" (online database). Digital image s.v. "Hannon, Owen," 1900. *Ancestry.com*. https://www.ancestrylibrary.com/imageviewer/collections/7602/images/4115197_00451?pid=58666293&usePUB=true&_phsrc=VNq698&_phstart=successSource&usePUBJs=true.

———. Digital image s.v. "Hannon, Owen," 1910. *Ancestry.com*. https://www.ancestrylibrary.com/imageviewer/collections/7884/images/4450056_00074?pid=136067768&usePUB=true&_phsrc=VNq698&_phstart=successSource&usePUBJs=true.

———. Digital image s.v. "Wojenski, Theresa," 1940. *Ancestry.com*. https://www.ancestrylibrary.com/discoveryui-content/view/24080068:2442.

2119 North Front Street

"Action Line; Dial CO 3-7000." *Philadelphia Inquirer*, July 4, 1970. https://www.newspapers.com/image/179951352.

Department of Records, Philadelphia City Archives. 2119 North Front Street deeds (map registry nos. 18N240086, 18N240087, 18N240043). Various dates.

"Destroyed What They Could Not Steal." *Philadelphia Times*, April 28, 1896. https://www.newspapers.com/image/53789134.

"J. Cavanaugh." *Philadelphia Inquirer*, July 1, 1901. https://www.newspapers.com/image/168403349.

"Male Help Wanted." *Philadelphia Inquirer*, August 18, 1958. https://www.newspapers.com/image/176693345.

Malnic, Eric. "Francis X. Bushman Dies; Film Lover, 83." *Philadelphia Inquirer*, August 24, 1966. https://www.newspapers.com/image/179786699.

"Painting and Paperhanging." *Philadelphia Inquirer*, March 18, 1917. https://www.newspapers.com/image/169063964.

"Permits Issued Yesterday." *Philadelphia Inquirer*, March 13, 1902. https://www.newspapers.com/image/168210285.

"Spring Time Is Wallpaper and Paint Time." *Philadelphia Inquirer*, April 2, 1950. https://www.newspapers.com/image/173733627.

"Throttled by a Pawnbroker." *Philadelphia Times*, September 21, 1878. https://www.newspapers.com/image/52212930.

"2119 N. Front Street: Zoning Permit Documents." *City of Philadelphia Atlas*. Accessed January 10, 2023. https://s3.amazonaws.com/lni-zoning-pdfs/219-166441.pdf.

2101 North American Street

"Activities of Day in Real Estate." *Philadelphia Inquirer*, December 31, 1941. https://www.newspapers.com/image/171765429.

"Advance Construction News." *Philadelphia Real Estate Record and Builders' Guide*, July 21, 1915. *Greater Philadelphia GeoHistory Network*. http://www.philageohistory.org/rdic-images/view-book-uv.cfm/PhilaBuildersGuide_v30_1915#?ft=&q=%22american%20and%20diamond%22&c=&m=&s=&cv=573&xywh=-3329%2C-1%2C14663%2C4968.

"Annual Meetings." *Philadelphia Inquirer*, December 10, 1936. https://www.newspapers.com/image/176094250.

"Ask Your Grocer for Sun-Lite Brand." *Philadelphia Inquirer*, May 6, 1919. https://www.newspapers.com/image/162835806.
"Building and Real Estate Notes." *Philadelphia Real Estate Record and Builders' Guide*, January 25, 1905. *Greater Philadelphia GeoHistory Network*. http://www.philageohistory.org/rdic-images/view-book-uv.cfm/PhilaBuildersGuide_v20_1905#?ft=&q=%22american%20and%20diamond%22&c=&m=&s=&cv=50&xywh=3234%2C2689%2C7027%2C1517.
"Building Permits." *Philadelphia Inquirer*, August 17, 1882. https://www.newspapers.com/image/247862230.
———. *Philadelphia Real Estate Record and Builders' Guide*, January 31, 1887. *Greater Philadelphia GeoHistory Network*. http://www.philageohistory.org/rdic-images/view-book-uv.cfm/PhilaBuildersGuide_v2_1887#?ft=&q=%22american%20and%20diamond%22&c=&m=&s=&cv=55&xywh=-3450%2C-1%2C14120%2C4784.
———. *Philadelphia Real Estate Record and Builders' Guide*, April 19, 1905. *Greater Philadelphia GeoHistory Network*. http://www.philageohistory.org/rdic-images/view-book-uv.cfm/PhilaBuildersGuide_v20_1905#?ft=&q=%22american%20and%20diamond%22&c=&m=&s=&cv=249&xywh=-3527%2C-1%2C14569%2C4936.
"Building Permits Issued." *Philadelphia Times*, March 22, 1893. https://www.newspapers.com/image/53790088.
"Cape May." *Philadelphia Inquirer*, July 28, 1895. https://www.newspapers.com/image/168331443.
"Conveyances." *Philadelphia Real Estate Record and Builders' Guide*, January 30, 1901. *Greater Philadelphia GeoHistory Network*. http://www.philageohistory.org/rdic-images/view-book-uv.cfm/PhilaBuildersGuide_v16_1901#?ft=&q=%22american%20and%20diamond%22&c=&m=&s=&cv=729&xywh=-3573%2C0%2C14938%2C5060.
"Conveyances: Philadelphia." *Philadelphia Real Estate Record and Builders' Guide*, November 6, 1901. *Greater Philadelphia GeoHistory Network*. http://www.philageohistory.org/rdic-images/view-book-uv.cfm/PhilaBuildersGuide_v16_1901#?ft=&q=%22american%20and%20diamond%22&c=&m=&s=&cv=76&xywh=3020%2C2433%2C5907%2C2001.
Department of Records, Philadelphia City Archives. 2101 North American Street deeds (map registry nos. 28N180208, 28N180210, 28N180042). Various dates.
"Fire Commissioners." *Philadelphia Inquirer*, February 27, 1878. https://www.newspapers.com/image/167946104.
"Historical Review: An Epitome of the Manufacturing Industries, Commercial Enterprizes and Representative Business Houses of Philadelphia." In *Pennsylvania Historical Review: Gazetteer, Post-office, Express, and Telegraph Guide, City of Philadelphia, Leading Merchants and Manufacturers*. New York: Historical Publishing, 1886. *Google Books*. https://www.google.com/books/edition/Pennsylvania_Historical_Review/6ZFDAQAAMAAJ?hl=en&gbpv=1&bsq=eldridge.
La Croix, Harry J. "Delaware Valley: 18th Expansion under way at Synthane Corp." *Philadelphia Inquirer*, October 10, 1966. https://www.newspapers.com/image/179796073.
"The Latest News in Real Estate." *Philadelphia Inquirer*, May 14, 1895. https://www.newspapers.com/image/168184443.
———. *Philadelphia Inquirer*, January 4, 1905. https://www.newspapers.com/image/168330931.
Philadelphia Department of Records. *PhillyHistory.org* (online database). Various dates.
"Real Estate News." *Philadelphia Inquirer*, January 17, 1957. https://www.newspapers.com/image/176088705.
"2101 N. American Street: Zoning Permit Documents." *City of Philadelphia Atlas*. Accessed January 10, 2023. https://s3.amazonaws.com/lni-zoning-pdfs/27-321303.pdf.
"U.S., City Directories, 1822–1995" (online database). Digital image s.v. "American Stone & Building Supply Co.," 1900. *Ancestry.com*. https://www.ancestrylibrary.com/discoveryui-content/view/177434238:2469?tid=&pid=&queryId=8a7eedac3da63d20e14d04df0febc0cb&_phsrc=VNq708&_phstart=successSource.

1209–1211 North Hancock Street

"Affairs That Interest the Society World." *Philadelphia Inquirer*, March 5, 1905. https://www.newspapers.com/image/168015277.

"Building Permits." *Philadelphia Real Estate Record and Builders' Guide*, July 13, 1904. *Greater Philadelphia GeoHistory Network*. http://www.philageohistory.org/rdic-images/view-book-uv.cfm/PhilaBuildersGuide_v19_1904#?ft=&q=%22hancock%20st%22%20AND%201209&c=&m=&s=&cv=458&xywh=1404%2C747%2C8489%2C2876.

"Business Opportunities." *Philadelphia Inquirer*, March 3, 1912. https://www.newspapers.com/image/169036568.

Department of Records, Philadelphia City Archives. 1209–1211 North Hancock Street deeds (map registry nos. 9N110069, 9N110070). Various dates.

"Extradition Set for Gyp Suspect." *Philadelphia Daily News*, July 8, 1977. https://www.newspapers.com/image/185729269.

"Female Help Wanted." *Philadelphia Inquirer*, July 16, 1923. https://www.newspapers.com/image/170745824.

"Fire Record of the Day." *Philadelphia Inquirer*, December 3, 1938. https://www.newspapers.com/image/171590939.

"In Memoriam: Philip Hammerschlag." *Jewish Exponent*, September 13, 1901. *ProQuest Historical Newspapers*. https://proxy.library.upenn.edu/login?url=https://www.proquest.com/historical-newspapers/memoriam/docview/892027031/se-2?accountid=14707.

"Male Help Wanted." *Philadelphia Inquirer*, October 28, 1908. https://www.newspapers.com/image/168437598.

———. *Philadelphia Inquirer*, February 19, 1925. https://www.newspapers.com/image/171063804.

———. *Philadelphia Inquirer*, August 18, 1936. https://www.newspapers.com/image/176080771/?terms=%221209%20n%20hancock%22&match=1.

———. *Philadelphia Inquirer*, October 19, 1953. https://www.newspapers.com/image/172685495.

"Matzos." *Jewish Exponent*, March 23, 1888. *ProQuest Historical Newspapers*. https://proxy.library.upenn.edu/login?url=https://www.proquest.com/historical-newspapers/display-ad-7-no-title/docview/891875678/se-2?accountid=14707.

Morris, William, and Isaac Feinberg. "Resolutions: Mickve Israel Congregation." *Jewish Exponent*, September 13, 1901. *ProQuest Historical Newspapers*. https://proxy.library.upenn.edu/login?url=https://www.proquest.com/historical-newspapers/resolutions/docview/892034954/se-2?accountid=14707.

"Obituary." *Philadelphia Inquirer*, May 25, 1950. https://www.newspapers.com/image/173760718.

"Pennsylvania, U.S., Death Certificates, 1803–1915" (online database). Digital image s.v. "Hammerschlag, Philip." *Ancestry.com*. https://www.ancestrylibrary.com/discoveryui-content/view/1321379:2535?tid=&pid=&queryId=57bf5dc1c7ea80ddb9d310d36fe3ed45&_phsrc=VNq719&_phstart=successSource.

"Pennsylvania, U.S., Wills and Probate Records, 1683–1993" (online database). Digital image s.v. "Hammerschlag, Philip." *Ancestry.com*. https://www.ancestrylibrary.com/imageviewer/collections/8802/images/004431804_00248?pid=2361202&usePUB=true&_phsrc=VNq719&_phstart=successSource&usePUBJs=true.

"P. Hammerschlag & Co., 'Phone.'" *Jewish Exponent*, January 12, 1906. *ProQuest Historical Newspapers*. https://proxy.library.upenn.edu/login?url=https://www.proquest.com/historical-newspapers/display-ad-5-no-title/docview/892054997/se-2?accountid=14707.

"Real Estate for Rent: City Property." *Philadelphia Inquirer*, March 20, 1910. https://www.newspapers.com/image/167226173.

"Real Estate for Sale: City Property, Factories." *Philadelphia Inquirer*, March 20, 1910. https://www.newspapers.com/image/167226103.

"Society: Weddings." *Philadelphia Inquirer*, June 5, 1898. https://www.newspapers.com/image/167860405.

"1209–1211 N. Hancock Street, 'Phone.'" *Jewish Exponent*, October 21, 1904. *ProQuest Historical Newspapers*. https://proxy.library.upenn.edu/login?url=https://www.proquest.com/historical-newspapers/display-ad-5-no-title/docview/892039929/se-2?accountid=14707.

"2101 N. American Street: Zoning Permit Documents." *City of Philadelphia Atlas*. Accessed January 10, 2023. https://s3.amazonaws.com/lni-zoning-pdfs/219-185186.pdf.

"U.S., City Directories, 1822–1995" (online database). Digital image s.v. "Hammerschlag, Henrietta," 1905. *Ancestry.com*. https://www.ancestrylibrary.com/imageviewer/collections/2469/images/2851207?pid=1198394779&usePUB=true&_phsrc=VNq717&_phstart=successSource&usePUBJs=true.

——. Digital image s.v. "Hammerschlag, Henrietta," 1905. *Ancestry.com*. https://www.ancestrylibrary.com/imageviewer/collections/2469/images/2790465?pid=166219050&usePUB=true&_phsrc=VNq716&_phstart=successSource&usePUBJs=true.

——. Digital image s.v. "Hammerschlag, Philip," 1898. *Ancestry.com*. https://www.ancestrylibrary.com/imageviewer/collections/2469/images/2860774?pid=175842358&usePUB=true&_phsrc=VNq716&_phstart=successSource&usePUBJs=true.

"U.S. Federal Census" (online database). Digital image s.v. "Hammerschlag, Philip," 1880. *Ancestry.com*. https://www.ancestrylibrary.com/imageviewer/collections/6742/images/4244462-00508?pid=118461&usePUB=true&_phsrc=VNq719&_phstart=successSource&usePUBJs=true.

"U.S., IRS Tax Assessment Lists, 1862–1918" (online database). Digital image s.v. "Hammerschlag, Philip," 1862. *Ancestry.com*. https://www.ancestrylibrary.com/imageviewer/collections/1264/images/rhusa1862_101960-00135?pid=7375902&usePUB=true&_phsrc=VNq721&_phstart=successSource&usePUBJs=true.

1407 Marlborough Street/309 Belgrade Street

"Death Near after 92 Years of Life." *Philadelphia Times*, June 3, 1900. https://www.newspapers.com/image/52375563.

Delaware Historical and Cultural Affairs. "Details in Delaware: Serpentine Stone." Accessed May 25, 2023. https://history.delaware.gov/2022/08/16/details-in-delaware-serpentine-stone.

Department of Records, Philadelphia City Archives. 1407 Marlborough Street deeds (map registry nos. 18N010014, 18N010066). Various dates.

"1407 Marlborough Avenue: Zoning Permit Documents." *City of Philadelphia Atlas*. Accessed January 10, 2023. http://s3.amazonaws.com/eclipse-docs-pdfs/zoning/ZP-2020-002040.pdf.

"Independent Churches." *Philadelphia Times*, December 27, 1877. https://www.newspapers.com image/53239131.

Maule, Bradley. "Take 'Er Easy, Pilgrim Congregational." *Hidden City Philadelphia*, December 22, 2014. https://hiddencityphila.org/2014/12/take-er-easy-pilgrim-congregational.

Scharf, J. Thomas, and Thompson Westcott. *History of Philadelphia, 1609–1884*, vol. 2. Philadelphia: L. H. Everts, 1884.

NORTHWEST AND NORTHEAST PHILADELPHIA

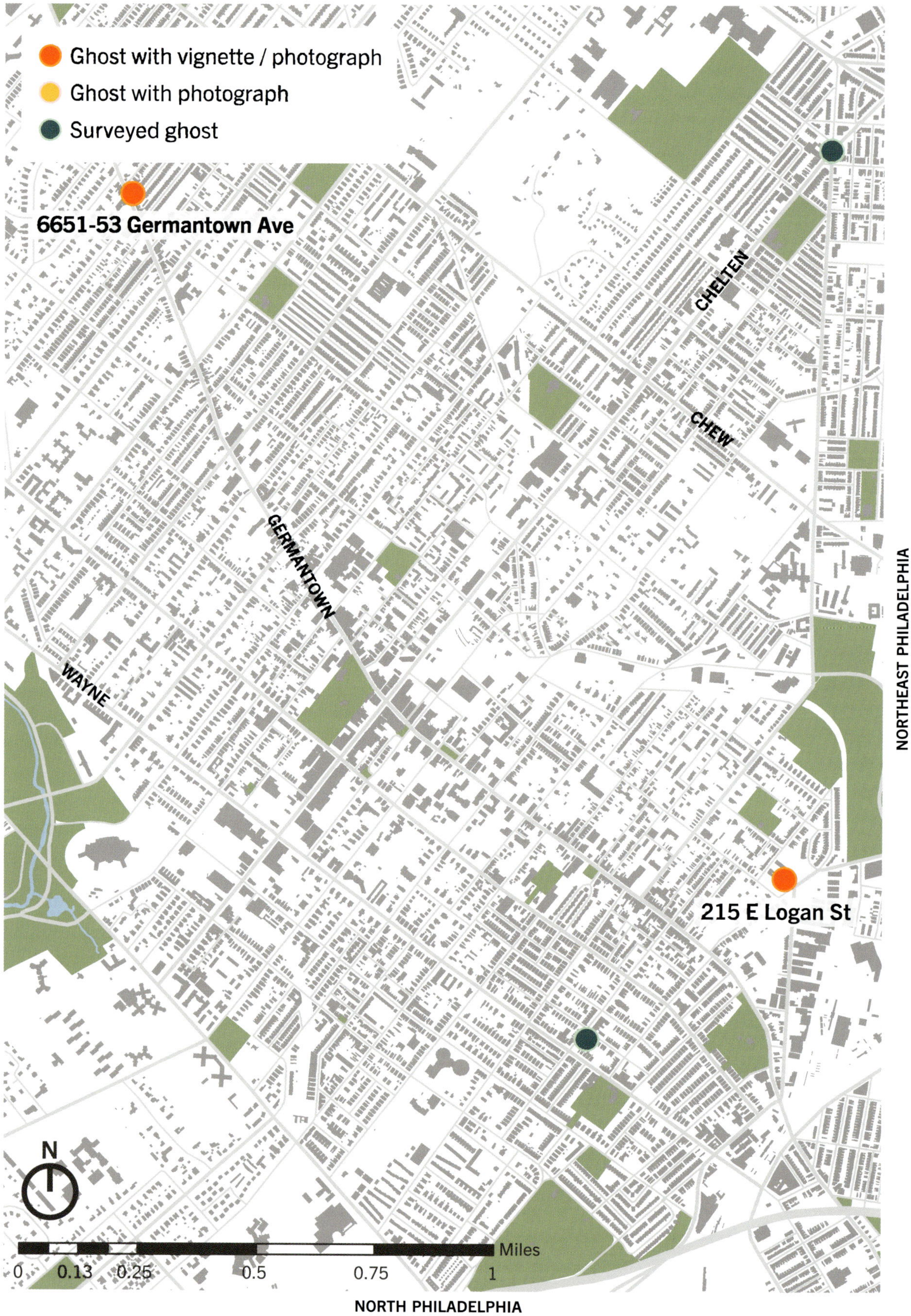

Designed by Kaitlyn Levesque.

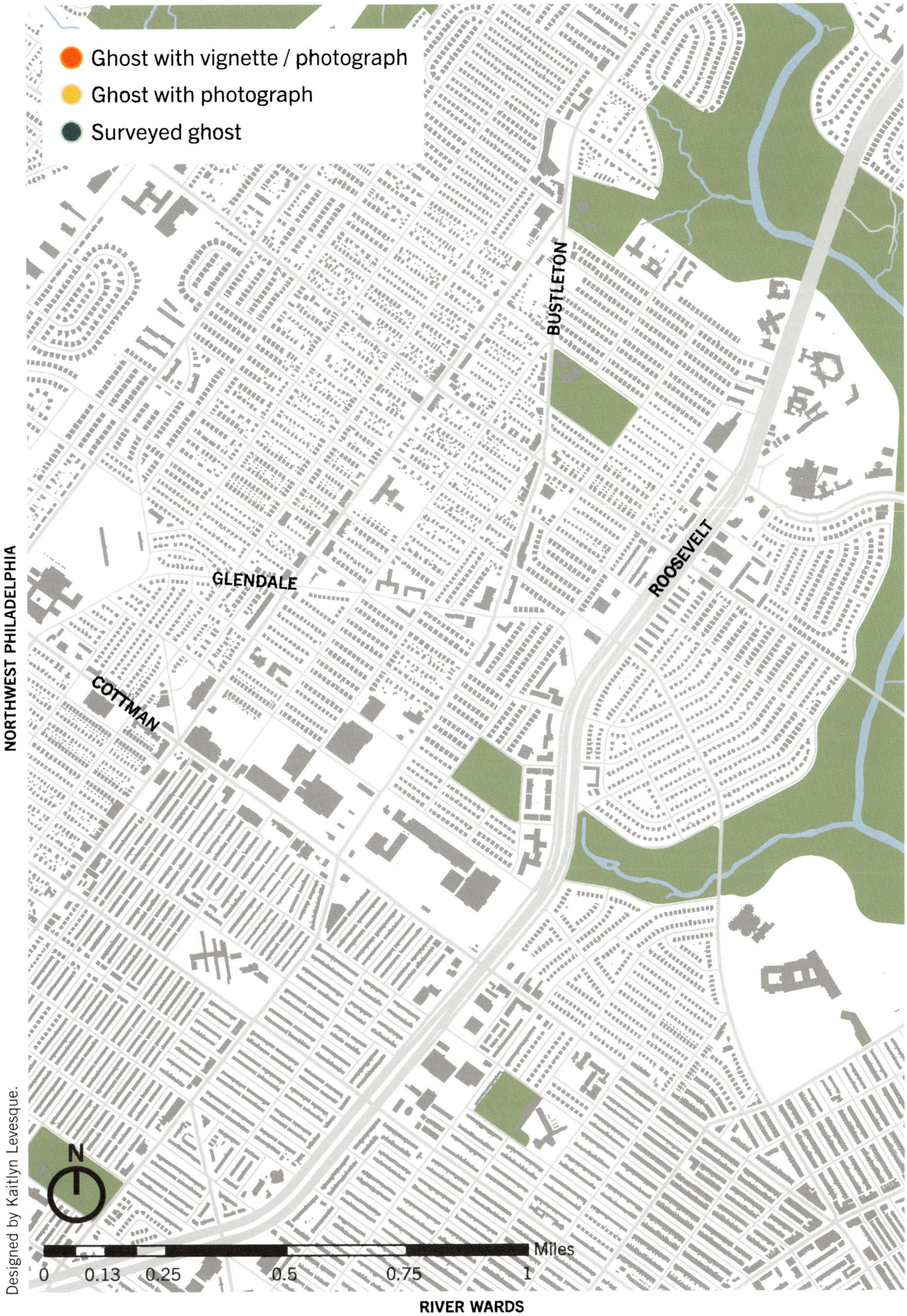

Designed by Kaitlyn Levesque.

It takes persistence to find a building ghost in Northwest or Northeast Philadelphia. Block after block, street after road and pike after avenue, ghosts are a rarity in the upper corners of the city. In so many other physical, demographic, and socioeconomic ways, the Northwest and Northeast would seem to be distinct from each other. Yet for all their differences, the swaths of Philadelphia mirrored across the northern extents of Broad Street share one undeniable reality: ghosts simply don't appear here.

In many areas of Northwest Philadelphia, the age of the building stock would seem to lend itself to ghosts; the roots of Germantown, after all, are as old as the city itself. In the upper western reaches of the city, as in many other parts of Philadelphia, the nineteenth century's industrializing surge translated to extensive development in Mount Airy, Wissahickon, and other Northwestern enclaves. Yet most of the equivalent industrial-era neighborhoods elsewhere in the city are pockmarked by many more building ghosts than the Northwest can claim. Why would that be?

The answer is in the type of building stock, not the age. The green space that defines much of the Northwest buffers mostly detached single-family homes; without a party wall, the Northwest's buildings cannot produce ghosts. This is most obvious in the upscale and scaled-up houses of Chestnut Hill and West Mount Airy, but it's also generally true of the buildings in West Oak Lane, Tulpehocken, Stenton, and elsewhere. Some neighborhoods west of the Wissahickon would seem to belie the pattern (Manayunk comes to mind), but even there the smallest sliver of daylight between buildings—those precious bits of lawn or sidewalk that separate buildings at any scale—can preclude a building ghost from ever existing in the Northwest.

The Northeast, on the whole, would not seem to share this architectural reality; communities such as Mayfair, Holmesburg, and Summerdale are undeniably dense. Nearly one in three Philadelphians lives in the Northeast, so clearly there is some measure of living shoulder to shoulder in this part of this city.[1] The physical conditions of the built environment would seem, then, to lend themselves to ample building ghosts—and yet they don't.

Unlike its analogue in the Northwest, the Northeast's dearth of ghosts can be explained by patterns of building age, not type. This is not to say that the cultural landscape in the Northeast isn't rich with centuries of history and development. In Frankford alone, the Lenape band of Native Americans lived on the land long before Swedish colonists arrived, not to mention the establishment of any colony in the name of William Penn and his woods. But despite these layers of embedded history, much of the extant building stock of Northeast Philadelphia is decidedly more recent fare.

In a city where much of the building stock originated in the eighteenth and nineteenth centuries, the urban fabric in the Northeast is generally newer. These neighborhoods saw accelerated development in the mid-twentieth century, spurred by the completion of Roosevelt Boulevard and the demand for new housing after World War II. Some of the postwar housing developments replicated the spacing of suburban developments (some also echoed the racist covenants of their suburban counterparts); this configuration does not lend itself to building ghosts. But several other developments adapted the classic Philadelphia rowhouse for the postwar era, capitalizing on the form's efficiencies to produce dense housing for a booming population. Even on these blocks, though, building ghosts are rare (or even nonexistent) for one simple reason: the buildings aren't yet old enough to seem disposable. They don't come down at the same rate as their older siblings in other areas of the city, because in the timeline of a centuries-old city, they only just went up.

There is an additional explanation that rationalizes the relative absence of building ghosts in the Northwest and Northeast—one that links them rather than distinguishes them—and that is their preponderance of *middle neighborhoods*. It's a term popularized by the planner Paul C. Brophy, a native of Hunting Park in Philadelphia, and it describes several neighborhoods in these sections of the city: West Oak Lane, Stenton, some areas of Germantown, and so on in the Northwest; Mayfair, Oxford Circle, and others in the Northeast.[2] While much urban policy is consumed with gentrification and growth, on one hand, and decline and disinvestment, on the other, middle neighborhoods are sus-

1. Joseph Minardi, *City of Neighborhoods: Philadelphia, 1890–1910* (Atglen, PA: Schiffer, 2020), 57.

2. Emily Dowdall, Jacob Rosch, and Ira Goldstein, *Philadelphia's Middle Neighborhoods: Demographic and Market Differences by Race, Ethnicity, and Nation of Origin* (Philadelphia: Reinvestment Fund, May 2017), 3.

pended in-between: neither the richest nor the poorest sections of the city, defined neither by rapid development nor equivalent decline.[3] They are defined by their relative stability, yet they face their own risks of falling through the cracks while decision makers are looking (and spending money) elsewhere.

Middle neighborhoods exist in other parts of the city, but in the context of the Northwest and Northeast specifically, they add another dimension to the factors that work against building ghosts in these areas. The comparative stability of middle neighborhoods results in a certain stasis in the built environment; without acute pressures from either side of the development equation, middle neighborhoods see less churn than their more dynamic counterparts. It's not enough, then, for the buildings in the Northwest and the Northeast to be both old and attached. For a building ghost to materialize, middle neighborhoods would have to experience the turnover that comes with demolition.

Northwest and Northeast Philadelphia bear out the principle that building ghosts are an artifact of space *and* time, people *and* place. The exceptions in these neighborhoods underscore the ubiquities in others (and vice versa); the conditions of geography, architecture, history, and change must all align to produce the building ghosts we encounter in our cities. So if building ghosts are the remnants and reminders of demolished buildings, then are Northwest and Northeast Philadelphia better or worse off for not having them?

3. Inga Saffron, "The Death and Life of Philadelphia's 'Middle Neighborhoods,'" *Philadelphia Inquirer,* March 16, 2017, https://www.inquirer.com/philly/columnists/inga_saffron/Tacony-Middle-Neighborhoods-gentrification-inga-saffron.html; Mark Dent, "Philly's Forgotten Middle: Places like West Oak Lane, Tacony Endangered," *Billy Penn*, February 22, 2017, https://billypenn.com/2017/02/22/phillys-forgotten-middle-places-like-west-oak-lane-tacony-endangered; Sandy Smith, "Some Philadelphia Neighborhoods Are Walking a Line between Boom and Bust," *Next City*, May 15, 2017, https://nextcity.org/features/philadelphia-middle-class-neighborhoods-mount-airy.

6651–6653 Germantown Avenue

Constructed in 1922
Demolished in 2020

There was a time in the early twentieth century when Eugene Raymond Jr. dabbled in buying and selling single parcels. By the 1920s, though, the lawyer and developer had larger ambitions: a handful of commercial properties here, a few dozen dwellings there. He carved out a particularly large domain in Germantown, penciling out lots for houses on both sides of Hortter Street and developing two-story retail fronts and apartments around the corner on Germantown Avenue. By November 1922, he was advertising the completion of nine storefronts at 6639–6653 Germantown Avenue. (For many of his other projects, scattered throughout Philadelphia, Raymond made sure to mention the architect in newspaper notices; for these relatively modest mixed-use buildings on Germantown Avenue, however, he was mum.) In Eugene Raymond Jr.'s words, they presented a "wonderful opportunity for gent's furnishings, meats and provisions, barbershop, hardware and paint, baker, auto accessories, etc."

The advertisement was practically a premonition: in the ninety-eight years that 6651–6653 Germantown Avenue stood, it hosted half of those exact commercial uses, as well as a variety store and an amusement arcade (both of which would seem to fall under the "etc." of Raymond's notice).

The first up was a salon, extant at number 6651 by 1924, if not earlier, under the care of Katherine Rayner. The daughter of Northern Irish immigrants, Katherine (née Brown) had been married to Thomas Rayner (a son of English immigrants) since 1913. They lived a typical life "over the store" on Germantown Avenue, with Katherine commuting downstairs while Thomas left for his job as a clerk.[4]

In late 1939, Thomas Rayner died at fifty-eight; Katherine's brother, Robert Brown, moved in with her above the salon. Brown was not home on New Year's Day in 1940, though, when a fire broke out in the apartment of number 6651, sparked by a forgotten cigarette or a short circuit in a lamp. (Investigators never determined the actual cause.) A passerby saw the flames in Katherine Rayner's apartment and called for fire trucks; that neighbor was too flustered, though, to name the right address, sending firefighters to 5614 Germantown Avenue instead—ten blocks away.

The delay was deadly.

While the firefighters raced more than a mile in the wrong direction, neighbors watched in helpless horror as Rayner appeared at the second-floor window several times,

4. Meanwhile, the Dougherty family lived next door at number 6653, with mother Mary as the head of household; seventeen-year-old daughter Mary was the only one old enough to help support the family, contributing income from her job at a hosiery mill.

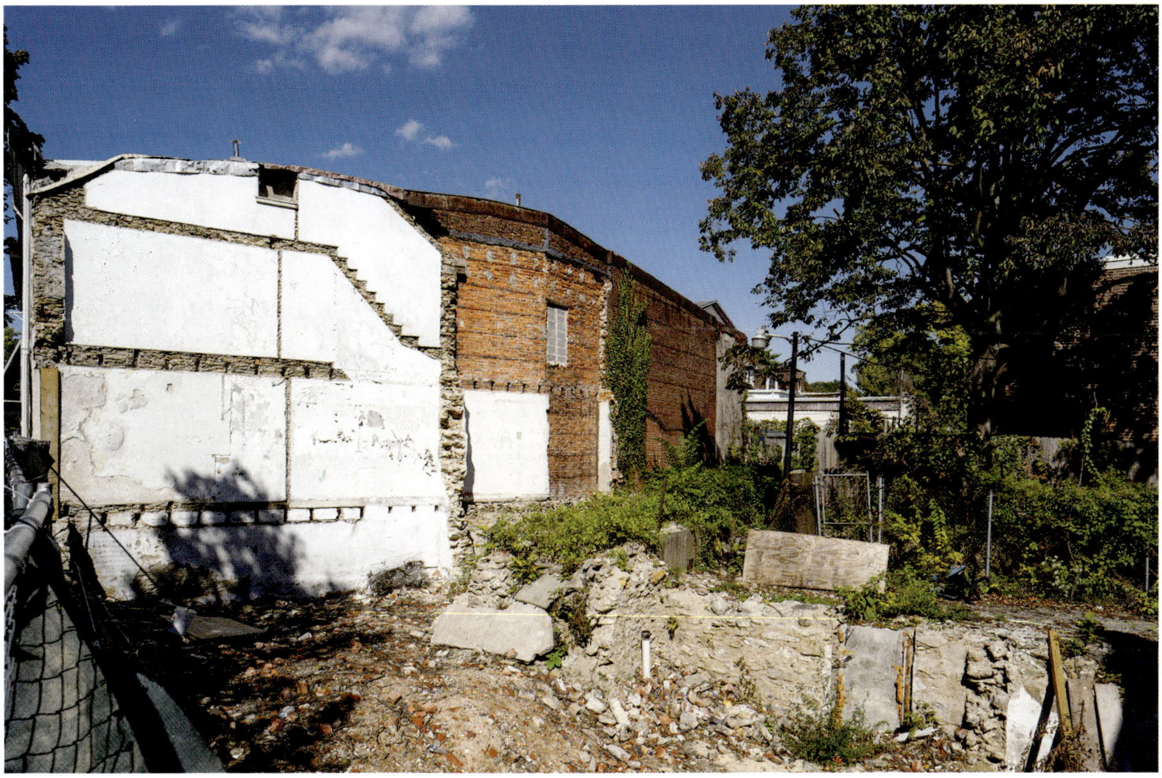

6651–6653 Germantown Avenue. (Photographed October 9, 2020.)

screaming and trying to break the glass as her clothes caught fire. (A newspaper gruesomely described her as "a human torch.") When the fire trucks finally arrived and crews threw ladders against the building to reach her, they confronted the realities of a fire in January: one ladder slipped on the icy pavement, and a firefighter fell twenty feet to the sidewalk, fracturing his heel. By the time they finally gained access to the apartment over the salon, Rayner was unconscious and burned almost beyond recognition. She was pronounced dead before the ambulance even reached Germantown Hospital. Her family and friends gathered a few days later at St. Madeleine Sophie Church in Mount Airy, burying Katherine Rayner just six months after doing the same for her husband, Thomas.

Somehow, life at 6651 Germantown Avenue continued after the grim events in 1940, and the address became associated once again with happy occasions. Two years later, Helen Breiner used the address to apply for a marriage license with Walter Simon Jr. Her parents (Lawrence and Catherine Breiner) had purchased the building from Robert Brown and opened "Graham's Variety Store" where Katherine Rayner's salon had been. While their twenty-two-year-old daughter married and presumably moved away, the Breiners seem to have lent some stability to the building again. They owned and operated Graham's Variety Store for more than two decades, maintaining the apartments on the (restored) second floor above.

By the early 1970s, the Breiners had both died (Lawrence in 1973 and Catherine just a year later), and the building's new owner applied for a permit to repurpose 6651 Germantown Avenue as an amusement arcade. Living in the apartments "over the store" would now mean living above a series of coin-operated pinball machines.

Whether it was the noise or some other reason, the amusement arcade was relatively short-lived. By 1978, a new building permit proposed to use the retail space as a paint store "for autos only"—two of Eugene Raymond Jr.'s "wonderful opportunities" combined into one, it would seem. For the next several decades, the building's retail space passed in and out of vacancy (on at least one Election Day it served as a polling place) before being demolished in 2020. As of 2023, after a few years of pandemic-related delays, the local community development corporation Mt. Airy CDC plans to construct a mixed-use building on the site, including rental housing on the upper floors and commercial space on the ground floor. Perhaps a bakery or a "gent's furnishings" shop will move in, and Eugene Raymond Jr.'s forecast will be complete.

215 East Logan Street

Constructed ca. 1866
Demolished ca. 1995

Designed and constructed together in the 1860s, the residences at 213–215 East Logan Street must have been complementary in every way. By 2020, though, only 213 East Logan Street could show off the trademarks of their original Italianate design—the projecting first-story bay, with its arched windows; the stacked quoin stones at the corner edges of the building; the bracketed cornice and vaulted mansard roof that both met an unceremonious end where 215 East Logan Street used to start. All of these distinctive features had been missing their twins (identical or otherwise) since the 1990s, when 215 East Logan Street was severed from its companion, leaving only a jumbled, plastered building ghost on their brick party wall.

For more than a century, the twins shared a fate. Built together as outlying farms became suburban residences for well-to-do Philadelphians, they moved up and down on the economic ladder in tandem with the prosperity or impoverishment of their Germantown neighborhood. When one side hosted craftsmen and stenographers and curators in the early twentieth century, the other was home to a minister and an engineer; as one half was subdivided into tenement housing in the mid-century, the other was partitioned, as well. (Only 213 East Logan Street, though, could claim a future Supreme Court justice among its generations of residents: Owen Josephus Roberts, named to the court in 1930 by President Herbert Hoover, lived there around 1899, just after graduating from the University of Pennsylvania's law school.)

By 1940, the buildings shared a party wall *and* an owner. Herbert Walter Sims and his wife, Delia, purchased number 215 in 1937 and number 213 three years later. With both halves in hand, the duplex became a compound of sorts, expanding in footprint and families over the next decade as multiple generations of the Sims family either moved in themselves or collected rent from other tenants.

At number 215, the trajectory started with a new garage, the permit for which was approved in 1938. As of that application, the house ostensibly hosted just one family. Within two years, however, it was home to five families, and Herbert Sims was applying for a building permit to nudge a sixth family into the address. (Given this acceleration toward what would officially be declared "tenement housing" in 1941, one wonders whether the 1938 permit application was fudging the truth of its use a bit.) The city's Zoning Board initially denied the permit, concerned that the property could not house so many people safely in its current condition. So the new garage—built just a few years earlier—had to go, along with a portion of the existing porch, in order to erect a one-story addition using fireproof materials. Once those changes were made, the expanded use appears to have passed muster, and the patchwork of plastered

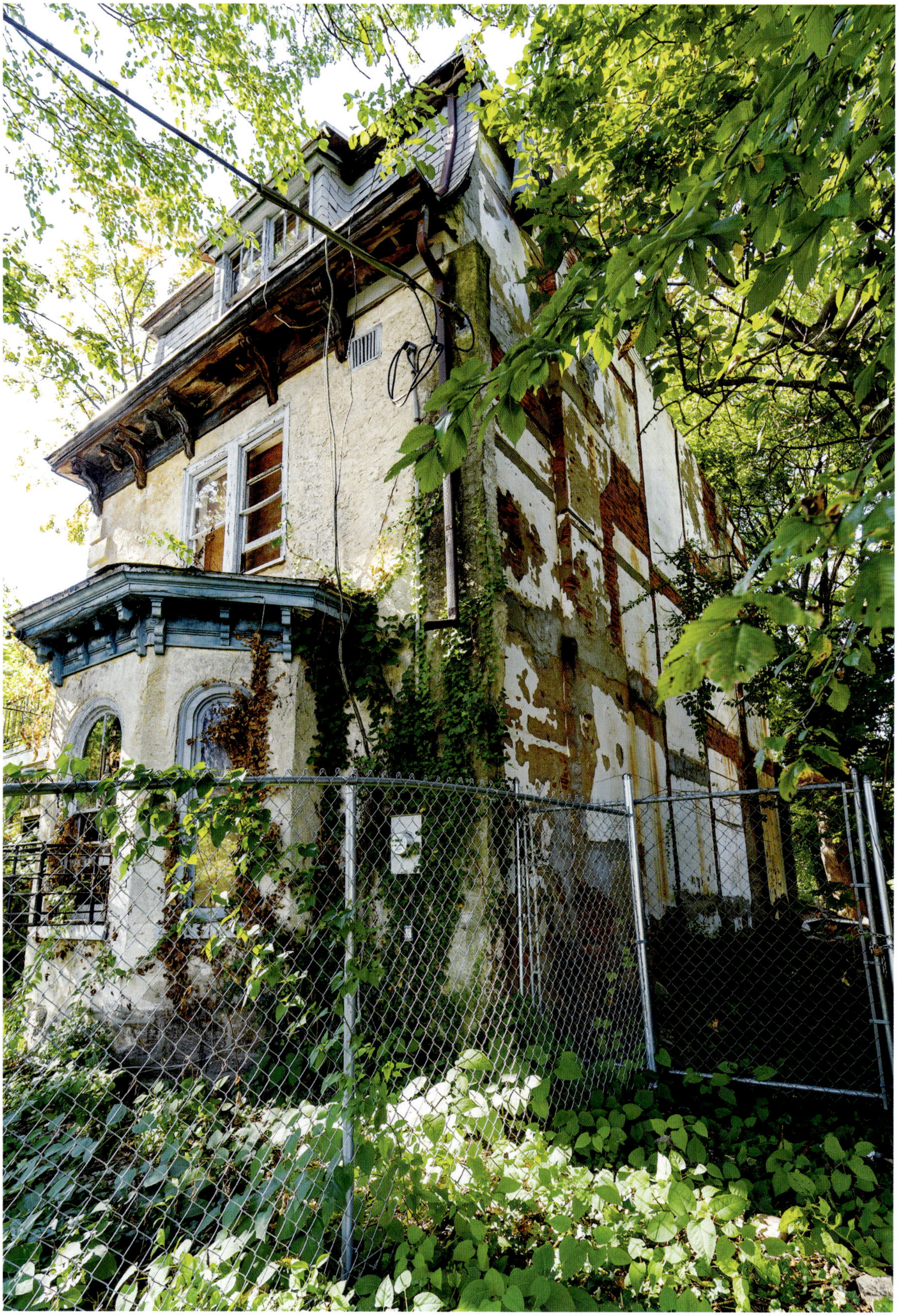

215 East Logan Street. (Photographed October 9, 2020.)

closets, hallways, and bedrooms visible in the eventual building ghost now served six families rather than five.

Among them were Herbert and Delia Sims themselves, who lived in number 215 while their adult son Atwood Arthur Sims lived with his family on the other side of the brick wall, at number 213. When thirty-one-year-old Atwood registered for the draft in October 1940, just a few months after Herbert and Delia purchased number 213, he updated his registration card to reflect his new address on Logan Street. When asked to vouch for someone who would be able to track him down in case of an emergency, he listed his father, residing just next door.

By the late 1940s, Atwood's younger brother Clyde also got involved in managing the twins on Logan Street, after returning from five years of active duty in the U.S. Army during World War II. In 1948, he and his father negotiated several real estate transactions related to number 215, and in 1950, he was responsible for an effort to expand number 213 from five families to seven. With members of the Sims family installed on both sides of the duplex, they could collect rent from up to eleven other families at a time.

The Sims father and sons apparently leaned on one another as much as their buildings at 213–215 East Logan Street did. Even after they sold the buildings and moved apart (Herbert relocated to Florida and Atwood relocated to Chestnut Hill, while Clyde lived on East Penn Street in Germantown), their deaths turned out to be as intertwined as their lives and structures on Logan Street once were. In January 1967, Atwood Arthur Sims died at fifty-seven. Five months later, his father, Herbert, passed away. In October of that same year, Clyde suffered a fatal heart attack. Within a single year, all of the men in two generations of the Sims family had died.

Meanwhile, the inseparable houses on Logan Street fell into increasing disrepair, together. In 1979, city inspectors noticed concerning conditions at the rear of both properties and published a warning notice in the *Philadelphia Inquirer* mandating that the structural issues be repaired within ten days or risk being demolished by the city at the owners' expense. In actuality, it took fifteen or so more years before the threat materialized, but sometime in the 1990s, 215 East Logan Street was demolished, severing it from its twin after 130 years. The surviving side, meanwhile, was included within the outer edges of the local East Logan Street Historic District in 2010, but the designation could not counteract an accumulating pile of building code violations and failed inspections. (How many of 213 East Logan Street's structural issues were the result of the loss of its twin?) In 2020, the owner, a real estate holdings limited liability company, pulled a demolition permit for 213 East Logan Street. When number 213 was torn down, taking the ghost of number 215 with it, the buildings' twin fates converged once again—this time for good.

Northwest and Northeast Philadelphia References

General Resources

Baist, G. Wm. *Baist's Atlas of the City of Philadelphia, Complete in One Volume*. Philadelphia: G. Wm. Baist, 1888. Athenaeum of Philadelphia, *Greater Philadelphia GeoHistory Network*. https://www.philageohistory.org/rdic-images/view-image.cfm/BST1888.Phila.040.Plate33.

Bromley, George W., and Walter S. Bromley. *Atlas of the City of Philadelphia, Complete in One Volume, from Actual Surveys and Official Plans*. Philadelphia: G. W. Bromley, 1910. Athenaeum of Philadelphia, *Greater Philadelphia GeoHistory Network*. https://www.philageohistory.org/rdic-images/view-image.cfm/237%2DMP%2D022.

Hopkins, G. M. *Atlas of the Late Borough of Germantown, 22nd Ward, City of Philadelphia*. Philadelphia: G. M. Hopkins, 1871. Athenaeum of Philadelphia, *Greater Philadelphia GeoHistory Network*. http://www.philageohistory.org/rdic-images/view-image.cfm/GMH1871.Germantown.016.Plate13.

Smedley, Samuel. *Atlas of the City of Philadelphia*. Philadelphia: J. B. Lippincott, 1862. Map Collection, Free Library of Philadelphia, *Greater Philadelphia GeoHistory Network*. http://www.philageohistory.org/tiles/viewer.

6651–6653 Germantown Avenue

"Activities of Day in Real Estate." *Philadelphia Inquirer*, July 28, 1921. https://www.newspapers.com/image/170680588.

——. *Philadelphia Inquirer*, August 4, 1922. https://www.newspapers.com/image/171017746.

——. *Philadelphia Inquirer*, August 6, 1922. https://www.newspapers.com/image/171020207.

"Advance Construction News." *Philadelphia Real Estate Record and Builders' Guide*, December 21, 1921. *Greater Philadelphia GeoHistory Network*. http://www.philageohistory.org/rdic-images/view-book-uv.cfm/PhilaBuildersGuide_v36_1921#?ft=&q=%22eugene%20raymond%22&c=&m=&s=&cv=1015&xywh=-3389%2C0%2C14303%2C4846.

——. *Philadelphia Real Estate Record and Builders' Guide*, August 30, 1922. *Greater Philadelphia GeoHistory Network*. http://www.philageohistory.org/rdic-images/view-book-uv.cfm/PhilaBuildersGuide_v37_1922#?ft=&q=%22eugene%20raymond%22&c=&m=&s=&cv=689&xywh=-3410%2C0%2C14339%2C4858.

"Apartments: City: Germantown." *Philadelphia Inquirer*, September 22, 1957. https://www.newspapers.com/image/178018886.

"Applications for Marriage Licenses." *Philadelphia Inquirer*, February 7, 1942. https://www.newspapers.com/image/172125666.

"Death Notices: Breiner." *Philadelphia Inquirer*, November 19, 1974. https://www.newspapers.com/image/173547832.

"Delaware Valley Deaths: Breiner, Lawrence S." *Philadelphia Inquirer*, June 21, 1973. https://www.newspapers.com/image/180061366.

Department of Records, Philadelphia City Archives. 6651–6653 Germantown Avenue deeds (map registry nos. 52N080215, 52N080337). Various dates.

"Died." *Philadelphia Inquirer*, January 5, 1940. https://www.newspapers.com/image/166608318.

"Female Help Wanted." *Philadelphia Inquirer*, July 9, 1924. https://www.newspapers.com/image/170754082.

"Fire Kills One, Fells 25 in S[outh] Phila[delphia]." *Philadelphia Inquirer*, January 2, 1940. https://www.newspapers.com/image/166598384/?fcfToken=eyJhbGciOiJIUzI1NiIsInR5cCI6IkpXVCJ9.eyJmcmVlLXZpZXctaWQiOjE2NjU5ODM4NCwiaWF0IjoxNjIwNzgwOTQxLCJleHAiOjE2MjA4NjczNDF9.km-ijltgKGitFOli1nVzF2pVpTi5beVveltJ4OI7DXI.

"Honeywell Introduces Tap-Lite." *Philadelphia Inquirer,* October 27, 1957. https://www.newspapers.com/image/178346273.
"The Leading Beauticians Feature Frederics New 50% Coolers Permanent Wave." *Philadelphia Inquirer,* June 16, 1935. https://www.newspapers.com/image/174630809.
"Now! Two Brand New Premier Vacuum Cleaners for Complete Home Cleaning!" *Philadelphia Inquirer,* October 23, 1947. https://www.newspapers.com/image/174454818.
"Obituary: Eugene Raymond, Jr." *Philadelphia Inquirer,* July 30, 1956. https://www.newspapers.com/image/175820580.
"Pennsylvania, U.S. Marriages, 1852–1968" (online database). Digital image s.v. "Rayner, Katherine E.," 1913. *Ancestry.com.* https://www.ancestrylibrary.com/discoveryui-content/view/900145173:61381?tid=&pid=&queryId=82f2d5be5b343601c6820d3aa678cb09&_phsrc=VNq199&_phstart=successSource.
Rybak, Sue Ann. "Mt. Airy USA Completes Renovation on Mixed-Use Building." *Chestnut Hill Local,* March 29, 2013. https://www.chestnuthilllocal.com/stories/mt-airy-usa-completes-renovation-on-mixed-use-building,3167.
"6651–53 Germantown Avenue: Zoning Permit Documents." *City of Philadelphia Atlas.* Accessed January 10, 2023. https://s3.amazonaws.com/lni-zoning-pdfs/219-171000.pdf.
"Stores." *Philadelphia Inquirer,* November 19, 1922. https://www.newspapers.com/image/171035441.
"U.S., World War I Draft Registration Cards, 1917–1918" (online database). Digital image s.v. "Rayner, Thomas." *Ancestry.com.* https://www.ancestrylibrary.com/discoveryui-content/view/26180897:6482?tid=&pid=&queryId=7eae2069b45ebdb874909a80976762f8&_phsrc=VNq204&_phstart=successSource.

215 East Logan Street

C. E. Howe Company. *Boyd's Philadelphia Blue Book Elite Directory.* Philadelphia: Boyd's Directory Office, 1906. *Google Books.* https://www.google.com/books/edition/Boyd_s_Blue_Book/PwICAAAAYAAJ?hl=en&gbpv=1&dq=%22215+e+logan%22+philadelphia&pg=PA400&printsec=frontcover.
Department of Records, Philadelphia City Archives. 215 East Logan Street deeds (map registry no. 54N150163). Various dates.
"Female Help Wanted." *Philadelphia Inquirer,* October 3, 1912. https://www.newspapers.com/image/169036218.
"Legal Notice to the Following Persons, Whose Last Known Addresses Are as Follows." *Philadelphia Inquirer,* September 20, 1979. https://www.newspapers.com/image/174922851.
"Pennsylvania." *National Shorthand Reporter* II, no. 12 (December 1914): 286. *Google Books.* https://www.google.com/books/edition/The_National_Shorthand_Reporter/ZN0CAAAAYAAJ?hl=en&gbpv=1&bsq=%22lewis%20hopper%22%20.
"Social and Other Feminine Themes: People You Know." *Philadelphia Inquirer,* July 13, 1935. https://www.newspapers.com/image/174688284.
Society of Arts and Crafts. *Annual Report of the Society of Arts and Crafts, Boston Massachusetts for the Year 1914.* Boston: Society of Arts and Crafts, 1915. *Google Books.* https://www.google.com/books/edition/Annual_Report/kuUYAAAAYAAJ?hl=en&gbpv=1&dq=%22215+e+logan%22+philadelphia&pg=RA11-PA49&printsec=frontcover.
"215 E. Logan Street: Zoning Permit Documents." *City of Philadelphia Atlas.* Accessed January 10, 2023. https://s3.amazonaws.com/lni-zoning-pdfs/219-232781.pdf.
"U.S., City Directories, 1822–1995" (online database). Digital image s.v. "Cooley, Franklin," 1899. *Ancestry.com.* https://www.ancestrylibrary.com/discoveryui-content/view/175550475:2469?tid=&pid=&queryId=634e4b3f959c0e7efcb12f487aed5a14&_phsrc=VNq83&_phstart=successSource.
———. Digital image s.v. "Cooley, Franklin," 1900. *Ancestry.com.* https://www.ancestrylibrary.com/discoveryui-content/view/177471602:2469?tid=&pid=&queryId=634e4b3f959c0e7efcb12f487aed5a14&_phsrc=VNq83&_phstart=successSource.

——. Digital image s.v. "Heron, Caroline J.," 1909. *Ancestry.com.* https://www.ancestrylibrary.com/discoveryui-content/view/1194279297:2469?tid=&pid=&queryId=df4623ec179f26db45fb710d197aafcd&_phsrc=VNq87&_phstart=successSource.

——. Digital image s.v. "Hopper, Lewis," 1908. *Ancestry.com.* https://www.ancestrylibrary.com/discoveryui-content/view/166239615:2469?tid=&pid=&queryId=634e4b3f959c0e7efcb12f487aed5a14&_phsrc=VNq83&_phstart=successSource.

——. Digital image s.v. "Hopper, Lewis," 1917. *Ancestry.com.* https://www.ancestrylibrary.com/discoveryui-content/view/160150562:2469?tid=&pid=&queryId=634e4b3f959c0e7efcb12f487aed5a14&_phsrc=VNq83&_phstart=successSource.

——. Digital image s.v. "Ray, Jno. L. (Rev.)," 1901. *Ancestry.com.* https://www.ancestrylibrary.com/discoveryui-content/view/1188994564:2469?tid=&pid=&queryId=df4623ec179f26db45fb710d197aafcd&_phsrc=VNq87&_phstart=successSource.

——. Digital image s.v. "Sims, Atwood," 1950. *Ancestry.com.* https://www.ancestrylibrary.com/discoveryui-content/view/1197815082:2469?tid=&pid=&queryId=df4623ec179f26db45fb710d197aafcd&_phsrc=VNq88&_phstart=successSource.

——. Digital image s.v. "Sims, Herbert," 1950. *Ancestry.com.* https://www.ancestrylibrary.com/discoveryui-content/view/1197819121:2469?tid=&pid=&queryId=634e4b3f959c0e7efcb12f487aed5a14&_phsrc=VNq83&_phstart=successSource.

CODA

Puncturing the urban fabric and giving us pause, building ghosts offer evidence of patterns that are neither accidental nor incidental. They somehow manage to remind us of a structure's disposability *and* its permanence, speaking in the same breath to a city's development and its destruction. Such dynamism is essential to the understanding of Philadelphia (and any other city); the stories and lives excerpted in this book would not exist without it. Marking and mourning the presence of building ghosts, then, is not about stopping time or halting change. These ghosts are proof of the very futility of such an endeavor.

In the end, building ghosts are an insistence that these places are not blank slates or empty canvases. (What place is?) They are fragments that will simply be folded into the kaleidoscopic city around them—a century in the future, a year away, an hour from now.

Acknowledgments

The idea for this book took root more than a decade ago, and thirteen years' worth of colleagues, friends, and advocates have helped bring it to life. First and foremost, we thank the staff and board of the Sachs Program for Arts Innovation at the University of Pennsylvania—in particular, John McInerney, Chloe Reison, and Tamara Suber. Their support (both creative and financial) propelled the idea from an imagined notion to (at last) something very real.

In the early years of wandering around the city, developing the concept and the questions, we also benefited tremendously from the encouragement of Randy Mason and Julie Donofrio. They understood the intention, and their provocations helped to hone it even further. As respected, much loved friends and colleagues, their belief was—and is—fortifying. Ashley Hahn was a creative sounding board in key early moments; our "book club" conversations helped to dream up this very tome. Michael Grant, John Caperton, Frank Matero, David Hollenberg, Micah Dornfeld, and Laney Myers have stayed curious about this project for several years; their steady interest has given us stamina. Our thanks also go to Conrad Benner, Patrick Grossi, Sarah Kaizar, Bruce Laverty, Ellen Ryan, Ben Volta, and Shira Walinsky, whose work has intersected in some way with building ghosts and who were generous to give their time in talking through the artistic and intellectual overlaps between our work.

Once the @buildingghosts Instagram account launched, it quickly grew beyond our own finds, thanks to crowdsourced submissions from friends and strangers alike. Special thanks to Lynn Alpert, Charles DiSanto, Andrew Hart, Libbie Hawes, Samantha Kurland, Bradley Maule, Kevin McMahon, and Amelia Popovic for their frequent submissions, along with the many, many others we know and appreciate only as usernames.

With the archival research underway, our indebtedness grew. The very accommodating staff at the Philadelphia City Archives brought cart after cart of files to the reading room; infinite thanks for the infinite patience of David Baugh, Joshua Blay, and Kenneth Rice. John Hinchman tracked down a research paper from years ago to fill a persistent knowledge gap. And then there's Larry Santucci, who led a significant research study for the Federal Reserve of Philadelphia and then, several years later, fished out the very obscure research file from his study that related to one of our building ghosts. In a year's worth of research finds and failures for this book, that was a thrill of a day, and we thank him profusely.

Kaitlyn Levesque is the multihyphenate talent who created the maps and illustrative photomontage for the book. Her graphics elevated our scrappy fieldwork maps, complementing the book's photographs by interpreting their larger contexts. Thanks also to Jacob Torkelson for technical assists in the mapping process.

We reserve some of our deepest gratitude for the colleagues at Temple University Press who ushered this concept from proposal to publication: Mary Rose Muccie and Aaron Javsicas, along with Will Forrest, Gary Kramer, Kate Nichols, and Ashley Petrucci. We also thank freelance copyeditor Susan Deeks.

Several dear friends were a brain trust when the writing was going well—and happy hour companions when it was not. We thank especially Kimberly Chantry and Laura DiPasquale Zupan, who reviewed drafts of this manuscript.

Finally, on a personal note, Michael gives a special shout-out to Peter Woodall and the many writers, researchers, and photographers who have contributed to Hidden City Philadelphia, exploring the city's forgotten history and uncovering stories about people and places that otherwise would go untold. He also thanks Kate for her positivity and moral support during the project's challenging photo documentation process; it was an incredible journey. Molly thanks her guideposts in life: Heather, Jenny, and Francesca. But most of all, and with all the love that can be distilled onto a page, she thanks her family.

Index

MARGARET (MOLLY) LESTER is Associate Director of the Urban Heritage Project at the University of Pennsylvania Weitzman School of Design and the coauthor of *Minerva Parker Nichols: The Search for a Forgotten Architect.*

MICHAEL BIXLER is the Editorial Director and Chief Photographer of Hidden City Philadelphia.